Spiritual Conferences

Monsignor Tony Philpot

Photograph by Fr Bob Rainbow of the Jesus Caritas Priests' Fraternity

Spiritual Conferences

Mgr Tony Philpot

edited by

Fr Gerard Skinner

GRACEWING

First published in England in 2018
by
Gracewing
2 Southern Avenue
Leominster
Herefordshire HR6 0QF
United Kingdom
www.gracewing.co.uk

ISBN 978 085244 938 7

Typeset by Word and Page, Chester, UK

Cover design by Bernardita Peña Hurtado

Front cover:
The Holy Trinity with St Thomas of Canterbury and St Edmund of East Anglia, known as The Martyrs' Picture—Durante Alberti, 1581.
Reproduced by kind permission of the Rector, Venerable English College, Rome.

Back cover:
The Martyr's Chapel, Venerable English College, Rome.
© Fr Lawrence Lew, OP.

CONTENTS

INTRODUCTION

A few years before he died I invited Mgr Tony (Tony, never Anthony) to give a spiritual conference to the junior clergy of the Archdiocese of Westminster. It's a cliché but it has to be said that as he spoke you could have heard a pin drop. At the end of the talk a young priest who had never heard Tony before turned to me and said, 'He's the real thing'. He was, and those of us who were blessed to hear him week after week giving spiritual conferences in Rome or who heard him giving retreats or homilies in other settings did not doubt that what we were hearing was the fruit of the prayer and reflection of a priest who knew both God and humanity well.

Anthony John Philpot was born in Croydon on 24 March 1935. A few years later his family moved to Bedford, where Tony was educated at Bedford School, the alma mater of John Bunyan. In 1953 Tony's 'Pilgrim's Progress' brought him to the Venerable English College, Rome. During his years of study he occasionally wrote articles for *The Venerabile*, the College's journal, and not infrequently acted in College plays. He was a member and, for one year, chair of the Mezzofanti Society, a group that held talks and debates in any language possible, except English: Tony's gift for languages also presumably came to the fore in a talk he gave that *The Venerabile* records as being 'a lively portrait of Paul Verlaine, with the emphasis on quotations from his poetry at some length'.

A further year of study in Rome followed Tony's ordination to the priesthood in 1959 after which he returned to his home diocese, Northampton. He served in St Joseph's, Bedford, and Northampton Cathedral before being appointed Parish Priest of Leighton Buzzard. For the rest of his life Tony was to serve in parishes that were later to become the newly formed Diocese of East Anglia: in Ipswich, Newmarket and then, for fourteen years, in Our Lady of the English Martyrs, Cambridge.

With the establishment of the new Diocese of East Anglia, Tony was asked to take charge of religious education before being appointed as one of the Diocese's Vicars General. For a man of Tony's sensibility, such a role must have been a severe trial: he once told me that as a Vicar General 'you find out too much about what you don't want to know, and too little about what you do want to know'! More to Tony's liking was being given responsibility for the Diocese's 'Ministry to Priests' programme. In a similar field, he became the international 'responsible' of Jesus Caritas, a fraternity inspired by the spirituality of Charles de Foucauld.

From Cambridge, Tony returned to Ipswich, before being appointed the director of Palazzola, a former monastery on the edge of Lake Albano, near Rome, that belongs to the English College. Palazzola is a place of prayer and hospitality that is used by the students of the English College and many English pilgrims to Rome. It was a most obvious and natural appointment when, in 2001, Tony was appointed Spiritual Director of the English College, a post he held for five years. As one former student recorded, 'Always first in chapel in the morning, his constancy has been a great help and encouragement. Many a tired head has been lifted from its slumbers when he has preached at the 6.45am Mass. His homilies are more than just a thought for the day: they carry a weight that makes their listeners try to adapt their lives for the better.' His weekly spiritual conferences brought his hearers closer to God through his prayerful insights into life in Christ and his compassionate understanding of human nature. Deep erudition was imparted with self-deprecating humour and a lightness of touch, a conference often beginning with 'This one's about …'.

On leaving the English College Tony was asked by his bishop to minister to the Portuguese community in Peterborough, so Tony set about learning Portuguese. After one more spell as a seminary spiritual director (once again in Rome, but this time for the Beda College) Tony retired to London in order to be nearer to his sisters Margaret and Cathie. It was there where he died on 16 July 2016, having been cared for in his last illness by the Little Sisters of the Poor at St Anne's, Stoke Newington.

I am so grateful that Margaret suggested that it might be a good idea if a large collection of Tony's spiritual conferences were published. During his lifetime Tony's words were published on a number of occasions, most notably in two previous collections of spiritual conferences, *Priesthood in Reality* and *You shall be Holy*. Most people who heard him were left with the impression that Tony was holy, that he was indeed 'the real thing'. May he rest in peace and rise in glory.

✠

SETTING THE SCENE

When we come on retreat we dare to do what, for most of our life, we have been trained not to do: daydream, waste time, even allow ourselves to be bored. Keen schoolteachers at the start of our lives would have glinted at us through their rimless glasses and written 'lazy' on our reports.

But there is a difference. This is inactivity, but it is alert inactivity. It is the inactivity of one who waits. It is the inactivity of one who is open and receptive, inviting communication. Colossians 4:2 says: 'Devote yourselves to prayer, keeping alert in it with thanksgiving.' It is the inactivity of one who reflects on scripture while he is waiting, so that when the communication does come he will recognize the language.

In the politically incorrect days of tiger hunting, one cruel trick was the trick of the Judas goat. You put your sacrificial goat out in a clearing, tethered so that he couldn't get away. And you left him there. Inevitably, after a while he started to bleat. And the hungry tiger, far away in the jungle, heard his bleating and began to head for the clearing. On arrival he would spy out the land, and once he was satisfied that no-one else was interested in the goat, he would attack; which, of course, put him at the mercy of the hunters, and turned him into a rug in the colonel's drawing room.

Drain the triple cruelty out of this … double cruelty to the goat, and bitter deception of the tiger … and you have a notion of what happens on a retreat. We tether ourselves out in the open where God can find us. We call out to him, and then we wait. And in the end, once he's satisfied that we are genuine, he comes, and, to quote the hymn, he takes possession of our souls and makes them all his own. The point is that in this whole dialogue it is God who acts, not us. He is the senior partner, he calls the shots. Our job is to make ourselves available. The silence is this—making yourself available to God, screening out all other distractions, so that you can call out to him and he can speak to your soul. In this instance it is the tiger, not the colonel, who wins.

When I say 'God speaks to your soul' I don't mean that you will hear voices. Joan of Arc heard voices, so did Teresa of Avila. It is possible, in cases of advanced sanctity. As a priest in a parish, however, you will get to recognize the kind of person who asks for an interview because God has spoken to them. It's usually a pretty plain indication of schizophrenia, and not sanctity at all. No, God will speak to you, but it will be by way of intuition and conviction, things suddenly becoming plain which before were confused, a release of spiritual energy in an area where previously you felt drained. By the end of the retreat you will be able to say 'I have moved along' though putting words to it may not be easy. If we sincerely make ourselves available, he acts.

In our particular context we are thinking ahead to priesthood. When we think of priesthood we add the rider 'If that is God's will.' We might find it hard to imagine ourselves doing anything else, and have the feeling that our whole life has been leading up to priesthood, and be pretty sure that this is our vocation, but nevertheless we must open the whole thing to God, submitting our will to his. If it's a calling, there has to be a caller. Right and proper at this stage, well on in our seminary formation, for us to consult the caller and check that we've got it right. Our greatest desire should be that God's will be done, not that we get what we want. Ignatius called this 'indifference', meaning not off-handed couldn't-care-lessness, but a realization that in God's will is our only good. If God doesn't want me for a priest but for something else, then to continue would be madness, bringing unhappiness to me and disaster to my people. So this retreat is different from other College retreats; this is, so far as we can make it so, a retreat of discernment. We dive deeper and it takes longer. Adrienne von Speyr in *They Followed His Call*:

> Surrender to the Lord—perfect, unconditional surrender—is an ascetical deed that contains in itself, or at least *should* contain in itself, everything having to do with the Lord's plans for a person. And so, the first quality of this deed is readiness, an open readiness that is not always trying to calculate what for us is possible, then just possible and finally impossible.

This courage has an openness about it that has the courage of leaving to the Lord what is his.

You would be surprised how much the College staff are concerned about men after their ordination—where they are sent, whether they are happy, whether they have a 'soft landing', a fruitful apostolate, a sense of fulfilment. Ninety-nine per cent of the time, thank God, the news is good. But just occasionally it's bad. You get news filtering back of discontent and disillusion, and even of things that are worse. In recent years, quite a number of priests—from a variety of seminaries—have checked out within a couple of years or ordination. It is always a tragedy, in the way that a broken marriage is a tragedy, and like a broken marriage it brings scandal and strain and distress to a lot of people. We have to ask 'Why?' Sometimes the men were insufficiently mature to picture the reality of priestly life, they were caught up in the externals of vestments and processions. Some of them were fatally skewed by a human relationship which filled their whole horizon. Sometimes they hadn't done this honest exercise in discernment. Old Bishop Clark [of East Anglia] used to snort, when some young priest had objected to an appointment, 'Some of these people seem never to have heard of the Cross!' It's true—sometimes they had never really confronted the living Christ and accepted the need, indeed the inevitability in grown-up life, of sacrifice and the Cross. To embrace the priesthood in the twenty-first century we need to be, to quote the Book of Numbers, 'Men with far-seeing eyes'.

My prayer for you is that in these eight days you will be objective, sincere, persevering, undistracted by any irrelevant issue, open to the living God. On this occasion we can say 'Grace is all'. The result of the retreat will not be the result of your brainwork, but of the sheer loving grace of God.

Scripture for reflection

I Samuel 3:1–11   Psalm 94/5:7–8
I Kings 19.11–13   Mark 1:35
Hosea, 2:14–15

✠

WHAT WAS JESUS LIKE?

What was Jesus like?

We are stuffed full of theology about him. We are good at Persons and Natures. We can say, quite correctly, that the Church is his Body on earth. We can define what is meant by the Real Presence in the Blessed Sacrament. We can say, with Pope Francis, that when we meet poor people with loving attention and generosity, then we are meeting Jesus. All this is the bread and butter of our training.

But the very human question remains, and it can be asked by the simplest and most uneducated Christian—what was he really like? What was he like to know? How did the Apostles perceive him? What bound them to him?

The answer lies in two sentences you and I say every day, rather automatically. 'This is my Body, which will be given up for you.' 'This is the chalice of my Blood, which will be poured out for you.' Given up, poured out. That's what he's like.

When John the Baptist sees him in the crowd, he says 'There is the Lamb of God.' The lamb is the symbol of gentle but total self-surrender. Francisco de Zurbarán painted a deeply moving picture of the Lamb, his legs tied, awaiting the butcher's knife: but most moving of all is the expression in the Lamb's eyes, full of awareness and patience and self-gift.

Christ's gift of self for others was never measured, never calculated. And indeed, if you take a bird's eye view of the Gospels, you can say that all the time he is pushing his loving service of men and women to the outside limits compatible with being human. And it's catching. Listen to the call of Levi. 'He noticed a tax collector, Levi by name, sitting by the customs house, and he said to him, 'Follow me.' And leaving everything he got up and followed him' (Luke 5:27). It's clean and decisive.

Our priesthood runs the risk of being humdrum and boring, if we turn it into a profession. It is after all as respectable as being a lawyer or

5

a doctor, and within the confines of the Catholic body it shares the same kind of kudos. We have a battery of letters after our names to show what it cost us to qualify. No-one will blame us if we live it in a reasonable but non-enthusiastic way, middle-class professional men occupying an esteemed place in the eyes of our people, doing our duty with style and decorum. But that's not like Levi. Nor is it like Jesus.

Here's von Balthasar, writing in 1954:

> Yes, a priest stands at the altar, all the way at the front, distracted and tired. Behind him in the nave he senses the absent-minded crowd with its dull confidence that 'up there something's happening that somehow (we don't know exactly how) concerns us, too. Up there a man is at work and surely he knows what he's doing. He holds the office: he has the responsibility.' But how is a man, even if he is a priest, to bear the burden of the whole community? He too is (fortunately) only a human being, only a sinner. At one time he had indeed attempted to give himself wholly, to hold nothing back. But everything has turned out very differently from what he had expected.*

I think von Balthasar is imagining a young priest in Switzerland, before the liturgical changes of the Council. The bloom has definitely worn off this man's vocation. But fifty years later, here is John Paul II in his *Maundy Thursday Letter to Priests*: 'From the Upper Room, Christ tirelessly seeks and calls.' The bloom doesn't have to wear off. Given up; poured out.

'I used to say, 'I will not think about him, I will not speak his name any more.' Then there seemed to be a fire burning in my heart, imprisoned in my bones. The effort to restrain it wearied me, I could not bear it.' That's Jeremiah (20:9). Poor Jeremiah seemed to get the rough end of the stick in every possible way, and we can empathize with him when he cried out to God. But for all his anguish, he had that bounce-back factor which made him so great a prophet. God was the source of his

---

* *Heart of the World*, ch. 5.

courage and the reason for his ultimate joy and trust, the reason why he could still sing for joy and glorify the Lord. Of all the prophets, he would have understood what Jesus meant at the Last Supper with those words: Given up, poured out.

I was once spiritual director to a monk. How much help it was to him I don't know, but it taught me something very important. He was coming up to diaconate, which by any standards is a pretty decisive moment, but I detected in him a certain off-handedness about the whole proceeding. Yes, it was a means to the priesthood. And priesthood would mean coming at last out of the pupillary state, returning to his monastery, being a full-blown monk. But diaconate? He could take or leave it. I confronted him with this, and he said, 'But Father, I have just made my solemn profession, and that was the high point of my life, the moment at which I embraced celibacy, the point of definitive commitment; how many definitive commitments can a man make?' And he was right. With those solemn vows he had taken the prophetic step. It wasn't a sacrament, but in terms of his human experience and witness to the world it was the climax. It was his Levi-moment. That was when he got up and left the table with the money on it, and followed Jesus blindly.

Secular priests don't have a solemn profession, because we don't make vows. We have candidacy, which is serious commitment, but compared to solemn vows it is rather anaemic. Diaconate for us means the promise of celibacy, yes, but then you're already into the liturgical functions of the deacon, the whole business of vestments and so on: a great distraction. My early experience training permanent deacons taught me a lot. Service at the altar was what loomed largest for them, however much you thought you had trained apostles for the community. It was the dalmatic that counted. They were good, good men; but their ordination did not mark the moment of conversion.

I think we secular priests miss out by not having a solemn profession. The *Letter to Religious* at the start of the year for Consecrated Life [2015] included this passage: 'It is Christ who called you to follow him in the consecrated life, and this means continually making an 'exodus' from yourself in order to centre your life on Christ and on his Gospel, on the will of God, laying aside your own plans.' An exodus from yourself.

Think of the first exodus—the hurried packing-up, the heading off into the desert in the middle of the night with pots and pans and sleeping mats, the continuous herding of the children so that they didn't get lost, and above all the uncertainty. Hoping in God and trusting Moses. Life would never be the same again. The garlic and the onions, for better or worse, were a thing of the past. There was no way back. Exodus requires risk-taking, and courage, no less today than it did thirty-five centuries ago. And that challenge to exodus isn't just for religious.

In his *Confessions* Augustine describes his conversion (ch. 10). He describes the monumental fight which went on inside him—intellectually he was convinced about the Catholic Faith, but old habits of lust held him tight, anaesthetized him almost. Then he relates the famous scene in the garden when a voice which seems to come from next-door says repeatedly 'Tolle, lege.' 'Pick up the book and read.' He has the writings of St Paul on the garden bench beside him; and the page falls open at Romans 15: 'Put on the Lord Jesus Christ and make no provision for the flesh or the gratification of your desires.' Suddenly the sense of enslavement to sin falls away, and he knows that he is ready to submit to Christ, 'putting him on' in baptism. He compares this with the experience of St Antony, hearing the words 'Go sell all you possess and give the money to the poor: you will have treasure in heaven. Then come, follow me.' Antony made a radical break with his old self; so did Augustine. In both cases, an exodus. In both cases, a work of grace. Only the Holy Spirit can supply us with this great spurt of spiritual energy, so that other people can finally use those words of us: he was given up, he was poured out.

Francis had not been Pope more than forty-eight hours when he celebrated Mass with the cardinals, and preached them a homily which was deliberately disturbing. 'When we journey without the Cross, when we build without the Cross, when we profess Christ without the Cross, we are not disciples of the Lord, we are worldly. We may be bishops, priests, cardinals, popes, but not disciples of the Lord.' To those elderly gentlemen he was preaching exodus: go out of yourself, forget yourself in serving others, take on board the pain and the uncertainty, sharpen up your trust in the living God, be men of sacrifice. You and I cannot risk becoming sleepy and lethargic, he's saying, vaguely self-satisfied, like people on a cruise. There are people at our door with wounds which need binding, and beyond them, there is a world to convert.

The history of the Church is a history of light and shade. It needs saying that there never was a golden age. If we are ashamed now about child abuse and financial corruption, has there ever been a century when there wasn't something to be ashamed of? The disgraceful trials of strength between Italian gangster families to see who could gain the papacy and hold on to it; the disgusting behaviour of some of the Crusaders; the gross wealth of the Renaissance Church; the cruelty of the Counter-Reformation (think of the Thirty Years' War); the carelessness about the poor which contributed to the French Revolution; the obsession with territory which led to the war over the Papal States.

Yet in all these dark periods there have been blinding shafts of light—great saints, men and women of heroic life, deeply wise people. They rose above the mess. They kicked away the props of class and wealth, they dared to be counter-cultural. They were men and women of exodus. They were given up, poured out.

Women like Catherine of Siena and Bridget of Sweden, who could think outside the box, so to speak, and advise popes; or like Mary Ward, who started the order now known as the Congregation of Jesus, right in the middle of the perilous penal period, making impossible journeys across Europe, taking on the Vatican authorities when they tried to cloister her English nuns, and doing it while still remaining loyal to the Church. Madeleine Hutin, who founded the Little Sisters of Jesus in spite of appalling health, and said afterwards, 'He took me by the hand, and blindly I followed.'

Francis de Sales, who could have cashed in on his aristocratic status, but instead underwent enormous discomfort and risk reconverting his diocese from the Reformers. Charles de Foucauld, who had great social and military advantages which he cheerfully jettisoned in order to live poorly among the Algerian Arabs and Touareg. Oscar Romero, who had the courage radically to change his mind and his way of being a bishop, and paid for it with his life. I could add scores of other examples and so could you. What all these people have in common is a refusal to be trapped on the treadmill of banality, which can so easily infest the Church. *Caritas Christi urget nos.* They were driven men and women, and the driving force was love. Love forced them into originality and risk. Their decision to be disciples was clean and decisive. Given up, poured out.

At the start of Mark, there is a bald description of Jesus before sunrise (Mark 1:35). We don't really know him yet, so every action of his is significant. 'In the morning, while it was still very dark, he got up and went out to a deserted place and there he prayed.' The Greek is more graphic. It uses three verbs: *anastas* means 'having got up'; *exelthen* means 'he went out' of the house—stood in the garden, so to speak, sniffed the breeze; and then *apelthen*—'he went off'; he decided what he was going to do, and he went and did it: he found an *eremos topos*, a 'hermit-place' and there he prayed. He didn't wait for circumstances to overtake him and dictate his day. He had his priorities. These perplexed the disciples, who didn't really get the prayer thing, and felt he was neglecting his public. Tough. Already we see in Jesus a steely resolve, a clarity of vision. Clean and decisive.

We find the same quality described in Luke. It's the end of the Galilean ministry and the start of the walk to Jerusalem. 'He resolutely set his face towards Jerusalem' (Luke 9:51). The Greek is *prosopon esterisen*—literally 'he made his face firm'. Knowing what awaited him there, he moved decisively, cleanly, deliberately southwards.

Listen to St Edmund Campion. He wrote to the Privy Councillors of England in 1581 the document known as 'Campion's Brag'. You will find in it the qualities we have been highlighting. Here is a man who is given up, poured out. Here is a man who has chosen his direction cleanly and decisively, who has made a definitve exodus from academic life in Oxford, and chosen a higher cause. *Prosopon esterisen*.

> My charge is of free cost to preach the Gospel, to minister the sacraments, to instruct the simple, to reform sinners, to confute errors—in brief, to cry alarm spiritual against foul vice and proud ignorance, wherewith many of my dear countrymen are abused. Hearken to those who would spend the best blood in their bodies for your salvation. We [Jesuits] have made a league, cheerfully to carry the cross you shall lay upon us, and never to despair your recovery, while we

have a man left to enjoy your Tyburn, or to be racked with
your torments, or consumed with your prisons. The expense
is reckoned, the enterprise is begun.

The expense is reckoned, the enterprise is begun.

The enterprise for us, 430 years later, is the same. It is still to preach
the Gospel, to minister the sacraments, to instruct the simple, to reform
sinners, to refute errors—in brief, to cry alarm spiritual against foul
vice and proud ignorance, wherewith may of our dear countrymen are
abused. In order to do it we must be men of prayer, able easily to slip
into prolonged and silent union with Our Lord. We must be men with
a heart for the poor. We must be men who know their stuff, who read
intelligently, who don't stop thinking. We must be men who really trust
God to send his Spirit on this benighted country, and reclaim men and
women for himself. Trusting God is demanding. Jesus often asks for
trust from those he helps in the Gospel, doesn't he? 'Do you believe
that I can do this?' If we pray the psalms with care, we will find there
innumerable expressions of trust. We must be men who operate within
the discipline of the Church, not mavericks. But this still leaves us with
ample liberty to choose our path, our style, to be self-motivated and
not cogs in a machine.

If we listen, the invitation is clear. May our decision to preach the
Gospel be clean and decisive. May we be able to say 'The expense is
reckoned, the enterprise is begun', May we answer the call to daily exodus
from ourselves and our securities. May we be men who are given up,
poured out. Because that is what Jesus is like.

✠

EASTER

I want to talk about Easter. You may think there is not much point in this because Easter, at least for 2004, is over and done with, and we are now in the green period after Pentecost, thinking about first communions and the summer season. The RCIA [Rite of Christian Initiation of Adults] is safely tucked away, and Easter is just a memory. But Easter should never be just a memory. It's Easter we're on about every time we celebrate Mass. It's the risen Christ we're talking to—or through—when we say our prayers. It is the empty tomb we're pointing to every time we do a funeral. Easter impregnates our pastoral and spiritual lives. It is never off-season to talk about Easter.

Let us expose ourselves to the power and the light of Easter. This feast carries an impact like no other. It is not just a matter of understanding. It is also a matter of experiencing. This is no ordinary feast, a memorial of things past. No—we are celebrating Christ who is alive, who is actual, who is present, and who is powerful. Let us focus on him. 'Let us not lose sight of Jesus, who leads us in our faith and brings it to perfection: for the sake of the joy which was still in the future, he endured the cross, disregarding the shamefulness of it, and from now on has taken his place at the right of God's throne.' It is the risen and ascended Christ on whom our gaze is locked. The bishop when I was young used to preach in the Cathedral on Easter morning. He made his way up the steps into the pulpit in an alb, two dalmatics, chasuble and mitre, and with his crozier: it was a struggle. From somewhere under the layers of vestments he produced his sermon notes. 'Joy to you all at Easter!' he would say, 'And another thing.' Well, my purpose this evening is to convince you that there isn't 'another thing.' The grace and the reality of Easter is everything.

Pius XII used to come on to the loggia of St Peter's on Easter morning, and proclaim in his bell-like voice, 'Cristo è risorto ... Christos anesti!'

13

Two languages instead of the fifty-five of John Paul. For East and West, Pius was saying, Christ is risen. He is alive now for men and women of east and west, for Latin and for Greek. For men and women of both east and west Christ made these promises: 'I will not leave you orphans, I will come back to you' and 'Know that I am with you always; yes, to the end of time.' No-one is omitted; no-one is left out; from the rising of the sun to its setting, blessed be the name of the Lord.

Our greatest enemy is despair. Perhaps we were tempted to despair when the war in Iraq went ahead, in spite of all our prayers. Perhaps despair grips us when the talks in Northern Ireland break down, or the Holy Land flares up yet again in bloodshed and bitterness. Maybe the news from our diocese of a new case of child-abuse really chills our heart. Maybe our personal weakness and repetitive sinfulness pulls us down more than anything else, and floods us with sadness and hopelessness. To all of us Jesus says, as he said to the Apostles in the Upper Room, 'Peace be with you,' and he shows us his hands and his side. To all of us Jesus says 'I have told you all this so that you may find peace in me. In the world you will have trouble, but be brave: I have conquered the world.' It's a message for humanity as a whole, and it's a message for you and for me. He says, 'I have plumbed the depths of evil. I recall the unspeakable agony of the Mount of Olives. My heart was broken when my own disciples deserted and betrayed me, and my own people demanded my crucifixion, and when I saw the sorrow of my Mother. I still bear in my body the marks of the nails and the spear. I have run the gamut of human suffering and disillusionment. But look, I am alive. I have overcome all the evil the world could throw at me, even death. Take my hand, and I will care for you, I will bring you safely through whatever worries or frightens you or weighs you down. Do not be afraid; it is I, the First and the Last; I am the living one, I was dead and now I am to live for ever and ever, and I hold the keys of death and of the underworld.'

See how the Risen Christ attends first of all to our deepest need, that of forgiveness. He knows where the pain is worst and the burden greatest. It is our self-knowledge, the knowledge of our own track-record, isn't it? It produces in us a chronic diffidence: I have messed up so often in the past, what chance is there that I will not mess up again?

Forgiveness is the first thing on his agenda when he rises from the tomb. Thinking of us Jesus says to the Eleven, 'Receive the Holy Spirit. For those whose sins you shall forgive, they are forgiven; for those whose sins you retain, they are retained.' The only thing that could cause our sins to be retained is a refusal even to try again, and that is another name for despair. The pardon we receive in confession is the direct result of Easter, the first-fruits of Easter, the feast of hope. 'O happy fault, O necessary sin of Adam', they sang to us on Easter night, 'which gained for us so great a Redeemer.' A Redeemer who is so great, and so intuitively wise, who prescribes for us like the wisest of doctors: what you need, he says, is forgiveness and hope, and these I gladly give you, because they are in my gift.

The grace and power of Easter are conveyed to us by baptism. Infant baptism has this disadvantage, that at the time we are not aware of it, and afterwards we cannot remember it. Infant baptism can be a very prosaic and matter-of-fact thing, especially if it is done on a wet Sunday afternoon at the back of the church, and most of the onlookers are not believers so much as photographers. Nevertheless, it is the hinge-moment of our lives. The real drama and beauty of baptism comes home to you, as you know, when you have adults to baptize at the Easter Vigil. It is then that you realize most starkly and vividly that baptism *is* Easter, applied to the individual soul. The sheer calm might of God, which raised Jesus from the tomb very early on the Sunday morning, is the same might which raises this person now to adopted status in God's family, flooded through with the grace of God, transformed by being baptized into the death and resurrection of the Lord, equipped to cope with whatever comes. Listen to St John Chrysostom, preaching on the Pasch:

> As when a very good trainer of the gymnasium accepts some weak and wretched athlete, and when he has massaged him, taught him, and strengthened his body, he does not allow him to remain idle, but bids him enter the contests, so as to learn from experience what strength he has acquired, so has Christ also done. He could have removed the enemy from our midst, but that you may learn the superiority of his grace, the greatness of the spiritual strength you have received in

your baptism, he allows him to attack you, giving you at the
same time the opportunity to gain for yourself many victories.

That's the antidote to despair, that's the language of hope, and confidence,
isn't it? Paul says to the Romans, 'With God on our side, who can be
against us?'

Easter means that while we live in this world, we have one foot in
heaven. Christ resurrected is already glorified: he stays with his friends
a little longer, but already, you might say, he has a faraway look in his
eyes, and his bags are packed: he is on his way home. The same is
true of you and me, even if we cannot walk through closed doors and
disappear from dinner tables. We are built into Christ, and Christ's
real home now is with his Father. If he is in this world but not of it,
then so are we. This alters our attitude to so many things, if we follow
it through. To relationships, for instance: every relationship, however
intense, every attraction, however strong, ultimately has to give way
before the supreme relationship. Nothing has the durability of my
sonship of God, which Jesus has won for me and shares with me. And
then, to property. My ownership of goods and money is such a fleeting
thing that to give them away should not distress me; I set a different
value on them from the one the world sets. My association with what I
have is so casual and so passing, compared with my possession of God
who dwells within me. Because of my faith in the risen Christ and my
identity with him, I will probably surprise my friends and relations by
my priorities, priorities which are not theirs. I will be serious about
things they feel are unimportant; I will treat as marginal things which
for them are the breath of life. The *Epistle to Diognetus* expresses this
beautifully. Remember how early a document this is. It is an anonymous
author's explanation of the manner of life practised in the Christian
communities of the time of the Emperor Hadrian, or possibly Marcus
Aurelius. The manuscript was not copied until the sixteenth century, and
it was fortunate that this was done, because the original was destroyed
during the Franco-Prussian War. Listen to what it says:

Though they are residents at home in their own countries,
their behaviour is more like that of transients; they take

their full part as citizens, but they also submit to anything and everything as if they were aliens. For them, any foreign country is a motherland, and any motherland is a foreign country ... Though destiny has placed them here in the flesh, they do not live after the flesh; their days are passed on earth, but their citizenship is above in the heavens.

And then, promotion recognition and success. I am a member of that Christ who by the world's standards was a failure, but by the standards of eternity the destiny of the world hangs on him. Human approval and endorsement are very puny things compared with the interior life I have, I dwelling in Christ and he in me. I know from simple observation that people in public life, politics, the army and so on, get promoted beyond their abilities, and that human instinct in this regard can easily be faulty. A glamorous uniform can be a cover for a personality which is sterile and empty. But my intimate knowledge and love of the risen Christ, my discipleship of him, will never disappoint and can never prove hollow. Thus Easter drives a horse and cart through the world's assessment of what is great, or enjoyable, or desirable. Easter offers me a glorious freedom. 'Those whom the world thinks common and contemptible are the ones that God has chosen.'

The other thing about Easter is the effect it has on our long-term prospects; I don't mean our chances of a leg up the ladder, but our chances of life after death. The way Paul describes it in I Corinthians make it seem as if Jesus had broken through a wall by his resurrection, and the hole he made is big enough for us all to follow him through. 'But Christ has in fact been raised from the dead, the first-fruits of all who have fallen asleep. Death came through one man and in the same way the resurrection of the dead has come through one man. Just as all men die in Adam, so will all men be brought to life in Christ.' This is the lasting truth about us. The ultimate question will not be 'Did he become a general, an archbishop, the managing director of a chocolate factory?' but 'Did death blot him out, or is he enjoying eternal life?' Easter answers this deepest of all questions.

Finally, as I said at the start of this talk, Easter doesn't stop. When John Chrysostom had been away from Constantinople over Easter 402, inspecting the Churches in Asia Minor, his loyal laypeople grumbled. Someone else had done the adult baptisms at the Vigil, and they felt that the converts had been short-changed. When he returned to the City they complained, 'We wanted to observe Easter with you.' And he replied 'Observe Easter with me today ... My point is that just as the sun is constantly rising and we don't see numerous suns—just the one rising day after day—so the Paschal feast too is constantly being celebrated, and yet all the time it's the one Pasch that is being observed.' We, after Easter, have a string of feasts. Divine Mercy, the Ascension, Pentecost, Corpus Christi, the Sacred Heart, SS Peter and Paul. Each of these feasts is the consequence of Easter, or the spinning-out of the meaning of Easter.

* The Ascension completes of the glorification of which John speaks so often in his Gospel: the Risen Christ is given the title above all others, that of Lord, which might make him sound remote and formidable, like a Roman Emperor; but the reverse is true, because by virtue of the Ascension he becomes *Our* Lord, intimately close to you and to me.

* Whit Sunday brings the Spirit, unpredictable and mighty, into the centre of our lives. What for? So that we may experience and live out and proclaim to the world the results of the Resurrection.

* Corpus Christi gives us the Risen Christ under the appearance of bread and wine, so that we may truly be branches on the living Vine.

* Saints Peter and Paul represent the Church, which is God's way of announcing the Resurrection to the world. 'Their voice goes out through all the earth, and their message to the ends of the world.'

* The Resurrection is evidence of the divine mercy. In raising Christ to life the Father mercifully includes us, undeserving though we are. Baptism is the sovereign act of divine mercy: the uniting of the saved with the Saviour.

* The Feast of the Sacred Heart reminds us that the Lord to whom we relate now is the Jesus who has lived the Passion and Death of Calvary, whose heart was pierced by the lance, who has experienced Easter morning, and is now seated at his Father's right hand. There is no other Jesus. And this Jesus, proclaims the Church, has a warm and tender heart for humanity. He asks of us a response in kind—a response not simply of the head but also of the heart.

✠

EUCHARIST IN A TIME OF CHANGE

'The Lord said to Moses and Aaron in the land of Egypt: This month shall mark for you the beginning of the months: it shall be the first month of the year for you.' Thus the narration of the Passover begins with a brand-new calendar (Exodus 12:1, NRSV). This month, says God, counts as the first month of the year. And these instructions of God to Moses and Aaron proceed to describe, in great detail, the eating of the Paschal Lamb. 'This is how you shall eat it: your loins girded, your sandals on your feet, and your staff in your hand; and you shall eat it hurriedly. It is the passover of the Lord.' Ready to march out at any moment, eating in haste, the Israelites contemplated an uncertain future in which all their familiar props and supports would no longer be there: gone for good. This meal marked a seismic shift in their lives, from forced labour with a degree of security, to a nomadic existence in which God alone would sustain them. 'It shall be the first month of the year for you.' The Passover made all things new.

The Last Supper shared by Jesus with the Twelve marked a similar moment of transition. Within a few hours Jesus would embark upon his Passion, and nothing would ever be the same again: the whole history of the planet was about to take a dramatic and permanent turn. The death and resurrection of Christ would re-constitute not just the Jews, but the whole People of the New Covenant and potentially the whole human race, as redeemed instead of damned, as adopted instead of alienated. Here is Paul to the Ephesians: 'Remember that you were at that time without Christ, being aliens from the commonwealth of Israel, and strangers to the covenants of promise, having no hope and without God in the world. But now in Christ Jesus you who were once far off have been brought near by the blood of Christ … So then you are no longer strangers and aliens, but you are citizens with the saints and also members of the household of God' (Ephesians 2:12–13, 19). By the blood of Christ we are brought near. We receive the Blood of Christ at Mass, and it makes us members of the household of God. Nothing less than that. This radical rescue of you and me from a loveless and purposeless futility, this insertion of you and me in God's domestic circle, also started with a meal. It started with the Last Supper.

There is, inset in the Eucharist, in every celebration of the Eucharist, a summons to march out, to change, to embrace a new reality. The Eucharist is never a placid celebration of the *status quo*. The French bishops, planning the Eucharistic Congress in 1981, were at pains to emphasize the dynamism contained in the Eucharist, a dynamism which they describe most forcefully. 'In offering his life for us, Christ opens humanity to the coming of a world transformed in his image and renewed by the power of his Spirit.'* And they speak of 'Jesus Christ who died and was raised to life, present and active in the sacrament of the Eucharist so as to transform our life in its entirety.'† A world transformed; our life transformed. When we think of it like that we may well be filled with despair. We feel so impotent to tidy up our own lives, let alone reform the world. But the Spirit is present in the Eucharist, with force and with power. 'For nothing will be impossible with God' (Luke 1:37). Every time we celebrate Mass, we expose ourselves to the power of the Spirit, we join in a great act of hope, and at the same time hear again the call to conversion. This is expressed in the penitential rite at the beginning: our trust in God's merciful forgiveness, our plea for grace that we may change.

It is interesting to reflect a little on the key idea of 'assembly' in our religious history. In France and Italy now, people talk easily of 'the Sunday assembly', meaning the coming-together of the people for Mass. In English it still sounds strange. Is this because we still think of Mass-attendance as primarily an individual duty? Surely the primary obligation is on the people as a whole, to come together to hear God's word in obedience and to celebrate his goodness with thanksgiving? It is as part of the people that the obligation trickles down to us as private citizens. Another slant on the theme of assembly is this. Christ is present

* *Jésus Christ, pain rompu pour un monde nouveau* (Paris, 1981), p. 18.
† *ibid.*

in the assembly, just by virtue of its being there; this is what he promised, and he keeps his promises. It is a fact, not just an aspiration. The Gospel ('Where two or three …') gives priority to the assembly.

Well, if the drawing-together of the people is so important, then there has to be a convener, someone to call them. That key person is you. Long before you get to the preaching of the word, or what we used to call the 'confection' of the sacrifice, you have done something of huge significance. You have called the people together. You have greeted them as what canon lawyers would call a moral person, an entity. In *Pastores Dabo Vobis* Pope John Paul II said 'In so far as he represents Christ as Head, Shepherd and Spouse of the Church, the priest places himself not only in the Church, but at the front of it.'* This is true both metaphorically and literally. You place yourself at the front of the Church as Moses placed himself at the front of the Israelites at the Exodus, showing them at a time of profound change and bewilderment that God can and must be trusted, for he will never abandon his people. You summon them to put their faith in God.

A fine example of this is found in an Elizabethan document called the 'Relation of the Sufferings of Mr Thomas Woodhouse'.† Thomas Woodhouse was one of the martyrs who was later beatified. This is the story as told by one of his flock.

> He said Mass daily in his chamber and the heretics knew it well and yet he would never leave it, although the Doctors [the divines of the Established Church] willed him not to be so bold. Once being at Mass with him, a heretic lodged in the next room having perceived he struck fire [to light the candles] did call the rest of his friends and had thought to have taken us all, who were eight in number, and came and bounced at the door several times so hard as the door was like to be laid on the floor. Mr Woodhouse turned unto us before consecration, and bade us be of good cheer for (his life upon it) they should have no power to take us: after which

* *Pastores Dabo Vobis'* n. 22.
† cf. Caraman, *The Other Face* (London, 1960), p. 91.

words we all thought ourselves so sure as if we had been in a castle, and as he promised we were safe, for they went away.

I quote again from the French bishops:

> This great initiative of God [meaning the celebration of Mass] is exercised through the agency of men. To bring his people together and to preside at the Eucharist Christ continues to choose servants for himself in the line of the Apostles. He makes a gift of them to his Church so that she may never forget that she is not a club, but a summoned gathering. It is Jesus Christ who invites us and brings us together. The man who receives ordination, and for whom the Church asks the gift of the Spirit, does not act simply out of his personal talents, but in the name of Christ who sends him. In his whole person he becomes the living sign through which the Christian community is called to recognize its true identity.

Summoning, convoking, convening, drawing together, inviting, calling. That's us. It is because of this that the liturgical language of the present time talks about 'presiding at Mass' rather than 'saying Mass'. If you are going to convoke the assembly of God's people, you have to be visible, you have to be aware of the great dignity bestowed upon you, you have to remember that the Church has formally asked God to grant you the gift of the Spirit, and you have to do your presiding with a certain self-confidence and solemnity, while avoiding like the plague anything so self-indulgent as a theatrical ego-trip. This is a huge, awe-inspiring thing that is happening. In your parish on a Sunday there may be several hundred people there. They have dropped their normal pursuits and made their way to this particular church in order that through the Eucharist the Holy Spirit may fill them with hope, and enable them to alter their lives and transform their world. To preside over that is the greatest of privileges.

If you want a hint of the importance of convoking and presiding, look at Moses in Exodus:

> On the morning of the third day there was thunder and
> lightning, as well as a thick cloud on the mountain, and a
> blast of a trumpet so loud that all the people who were in the
> camp trembled. Moses brought the people out of the camp to
> meet God. They took their stand at the foot of the mountain.
> Now Mount Sinai was wrapped in smoke, because the Lord
> had descended upon it in fire; the smoke went up like the
> smoke of a kiln, while the whole mountain shook violently.
> As the blast of the trumpet grew louder and louder, Moses
> would speak and God would answer him in thunder.

Well, that's you. You bring the people out of the camp to meet God;
and you speak to God on their behalf, like Moses. And in this way you
help the people of God to manage inevitable change, to keep their faith
alive in spite of change, even to plan change, change for the better. The
Eucharist is their strength—and yours. It is not an expression of the
immutability and cosiness and sameness of things. Far from it. In his
recent Encyclical *Ecclesia de Eucharistia* Pope John Paul, talking about
the uphill path of ecumenism, insists that Catholics will be strengthened
for this by the Body and Blood of Christ. He says 'We have the Eucharist,
and in its presence we can hear in the depths of our hearts, as if they
were addressed to us, the same words heard by the Prophet Elijah:
'Arise and eat, else the journey will be too great for you.'' Well, it isn't
just the journey of ecumenism which might be too great for us, is it?
It is the journey of finding a language to communicate the faith in a
secular world. It is the journey of keeping the parish and the diocese
alive despite falling numbers and few vocations. It is the journey of
wading through the atmosphere engendered by child abuse. It is the
prospect of a different shape of Church which it falls to us to bring to
birth. 'Arise and eat, else the journey will be too great for you.' In the
same letter the Pope, thinking back on his priestly life, says: 'Each day
my faith has been able to recognize in the consecrated bread and wine
the divine Wayfarer who joined the two disciples on the road to Emmaus

---

* *Ecclesia de Eucharistia*, n. 61.

and opened their eyes to the light and their hearts to new hope." On a Sunday, from the president's chair, you beckon dozens of diverse people into unity, so that the Eucharist may open their eyes to the light and their hearts to new hope.

The Christ who is present in tabernacle and monstrance is the Risen Christ. This is his present reality. The French bishops talk about 'the great liturgy of the Kingdom where Christ, standing before the throne of God, surrounded by his apostles and a numberless crowd of witnesses, gives thanks on behalf of a saved humanity; from now on this humanity shares in the life of God and pleads for the coming of a world made new.' The Eucharist, they say, reflects this present reality: Christ standing before the throne of God. So: not Christ in the manger, or Christ on the lake. The Pope, talking about the Mass in his encyclical, makes the same point. 'The eucharistic sacrifice makes present not only the mystery of the Saviour's Passion and Death, but also the mystery of the Resurrection which crowned his sacrifice. It is as the living and risen one that Christ can become in the Eucharist the "bread of life".'† No wonder St Ephraim could say of holy communion, 'He who eats it with faith, eats Fire and Spirit.'‡ 'With faith.' It is so easy for you and me to celebrate Mass correctly and genially, but without any great expectation. Routine takes over. The small-scale nuts and bolts of the operation can dominate us, the coordinating of music and servers and readers, the conducting of the orchestra. But of course, the greatest conductors are swept away by the beauty and the majesty of their music, and rise above the mechanics of the job. So must you and I. We are feeding our people with the Risen Christ, the principle of resurrection for their lives and for their society. We are feeding them—and ourselves—with fire and Spirit. Let us renew our faith in what we are doing, let us believe in the grandeur and the power of it.

In Deuteronomy 16, when God is telling the people through Moses how they are to keep the great feast of the Passover, he says they are to eat unleavened bread for seven days. And he says that this is—and here

---

*   *ibid.*, n. 59.
†   *ibid.*, n. 14.
‡   *Sermo IV in Hebd. Sanct.*

is the NRSV translation—'the bread of affliction'. The French Jerusalem Bible talks about *le pain de misère* and the Italian Paulist Bible says *il pane di miseria*. But the English Jerusalem Bible talks about 'the bread of emergency'. Now I don't know Hebrew, and I cannot say which is the best rendering. But all these words—affliction, misery, emergency—express something extreme. An extreme situation, extreme emotions. In later years, when the Hebrews observed the Passover in their families, and shared unleavened bread, they re-lived that extreme situation and those extreme emotions. Their Passover took place at a time of anguish and of risk.

So does ours. Things are changing very fast, almost faster than we can plan for. Our parishes are merging, laypeople are being asked to take more of the load, the average age of the priests in each diocese is rising sharply, and men who in times past would have waited twenty years to become parish priests may now achieve these dizzy heights in two. And quite apart from the clerical scene, the media have become sharply critical of us and the public has moved away from all kinds of institutional religion. We are aware for the first time that our project is not simply a reclaiming of Catholics who have drifted, or the convincing of Anglicans, but the re-evangelization of a whole country. It's a new scene, and becomes newer each year. What will the Church in England and Wales look like in twenty, thirty years? What kind of people will want to join it? It is only the Eucharist which will energize and enthuse us for these coming decades. 'From the perpetuation of the Sacrifice of the Cross and the communion with the Body and Blood of Christ in the Eucharist, the Church draws the spiritual power needed to carry out her mission,' says the Pope.[*] It is vital that we celebrate the Eucharist with expectant faith and with joy in the power and mercy of God, while facing, like the people of Israel on the night of the Passover, like the Apostles on Maundy Thursday, an opaque future. Opaque, but shot through with hope. In spite of all appearances, we lead our people under God towards the Promised Land. The French bishops said this in 1981, and it is true today. 'We live today in a world marked by uncertainty, a world with enormous needs. However, this world continues to be enveloped

---

[*] *Ecclesia de Eucharistia*, n. 22.

by and soaked in the tenderness of God who holds the ravines and the mountains in the palm of his hand, and who promises to wipe away every tear from our eyes."

* *Jésus Christ, pain rompu pour un monde nouveau*, p. 37.

✝

Holding the Charge

Like a lot of people of my age I make heavy weather of mobile phones and information technology. I am not as bad as the late Bishop Clark, who when we tried to persuade him to get a laptop said, thunderously, 'This is a step too far' but I'm not very quick on the uptake. I complained the other day to one of our seminarians that my mobile and my portable computer were losing their charge far too quickly. 'That,' he said, with more than a smidgeon of pity in his voice, 'is because, when you first bought them, you didn't run them down once a week.'

I find that analogy of losing the charge useful. It sums up the malaise and unease which afflicts priests. We have events like this—retreats, in-service sessions and so on—which are good as far as they go. We make resolutions and formulate plans. But there is something inexorably grinding about real life when we get back to it. It is as if the deanery, the desk, the school and the phone were sitting there laughing at us on Friday evening as we go through the door. 'So,' they say, 'you thought things might change, you thought you'd take a deep breath and do things differently, did you? We'll soon see about that.' And after a few post-retreat experiences of losing the charge within days, we become cynical: nothing ever changes, nothing can change, things are as they are. Fatigue and demoralization are built-in factors of priestly life. So now we come on retreat with low expectations.

I could wish for nothing better than for this retreat to give you a charge you could hold. I would be pleased if it moved you on a bit, changed you in some way that was permanent. I truly believe this is possible. I don't think the secret lies in learning new tricks of the trade, new pastoral techniques, even new methods of prayer. I think it lies in acquiring a new way of being, a new way of feeling about yourself, a new way of seeing yourself in relation to God, a new way of situating yourself in the sight of God. If you can do that, it will be like the undoing of a great knot in your life. If you can do that, things need never be quite the same again.

I may be jumping the gun by presuming that fatigue and demoralization play a part in your life. But if they do, might I suggest that the reason is quite a profound one. It is to do with the way we are all brought up. We are educated to be in charge. This is a western thing. If we end up in a job without responsibility, our friends and relatives say 'What a tragedy, he's wasted his life.' Being in charge is a sign of success. I remember a fellow-seminarian, back in the fifties, being driven to the airport by his disgruntled father, who saw priesthood as a dead-end job. 'I shall expect you at least,' he said, as they unloaded the suitcase from the boot, 'to do your best to get on: become a papal nuncio, something like that.' Well, being in charge is all very well, but it makes us feel, like President Truman, that 'the buck stops here.' Being in charge is the trigger for anxiety, and Holy Mother Church sure as hell expects us to be in charge.

Canon law nails us down at all four corners. When I was preparing this talk I looked up, just for fun, what canons 528, 529 and 532 had to say. I should, of course, know them off by heart, as I was a parish priest myself for nearly thirty years, but unaccountably some of the details had slipped my mind. Here's the list. Word of God to be proclaimed in its entirety; catechetics; social justice; Catholic education; outreach to the lapsed; primacy of the Eucharist; promotion of confession; family prayers; liturgical abuse to be watched out for; house-visiting; prudent correction of the wayward; care of the sick and dying; care of immigrants; care of the poor; support of marriage and family life; support of lay apostolate; good relations with the bishop and presbyterium; promotion of parish atmosphere and community-feeling. And the parish priest has got to administer the parish goods with the diligence of a good householder.

My God! No wonder we feel fatigued and demoralized. Just reading that stuff makes me feel like a building without a lightning conductor which is suddenly struck by a thunderbolt. No-one can carry that kind of responsibility by himself. And the joke gets even worse when the Bishop asks you to take on two parishes instead of one. The guy portrayed in the Code is a monster. He is vigilant, prudent, diligent, solicitous, correct, learned, efficient and caring, suave and diplomatic all at once. The Code doesn't say anything about a sense of humour. Perhaps he hasn't got one. Nor does it say anything about congenial and supportive company, or a day off. Who in his right senses would volunteer to be solely accountable in all these ways?

Let's step back from this load-bearing model of responsibility. Let's realize first of all that it is quite unreasonable to pile responsibility on a man unless you also give him at the same time the means of discharging that responsibility. I recall being furious with professional appealers who came to the parish and wheedled permission out of me to preach on Sunday—in aid of projects in Romania or Paraguay or Ethiopia. They would go off with bumper collections. They were very proud of their work, and felt that I should congratulate them. On the contrary, before long I was turning down all such appeals. They did what they did by making the parishioners feel guilty, and then allowing them to assuage their guilt by writing cheques. This was manipulative, and dishonest. The parishioners should not have felt guilty because the Ethiopian children had flies in their eyes, or the Romanian orphans had no-one to wash them, or the mud-brick schools in Paraguay were leaking. Keen and most willing to help, yes: but guilty, no. There is, humanly speaking, nothing that the people in our parishes can do about these things, apart from writing to their MP or sending a letter to The Times. So they're not responsible, and should not be made to feel guilty.

The same applies to us. Placed as we are, we have not the time or the energy to do all the things the Code says. We can do a few of them all the time, and most of them some of the time, and a few of them from time to time. We can do our reasonable best, given the nature of the secular society in which Providence has placed us. But at the end of the day, anyone who tries to tell you that therefore you are under-achieving, and responsible for the sad state of the Church, is being manipulative and dishonest. Much of our fatigue and demoralization stems from the size of the job we would like to do, and our sheer inability to do it. Well, if we cannot do our job with a light heart, something is wrong. If the feeling of inadequate performance, and of always having to run to catch up, are endemic in the job, then there is something wrong with the job, not with us.

The guy in the Code is good at everything. He is a liturgical, social, catechetical, financial performer of the highest order, a sickening whizz-kid. The only thing is, he doesn't exist. All of us were issued, at birth, with a limited gamut of gifts. None of us has them all. You can't be good at everything. It is permitted to be bad at things. Blind spots are allowed for. When we know that, we should be able, with a smile, to ask someone else to look after certain areas of parish life, or even face the fact that this time round they won't be looked after at all. And to do it without shame. I shall render my parishioners a much greater service by maintaining a positive and upbeat morale, than by trying unsuccessfully to do everything. We have, in other words, to grow a shell against unreasonable responsibility which others try to impose upon us. Even after we have done all the proper things about collaborative ministry, collaborating that is both with our brother priests and with the laypeople in our parishes, there will still be some items on our plate which we honestly cannot cope with. So be it. 'So with you' says Jesus: 'When you have done all you have been told to do, say, 'We are useless servants: we have done no more than our duty' (Luke 17:7, NJB). The Greek used by Luke is very strong: *douloi achreioi*, good-for-nothing slaves. But Jesus isn't calling us names; he is talking to all his disciples, not just priests, and saying 'Let your service be humble and unassuming'. That's what the Gospel says. It emphatically doesn't say you've got to be good at everything, or else you can't be an apostle.

Collaborative ministry has always been important, and it is becoming more important by the day. A great deal of work is better done by other members of the people of God, than by us. But they have to be recruited, and they have to be encouraged, and we have to remember that they have partners, families, jobs ... and that they too can get fatigued and demoralized. Even if we take seriously the doctrine of limited and reasonable responsibility, we must not compensate by dumping the load on folk who are already carrying a load. We are still the only full-timers on the block. Hence the ultimate responsibility, and the fact that it can weigh heavy.

Being in charge is one of the tricks our civilization plays on us. The other one is being in competition. We are taught from our earliest years to compare ourselves with others. Class lists, first elevens and second fifteens, that sort of thing. Do you remember the humiliating experience of being picked up, as they called it, for the cricket teams on a summer afternoon; or rather the humiliating experience of not being picked up, and being the only boy left in the arena, not wanted by either side? The iron can enter the soul at a very early age. And then at university, the different classes of degree. In my last parish but one we converted a failing comprehensive school into an ecumenical college, and the board of governors became half Anglican, half Catholic. The magnitude of the change only struck me when we started short-listing for appointments. In the good old Catholic days, I would have scanned the references to see whether the candidate had the Catholic Teachers' Certificate and a letter from the parish priest saying that he was practising his faith. In this new and headier atmosphere, my opposite number in the Anglican diocese could be heard to complain of an applicant, 'Well, he is an Oxford man, but he only has a third from Balliol.' Competition, ever since we were four years old, has had a jagged edge to it. Unless we are supermen we are constantly comparing ourselves with those more talented than ourselves, and feeling to blame because we cannot deliver what they can deliver, and cannot be promoted as they have been promoted. This is a cause of fatigue and demoralization. As Ecclesiastes said in his inimitable dry and vinegary way, 'I see that all effort and all achievement spring from mutual jealousy. This, too, is vanity, and chasing after the wind' (Ecclesiastes 4:4). It also has nothing, absolutely nothing, to do with the Gospel. Indeed the Gospel is very severe about this. Remember the argument which broke out halfway through the Last Supper about who was the greatest, and how Jesus slapped it down. 'Among the Gentiles it is the kings who lord it over them, and those who have authority over them are given the title Benefactor. With you this must not happen' (Luke 22:25, NJB). God is very happy with me the way he made me, with my strengths and weaknesses. He does not compare me, to my disadvantage, with others. Why should I? In Matthew 25 he says 'Well done, good and faithful servant', affirming us in the way we should be affirming one another; not saying 'I'm sorry, you came a poor second.'

If we apply to ourselves, working in the Church, the criteria of excellence which belong to a non-Christian society, we shall end up with a whole series of mismatches. Our energy will be depleted, and we shall get depressed.

In the Church we are dealing here with spiritual realities, not political ones. The Church is a spiritual reality. It is all the things *Lumen Gentium* says it is. It is the Body of Christ, which is certainly a spiritual reality. It is the Father's vineyard, and he is the vinedresser. It is the People of God, called forth by him, and led into an uncertain future by him, pillar of cloud by day and fire by night. Moses is no more than a conduit for the word of God, a channel of communication. It all starts at the Burning Bush (Exodus 3:7). God trades on Moses' curiosity. As soon as Moses comes to investigate the Burning Bush, God takes the initiative, and after that he holds on to it and never lets it fall. 'I have indeed seen the misery of my people in Egypt, I have heard them crying for help on account of their taskmasters ... I have come down to rescue them ... and bring them to a country rich and broad, a country flowing with milk and honey.' The responsibility for the people rests with God, and he retains it, whether Moses is faithful or not, whether Aaron is faithful or not. Moses doubting God at Meribah, Aaron conniving at the Golden Calf, do not deflect God one iota from his plan. He knows what he means to do with his people. The only thing he allows Moses to do, on this level, is plead for them, as when the Egyptians put pressure on the Hebrew foremen. 'Moses went back to Yahweh and said, "Lord, why do you treat these people so harshly? Why did you send me? Ever since I came to Pharaoh and spoke to him in your name, he has ill-treated this people, and you have done nothing at all about rescuing your people"' (Exodus 5:22–3, NJB). After the crossing of the Red Sea Moses appeals to Yahweh about the bitterness of the water. After the episode of the Golden Calf he appeals to the Lord to forgive the people. God does not mind being interrogated, moaned at, badgered even by his minister, and happily enters into dialogue with him. 'Yahweh would talk to Moses face to face, as a man speaks to his friend' (Exodus 33:11, NJB). But he never lets Moses make the policy decisions.

It's God's Church, it's God's diocese, and it's God's parish. The God who raised Jesus from the dead can deal with my patch with one hand tied behind his back. What he looks for in me is not increased activity but increased faith, increased closeness to him, increased trust. This is what I mean by 'holding the charge'. If, this time next year, you can look back on 2004–5 and say 'By and large, I have lived my life with a greater measure of peace. The old tense anxiety and apprehension has given way to something else—a resignation to the will of God, and a willingness to place my people in his merciful hands' ... if in May 2005 you can say that, you will have moved on in no uncertain terms. It is all a matter of seeing God as a hands-on God, a God who knows, sees and cares. What will give might to his arm is not a new programme of evangelization, good though this might be; his arm is already mighty. What will unleash that might is our daily renewed confidence in him.

I am sure that one of the things which wears us down is the contrast between the culture of religion and the culture of the modern world. It is so painful to see our youngsters swept away by the tidal wave of secularism, abandoning the truths by which their forefathers and ancestors lived. Values like regular worship, faithfulness in marriage, scrupulous honesty in private and public life, humble acceptance of the Church's teachings. The news spread by the internet and the television is in-your-face secular, materialist, and often tasteless and vulgar when not downright pornographic. And yet to stand aloof from it all makes us very lonely, like the bird in Psalm 102:6–7 (NJB): 'I am like a desert-owl in the wastes, a screech-owl among ruins. I keep vigil and moan like a lone bird on a roof.' Do you feel like a screech-owl among ruins? It is worthwhile remembering that the Old Testament Hebrews suffered similarly from the contrast with pagan cultures all around them. Half-appalled, half-fascinated, they were. Every time you read in the breviary about 'the nations' you have a match for your own time, in your own parish. 'He frustrates the designs of the nations, he defeats the plans of the peoples' (Psalm 33:10, Grail). God can take on the gruesomeness of the modern media. He is my strength, my rock, my fortress, my Saviour, the rock where I take refuge, my shield, my mighty help, my stronghold. He will bring us forth into freedom; he will save us because he loves us (cf. Psalm 18, Grail). If I can believe this, it will be like the undoing of a troublesome and tightly compacted knot, and the cord will come free at last. I shall work as hard as ever I did, but with great peace. We should not underestimate the size of the opposition. But the responsibility for taking it on is not mine alone, or even principally mine. I lend my hands and my voice and my brain: the rest is up to God.

The prophet Habakkuk might sound like an unlikely place for us to find the support we need, but his third chapter bears reading and meditating upon. In the Jerusalem Bible it is headed 'A Plea to Yahweh for Deliverance' which certainly matches the prayer of the Church in a secular society which is sour, sex-sodden, cynical, thriving on scandal, relentlessly pessimistic and savagely derisive of anything like organized religion. The chapter describes God striding to help his people, to save his anointed; and Habakkuk says 'Yet I calmly wait for the doom that will fall on the people who assail us.' It isn't that we wish doom on individual people. But we do wish doom on a whole culture which is so destructive of human values. And Habakkuk goes on with a sublime act of hope which we should make our own. 'For even if the fig does not blossom, nor fruit grow on the vine, even though the olive crop fail, and fields produce no harvest, even though flocks vanish from the folds, and stall stand empty of cattle, yet I will rejoice in the Lord and exult in God my Saviour. The Lord God is my strength. He makes me leap like the deer, he guides me to the high places.' A great friend of mine who is a retreat-giver and spiritual director in Australia says that the word 'yet' in that passage is the most important word in the whole Bible. An act of hope in a three-letter word. If we can own it, we will hold the charge.

✠

The Presbyterium

One of the most enigmatic components of my priestly life has been my relationship with fellow-priests. At times it has been hugely enriching. At times it has been very disappointing.

We are ordained not in a vacuum but into a presbyterate. Concretely, this means into a diocese, into the clergy of a diocese. If we are ordained in our home parish, the chances are that quite a number of the clergy will show up for the ceremony, and concelebrate, and impose hands at the correct moment. At the sign of peace they will file past again for a brotherly embrace, while the bishop looks benignly on. It all looks like a good beginning, like adoption into a close-knit and fraternal family. Experience shows that the experience falls somewhat short of this. I am not being cynical—just realistic.

I think we can do a fruitful reflection on how the whole thing works, why it works the way it does, why sometimes it doesn't work, and how we can make it better.

I am going to treat you to a lightning description of something called 'transactional analysis'. You may be familiar with this already. If so, you will know that it is not holy writ or an article of faith. It is simply one way of describing human behaviour. It is one that I have found helpful. You are perfectly at liberty to reject this. You may regard it as psychobabble and mumbo-jumbo, and that's OK. But if you do, you will probably concoct your own version of it, simply by observing how other people interrelate. We come to our own conclusions about human chemistry, and priests are generally pretty wise about this stuff. So this is just one set of conclusions. They seem to me pretty near the mark. Bear with me for a moment.

We are built in layers, like a Black Forest gateau. There is in every one of us a child. By and large we grew out of childish behaviour when our voices broke, but not entirely. Bits got left behind. Bits resisted incorporation into the man we were becoming. We are still capable, on occasion, of acting childishly. We do this when we appeal winsomely for assistance. 'I am so helpless, I don't know what to do,' and people rush to help us. We do it when we say to someone more powerful or important than ourselves, 'But you promised...', which is a sort of blackmail (if you don't do what I want you are not a man of integrity). Violet Elizabeth Bott, the girl in the 'Just William' stories, would say when thwarted, 'I'll scream and I'll scream and I'll scream till I'm sick' and some grown-up people say something very similar. We act childishly when we complain, 'Nobody loves me' and wait for someone to say 'Oh, but I love you.'

There is also in us a parent. A father manqué, even if our idea of how to be a father is hopelessly out of date, and would alienate any self-respecting son or daughter. This parent wants to say to people, 'Now just listen to me and I'll tell you how it is.' This parent curtails argument by saying 'I'm in charge here, and I make the decisions.' This parent wants to put people straight, either from the standpoint of superior scholarship, or because he's got more pips on his shoulder. I had a boss once who could not bear theological statements at the dinner-table. However much sense they made. He could not abide discussion or argument. All he wanted was to hear you quote your authority for saying what you said, and see whether it out-trumped his authority. It was a kind of perverted nominalism. Truth had no rights in itself. Things were true because a pope, or a council, had said them; there was no other kind of truth.

The third, and most important layer in us is the adult layer. This is the part of our character which gives other people the credit for also being adults; whether I am talking to the cardinal or the dustman, whether it's a university lecturer or an illiterate Romanian gipsy, this is another human being who deserves my respect, and—more important—deserves a courteous hearing. I might just learn something I didn't know before. At the same time, I expect from this other person the parallel courtesy of being treated with respect, as an equal, and to have my views and experience taken seriously. Adults are capable of offering one another real support. They don't treat one another either as contemptible inferiors, or as superiors to be wheedled, bribed and feared. A truly adult relationship is one on which fraternity can be built. The only one.

The first half of my priestly life was dominated by what I might call the hierarchical principle. Without knowing it, people were acting as parents and children; seldom as adults. Older priests in the diocese were determined to keep the younger ones in their place, rather like prefects at a public school with the new boys. So they barked at us quite a lot. I think, in retrospect, that some of us gave them good reason to bark, and I do not altogether blame them. My impression of myself in the 1960s is of an opinionated and priggish young man, cynical and satirical in a rather adolescent way, un-tellable because I knew the answers, too clever by half, resenting authority and manipulating it with sulks and pouts, impossible to deal with. I am not surprised that some of the older brethren occasionally lost their cool with my generation, and especially with me. In semi-justification, I would say that the system was partly to blame. If you treat men in their twenties like children, they will regress and behave like children: if you look for footprints in the snow to see if anyone came in after eleven o'clock, you must expect your subordinates to nip round the back and climb in through the toilet window. I think both my seminary and my two curacies seriously arrested my development as an adult human being. And if you're not fully adult, it is hard for you to relate in an adult way to other adults. If you behave in a childish way, you cause the other person to turn into a parent and wag his finger. And conversely, if you are supercilious and condescending, you can bring out the infantile streak in the person you're dealing with.

Some people are impossible to deal with because they spend a lot of time being dictatorial and reproachful, but then they unexpectedly topple over into being depressed and pathetic. Many, many years ago I knew a bishop like this. For much of the time he was clouting his men over the head with episcopal authority; it was a card he played very early in any conversation. He would also invoke the magisterium with fatal ease. Invoking the magisterium is a way of winning, but it's also a total show-stopper. (But Father, the Council of Trent is quite clear on the matter ... OK, so now what shall we talk about?) So, inevitably, his priests treated him warily, took him on his own terms, gave him a wide berth. A hard man to make friends with. But then, out of the blue, would come his other bit. Oh dear. Have I lost the trust of the clergy? Should

I resign? I can't do all this by myself. Help me, somebody. And then the guys had to weigh in with a lightning vote of confidence, because he needed soothing and stroking like any child. What he found it very hard to do was look them in the eye and listen unjudgmentally, and with interest, to what they were saying. He had to break in and correct them. He found it hard to accept criticism or advice from those below him in rank, but could be quite superstitiously impressed by those above him. Too much parent, too much child, not enough adult. Before I pillory this particular prelate, I have to face the fact that on my small stage I have acted very similarly for a large part of my life, both as a curate and as a Parish Priest. It reminds me of that verse in Jeremiah in the King James version 'To whom shall I speak and give warning, that they may hear? Indeed, their ear is uncircumcised, and they cannot give heed.' I think there is something in the clerical psyche which gives us uncircumcised ears. We listen badly, and are impatient. We too easily think we know best.

John Paul II says, in *Centesimus Annus*, 'When man does not recognize in himself and in others the value and grandeur of the human person, he effectively deprives himself of the possibility of benefiting from his humanity, and of entering into that relationship of solidarity and communion with others for which God created him.' The value and grandeur of the human person. Pause there. The man you secretly believe to be stupid and unenlightened; the man whose liturgical style makes you cringe; the man whose theology you feel to be on the level of the Beano and the Dandy ... this man has value and grandeur, and God created you to live in solidarity and communion with him. It doesn't mean you have to agree with him. But it does mean that you may never write him off. If you do, you cease, yourself, to benefit from your own humanity. This is sobering stuff. It elevates the imperative for priestly fraternity to a previously unheard-of level. It is no longer an optional extra.

Let me base this where it needs to be based, which is in no other place than the Blessed Trinity itself. We speak of Islam, Judaism and Christianity as the three great monotheistic religions. But Christianity is fundamentally different from the other two because of our belief in the Trinity. When I say I believe in Father, Son and Spirit, what am I really saying? I am saying that God lives in relationship, indeed that God *is* relationship. We name each Person of the Trinity for his stance towards the other two. The first Person is known as Father: he has no other name, and this is right, because we believe that he is totally consumed by the act of self-expression and love which generates the Son—his raison-d'etre is this. And similarly the Son is called that because he receives his whole self from the Father, and in freedom dedicates himself to the Father in unforced filial obedience. The love between these two is the most real thing in the universe, or even outside the universe. It is an infinite, vibrant, knowing, comprehending love, personified in the Spirit. The Spirit has no meaning apart from the Father and the Son. He relates to them with his whole self, his whole being, his whole meaning. So that each Person is unthinkable without the others. It isn't as it is in a human family, where you have family members who are separate and apart, and who happen either to love one another to not, who can go off to the South Pacific and sever contact, who can have rows and divorce one another, and still survive as individuals. The Persons of the Trinity are distinct from one another, but fit into one another as a hand into a glove; if they were made, one would say they were made for one another; but human words falter and fall short of the truth. All one can say is, there is a drama of love and self-gift going on in heaven, a conversation of altruism, which is absolutely necessary, which has to be, and would blind us by its brightness.

Well, this God has made us in his image and likeness. This potential for relating, for going beyond myself in favour of the other, is part of the kit I was issued with when the sperm hit the egg, and I came into being. It's more than good manners. It is in my blood and bones. I am made for this. I am made to relate in love. Some people, like Mother Teresa, St Thérèse of Lisieux and St Vincent de Paul, seem to have known this instinctively. Some of us, for reasons which may not be our fault, make heavier weather of it. If the Catholic Church has a high theology of marriage it is because of this. She knows what men and women are capable of in terms of unselfishness, because she knows where they came from, whose fingerprints are on them.

What is true of me individually is true of the Catholic Church corporately. The Church is not just an association of like-minded people who happen to converge on a Sunday morning. The Church is the

Father's vine, which he has planted and which he tends. It is Christ's body, fed with the eucharist; and it is made alive by the Spirit. The Church is soaked in the Trinity. Without the constant living presence of the Trinity it would collapse in a heap. If it is anything at all it is a spiritual reality. And I am referring not to some Platonic ideal Church floating around in the stratosphere; I am referring to the Church we know, our diocese, our parish, with all its spots and wrinkles. This is the only Church there is. There is no other. In all its concrete clumsiness, and in spite of its human inadequacies, this local Church reflects the Trinity, reveals the Trinity. Rublev's icon of the three persons seated on a single throne around a single chalice is an image of the Trinity, Father Son and Spirit with a united will, a united wisdom. But this icon was painted for a monastery, to remind the monks what God expected of them, too. Benedict had the same truth at heart when he wrote his Rule, with the long-term purpose of enabling the men to live together in charity, above all in charity; all else would be secondary. And a century or so before Benedict, St Basil, who was a monk dragooned into being a bishop, recalled the early Christian community described by St Luke as having all things in common, one heart and one soul, and commented 'Humanly speaking, and by birth, you would expect them to resist this kind of unity'. The unity of the Church was, for him, a miracle. One of the things that would prolong the miracle was the unity of monastic communities, which modelled for the rest of the Church how things ought to be. Well, we could say the same thing about the presbyterate of a diocese. It's like Russian dolls. If in spite of human differences we priests can model for the rest of the Church what it means to live together in charity and loyalty within the local Church, there is more chance that the Church in its turn will be what *Lumen Gentium* says it ought to be, an example of unity and peace for the human race. 'All those who in faith look towards Jesus, the author of salvation and the source of unity and peace, God has gathered together and established as the Church, that it may be for each and everyone the visible sacrament of this saving unity.' A hell of a lot hinges on how we priests treat one another, and how we treat the bishop, and how we are willing to work with one another and with the bishop, and how much forgiveness and milk of human kindness there is in us.

How often have you heard in a panegyric at the crem., 'He wouldn't hurt a fly; he never did harm to anybody, all his life long.' Not hurting a fly is doubtless very fine, but it is not charity. To refrain from scratching and biting and suchlike dirty tricks is commendable, but in itself it is not charity. We can live in placid indifference to our fellow-clergy, not caring whether they sink or swim, but that's not charity. These are the brothers God has given me to love. I might have chosen other brothers, more congenial, more like myself, but the fact is that these are the ones. I need in some way to manifest my care for them, to be hospitable, to be collaborative, to be generous. With a bit of planning it is not too hard to throw a party and invite the local brethren; there's always an excuse for that. With a bit of rearranging one can take the hospital pager and give the chaplain a rest. Without too much drama one can run a neighbouring priest to the airport, or meet him off a plane. These are what the old moral theologians would have called 'the common signs' of charity. What is harder, because it touches us more intimately, is to share our faith with a brother. It is harder because it involves a measure of self-disclosure, which for the British, at any rate, is agonizingly difficult. And yet it is the greatest charity of all, and the most supportive thing of all. Often we can't do it without a framework within it happens more easily, a kind of catalyst, and I want to describe one to you. It is called the 'Jesus Caritas' fraternity, and I only mention it because it is the one I know best, and have been involved with it for going on twenty-five years. It is not the only one, and I am not doing a commercial here: it's not everyone's cup of tea. All I can say is, it's been good for me. Let me describe it.

At the end of the nineteenth century and the beginning of the twentieth there was a French army officer who underwent a profound conversion and became first a monk and then a hermit in the Sahara. His name was Charles de Foucauld. He did everything on a generous scale. He didn't just pray, he prayed a lot, and he wrote a lot of his meditations down, if only to keep himself awake. He didn't just fast, he fasted a lot, and in fact the rule he wrote for the religious order he wanted to start was so strict that nobody joined. He wasn't just hospitable, his hermitage door was open day and night to French soldiers, to Arabs, to Touareg tribesmen, and he was sometimes besieged by visitors. He wasn't just humble, he came right down to the level of the people among whom he lived, learned their language, dressed like them, ate like them, and said 'I want to be a universal brother.' His aim was to convert the Sahara not by preaching but by goodness of life, being being Christlike rather than by talking about Jesus.

He was murdered in 1916 without achieving any of his aims: No order, no conversions. By human standards his life was an eccentric failure. But his friends reflected on his life and his writings, and reckoned that there was something new here, a new way of living the Gospel. Seventeen years after his death, a group of Frenchmen inspired by him formed a new congregation they called 'The Little Brothers of Jesus'. It went through various teething troubles, but when it settled down it, too, was something radically different in the Church of the time. The brothers got jobs, very menial jobs, with no hope of improvement or promotion, so that they could be alongside the poorest and most hopeless members of the working class. The aim was to evangelize not by persuading, but by presence. The manual work might be in a factory, on a farm, in a fishing fleet; it might be sweeping the streets or the corridors of a school, a hospital; but wherever it took place, it was accompanied by long periods of contemplative prayer, centred on the Eucharist. The brothers would live in threes and fours in tiny flats and cottages they called 'fraternities', and a room would always be set aside for the chapel, so that they could have eucharistic adoration. These flats are often in the most violent, run-down, red-light sectors of big cities. I remember visiting one in Warsaw. As you went up the stairs you realized that there was no glass in the windows, and this was at the heart of winter. You also realized that all the families had steel-plated doors so that they could not be smashed in with axes. A glimpse through the odd doorway revealed whole families separated from one another by flimsy curtains; it was like the beginning of Dostoevsky's *Crime and Punishment.* The Little Brothers were placidly setting up home on the top floor of all this. They said that they could not go out at night—no-one could—because of the number of drunk Russian hucksters roaming the streets looking for people to mug and rape. Not surprisingly, they have developed a huge solidarity with the oppressed people of the industrial world. They were very much at home in the France of the early 1950s, with its industrial missions and worker priests. (These days, of course, if you want to identify yourself with the most abandoned people on earth, you join the dole queue.) After the Second World War a parallel order was founded for women, and this is now much bigger than the Brothers.

In the early fifties, a group of priests decided that they wanted to incorporate these values into the diocesan priesthood. They wanted to do it while remaining diocesan priests. They wanted it to be their way of living the Gospel. They wanted to turn their backs on careerism, they wanted to live very simply and hospitably, they wanted to centre their lives explicitly on the eucharist and deepen their prayer life, they wanted to be in constant and affectionate relationship with those the Church had lost touch with, the really poor and marginalized; and—perhaps most importantly—they wanted to support one another.. So they started a movement for secular priests called 'Jesus Caritas', which was one of the slogans minted by Charles de Foucauld in the desert: 'Jesus is love'. The movement grew at speed, and became international within a few years.

The way it works is this. In your area, your diocese, or your part of your diocese, a group of five or six men will meet once a month. The meeting takes a number of hours and it may include an overnight stay somewhere. At this meeting the men pray together before the Blessed Sacrament for an hour; they may read the gospel together and share their reactions to it; and then they make a Review of Life. Usually there's a meal together, and this can be pleasantly uproarious. A Review of Life is a glance back over the preceding month, with its highs and lows, its successes and failures, and an assessment of these in the light of the Gospel. It isn't public confession, and nobody's confidence is forced; but it does involve a degree of self-disclosure. Confidentiality is assured, and so is what we would call 'good listening'. Each man really focuses on what his brother his saying and sharing, and offers his reaction and his support. As the years pass and the group matures, an astonishing degree of trust develops, and people feel free to talk about quite deep and personal things. It is really like a diffuse spiritual direction. You know that whatever your companions say to you, they say as the fruit of prolonged prayer, and with real sincerity. And you know they are there for you whatever happens. There is a skeleton organization at national and international level, with occasional meetings: but nothing pushy. The real life happens at ground-floor level where the priests meet.

Interestingly, the people who end up in a fraternity together might not be obvious mates. They might not choose to go on holiday together. They might have different standpoints on liturgy, on theology, on politics. None of this matters, because the level on which they meet is deeper than any of these. Without being in the least pious or sentimental, you know the depth of faith and love of Jesus in the heart of each one of them, and that is all that matters. They share a love of the desert—they're not necessarily addicted to sand dunes and camels, but to a regular day of quiet prayer and reflection somewhere; they are Nazareth men rather than Jerusalem men. I belong to a group in Rome which includes the international chaplain to the Young Christian Workers, the priest who does the Portuguese broadcasts on Vatican Radio, two hospital chaplains, a university professor, a Peruvian immigrant who looks after a tiny parish in central Italy, the man who used to look after the gypsies in the Rome area, a South African oblate, and the chaplain to l'Arche.

As I said, there are other ways of achieving the same ends, and I am not a fanatical proponent of my own club. But whatever we do by way of 'clotting', we shall be acting in a trinitarian fashion, realizing that we can't do this job without relating to others in a quite intimate way. Diocese has to be more than a slice of the Church described in canon law. DIY priesthood is an oxymoron, it doesn't make sense. Collaborative and supportive priesthood, on the other hand, is based in the proper place, it's based on God and on his way of being. It makes demands on us, of course. We may be temperamental loners, and that's why we joined the diocese and not the Franciscans. But the fact that I, a temperamental loner, am willing monthly to set aside an afternoon and evening for a bunch of colleagues, speaks worlds. It means my priorities are right.

It also means, please God, that I have the child in me and the parent in me under reasonable control, and that I spend most of my time behaving in an adult way with other adults. Not dominating, not manipulating, not creating unhealthy dependencies, but discovering how to be a real brother in a relationship which will survive the ebbs and flows of diocesan life.

✝

INTRODUCTION TO RETREAT

It helps if we can square up to what the next few days are going to contain, so that we don't just drift into the retreat without any focus.

I'd like to start by saying that I think that the pastoral clergy of a diocese are the salt of the earth. I know the kind of difficulties you're up against, and I think that for sheer perseverance and long-term courage you take a lot of beating. For half a hundred reasons, yours is not an easy job. I want to praise you for your tenacity and your faithfulness. I often want to say to the lads in the seminary that the secret is not just preaching brilliant sermons and charming the youngsters in the secondary school: it is that whatever happens you are still there each time when the dust has settled.

That tenacity and faithfulness need to have a reason. A retreat is a time for bringing that reason to the forefront of the mind. Why do I do what I do? Why do I keep on doing it? I do it for God. I do it because I believe in him. I do it because I think he wants me to do it. I do it, in other words, because I believe I have a vocation.

At intervals, then, it is vital for me to focus on this Lord who has called me. During the next three and a half days we are going to attempt this.

If it were a purely secular exercise we could do it via a series of seminars and workshops. But it is not a purely secular exercise. If my awareness of the God who calls me is to be heightened, I have to give him access to me. I have to silence the other noise in my life. Some of the noise is straightforward, physical racket: decibels. Luxuriate in the absence of the phone and the doorbell, and the car doors slamming at midnight as people leave the parish club. You've left all that behind. A retreat is a time for pools of silence in which God can speak to my heart, often in ways which won't go into words at all. He speaks to me in intuitions and convictions. He can't do this unless I limit the noise in my life, and especially the amount of conversation with other people.

I know that one of the great values of a diocesan clergy retreat is that it enables men to meet, and in a diocese like Cardiff, with all its one-man parishes, this is particularly important. The last thing I want to do is stand in the way of that. All I am saying is that something else needs to be going on too, a desert experience, where the individual gets right away from distraction so that he can open himself to Almighty God. I know that in three and a half days none of us can get very far into the desert. But something substantial is still possible. I recommend to you three pools of silent prayer each day, in the morning after the talk, in the afternoon before or after your siesta if you take one, and possibly the Holy Hour at night. Times when you embark on prayer not with any great agenda, except that of humbly waiting upon God, making yourself flexible in his hands, using the words of the infant Samuel: 'Speak Lord, for your servant heareth.' You can do it in the grounds, in the chapel, in your room: walking, sitting or kneeling. The details are unimportant. It's doing it that matters.

There are other kinds of noise. Our worries and anxieties are a kind of noise, aren't they, noise inside our heads and hearts, and these too can crowd the Lord out. Our greatest weapon against these is trust. Whether your preoccupations are personal, or parochial, or both, try to hand them over to Our Lord in perfect trust this week. Too often we say with our people on Sunday 'I believe in one God, the Father, the Almighty' and then proceed to live as if God were too distant, or impotent, or uninterested, to make any difference. By our great anxiety we sometimes negate what we say in the Creed. Try then this week to realize that you don't carry the burden alone: God is near, he is close, he really cares about you, even if he doesn't crack all your problems in the only way which seems possible to you, and according to your time scale. Try to renew your trust, your spirit of self-abandonment, to the living Lord. 'Lord, tell me to come to you across the water.' He won't let you down.

On the side of an Italian All-Bran packet there is a little commercial telling you how good this stuff is for your 'internal gymnastics'. I have been on retreats where it was a bit like internal gymnastics: rosary in common, Stations of the Cross, something to fill every gap. Spiritual exercises of every kind, and no time left to daydream, or to browse over the Gospel. We do need those empty spaces, and to keep them empty; and if we experience boredom rather easily, we will discover that God is at the heart of the boredom, rather like the vein of gold at the heart of the lump of rock. People like Teresa of Avila and John of the Cross will tell you that it was in darkness that they established their most real link with God. Silence and solitude can feel a bit like darkness. But they are a darkness pregnant with promise.

I hope the talks are useful. But even if they're not, you can still make a good retreat: the talks are the icing on the cake. The cake is your relationship with God. This is intensely personal, and needs your personal attention. The Bishop can't have your personal relationship with God, and nor can I: it's yours. The conversation you have with the Lord in the next three days is privileged and private, but above all, it's yours. What I am saying is that we should each dare to take the initiative in taking our spiritual life by the scruff of the neck and sorting what needs sorting. We don't need anyone's permission for that.

I went on the Portsmouth retreat thirty-eight years ago. I was late in applying to my own diocese, and the accommodation was all used up. Imagine that, a diocesan retreat over-subscribed! Anyway, I went to Douai to be with the Portsmouth men, and the retreat-giver was a dynamic young monsignor who had just come back from the Vatican Council, where he had been a consultant and an expert, a *peritus*. His first talk was so full of theological jargon that when I came out into the garden there were two old canons standing and smoking and tapping their cigarettes into a bush, and one said to the other, 'Well, Paddy, it's clear that we're going to get no piety off this man; we'll have to supply our own.' I don't know how much piety you're going to get off me. I simply want to say that I am available to you this week, either in my room or for you to collar me out in the grounds, if you want a chat, or confession. You will be most, most welcome. And I wish you all a good retreat.

✝

Mary, Mother
and Model of the Church

Pope John Paul I said in his last public audience, the day before he died 'To love God is to go towards him with your heart'. It is an instinctive leap forward, in joy and trust. This leap on man's part is generous, simple, affectionate, confiding, warm in response to warmth. This movement of the heart is at the heart of the Catholic religion. All else is done and taught in order that this leap may take place. And no-one shows us this as Mary does. This love gives us endurance, patience, bravery, as it did her. Let me quote from the meditation for the Fourth Station in the 2005 *Via Crucis*.

> In her heart she had kept the words of the angel, spoken to her in the beginning: Do not be afraid, Mary. The disciples fled, yet she did not flee. She stayed there, with a Mother's courage, a Mother's fidelity, a Mother's goodness, and a faith which did not waver in the hour of darkness: 'Blessed is she who believed.'

We can very properly weave a network of theological reflection around the person of Mary. But at the centre of it all is sympathy, kindness, compassion, goodness, and above all, hope. The most inspiring memories I have of very many years spent in pastoral work are of the brisk, loving, competent mothers of large families. How fortunate we are to have such a Mother, and to recognize her.

It is a remarkable feature of Catholic and Orthodox spirituality, that Mary holds a major place in it. This is not simply due to sentiment. There is a solid theological foundation for it. Paul VI said: 'Every authentic development of Christian worship is necessarily followed by a fitting increase of piety for the Mother of the Lord." And he talks about the way God has placed within his family (the Church) 'as in every home, the figure of a Woman, who in a hidden manner and in a spirit of service watches over that family, "and carefully looks after it until the glorious day of the Lord".'†

Love of Mary is also a prime example of what we call the *sensus fidelium*. This means the instinct/intuition/awareness of the ordinary faithful, where the Holy Spirit is strongly present. Devotion to Mary is not driven from the top. It is not imposed. The clergy do not have to bully people into going to Knock, or Lourdes, or Walsingham (or Medjugorje), or into saying the rosary.

The key to Mary's importance is her *Motherhood*. Everything else stems from this. Dante writes in the *Paradiso* (xxxiii.4):

> *Tu se' colei, che l'umana natura*
> *nobilitasti sì che il suo Fattore*
> *non disdegnò di farsi sua fattura.*

> You are she who ennobled human nature to such a degree
> that its Maker did not scorn to be fashioned within it.

Mary was and is the Mother of Jesus. Her maker did not scorn to be fashioned within her. Hers, and no other, was the womb. But Jesus is the Second Person of the Trinity who became man for us. The Councils of Ephesus in 431 and Chalcedon in 451 insisted that Jesus is not two persons but one, although he has two natures. This sounds like a rather dry and abstract argument. But it has astonishing repercussions. If Jesus is just one person, and Mary conceived and bore that person, then Mary is really the Mother of God. She is not simply the mother of the human nature of Jesus—you can't be the mother of a nature. She, a human woman, was chosen to conceive and bring forth a divine person. In this respect she is simply different from any other human being who has ever existed. Her level of intimacy with God is far beyond anyone else's. Being

---

* Apostolic Exhortation *Marialis Cultus*, 1974: Introduction.
† *ibid.*

a mother is, to put it bluntly, a wet and messy business. Her knowledge of him, her bonding with him and her love of him exceeds anyone else's. It is hard for males to comprehend the personal bond experienced by mothers for the children they carry in their womb. That bond existed par excellence between Mary and Jesus. Ephesus described her as *theotokos* which is Greek for 'God-bearer'. This is why 1 January has been changed from the Feast of the Circumcision to the Solemnity of Mary, Mother of God. By worldly standards Mary was simple, undoctored, untutored. But by God's grace she had the capacity to contain and nurture this astonishing, unique and timeless gift. 'God so loved the world that he gave his only Son ...' And he gave him through Mary.

This motherhood has a consequence which has changed the shape of Christianity. We are told in St John's Gospel that he and Mary stood side by side at the foot of the Cross, and that Jesus, with his dying breath, gave them to each other. 'Son, behold thy mother' means that Our Lady becomes our mother as well. That bonding is transferred. Epiphanius, a rather fiery Cypriot bishop in the fourth century, and an ardent upholder of the faith of Nicaea, said that when Genesis 3:20 identifies Eve as the mother of all the living, it is in fact Mary who is being forecast, because while Eve is the carnal mother of all of us, Mary is the mother of life itself, of the Living One, and thus she is truly the mother of all the living, including us.

Much of the patristic reflection on Mary's motherhood stems from this comparison with Eve. The Fathers of the Church delighted in what they called 'recapitulation', which meant a New Testament return to something which in the Old Testament was left hanging, so that it could be completed, perfected and fulfilled by Christ. Mary recapitulates Eve. Irenaeus, the oriental who became the bishop of Lyons in the West, and was martyred in 177, lays it out with crystal clarity.* Eve is the woman who fell; Mary recapitulates her. Eve is the one seduced by a rebel angel; Mary listened to a faithful angel. Eve is the disobedient woman, Mary the obedient one. Eve caused death; Mary caused salvation. Eve brings forth in corruption and pain; Mary with neither. Following Irenaeus, we realize the greatness of Mary's motherhood when we reflect on the

---

* cf. *Adversus Haereses* V.19

enormous number of Eve's descendants, and on the damage she did to them all. If Mary recapitulates all this, as the Fathers say she does, her motherhood is on an awesome scale. And yet it succeeds in being personal and intimate, individual and special.

The Gospels do not tell us much about Our Lady, though what they do tell us is full of meaning. They give us the Annunciation, the Visitation, the Birth of the Lord, his Presentation in the Temple, and Mary and Joseph finding him after three days. They give us the marriage feast at Cana. They give us Mary standing outside the house where he was preaching, with the rest of his family, and asking for him. They give us Mary at the foot of the Cross. And the New Testament shows us Mary, after the Ascension, praying with the Apostles. There are very few words of Mary quoted in the Bible. 'My child, why have you done this to us? See how worried your father and I have been, looking for you' (Luke 2:48, JB). 'They have no wine.' 'Do whatever he tells you' (John 2:4–5). But the Church like Mary herself at Bethlehem, 'treasured all these things and pondered them in her heart' (Luke 2:19).

Our attitude to Mary is a prime example of the twin sources of revelation which are intertwined—scripture, and the constant teaching and practice of the living Church. 'Sacred Tradition and Sacred Scripture, then, are bound closely together, and communicate one with the other. For both of them, flowing out from the same divine well-spring, come together in some fashion to form one thing, and move towards the same goal.'* There was a Russian Orthodox theologian, a layman, called Vladimir Lossky, who lived in the first half of the twentieth century, mostly in Paris, because the Soviets expelled him from Russia. He expresses this truth wisely and beautifully, and applies it to Mary: 'If teaching about Mary belongs to Tradition, it is only through our life in the Church that we can share the limitless devotion offered to the Mother of God by the Church. The measure in which we share in this is the measure of our belonging to the Body of Christ.' It is fascinating to see how entirely an Orthodox believer can enter into the mind of the Church here; many Protestant believers would balk at this idea of sharing the Church's life. Lossky goes on 'Outside the Church, theology will stay

---

* Vatican II, *Dei Verbum*, n. 9.

dumb on this subject, and will not be able to justify the surprising glory of Mary—and that's why Christian communities which reject all notion of Tradition will also remain strangers to the cult of the Mother of God.' I have been infected, both by the scepticism of a materialist Britain, and by the rather suspicious kind of Protestantism which rejects what is not explicitly scriptural, and downgrades Tradition. I remember as a teenager wrestling with Catholic teaching on Our Lady, really because I did not understand the rich notion of Tradition, and living with the Church's life. I felt very strongly the derision, for example, of my French teacher, who had caught sight of a Catholic May procession through the streets of Bedford, 'and *men*, Philpot, with *beads!*'

In the West, the principal prayer to and through Mary is the Rosary. Of this John Paul II said it was 'a devotion directed to the Christological centre of the Christian faith.'* Saying the Rosary has been for centuries an everyday experience for millions of people. For centuries it was the main way of being present at Mass, for all but the most liturgically expert. It took the place of the missal and the psalter for most of the Church. It dates back to the Carthusians in the fourteenth century, who passed it on to the Dominicans, who propagated it. There is also a legend that Our Lady herself gave St Dominic the Rosary as a weapon against the Albigensians. Paul VI said 'By its nature the recitation of the Rosary calls for a quiet rhythm and a lingering pace, helping the individual to meditate on mysteries of the Lord's life as seen through the eyes of her who was closest to the Lord.'† The Feast of the Rosary was instituted by St Pius V after the defeat of the Turks in the naval battle of Lepanto (1571). John Paul II added five more mysteries. And those mysteries of light are full of hope.

The habit of counting prayers is very old. It is said of St Paul the first hermit in the Egyptian desert that he had a pocket full of pebbles, three hundred of them, and that he used to drop them as he prayed. By the fourteenth century, rosaries had become valuable presents. The King of France in 1389 gave his bride 'a string of paternosters' with beads of silver and gold, enamel and pearls. To start with, the beads were for

* Apostolic Letter *Rosarium Virginis Mariae* (2002), n. 4.
† *Marialis Cultus*, n. 47.

counting Our Fathers; the Hail Marys came a bit later. If you said all fifteen decades, that was 150 prayers, which corresponded to the 150 psalms chanted by the monks. (The daily office in those days was, you see, vastly more serious than it is today). As the rosary took on its present form, the Our Fathers between the decades were like the antiphons to psalms chanted in choir. Thomas Spidlik, in his book *The Mother of God,* suggests that we use the rosary as the eastern Christians use the Jesus Prayer: allowing our mind to dwell on all the causes closest to our hearts, all the needs of our friends and relatives, all the people for whom we wish to pray ... and to each reflection, each mental picture, adding an Ave. Such prayer, he says, presupposes simplicity, a simple heart, a heart close to God in all its thoughts. John Paul II refers, in his encyclical on the Rosary, to 'the richness of this traditional prayer, which has the simplicity of a popular devotion but also the theological depth of a prayer suited to those who feel the need for deeper contemplation.'* In other words, it works at all levels.

Mary is Mother of the Church in a special way. In the work of salvation, she stands in the same relation to Christ as Eve did to Adam. Eve was the helper Adam needed. Mary is the helper Christ needs. Augustine says 'She is clearly the mother of the members of Christ, since she has by her charity joined in bringing about the birth of believers in the Church, who are members of its head.'† In the Acts of the Apostles, we find Mary praying with the Apostles for the coming of the Spirit, for Pentecost: to Mary herself, the Spirit was, of course, no stranger. The more we comprehend the mystery of the Church as Christ's Body, the more we shall realize the protective motherly care Mary has for it. These mysteries—The Church as Christ's Body and Mary as the Church's mother—are intimately connected. The Pope, when he greeted the German pilgrims who had come for his installation, said 'Let us pray to Mary, the Mother of the Lord, that she may let us feel her womanly and motherly kindness, in which the whole depth of the mystery of Christ can open up for us.' Womanly and motherly. That's good. That's the key to the whole thing. *Lumen Gentium,* the Vatican II document on the

---

*   *Rosarium Virginis Mariae,* n. 39.
†   *De Virginitate* 6.

Church, calls her 'mother in the order of grace' because of the way she helps restore supernatural life to souls.* In fact the Byzantines have a feast of Mary's protective care. There's a sanctuary at Constantinople where, in the tenth century, two men had a vision of Our Lady sheltering all sorts of people under her cloak: you can see the same image in a fresco in the lower part of the monastery at Subiaco, where St Benedict lived: the all-embracing merciful cloak of Mary. She is Mother of the Church.

Mary is also seen—and this involves a bit of theological sophistication—as model of the Church. The way she is is the way the Church ought to be. The technical term for this, in Latin is *typus*. It means that in faith and charity she blazes the trail that we all ought to be following, not just personally but collectively. Here's the present Holy Father (Pope Benedict XVI), in the Stations of the Cross:

> Holy Mary, Mother of the Lord, you remained faithful when the disciples fled. Just as you believed the angel's incredible message, that you would become the Mother of the Most High, so too you believed at the hour of his deepest abasement. In this way, at the hour of the Cross, at the hour of the world's darkest night, you became the Mother of all believers, the Mother of the Church. We beg you: teach us to believe.[†]

On Calvary Mary is shown to us as both our mother and our pattern of belief.

Mary is, of course, herself a member of the Church, the first among her Son's disciples. Because she is assumed into heaven she shows us what the Church will be one day. The Catechism says, talking about the Church, that it is 'from the Church that the Christian learns the example of holiness, and recognizes its model and source in the all-holy Virgin Mary.'[‡] Yet we have to admit, humbly, that we've a long way to go. Another quotation from the Stations, underlining this starkly.

---

* *Lumen Gentium* 61.
† *Via Crucis* [2005], IV station.
‡ *Catechism of the Catholic Church*, 2030.

Lord, your Church often seems like a boat about to sink, a
boat taking in water on every side. In your field we see more
weeds than wheat. The soiled garments and face of your
Church throw us into confusion.*

But in spite of the spots and wrinkles, in spite of clerical sin, the Church
remains the authentic Body of Christ, full of grace as Mary is full of
grace. Our hope is not hope-against-hope. It's trust.

Mary is also the model for the Church in that she brought forth
Christ at Christmas, and the Church brings forth members for his Body
in baptism. You feel this as priests in a pastoral setting: the instructing
and baptizing of converts is a real bringing to birth, and will give you all
the joy of parenthood. Those of you who have worked in England will
have, maybe, more experience of this joy. As a priest, you share in the
delight of the Church as she contemplates her new-born babies ... even
if some of the babies are a bit old and whiskery by the time they get to
us. I remember receiving an old army major into full communion—I
think he was 90; in the evening his wife asked him 'How do you feel,
Hughie dear?' and he replied 'Considerably uplifted.' When we do this,
we are doing a Mary-like thing. In Spanish, to have a baby is *dar luz*'—to
give light. As Mary gave light to Jesus at Bethlehem, so you and I in the
name of the Church give light to his new members.

When I go into a church and see the sanctuary lamp burning before
the tabernacle, I have a sense of relief, of coming home. The same is
true when I think of Our Lady. How incredibly fortunate we Catholics
are to have these powerful, living resources: God who pitches his tent
among us, and Mary who is always mother, who brings tenderness and
mercy into the mix of the Church. Blessed art thou among women ...
and blessed are we to have you as our mother.

* *Via Crucis*, IX station.

✛

THE PRIEST IN HIMSELF

That is why I am reminding you now
to fan into a flame
the gift that God gave you
when I laid my hands on you.
God's gift was not a spirit of timidity,
but the spirit of power, and love, and self-control.
So you are never to be ashamed of witnessing to the Lord,
or ashamed of me for being his prisoner;
but with me, bear the hardships for the sake of the Good News,
relying on the power of God,
who has saved us and called us to be holy -
not because of anything we ourselves have done
but for his own purpose and by his own grace.

This talk is about you as an individual. Time now to look at the priest, the texture of his life, his hopes and fears, his feelings about the way things are. Things in the world; things in the Church; things in the diocese and in the parish.

In 1978 Cardinal Hume came to a big gathering of priests at Hopwood Hall, in Manchester. It was the start of the charismatic renewal among the clergy. He said to us what seemed at the time an extraordinary thing, but which was also deeply moving. 'Dear Fathers,' he said, 'Thank you. Thank you, not just for what you do, but for who you are.' I think we all agreed over lunch that this was the first time we had been thanked in this way by a bishop. I, though not a bishop, would like to echo what the Cardinal said. I have had jobs, both in my diocese and internationally, which have brought me into contact with hundreds and hundreds of pastoral clergy. Often they have been doing superhuman jobs on the slenderest of resources. Slender resources not just materially, but emotionally and psychologically too. I think the priest in the parish, the priest at the coalface of the apostolate, is the salt of the earth. This is true whether he is in Bangladesh or Argentina or Malta or Plymouth. The job, with its disappointments and consolations, is astonishingly alike wherever you go. Thank you, Fathers, for being the men who do this job, who hold the Church together, who provide the seedbed from which conversion and reconciliation and vocation can spring. What you do is of priceless worth, although it is unspectacular enough. Whether you are a priest or a deacon, thankyou not just for what you do, but for who you are.

And here is Pope John Paul one Maundy Thursday, in his message to priests [2001]. In his own way he is saying the same thing, and saying it better than I can say it.

> Today I wish to express to each of you my gratitude for all that you did during the Jubilee Year to ensure that the people entrusted to your care might experience more intensely the presence of the Risen Lord. At this time, I am also thinking of the work you do every day, work that is often hidden and, without making headlines, causes the Kingdom of God to advance in people's minds and hearts. I want you to know of my admiration for this ministry, discreet, tenacious and creative, even if it is sometimes watered by those tears of the soul which only God sees and 'stores in his bottle' (cf. Psalm 56:8). Your ministry is all the more admirable when it is tested by the resistance of a widely secularized environment, which subjects priestly activity to the temptations of fatigue and discouragement. You well know that such daily commitment is precious in the eyes of God.

To hear a pope using a word like 'admiration' is heartening.

It is important for you to see the hand of God in your personal history. Think of the way God chooses people, in both the Old and New Testaments. It is not always clear why, for instance, he preferred Abel to Cain, or Jacob to Esau, or Joseph to his brothers, or David to his brothers. Often it's the youngest, the least likely. Why did he choose the

Apostles? Why them and not twelve other local lads? Why Paul, who himelf says that he was a child born out of due time, and not another Pharisee, like Gamaliel? There is no point in asking, for you will never find the answer. The point is, *you* are one of those picked people, and God has confirmed his choice not just once, but several times. On the day you were baptized, thousands of others could have been baptized, and were not. You were: you were picked to die with Christ and rise with him to everlasting life. Your confirmation bore fruit; the Spirit came to life in you; in many others, he has been stifled. Your priestly or diaconal vocation is part of the same mystery of God's choice. 'For his own purpose and by his own grace' says Paul to Timothy, and 'not because of anything we ourselves have done.' Isn't that true? When I look at the hoops potential seminarians have to jump through these days, I know for a fact that I would not have got through, even to the starting tape. All I had to do by way of screening was spend ten minutes with the old Bishop, who said, 'Do you have diseases?' I said, 'Yes, I have asthma.' 'No, no,' he said, 'what you have is hay fever.' I discovered later that he had asthma, and maybe he didn't like other people having it too. So I got past that hurdle. Then, when I consider that I actually got through seven years of seminary, I am astonished. I can only think that the staff did not really know what I was like. My first boss in the parish, forty-two years ago, used to say, 'I am very sceptical when people talk about vocation. When I was at Oscott, four of us went out illegally to a coffee shop. Suddenly the Vice-Rector appeared. Two got away through a window and two didn't. The two that didn't got sacked. And now,' he preened himself discreetly, 'And now I'm a canon.' There is no doubt that God chose you, and me, for ordination, and gave us the mental and spiritual equipment to be a pastoral priest. Maybe not because of us, but in spite of us.

The choice of God fell on you, not for your own sake, but for the sake of the ten thousand or so people you would influence pastorally in the course of your life. They were destined to meet you. By preaching, by interview, by hospital or prison visit, at funerals and weddings: in God's plan, those people are lined up in a queue so that they may be be affected by you, by your sincerity, your faith, your unselfish service, your particular genius, character and gift. You may not think much of yourself, but God fashioned you so that you would be ripe for calling, ripe for the work. Your priesthood is not your own. Theologically priests share in the priesthood of the Bishop, we know this. Experientially however priests are a gift for folk who need the sacraments, whom God longs to heal and feed and teach. I recall a young priest who left the priesthood and became an Anglican, proposing to be employed as a priest in the Church of England. 'You can't do that,' we said to him. He replied 'It's my priesthood, and I'll take it where I like.' His theology was faulty. Divorced from the bishop and from the people to whom the bishop had sent him, his priesthood did not make sense. We cannot afford to be narcissistic about this. It's not a personal perk. Our job is to fit into God's plan like a piece into a jigsaw. God's plan is still in place, still unfolding. The plan still runs. The grace is still given, if we are disposed to accept it. Outside God's plan, priesthood would be an enormity. Within it, we have the potential to do so much good to so many people.

Paul says to Timothy that God has saved us and called us to be holy. Not just called us to be priests, but called us to be holy. Holy is an off-putting word, isn't it, and I am tempted to apologize for pushing it at you. But I shan't apologize, because it says what I want to say. We do our job most effectively by being holy. Note that I didn't say 'by being pious'. That's something quite different. I don't think that you, personally, necessarily have a vocation to be pious. I am certain, however, that you are called to be holy.

Being holy implies, first of all, being a man of prayer. I am talking here about private and personal prayer, the kind of thing which was called 'meditation' in the seminaries of the 1950s. Each of us will have his own approach to this. Some men are happy with the structured Ignatian model: if your imagination is constantly distracting you, it's a good idea to employ it in your prayer, put yourself with all your five senses into the gospel account and live it as vividly as you can, letting it turn into a conversation with Our Blessed Lord, imagining him talking to you as much as you talking to him. Some people are happier simply focusing on God, dispensing as far as they can with imagination, using a word or a phrase from the gospel as background. Cardinal Hume prayed a bit like this—he used to say that prayer was rather like being with someone you love, but in a very dark room. Some people are happier with traditional patterns like the Rosary. Some people—I suspect, quite a lot—have dispensed entirely with private and personal prayer, seeing it as a kind of seminary homework from which they are now, thankfully, free. I am sure this is a pity. Timothy Radcliffe, the Master General of the Dominicans, said in a recent book, 'Contemplation of the only-begotten Son is the root of all mission ... without this stillness there is no movement.' The point is that private and personal prayer has a transforming effect on you, although you may be the last person to detect it. It increases your pastoral effectiveness. It gives God the chance to make you holy.

Being holy implies treating other people right. That is, with both justice and kindness: having high standards of both fairness and charity. Clerical bull-sessions easily become, as we know from experience, anything but charitable, and sometimes they are unjust as well in the hatchet-jobs they do on people. Then, we need to have a highly developed sense of justice, and one going beyond our domestic situation or diocesan matters. We are citizens in a democracy, with entitlement to write to the papers, to address our MP, to dialogue constructively but critically with those in charge of our affairs. In the face of so much suffering on the surface of our planet, the rich/poor contrast becomes an affront to the gospel. It overflows politics and becomes a major moral concern. Concern for justice is a constituent part of holiness, on the micro and the macro level.

Being holy implies walking in the footsteps of the most holy person who has ever inhabited this earth, which is Christ. And Christ plants the Cross bang in the middle of our lives. If you want to be my disciple, he says, this is the deal. Pick up your cross and carry it. How do we confront the pains and inconveniences of life? With fury and impatience? Or can we see within them an invitation from the Lord? God knows that the life of pastoral clergy is littered with frustrations and disappointments, although there are the good moments as well. Can we weave the frustrations and disappointments into the texture, see them as part of an intended texture, of a life lived for God—that's the question. We are no strangers to fatigue, moral, physical and mental. I wonder if you know that poem of R. S. Thomas called 'The Minister'? In it he describes the recruiting of a new Nonconformist pastor for a Welsh mountain village.

> They chose their pastors as they chose their horses,
> For hard work. But the last one died,
> Sooner than they expected; nothing sinister,
> You understand, but just the natural
> Breaking of the heart beneath a load
> Unfit for horses. 'Ay, he's a good 'un,'
> Job Davies had said; and Job was a master
> Hand at choosing a nag or a pastor.

There are times when we feel more like nags than pastors. That's the eighth beggar at the door today. This is the third Thursday in a row that half the confirmation kids haven't turned up. The organist has gone neurotic on me yet again and resigned, and I have two weddings on Saturday. Christ tells us that none of this is without meaning, none of this is entirely dark. God speaks to me when Paul talks to Timothy about bearing hardships for the sake of the Good News, and these are the hardships he means. Do we really believe this?

'With me, bear the hardships for the sake of the Good News.' I think the greatest of these is the fact that wedges can be driven between us. When you read the story of our Martyrs, you get the impression that there were no wedges. The Council of Trent had seen to that. Uniform liturgical outlook, uniform theology. The Martyrs could get Calvinists and Lutherans and Anglicans in their sights and say 'That's the enemy.' The enemy was outside, never inside. Caraman describes, in *Henry Garnet and the Gunpowder Plot,* how Garnet would convene the young Jesuits from all over England. They would come secretly to a house in the fields just north of London. They said Mass, serving one another's Masses. They went to confession. They asked one another's advice about difficult cases. They rejoiced in one another's company. Then Garnet would say, quite suddenly, 'Fathers, from now on I cannot guarantee your safety—I advise you to disperse, and we will meet again in a year's time.' His instinct was infallible. As they slipped out of the back door and away down the country paths, the priest-hunters would come thundering up the road to the front door. Those young men were energized and heartened and prepared for martyrdom by the unity that reigned among them. Of course it is possible to paint too rosy a picture. Even in the sixteenth century there were ferocious rows, for instance, between the Jesuits and the secular clergy, or people who supported the Archpriest and people who didn't. Are there things which divide us? Standpoints on liturgy, justice and peace, Church authority, where a difference of opinion destroys our respect and esteem for another man?

John Chrysostom said in one of his homilies,

> For then especially will the Devil attack us when he sees us alone and separated from each other. It was in this way that he tempted the woman in the beginning: approaching as she was alone, and her husband absent. For when he sees us in the company of others, and united, he does not dare attack us. For this special reason should we frequently come together: so that it shall be more difficult for the Devil to attack us.

When we experience those wedges, we are experiencing the Devil. The same applies to that feeling of jealousy when another man is promoted; or smouldering resentment at something the Bishop has done, or has not done, or the way he has done it. Jealousy and resentment are alive and kicking among Catholic clergy, aren't they? They are like scorpions which hide between the cracks in an Italian bathroom floor: you don't know they're there until they bite you. The deeper truth, if only we can attend to it, is that we need one another. The Lord has given us to one another to be brothers. There are no other brothers on offer. Let no-one and no thing ever take that from us.

Being holy implies what Paul calls 'living in the Spirit'. If you have received the Spirit, then, he says, for God's sake live in the Spirit. Dare to see the whole drama of human existence, your own and other people's, from God's point of view and in the light of eternity. Believe that God is a hands-on God who is very close to you, who knows all the details of your life, both private and professional, and who loves you to distraction. You can converse with God, interrogate him even, over the greatest and the smallest things. The Spirit enables you to see God as your good Father. This intimate relationship is the dominant factor in your life. Don't let it cool.

The best result from these few days together would be what Paul recommends to Timothy: a fanning into flame of the gift we have all received. The Greek word is more like 'giving the fire a poke', stirring it up from the embers: it's still there, like a sleeping giant, but it might need awakening. We should not be afraid of doing this, and landing ourselves with more work, more risk of disappointment and disillusion, because this time we shall be—to quote Paul again—relying on the power of God, and God cannot be tripped up. The sky's the limit. He can be blocked by the hardness of a human heart, but that's about all. If my heart has got hardened by bad experiences, or by tiredness, or by resentment, now is the moment to soften it again. The outcome, for me, my diocese and the whole Church, could be quite fantastic.

✠

THE PRIEST IN THE CHURCH

That is why I am reminding you now to fan into a flame
the gift that God gave you when I laid my hands on you.
God's gift was not a spirit of timidity,
but the Spirit of power, and love, and self-control.
So you are never to be ashamed of witnessing to the Lord,
or ashamed of me for being his prisoner;
but with me, bear the hardships for the sake of the Good News,
relying on the power of God who has saved us
and called us to be holy—
not because of anything we ourselves have done
but for his own purpose and by his own grace.

This is really a meditation on what the Church is anyway. It is a necessary meditation to offset the sadness and depression which can overtake us. We feel responsible for the Church. We compare it with the boom years of the past. We wonder what it is that our generation has done wrong, while all the others appear to have got it right. When vocations fall sharply, when scandals break in the media, when the numbers at Mass decrease and the young vote with their feet, we priests feel responsible, but at the same time we don't know what to do. Responsibility without any way of discharging it is the very worst fate that can befall anyone. If the Church isn't functioning well, if it is criticized in the press and on the television, we can become ashamed of witnessing to the Lord.

At the beginning of the decree *Lumen Gentium* in Vatican II there is a whole list of analogies which help us understand the Church. No longer are we hemmed in by the penny catechism definition 'the one ark of salvation for all'. The biblical images crowd in upon one another—heavenly Jerusalem, vineyard, sheepfold, body, bride. But the preferred image seems to be that of the messianic people on pilgrimage. The Church is dynamic, travelling somewhere with a sense of purpose. The clear likeness is to the Israelites in the desert after the Passover. It has not yet arrived but is 'in search of a future and permanent city (cf. Hebrews 13:14)'. Meanwhile, it is Christ who has purchased the Church with his own blood. He has filled it with his Spirit. The members of the Church are people who look towards Jesus, the author of salvation and the principle of unity and peace.

So we are not alone. Just as the Israelites in the desert were in constant contact with God, and Yahweh spoke to Moses 'face to face, as a man speaks with his friend' (Exodus 33:11), so are we. We travel under God. We may let him down in various ways, as the Hebrews did, grumbling about the diet, pining for the fleshpots of Egypt, and he may show us his displeasure in various ways, as he did the Hebrews. Read Psalm 106 to get an idea of the chequered relationship. They defied him at the Red Sea. They sang his praises when he rescued them from the Egyptians, but then they forgot his achievements and challenged him again. They made the Golden Calf and worshipped it. They lost faith in his promise. They went in for false religions and human sacrifice. God punished them in various ways, he struck them with a wasting fever, sent them a plague, handed them over to the pagans, but he never abandoned them. For their sake he remembered his covenant, says the psalm, he relented in his great love. This is the heart of the matter. God had committed himself to them, he had invested so much in them that he could not draw back. A covenant is a covenant, and God is always faithful. There were times when Moses despaired of ever getting this motley and stubborn crowd across the desert to the Promised Land. Times when Moses himself lost confidence in the covenant. Times of what seemed like total eclipse for all his hopes. More often than not his problems arose not from marauding tribes, who could be dealt with by God's help, but from inside the Chosen People. (Clearly, the Israeli taste for politics, for breaking into contentious factions, dates back a long, long way.) Yet the one constant in this turbulent story is that Moses was never out of contact with God, and that God remained faithful to his covenant with his people.

We too are in constant contact with God, and we live under the new and everlasting covenant. In the light of this, all the woes and agonies of the present-day Church are only relative. God has pledged himself to this people. That is the source of our hope. The people may dwindle at certain stages of the pilgrimage. The marauding tribes may succeed in picking off a lot of stragglers. Some of our spiritual leaders may lose their nerve, or prove morally defective. It may be hard at some periods to recruit spiritual leaders at all. But the show goes on. I remember Archbishop Dwyer, thirty years ago, speaking after lunch to a group of priests. 'Please don't be too hard on the bishops', he said, 'We are doing our best. But if you do feel you have to go in for heavy criticism—well, the dogs may bark, but the caravan still goes by.' That describes the Church very accurately. The dogs may bark (media dogs, tabloid dogs, some Catholic dogs), but the caravan still goes by. It goes by because we are in constant contact with God, and we live under the new and everlasting covenant. We are part of a spiritual reality. The Church, for all its human spots and wrinkles, is a mystery, it is God's way of pitching his tent among men, and it cannot come to lasting harm. We haven't backed a loser. We do our little best, we contribute our sixpennyworth of effort and ingenuity at this particular point of the trek across the desert, but the ultimate responsibility is God's. It is he who has taken on this people. Do not be afraid.

The worst thing Moses ever did was to crack, at the waters of Meribah. The worst thing we as pastors can do is to lose confidence in God. That's worse than pedestrian liturgy, dismal preaching or bad catechetics. If we stop trusting God we are taking on our shoulders an impossible burden. If we try to make ourselves solely responsible for the Church, even the Church in our country or our diocese or our parish, we are literally attempting the impossible. If God called the Israelites a stiff-necked people in Exodus 33:5, it was because he knew them to be ungovernable, unleadable by any human agency. Had Moses attempted to do it by himself he would have been eaten alive. Yet sometimes we try to do it by ourselves. We forget to pray, to cast ourselves on God's mercy daily, and we try to run the Church as though it were a corporation. In his book *The Heart of the World*, published nearly fifty years ago, von Balthasar says:

Yes, a priest stands at the altar, all the way at the front,
distracted and tired. Behind him in the nave he senses the
absent-minded crowd with its dull confidence that 'Up there
something's happening that somehow (we don't know exactly
how) concerns us, too. Up there a man is at work and surely
he knows what he's doing. He holds the office, he has the
responsibility.' But how is a man, even if he is a priest, to bear
the burden of the whole community?

Do you have the feeling, I wonder, of bearing the burden of the whole
community? We need, don't we, to reclaim that profound, radical sense
of being God's people, utterly dependent upon him for everything,
pleading humbly for his direction. God is the dominant reality in this
Church, and going it alone is quite insane. 'Relying on the power of
God who has saved us' says Paul to Timothy. We need to ask ourselves.
'What do we rely on? Where is our centre of gravity? We say every
Sunday at Mass that we believe in one God, but do we *really* believe in
him? Really believing in him does not mean that we shall lie back and
do less work. It does mean that we shall do less worrying, and not feel
ashamed when times are hard.

I find comfort in looking at Bishop Challoner. Challoner was the Vicar
Apostolic of the London District for most of the eighteenth century. He
was a totally unimaginative man, emotionally level, who lived by a very
strict self-imposed routine: prayer, Mass, writing, reading, interviews,
visitations, hearing confessions at his house. He was not an exciting
person: 'dogged' is the word that comes to mind. The problems he had
to face were colossal. Catholicism, a tiny minority, was no longer being
persecuted in a bloody sense, but was still liable to periodic bursts of
unpopularity. In the 1760s, a vitriolic informer called Paine, a carpenter,
began a series of prosecutions of Catholic priests and schoolteachers,
invoking the letter of the law and getting Mass-centres closed. In 1780,
an unhinged Scottish nobleman started the Gordon riots, which was
really a march on Parliament that got out of hand, and unleashed a great
wave of violence, much of it against Catholics. The punitive stuff was
still on the statute books. Catholics tended to keep their heads down.
They were looked after by a motley bunch of priests. Poor Challoner

had problems with womanizing and actively alcoholic clergy, including an alcoholic retired bishop, on his patch. 'Fuddling about the country' was how Challoner described the more scandalous among the brethren. The wealthy laity claimed the right to choose their own chaplains and to control their activity. Some members of religious orders were not willing to accept the direction of the vicar apostolic, and had recourse instead to their own superiors. The seminaries, Challoner reckoned, were slack: he complained that at the English College in Rome the Jesuits were admitting 'unlikely persons' as ordinands. So the manpower truly at his disposal was terribly small. In addition to this, many of the prominent laity were losing their way. Several MPs renounced their Catholic faith in order to take their seats. If a Catholic landowner died and his successor was a Protestant, or if a Catholic landowner apostatized, then the Mass-centre in his house would be closed. 'A great decay of piety and religion amongst the greater part of our Catholics' Challoner remarked, and another writer said, that the 1700s were a 'century of depression, of lost hopes and discouragement, when numbers steadily, if slowly, dwindled away.' Newman, in his famous sermon on the Second Spring, alluded to the Catholics of the period as 'dimly seen, as through a mist or in a twilight, as ghosts flitting to and fro.' All these assessments were over-pessimistic, and things were not quite as bad as painted. Yet it was not a happy century for the Church in England.

In face of this, what did Challoner do? Well, the first thing was something he did not do. He did not lose his nerve. He went on with the work to hand, come rain come shine. Quite often come rain: I have my own picture of him, drenched and alone, riding his horse out of London on a chilly autumn afternoon, in the teeth of a gale and a slanting downpour, to administer confirmation to a handful of people hours away, in a village somewhere off the Great West Road, carrying his kit—crozier, mitre (he had a tin one), chrism, the lot—in a saddle-bag, the very opposite of the prince-archbishops of Liège and Cologne who were his contemporaries on the continent. He was a man who put up with discomfort and inconvenience with great long-term courage, and who did his duty with enormous patience. He undertook the updating of the Douai Bible and wrote many prayer-books and books of devotion for ordinary Catholics. He was supremely practical—he only did things that were useful. His prose style was leaden and unexciting. Yet what he produced kept the faith and the practice of the faith alive in hundreds of homes. He was a superbly pastoral bishop, in the face of what, as far as one could see, was a hopeless situation. He had what John Paul II would call 'pastoral charity'. By being who he was he did a lot to shape the Church in this country in the eighteenth century, and to prepare it for what he could not see, but was only just round the corner—a wave of conversions, Catholic Emancipation, massive Irish immigration and the restoration of the Hierarchy. You could have no greater contrast than that between Challoner and Wiseman. Wiseman rode the crest of the wave of the Second Spring. He was the Cardinal Archbishop, Rome-conditioned, baroque, flamboyant, emotional. There is nothing to say that Wiseman was better than Challoner, that he deserved more success and admiration. There was no personal merit in this. Simply, that in God's dispensation, it was Wiseman who inherited the hope and the prospects. It is, however, Challoner of whose canonization people sometimes talk.

Our mistake is to see the Church under the category of an earthly kingdom, or an earthly business. Earthly kingdoms and earthly businesses demand what you might call linear growth. They are supposed to develop at a steady percentage rate. How often do you hear on the stock market news some announcement like 'Heavy selling on the markets as such-and-such a firm predicts poor results for the current quarter'? How often do you hear the British Chancellor, in his budget speech, and no doubt this Irish counterpart too, talking of economic growth for the nation? This is how we calibrate success. Expansion good, contraction bad. Power good, powerlessness bad. So when we come to think of the Church, if we are not careful, we apply the same criteria. Growth, and influence. Here's von Balthasar again:

> The power of the Church also enters your ambitions. You want to see her great and beauteous and all-encompassing, and even if you do not yourselves rule, you look on with satisfaction when the Church tends the throngs like a herd. How acute is this drive to power in you! How greatly it lives on secretly in all those who have died to the world for my

name's sake! How sweet the song of the ancient serpent, 'You will have knowledge and be like gods!'

The Church, however, belongs to God, and power-criteria are not God's criteria. God seems, so far as we can tell, to specialize more in death and resurrection, in new beginnings, in shoots springing from stumps. That's his rhythm, that's his style.

Yahweh speaks, through Jeremiah, about the scattered flock of Israel (Jeremiah 23:3):

> The remnant of my flock I myself will gather from all the countries where I have dispersed them, and will bring them back to their pastures: they shall be fruitful and increase in numbers. I will raise up shepherds to look after them and pasture them; no fear, no terror for them any more; not one shall be lost—it is Yahweh who speaks!

The theme of the remnant is very important in the prophets, and I am sure learned theses have been written about it, and, to be honest, I haven't read them. The remnant of Israel gets threatened, as well as reassured: it's not all plain sailing. In spite of all this, we can hear—even in a prophet as pessimistic as Jeremiah—an insistent note: God may allow his people to be pared down, pruned, but he will not let anyone come and obliterate it. God may allow his people to be carted off to exile in Babylon, but that will not be the end of it. Always, always on the horizon there is light, and hope. God has invested so much in his people, and has bound himself to the people by his word: if the people were to perish, God would—and this is impossible—lose something of himself in the perishing. Mind, the exiles in Babylon could not see the shape of the Temple they would build when they got home, or what kind of nation they would construct. All they knew was, it would be quite different from the old one. The parallel with the Catholic Church at this moment, not just in the UK but in Ireland too and the whole of Western Europe, is striking. We must settle for a different shape of Church coming very soon, and having done so, reclaim the right to be men of hope.

✠

REMOVING THE ROADBLOCKS

In this talk I acknowledge my debt to a book by Gerald May called *Addiction and Grace*. I found it quite remarkable and thoroughly recommend it to you.

> In my Father's house there are many dwelling-places. If it were not so, would I have told you that I go to prepare a place for you? And if I go and prepare a place for you, I will come again and will take you to myself, so that where I am, you may be also. (John 14:2–3, NRSV)

This promise of Christ looms larger for me than it used to, because I am older, and naturally think about heaven, and judgment, quite a lot. It is a promise which fills me with hope, but it also causes me to review my life, and I do not altogether like what I see. I perceive more clearly than ever before the things that went wrong.

The things that went wrong can be grouped under a single heading—'addiction'. I don't mean by that, an irresistible craving for drugs or booze. I mean addiction in a much broader sense. Addiction is any kind of getting hooked. You can get hooked on praise and affirmation, really needing a periodic fix of admiration. You can get hooked on another person and dream about them day and night, without ever putting a foot wrong. You can get hooked on your own self-imposed daily routine, and be all at sea if it is interrupted. You can get hooked on having your own way, and turn very ugly if someone else's will prevails over yours, or if you are kept waiting or inconvenienced. You probably know the story of the priest who was so angry at the slow service in the hotel dining-room that he said to the young waiter 'Do you know who I am?' and the waiter replied, 'No sir, but I'm sure if you ask at the desk they'll be able to tell you.' You can get hooked on being right, and get very resentful if your public statements are questioned. You can be addicted to a hobby or a sport. You can get addicted to your property, to your hi-fi or your car, so that if these things are damaged or stolen you are devastated and depressed. You can be addicted to security—not to being rich, but to being safe, so that any question about your pension or your retirement plans sends you into a spiral of panic.

None of these forms of addiction will bring the Gardai to your door with the handcuffs, indeed they are all eminently respectable. Yet they are undue attachments. If we are doing our best to travel towards God, to grow in holiness, it is our attachments and addictions that will slow us down. So this talk is about claiming your freedom.

We do have a terrible tendency to get tunnel-visioned about things. When I was a young priest I was reluctant to go home on my day off because my mother had this crazy dog. For most of the day it behaved normally, but in the early evening it would growl, roll its eyes and seize some article of clothing and take it off into a corner. If it happened to be something you were likely to need in the next couple of hours, well, tough. Because it wasn't a game, it was an obsession, and in reclaiming your shoe or your scarf you could be quite badly bitten. Family members got no privileged treatment. The dog was, literally, obsessive. It could not see—how could it?—that its long-term interests would be served by laying off other people's property. Because it did not have that sort of intelligence, it had to be despatched by the vet before its time.

The dog didn't have the intelligence, but I have. I realize that my closeness to God, my union with God, will be impeded—and maybe fatally impeded—by undue attachments, whether to people or to things; and yet I still let them happen. (Maybe I'm the one who should have been taken to the vet). It is as though, somewhere in my heart, there were an adhesive strip or a piece of velcro which makes me possessive, which makes my heart stick to things. God says to me 'Son, give me your heart' and for much of my life I've had to say, 'By all means take my heart, but it is mortgaged.' I am not suggesting that we live devoid of preferences and recreations. Far from it. I think every priest should have at least one skill or talent, an absorbing interest, something that gives him and other people delight. But when the absorbing interest turns into a necessity that can't be done without, then we're in trouble.

The project of travelling home to the Father's house has encountered a roadblock.

St John of the Cross says in *The Ascent of Mount Carmel* (III.20):

> [The man who avoids attachment] will acquire liberty of soul, clarity of reason, rest, tranquillity and peaceful confidence in God and a true reverence and worship of God which comes from the will. He will find greater joy and recreation in [the] creatures through his detachment from them, for he cannot rejoice in them if he look upon them with attachment to them as to his own. Attachment is an anxiety that, like a bond, ties the spirit down to earth and allows it no enlargement of heart. He will also acquire, in his detachment from things, a clear conception of them, so that he can well understand the truths relating to them, both naturally and supernaturally. He will therefore enjoy them very differently from one who is attached to them, and he will have a great advantage and superiority over such a one.

John of the Cross is one of the all-time masters of the spiritual life, and whatever he says carries tremendous weight. It also has to be said that he was not a barrel of fun, and that his view of attachment, coming out of the religious culture of sixteenth-century Spain, seems to us excessively severe. But what the man says here is true. Attachment is an anxiety that, like a bond, ties the spirit down to earth and allows it no enlargement of heart. An anxiety. How much of our life is spent in anxiety? This has been my number one addiction, over forty-six years of priesthood. Anxiety about getting it wrong. Anxiety about what the bishop, or the parish priest, or the curate, would say or think. Anxiety about being correct, and safe from reproach. Anxiety about not upsetting the parishioners. Anxiety about the past, and about the future. Anxiety about how this article, or that talk, would be received. And these anxieties masked an undue concern about my image and my reputation: I was addicted to being blameless and being popular. My spirit was tied down to earth and had no opportunity to soar, because I was a chronically worried man. If you are full of apprehension, there is a concealed slavery somewhere, an addiction, an inability to let go.

Workaholics are addicted. What they do looks virtuous, but it's not. I remember when I was first ordained being warned against a fellow-curate: 'He always takes his day off.' I was suitably appalled. Today I would be delighted. The man who doesn't take time away from the parish or the desk is clearly convinced that he is indispensable, and that's an addiction if anything is. He's hooked on being necessary. He needs to be needed. His spirit is tied to earth by a misplaced sense of duty. Ego is filling his horizon. We have to remind ourselves again and again that it is not our Church but God's, and if we do our honest and reasonable best he will look after the rest. We do much greater service to the people by being relaxed and in good health, by letting the spirit soar, than by being lean and hungry perfectionists. Ultimately it doesn't boil down to being lazy or not being lazy. I'm not advocating laziness, of course I'm not, but that's not the issue. Laziness is a question of quantity of work. What really matters is how much faith you have, and how powerful and good you think God is. And that decides the quality of your work.

'He will also acquire, in his detachment from things, a clear conception of them.' A clear conception means being able to see round behind them and over the top of them. It means that nothing, and nobody (except God) becomes the be-all and end-all of your existence. It means that you can put everybody, and everything, in a context, so that the proportions don't get skewed. A good example would be the deep attraction we are bound to feel, from time to time, for someone in the parish. If we have a clear conception of things we will be able to name what's going on, admit it to ourselves and, ideally, someone else as well like a spiritual director or a brother priest. We will be able to accept it as a factor in our existence, at least for the moment, while realizing at the same time that our vocation and our ministry are far more important and far more durable than a hormonal response. We will, please God, be mature enough not to get hooked and start playing games of self-deceit, inventing reasons for seeing the object of our affections more frequently, or alone. In other words we fly neither into denial nor into surrender. Why? Because we believe that detachment is a fundamental quality for a priest, and by the grace of God we've got into the habit of it.

'He will therefore enjoy [things] very differently from one who has got attached to them.' There is enjoyment in store for the detached man, a lot of it. The world is his oyster. John of the Cross talks about 'joy and recreation'. It is not a joyless life that he is advocating. 'And he will have a great advantage and superiority'. Fine, so long as feeling superior does not itself become an addiction. A conviction that we are better than all the unfortunate addicts around us will be self-defeating in a big way. The essential companions of detachment are humility, which St John of the Cross would endorse, and a good sense of humour, and there I'm not quite so sure.

In his book, Gerald May makes the point that only the grace of God can rescue us from our addictions. Will-power alone will not do the trick. Naked resolution is its own worst enemy, because repeated failure only brings us depression and discouragement. All the puffing and blowing in the world will not break a habit of body or of mind, but the grace of God can do it, and do it easily, and there are countless examples of this on record. Every reason, then, to be full of trust about our personal future. None of us is stuck. We need, then, to put our energy into believing, and trusting. It is God's will that we should travel home to him, so surely it will be his will to break the shackles which impede our progress.

In 1547, Ignatius Loyola wrote a letter* to the young Jesuits who were studying at Coimbra in Portugal. They were the hope of the Order. He talks to them about 'the expectations which so many people have of you' and then he reflects with them on the grace they have received:

> God has not only 'called you out of darkness into His marvellous light' and transferred you 'to the Kingdom of his beloved Son', as with all other believers; it has also pleased Him to take you out of the dangerous gulf of this world, so that you can better remain pure and upright, and centre your affection on the things of the Spirit, the things of His service. Thus your consciences will not be at risk from the tempests often stirred up in us by the wind of desire, a desire at one moment for wealth, at another for being honoured, at

* Monumenta Historica Societatis Jesu, n. 169.

yet another for sensual pleasure, or else by the opposite of
desire, the fear that all this might be lost.

Addictions do not always come singly. If you are an addictive sort of
person, someone with a fatal propensity to say 'Yes' immediately to a
desire, you will understand this. Ignatius accurately detects one of the
ways in which addictions work: they fracture us. He describes a desire at
one moment for one thing, at another for another, so that we are pulled
about helplessly by our instincts, fragmented men, no longer masters in
our own house. The pleasures in such a life are only fleeting, and there
is very little peace, because we are not 'up together', we have lost our
centre of gravity, our fundamental unity. We are 'at risk from tempests'.
That is the dangerous gulf of this world from which we need rescuing,
and from which only grace can rescue us. You and I have to live our
lives, as diocesan priests, in the dangerous gulf. We can't cut ourselves
off from it. But we can learn to spot addiction, which is like a crocodile
swimming around in the gulf, and give it a wide berth.

About the same time as John of the Cross, Teresa of Avila wrote,
for her nuns, the famous book on prayer called *The Interior Castle*. She
says that the business of life is self-knowledge, which increases if we are
faithful to prayer, until we reach the deep-down heart of ourselves where
God dwells, and are united with him. So the key to self-knowledge is
prayer; if you don't pray you will never even begin. She pictures the soul
as a glass castle, with rooms opening one from another as we move from
the fringe towards the centre. Here she is talking about a man who is
just beginning this journey, a man in the outermost room of the castle.
And guess what, he is fighting his addictions.

> The room itself is light enough, but he cannot enjoy the light
> because he is prevented from doing so by these wild beasts
> and animals, which force him to close his eyes to everything
> but themselves. This seems to me to be the condition of a soul
> which, though not in a bad state, is so completely absorbed in
> things of the world and so deeply immersed, as I have said, in
> possessions or honour or business, that, although as a matter
> of fact it would like to gaze at the castle and enjoy its beauty,

it is prevented from doing so, and seems quite unable to free itself from all these impediments.*

'Quite unable to free itself'. She too would agree that the only way out of enslavement is God's grace. Although we can't manipulate this, or click our fingers so that it is served up to us on a plate, we can long for it, and really want it, ask for it constantly and rely on it. 'Lord, I want to reclaim my freedom. Lord, I want to be an integrated person so that I may love you and my neighbour with my whole heart, not just bits of it. Help me.'

The key example of non-attachment is Jesus. 'Who is my mother, and who are my brothers?' And pointing to his disciples he said, 'Here are my mother and my brothers! For whoever does the will of my Father in heaven is my brother and sister and mother' (Matthew 12:48–50, NRSV). And Paul, writing to the Philippians (2:6, NRSV), says:

> Let the same mind be in you that was in Christ Jesus, who though he was in the form of God did not regard equality with God as something to be exploited, but emptied himself, taking the from of a slave, being born in human likeness. And being found in human form, he humbled himself and became obedient to the point of death—even death on a cross.

Jesus models for us refusal to be attached. This passage, as you know, is an old hymn, and the scripture scholars have a fine old time arguing about the meaning of the Greek, especially where it says that Jesus did not 'regard equality with God a thing to be exploited'. The Greek word for 'a thing to be exploited' is *harpagmon*, which seems to mean in this context 'prey', something to be clung on to blindly and at all costs. Here we are in the stratosphere of the Trinity itself, and the light may well blind us. But it certainly seems from this passage that the Second Person of the Trinity, where the Incarnation was in view, was so detached that he was willing not to claim the advantages of godhead, but to go through the hoop of being born, raised, hungry, thirsty, tired, misjudged and murdered. Let the same mind be in you that was in Christ Jesus.

---

* *The Interior Castle*, I.ii

There aren't paragraphs in canon law condemning addiction. Nor
have there been encyclicals against it. It is too big a concept to be the
subject of legislation. Trying to condemn it would be like trying to
catch hold of quicksilver. Not all addictions are *ipso facto* sinful. Indeed,
I knew an old lady who was addicted to the recitation of the Rosary
on Vatican Radio, as you would realize if you ever tried to take her
Holy Communion at 11 o'clock on a Saturday morning. Addiction is
recognized with the spiritual eye of the soul, which is ultra-sensitive to
anything which threatens its freedom. Once you have tasted freedom,
once grace has liberated you, you are fiercely protective of what you have.
The Second Letter of Peter (2:20) says 'People are slaves to whatever
masters them'; and it lambasts false prophets in these terms:

> For if, after they have escaped the defilements of the world
> through the knowledge of Our Lord and Saviour Jesus Christ,
> they are again entangled in them and overpowered, the last
> state has become worse for them than the first.

I know what he means—I tried ten times to give up smoking before I
succeeded, and I know that even now I am an addictive person although
I have not had a cigarette for twenty years. Wild horses on their bended
knees would not get me to start smoking now. Knowing the discomfort of
actually having been addicted, I will fight like a tiger to stop it happening
again. If I do start again, my last state will be worse than my first. The
vice of the man who sells drugs to teenagers is that he takes away their
freedom, possibly for life: he reminds you of the spider who attacks
Frodo in Tolkien's *The Lord of the Rings* and binds him in her web. To
deprive other people of their freedom to travel home towards God is
a wicked thing to do.

Gerald May writes cheerfully that he still has at least fourteen
addictions himself. If we had none, we would be canonizable saints.
So there's nothing here to get depressed about. I am not trying to send
you on a guilt trip. But how good it is if we can call things by their
proper names. We need to call our addictions by their proper names.
It's half the battle, and opens the way up to the liberating grace of God.

✟

ST CHARLES BORROMEO

Today is Borromeo's feast day. It is also the day John XXIII chose for his coronation in 1958. He did that deliberately. It was a Wednesday, not a Sunday, and the diplomatic corps complained that it would interfere with their day-to-day duties; but John was adamant. As students we approved of his decision, because we got the day off the Greg. He preached at his own coronation Mass, which was an innovation, and he said this:

> The Lord's Church has had its moments of stagnation and revival (*stasi e ripresi*). In one such period of revival Providence reserved for St Charles Borromeo the lofty task of restoring ecclesiastical order. The part he played in implementing the reforms of the Council of Trent, and the example he gave in Milan and other dioceses of Italy, earned him the glorious title of Teacher of bishops, and as such he was adviser to popes and a wonderful model of episcopal holiness.

There are aspects of Borromeo's life which are relevant to ourselves, and he merits our knowledge and admiration. Let's have a look at him as we find him in April 1580; it was then that he housed three young priests from the English College, with Campion and Persons, as they walked home across Europe to danger and probable martyrdom. I quote from Evelyn Waugh's biography of Edmund Campion.[*]

> At Milan they spent eight days in the palace of Cardinal Borromeo, where a daily discourse was required of Campion. That huge and princely establishment was well accustomed to visitors of every degree; it numbered over 100 members of

---

[*] Evelyn Waugh, *Edmund Campion* (London, 1935), ch. 2.

the regular household; there were Chamberlains, Almoners, Stewards, Monitors, Oblates, Discreets of the Confraternity, Prefects of the Guest Chambers, all maintained and graded in hierarchical order under the Praepositus, the Vicar, and the Auditor-General. Three hundred guests, on an average, passed through these hospitable courts; there all the ways and passages of the vast ecclesiastical labyrinth seemed to intersect, and in the centre of it all, living in ascetic simplicity among the lavish retinue, eating his thin soup, sleeping on his folding bedstead, wearing his patched hair short, moving with halting gait, chilly even in the height of summer, speaking in a voice so subdued that it was barely audible, grave and recollected as a nun, was the dominating figure of the great Cardinal. The pilgrims were received, entertained, blessed and sent on their way, and the immense household went about it duties; in its splendour and order and sanctity, a microcosm of the Eternal Church.

Charles Borromeo knew how to maintain a princely household because he himself was noble-born, in 1538, in a town on Lake Maggiore. His family was connected with the Colonnas, the Gonzagas and the Medicis. He was a child of his age: at the age of twelve he was made the titular abbot of a monastery, enjoying its revenues. His uncle, Gian Angelo Medici, became Pope Pius IV in 1559, summoned Charles to Rome and made him a cardinal and secretary of state at the age of twenty-two. You might think this was an example of nepotism in the worst traditions of the Renaissance, but it resulted in enormous good for the Church. Charles was the reverse of a rich layabout. He was organized, and had a clear mind. He was a natural diplomat, and that was good for the Church, which was, as usual, suffering contrary pressures from Spain and France. He was a hugely energetic and hard worker, and he had something to get his teeth into, because the Council of Trent needed relaunching and then concluding. The Council actually met in Trent, which had not always been the case, and Charles could not be present, as his uncle demanded his constant presence in Rome, but he represented the mind of the Pope very forcefully in his letters to the legates. Trent provides us with the key to his whole life. He was to spend the next twenty-one years implementing it in his diocese of Milan. It was his theme-song, his great enthusiasm, the love of his life, and he lived off the decrees of the Council for the rest of his days. Due to him more than anyone else Trent became effective. Ecclesiastical discipline, style of episcopacy, liturgy, catechetics were gradually transformed across Europe from top to bottom, and from Europe the new atmosphere spread to the mission lands of Asia and Latin America. It was Borromeo who gave it all its initial boost.

One of the decisions of the Council had been to tie bishops to their dioceses. There had long been a tradition of their being absent from their sees, sometimes for many years at a time, on government or court business. Trent said this had to stop: a bishop's place was at home, with hands-on supervision of the Church's life on his patch. Borromeo had been made Archbishop of Milan by his uncle, but Pius IV—a pope with more than a whiff of the Renaissance about him—was not always logical in his decisions, and he would not let Charles leave Rome. Whether he liked it or not, he was an absentee from his diocese so long as Pius lived. Eventually, just before his uncle's death, he managed it. And at the next papal election, in which he played a major part, things changed radically. Pius V was a Dominican of austere life and burning zeal, who was intent on pushing through the reform of the Church, and under him Charles was able to establish himself in Milan and begin his life's work, which up to then he had carried out through assistant bishops and vicars general. He was the first resident archbishop for eighty years. He based his homily at the installation Mass on Luke 22:15: 'I have longed to eat this passover with you before I suffer.'

Borromeo might have been nothing more than a tiresome reformer. People with unlimited power, and the bit between their teeth, and a gift for hard work, can be a menace. The difference with Charles was that he was genuinely holy. He was not just a high-octane performer, there was a heart to all he did, and it was the heart of Christ. Early in his career he had been profoundly changed by the premature death of his elder brother; he was shocked, saddened and sobered by the loss. He said 'No human help can be of comfort under so terrible a blow. This event more than any other has brought sharply home to me the miseries of this life and the true happiness of eternal glory.' It was a moment of conversion. The family, including the Pope, put pressure on him, as the next in line, to marry; but he declined, and instead opted for the priesthood. He was secretly ordained in 1563. He wanted to enter a monastery, but a visiting Portuguese bishop, de Martyribus, himself a reformer in the spirit of Trent, persuaded him that the needs of Milan came first. When he got to Milan, the first things he did was reduce the archbishop's household. It is worth bearing all this in mind as we watch his meteoric progress across the north of Italy, his fights with the forces of entrenched self-interest, his incessant defence of the Church's rights against the Spanish governors of Milan, his clear vision of what the Church could be and ought to be, his organizational brilliance, that this was not just an ecclesiastical Napoleon, this was a saint.

His true holiness became apparent during the plague in Milan, in 1576. Typically, he was the first archbishop to set up viable and efficient systems of financial aid to the victims, well supplied and competently administered. But he was also personally present, moving among the dying and the bereaved, both in hospital and in their houses, with great compassion; and he persuaded a reluctant clergy to do the same. A procession was held through the City to implore God's healing, and Charles led the procession, walking barefoot, with a rope round his neck, carrying the Cathedral's most precious relic, a nail from the True Cross. One historian has said that he cast himself in the role of the suffering servant, the scapegoat, carrying the burden of his people's sins and imploring divine mercy. The plague ended in 1578 and from then on the ordinary folk of Milan looked on their bishop with veneration. There was almost a cult of him in his lifetime.

Some of his enactments make us smile. He was shocked to hear in the Holy Year that at Cremona, not far from Milan, erotic madrigals were being sung. A stop was put to the erotic madrigals. He regarded dancing on Sundays and feast days as such a grave sin that absolution was reserved to the archbishop himself. He would have been in sympathy with Pius V, who tried to stop the population of Rome going to taverns, saying they should be kept open only for visitors. Such strictness seems to us excessive. But his true greatness lay in his day-to-day journeys to the parishes of his vast territory, stretching from Genoa to the Alps;

his painstaking enquiry in each of them as to how Mass was celebrated, whether there were retreats and missions, whether the sacrament of penance was properly celebrated, whether there was good preaching in the parish, whether the people were being cared for. Which led him inevitably into examining the lifestyle of the clergy, whether they were living virtuous and prayerful lives, whether they were faithful to their promise of celibacy, whether they were an example to their flock. Many of the older priests were under-educated, because there had been no systematic theological training for them. Charles methodically set up seminaries, and staffed them from members of an order he himself founded, his own oblates, who rather like the Jesuits acted as a spearhead of reform and order in the Church.

He supervised the writing of the new Catechism, employing leading classicists so that the style would be elegant and worthy of the subject, and deliberately presented it to the world as a teaching pack for priests, so that even the old men would have good material on which to base their sermons. He formed a Confraternity of Christian Doctrine, for catechists, and might be regarded as the founder of the Sunday School. There is an inscription praising him for this in an unlikely place: at the Unitarian Church in Kensington. He attended to details: clear delineation of parish boundaries, and clerical incomes. He drew demarcation lines for the religious in his diocese, indicating where they came under his jurisdiction and where indeed they were exempt. The other cardinals once nicknamed him 'Cardinal Sacristan' because of his interest in church furniture and the design of vestments. He personally confirmed thousands of children. A visitation from Charles Borromeo was never a pushover.

Back in Rome there had been a further changing of the guard. Pius V died in 1572, and was replaced by Gregory XIII, Ugo Buoncompagni, a more worldly and easy-going man. But Gregory, too, recognized the need for reform in the Church, and Borromeo—though thirty-six years his junior—had a big influence on him. One historian says 'Charles Borromeo had a decisive impact upon both the interior and exterior life of Buoncompagni, weaning him away from the profane influence of the dying Renaissance.' It was Gregory XIII who, with the help of William Allen, founded the English College. At the time, a radical innovation.

In 1579 seminaries were still rare; seminaries abroad were still rarer. We were part of a new experiment stemming directly from the Council of Trent, an experiment which got its impetus from Borromeo. The courage to close down the old Hospice, open the new seminary, employ the Jesuits—themselves a brand new order—for the systematic theological formation of the men, may have belonged to Pope Gregory and Allen; but the impetus was Borromeo's. When the three young priests visited him on their way home to England in 1580, he must have felt a real sense of fulfilment: the programme of the Council was already bearing fruit.

I said at the beginning of this talk that Charles Borromeo has something to say to us, and let me spell that out.

The first thing that strikes you about him is that he was young. He was only forty-six when he died. He achieved the colossal work of reform and sanctification of his diocese in what, for many modern men, would be the first half of their lives. Evelyn Waugh's description of him makes him sound a gaunt old man; in fact, when the men from the College visited him, he was only forty-two. The fact remains that he was not afraid to get stuck in while still in his youth. He didn't wait. I am not suggesting that any of you become workaholics, and I am fierce defender of the day off and proper holidays. But there is something inspiring about his systematic, planned, attention to his diocese which we could well translate into our parishes when the time comes, which is soon. He saw things through. He didn't pick and choose his favourite things. He didn't get discouraged halfway through a job, because of a bit of opposition, and drop it. There was an allegedly pious association of well-to-do laymen in Milan called the Humiliati, who resisted the Conciliar reforms. He closed them down. An aggrieved member broke into his private chapel while he was at prayer and fired at him, luckily unsuccessfully. But he persisted in his decision, and eventually prevailed. On another occasion, the canons of a Collegiate Church, La Scala, asserted their exemption from his control, and he went to the Church to excommunicate them; he was fired on by their supporters, and the bullet hit the cross he was holding. But he saw it through. He had the grit and conviction to finish what he started. This is a spiritual thing, not just an operational one. It is needed as much in the twenty-first century as in the sixteenth. When I hear this, I have to examine my own conscience: how many half-read books are on my shelves? How many parish projects did I let trickle out into the sand? What diocesan jobs did I tacitly give up on? To follow through is a virtue, and we need it, in our youth as much as in our old age.

All his life he grappled with opposition. The Castello of Arona, his birthplace, was disputed territory between the French and the Spanish. As a young secretary of state he had to cope with the conflicting claims, pressures and threats of the French and the Spanish. As the Pope's legate for implementing the Council, he paid several visits to Switzerland, often travelling by mule, and there discovered the worst abuses, including witchcraft, and encountered the most extreme resentment and resistance. In Milan itself he was constantly at loggerheads with various Governors, asserting, like Thomas of Canterbury, the entitlements of the Church. He was a fine and natural diplomat, but diplomacy was not always enough. He was vilified and calumniated in private and in public. To deal with opposition and enmity patiently, with dignity, and with forgiveness, is a spiritual thing, not just a diplomatic one. A virtue, and you and I need it.

He was the most self-forgetful of men. Even in his final illness, dogged by fever and very weak, he continued to work. His travels took him across the lakes of northern Italy, which were damp and foggy, but there was not a trace of self-indulgence in him. He knew when he was dying, and summoned a Jesuit Father so that he could make a general confession; yet three days later he spent eight hours, the whole of the night, on his knees in prayer . . . and still he worked. We need to be self-forgetful. Not to take risks with our health—your bishops would not thank me for recommending that—but not being hypochondriacs, and not being self-indulgent and self-centred. Here again I have to examine my own conscience, and realize how preoccupied I am by even a slight illness, and how it can immobilize me. I occupy too much of my own horizon. There's a virtue to pray for here, in the twenty-first century as in the sixteenth.

Borromeo's great instrument of government was the synod. He must have held seven or eight diocesan synods, as well as a number of provincial councils. They were not, it must be said, democratic and parliamentary assemblies. They were occasions on which he could present to the whole diocese or the whole province the findings of his journeys and visitations, and the conclusions he had drawn from them, in terms of legislation. They were aimed at obtaining the assent and the agreement of the clergy, and also at making sure that everyone was informed. They must have been occasionally boring and sometimes quite conflictual: no class of men are as good at passive aggression as a bunch of priests. But they were a methodical way of rounding off each stage of his project, which was the implementation of the Council. You are going to be summoned to not a few meetings in your diocese and deanery, in the years to come. It is easy to become cynical about these, and discount in advance any good they might do. Cooperating with the business of meetings is a way of being a team player—of being what you will be ordained to be, a cooperator with the order of bishops. John Cleese stars in a brilliant video which does the rounds of board-rooms in the UK. It's called 'Meetings, Bloody Meetings'. We can all identify with that. However, remember that meetings may be the only way your bishop has of finding his way forward. Do support him. Don't sabotage them by dragging your feet. And don't discount the value of them in the parish, either.

Charles spent his life implementing the Council. He was viewed by his contemporaries as modern, a disturber of the *status quo*. Easy for us to forget this, since what he implemented then became the *status quo*. The Council of Trent took decades to fulfil its promise. The same is true of Vatican II. Vatican II demands our loyalty no less than Trent. Alberigo says that the Ecumenical Councils are the spinal column of the Church. This is as true of Vatican II as it was of Trent.

He was astonishingly modern in his social concern. The mediaeval thing was to toss coins to the poor, a little like Eva Peron in Argentina. But Borromeo's system was, as you would expect, a system. He took trouble over it. His almsgiving was not just a whim. He set up machinery for regular famine relief, and for help to plague victims. He regarded the poor as his responsibility. A hint to us. We cannot solve the problem of world poverty—it is bigger than we are. But we can be methodical and intelligent with our fund-raising—and with our personal almsgiving

And finally, he was *there*. He was a truly residential bishop, who resented being called to Rome (though he always went) and always hastened home. Psalm 15 says 'The measuring line marks out delightful places for me, for me the heritage is superb indeed' (Psalm 15:6, JB). Milan was for him a delightful place and a superb heritage. He was always totally loyal to the pope, whichever pope it was. But at the same time he had a terrific sense of place, and of local history. He fostered the Ambrosian rite of Mass in his diocese, and Ambrosian chant. He rejoiced in the particularity of Milan. We need to invest a lot of our love and energy in the place where we are, and not always be thinking of ways of getting out of it; whether it's seminary, or parish, or school, or tribunal, or hospital. We should be fiercely loyal to our diocese, and pitch in our lot with it. To be there in the full sense: focused, willing, anxious to live the Gospel on the spot where God has placed me, this is a virtue. And I need it.

✠

CHARITY

'The greatest of these is charity', says Paul (I Corinthians 13:13). I'm going to spend a little time in the stratosphere, but I promise you a concrete application before the night is out.

Charity is different from faith and hope. Faith and hope describe our relationship with God, but it's one-way. God can't have faith or hope in us. Charity on the other hand is two-way. We love God, but God is the great and original lover. Here is St John in his First Letter. 'This is the love I mean: not our love for God, but God's love for us when he sent his Son to be the sacrifice that takes our sins away' (I John 4:10). 'My dear people, let us love one another, since love comes from God and everyone who loves is begotten by God and knows God' (I John 4:7). So we are on the receiving end of God's torrential love for us, more massive than we can ever imagine. And the spin-off of being loved by God is that we love him, yes, but also that we are enabled to love one another: it's like an overflow of what we have received. We are expected to be simultaneously active and passive: on the one hand allowing God to love us, and of course believing that he loves us, and on the other truly caring for one another. Two sides of the same coin. The word John uses for God's activity and our activity is the same: *agape*. John makes *agape* the acid test of whether you belong or not: 'Anyone who fails to love can never have known God' (I John 4:8).

It's worth pausing in wonderment that God should be so loving, so positive. Genesis, in the first chapter, tells us that when God made the dry land and the mass of waters, when he made plants and trees, the sun and the moon, the fish and the birds, the wild beasts, cattle and reptiles, he found them good; and when he had made man in his own image and likeness, he looked at the whole of his creation and found it very good. He loved the work of his hands from the first moment. In other words, benevolence goes with being God. Love is the law of the universe because it is the law of the Trinity. God's way of being, in eternity, is love. 'Careless talk costs lives' said an old wartime poster. I suppose I am engaging in careless talk: how could I dare to use a word, love, which we kick around so casually here on earth, to describe the sublimest and purest activity, the very essence, of God himself, the earth's creator? Come to that, how can I pretend to know anything at all about how God is? My only excuse is what Jesus has told us. 'May they be completely one that the world may realize that it was you who sent me and that I have loved them as much as you loved me.' Within the Trinity there is love. That's how God is. Again, that word *agape*.

The Incarnation is a love story. The act of self-giving which this involves is staggering. The old Christmas carol says 'He came down to earth from heaven, who is God and Lord of all.' Paul says that he emptied himself to assume the condition of a slave, and became as men are. It was a gratuitous thing he did: there was no way we could have merited such a gift. Still less could we lay claim in any way to the Passion and death of Our Lord. It is an act of supreme condescension, condescension in the best sense, not the patronizing one. It stems from the compassion on the multitude which Jesus always had, but which is described especially in that passage in Mark 6:34, where he sees a large crowd, and takes pity on them because they are like sheep without a shepherd. That affection for ordinary people he never lost. His life and death were a continuous act of love. He played out on earth what was already true in heaven.

C. S. Lewis, in his book *The Four Loves*, distinguished between Need-love and Gift-love. Need-love is clearly where there is something in it for me. Need-love is not necessarily bad. A child's love for a parent, especially in the early days, is founded upon need. Many of our dealings with each other, at their best, have a mixed motive—there is true unselfishness there, but it is mixed up with a submerged desire, perhaps, to burnish our image or chalk up a success. We should not be too severe with ourselves, for the purification of motive is a lifelong task. Most of our dealings with God are founded upon Need-love, for example when we ask him to forgive us. For us ever to pretend that we love God as an equal, and are quite disinterested, as opposed to being his children and his creatures and his clients, would be madness. We *are* sheer need, incarnate need. Gift-love, on the other hand, is when we go out of ourselves in favour of the other, love for the sake of the other; it *is* disinterested, not seeking advantage for ourselves. And this is the way God loves us: here is Lewis again:

> In God there is no hunger that needs to be filled, only plenteousness that desires to give. The doctrine that God was under no necessity to create is not a piece of dry scholastic speculation. It is essential ... God, who needs nothing, loves into existence wholly superfluous creatures in order that He may love and perfect them. He creates the universe, already foreseeing—or should we say 'seeing'? there are no tenses in God—the buzzing cloud of flies about the cross, the flayed back pressed against the uneven stake, the nails driven through the mesial nerves, the repeated incipient suffocation as the body droops, the repeated torture of back and arms as it is time after time, for breath's sake, hitched up. If I may dare the biological image, God is a 'host' who deliberately creates his own parasites; causes us to be that we may exploit and 'take advantage of' Him. Herein is love. This is the diagram of love himself, the inventor of all loves.*

Lewis, having described so graphically and beautifully the way God loves us, then makes a startling point: God can and does bestow upon *us* the faculty of loving as He loves. It amounts to Love himself, working inside a man or woman. This love, if we have it, truly desires what is best for the beloved, even if this best does not fit in with any preconceived idea on the part of the lover. In other words if we love with true charity it won't be bossy. Although we shall long for our brother's eternal salvation, charity won't take the form of licking him into shape. Divine Gift-love enables us to love, for no advantage to ourselves, people who are not naturally lovable, and remain unlovable: lepers, criminals, enemies, morons, the sulky, the superior and the sneering. And finally, by a high paradox, says Lewis, God enables man to have a Gift-love towards God

* C. S. Lewis, *The Four Loves*, ch. 6.

himself—so that we give him the only thing we have to give, which is our will, our heart.

This ability to love in a superhuman way is sheer gift, sheer grace, and we rightly call it charity. St Thomas says 'It is plain that the act of charity is beyond the will's natural power" It is out of our nature to love like this, literally so. How could it be in our nature to be God-like? And so we use the clumsy but correct theological term 'supernatural'. It's like being dumbly and humbly aware that God has put into our hands, the hands of clumsy, jobbing carpenters, a tool of the most superb precision and of the highest worth, which will achieve results far exceeding our skill. By his death and resurrection, Jesus has purchased for me the life of grace in this world and glory in the next: and part of this package is the power to love as God loves, to be a man of charity.

Well, if it's been given to me, I am supposed to use it. Jesus makes this clear in the Gospel, talking to the Pharisee who was trying to trip him up: 'You shall love the Lord your God with all your heart, and with all your soul, and with all your mind. This is the greatest and first commandment. And a second is like it: You shall love your neighbour as yourself. On these two commandments hang all the Law and the prophets' (Matthew 22:37–40[†]). That could, of course, just refer to natural love and goodwill. If I am to live a moral life at all, if I am to be a commandment-keeping person, the whole operation has to be suffused by love. But then Jesus complements what he says to the Pharisee in Matthew by what he says to his friends at the Last Supper, in John: 'I give you a new commandment: love one another; just as I have loved you, you also must love one another' (John 13:34). There's a big difference, if you think about it, between 'love your neighbour as yourself' and 'love one another as I have loved you.' The second of these is the law of the new covenant. In other words, I can't go through life keeping my nose clean but being, basically, an unloving person, keeping the rules, but with a cold heart. I've got to let God inside me, so that he can love through me. Just look in I Corinthians 13: 'Though I should give away to the poor all that I possess, and even give up my body to be burned, if I

---

[*] *Summa Theologiae* 2a 2ae 23.6.
[†] cf. *Catechism of the Catholic Church*, 2055.

am without love, it will do me no good whatever' (I Corinthians 13, NJB).

In one presidential election in the US, the unsuccessful Democrat candidate, Walter Mondale, used to criticize his opponent's policies for being devoid of content. 'Where's the beef?' he used to ask. Well, you and I have now come to the beef of this reflection. I am a son of God, adopted by him, flooded with his Spirit, supernaturally endowed. How is this going to be worked out in my everyday life?

First of all, by my loving God. In practical terms, this involves prayer, lumps of it, repeated prayer, both in times of consolation and in times of dryness. Things like an hour of prayer before Office and Mass in the morning, or going to Exposition in the evening, are the bread and butter of charity. I am terrified by priests who are genial, smiling and efficient, but who never pray. I think their houses are built on sand. Watch Jesus in the Gospel, and see how he seized every moment to slip away from the disciples and from the crowds to be with his Father. The disciples would catch up with him and say, in effect 'You're wasting time. We're on a roll. Let's not waste it.' But Jesus's priorities were crystal clear. Right at the start of his public life, at the start of Mark, we finding him going quietly off to pray while everyone else was asleep. Before he chose the Twelve he spent the night in prayer, Luke says. Then, the Garden of Gethsemane was a place where he was accustomed to go: the Agony in the Garden was not the first time he had prayed under the olive trees. Luke says that after the Last Supper 'He then left to make his way *as usual* to the Mount of Olives' (Luke 22:39, JB) and John says 'Judas the traitor knew the place well, since Jesus had often met his disciples there' (John 18:2, JB). It is not fanciful to say that Christ prayed in the Garden regularly, and that was where his friends knew they would find him. Why was he so addicted to prayer, so Father-centred? The clue is in an earlier part of the Gospel, in John 7:28, where his enemies are already closing in, and he says 'There is one who sent me and I really come from him, and you do not know him, but *I know him because I have come from him.*' Jesus came from the Father in two senses. One was the Incarnation. But the most profound one was his generation by the Father in eternity. 'I know him' refers at least in part to this. We have to dare to think of the Trinity, to focus on it as best we can, although the light well-nigh blinds us. There is a timeless conversation of love within the Trinity, and Jesus couldn't help carrying this on, even in his time on earth. Well, the next stage is that by the gift of charity, he lets us in on that conversation too. We are enabled, in our tiny way, to love as he loves. You and I, adopted sons, are invited to take our place beside Jesus on the mountain and in the garden, like small boys with their elder brother, and watch what he does, and learn from him how to do it. Lord, teach me to love the Father as you do. Lord, teach me to love his will, so that when I say the Lord's Prayer I can really mean it. von Balthasar has this passage:

> Harassed by life, exhausted, we look about us for somewhere to be quiet, to be genuine, a place of refreshment. We yearn to restore our spirits in God, to simply let go in him and gain new strength to go on living. But we fail to look for him where he is waiting for us, where he is to be found: in his Son, who is his Word.[*]

Christ is uniquely Father-centred. I am invited to make Christ's prayer my prayer, and then I shall be loving with real charity, and not simply out of cupboard love. He will change my need-love into gift-love.

Bernard Lonergan was teaching at the Greg [Pontifical Gregorian University, Rome] in the 1950s. He once said to us in a lecture, 'If you want a 9 or 10 in the exams, then listen to what I'm going to be saying today and tomorrow; otherwise, you needn't bother.' I think he was trying out the first draft of his famous book 'Insight' and we were the guinea-pigs. Well, analogously, and in spite of everything we read in the Gospel, we sometimes treat brotherly love as an optional extra for the high-flyers, for those who want 9s and 10s. The way of the world is so ingrained in us that it seems natural to be contemptuous, to backbite, to gossip, to be sarcastic, to make wounding personal remarks, to crack unkind jokes to raise a laugh. We are so close to the poison of uncharity that we cannot identify it, and when we do it seems small stuff, of little importance. When I say 'we' I don't mean just we at the English College; I mean we of the developed world in the year 2004. Our media are full

---

[*] H. U. von Balthasar, *Prayer* (San Francisco, 1986).

of innuendos which crucify people, ostensibly in the public interest, and we take so much of our moral tone from the media. So it is worth saying in the context of tonight's talk that if we are really children of the Gospel and not just children of this fallen world we must be radically different. Not just a bit different, the same as everyone else with a bit of cosmetic tweaking, but radically different. Remember how John makes *agape* the acid test of belonging. 'Anyone who fails to love can never have known God.' Charity is the litmus paper of our seriousness.

And this should be verified above all in a community where all the people have the same belief and the same goal. Now I am talking about the English College. If you live in a group where non-believers and believers are mixed, possibly with the accent on the non-believers, then it is very hard not to take your tone from them. Here in the College, however, it should be possible for us to live charity well. It should be possible for us to take our tone from one another. If I am aware that the grace of God is working in me, and aware of the fact that the Father invites me to find Christ in my neighbour, then it should be possible to live charity to quite a deep level. I don't say 'easy' but 'possible'. The danger is that we shall be cynical even about that possibility, and say 'That's the sort of stuff spouted by spiritual directors, but wake up Grandad, this is the real world, a man has to defend himself, this is the jungle, people aren't all sweetness and light.' 'This is the real world.' Oh yes? Which *is* more real for us, the world of grace and the goodness of God, or the world of exclusion and discrimination, of mockery, of mindless violence and despair? Surely we have all come here because we believe that God's world is the real one, and that the spiritual values are the ones which will win out in the long run? I think people here make a real and genuine effort to be kind and patient to one another, so this isn't a critical talk. Inevitably, we sometimes slip, occasionally lose heart. Grudges and resentment can get a grip. Being Christlike inside a small community sometimes feels simply too much. Well, the good news tonight is that we can do it, and can continue to do it. Not from our own strength, but from the strength of Jesus, who gave himself for us and died for us, as Paul says, while we were still sinners (Romans 5:8). If he can do it, we can because he has given us the grace of *agape*, of charity. The gift is given, it only needs to be unwrapped.

✝

CHARLES DE FOUCAULD

The story of the Church in France is so different from that of our own Church. In the mid-nineteenth century we were struggling to establish ourselves: the hierarchy was restored only in 1850, we were very poor, dependent on a few wealthy families, and we didn't really figure in polite society. We were to a large extent a Church of immigrants, and thoroughly, even desperately working-class. In France, on the other hand, the Church was part of the establishment. The Revolution and the Napoleonic experience had lasted for twenty-six terrible years, but with the restoration of the Bourbon monarchy came the restoration of the Church. Restoration of privilege, restoration of prestige. The aristocracy, while not quite so flamboyant as that of Louis Quatorze, was still a force to be reckoned with, and Catholicism was part of its stock-in-trade. It was the Empress Eugenie, after all, who helped to put Lourdes on the map by visiting it in the 1860s. Imagine Prince Albert visiting Walsingham.

Short interlude now for a potted biography. It was into this restored Church that Charles de Foucauld was born at Strasbourg, in 1858. He was of the minor aristocracy, a viscount. He lost his parents in childhood and was brought up a good Catholic by his pious grandfather. His education followed the expected course for someone of his rank, and he concluded it in the military academy at Saint-Cyr and the cavalry school at Saumur. In adolescence, he lost his faith, and became an over-rich and rather pampered hedonist. He did not distinguish himself at the Military Academy or the Cavalry School, being known principally for riotous parties, but succeeded in getting a commission. In 1880 the Army posted him to Algeria. Charles de Foucauld was involved in one brief campaign there, but then fell foul of the authorities for importing and installing a girl-friend, and rather than give her up he got the Minister of Defence to put him on extended leave. (Viscounts can do that kind of thing.) He had all through his life to do battle with a colossal pride and stubbornness: at this stage he had not learned to master it. While he was vegetating near Lake Geneva, however, news reached him that his regiment was involved in a major push against the Arabs, and like the Prodigal Son he came to his senses, accepted the conditions imposed by the Army, joined up again and led his men in a heroic campaign. It is interesting that he never seems to have asked himself the question 'By what right are the French in North Africa at all?' Like many Englishmen of his period, he was an unashamed colonialist. He saw nothing but benefit for the Arabs in the French occupation. Father Lonergan at the Greg used to say that the greatest sin for the theologian was 'anachronismus'. The same is true for the historian: he must not judge yesterday with the insights of today, and neither must we.

His intellectual curiosity began to overpower him. He had been fighting the Arabs for years but he longed to understand them better. He asked for extended leave to go to the south of Algeria to do this, but leave was not granted, and he resigned his commission. So there he was in his mid-twenties, without employment, without faith and without much evident reason for living. At this point he fell in with a strange and inspiring character called Oscar McCarthy, who was a librarian in Algiers. With McCarthy (who was a great planner of expeditions which never quite came off) he devised a daring project. He would go in disguise to Morocco, at that time fiercely hostile to Christians, and he would map the unknown territories there using the latest scientific methods. He would go as an itinerant Jewish rabbi, and for this he had to learn Hebrew well enough to deceive even the Jews living in Morocco at the time, as well as Arabic. One begins to think that in another age he would not have done badly at the Biblicum. Fascinating to reflect that in the 1880s Jews were tolerated in this Muslim country, Morocco, while Christians were not.

He was so successful as a mapmaker that the Geographical Society in Paris awarded him their gold medal. During his time in Morocco, however, something much more important happened to him. He observed the simple, primitive and remote villagers at prayer, and their unquestioning faith began to touch him deeply. When he returned to Paris the feeling would not go away. He needed to encounter the God—if indeed he existed—who could inspire such single-minded devotion. He began to pray a paradoxical prayer: 'O God, if you exist, make me know it.' He began to drop into churches as he walked around the city. And most importantly, at a party given by his aunt, he met a priest called Father Huvelin. Huvelin at this time was not yet fifty, but in spite of recurrent sickness was known as one of the best spiritual directors in Paris. (He used to talk to people, and listen to them, incidentally, with a cat on his lap. I am thinking of acquiring a Siamese.) He had an infallible memory for names and faces. Like Padre Pio and the Cure of Ars, he also had the reputation of knowing your secrets before you disclosed them. His acquaintance with Charles de Foucauld developed into one of the great spiritual friendships, one that was to last till Huvelin's death in 1910. One October evening, Charles came into the confessional, and without kneeling down bent and spoke through the grille: 'Father, I have no faith, I have come to ask you to instruct me.' Huvelin said to him, 'If you make your confession now, you will believe.' 'But I did not come for that.' 'Make your confession.' And he did, a confession of his whole life. Immediately Huvelin took him up to altar and gave him Holy Communion. It was the moment of conversion for which, without knowing it, he had thirsted for so long. He later said of this moment, 'As soon as I realized that there was a God, I knew I had no alternative but to give him everything.'

In 1890 he joined the Cistercians, at an abbey high up in the mountains in south-eastern France called Notre Dame des Neiges, Our Lady of the Snows. Here, as a novice, he learned humility. The regime was very tough: not much food, and a lot of manual labour. He later said, 'Neither fasting, nor vigils, nor work ever inconvenienced me. The only thing that was difficult for me was obedience.' That colossal pride was beginning to be tamed.

Before joining the monastery he had been on pilgrimage to the Holy Land, and the place which most impressed him was Nazareth. He was deeply moved by the thought of the hidden life of Jesus, by the great poverty in which the Holy Family lived, and by the ordinariness of their life. He saw their poverty as a kind of abjection, of abandonment, and he longed to join them in it: like Jesus, to choose 'the lowest place.' So he volunteered to go the daughter house of Notre Dame des Neiges, a monastery at Akbes in Syria, which was even more austere. He describes the place as he saw it on his arrival after a day and a night riding up from the coast on a mule: 'a mass of small houses of boards and clay, covered with thatch ... a tangle of barns, cattle and little houses crowding quite close to one another for fear of raids and robbers; it is shaded by tall trees and watered by a spring which comes out of the rock.' The monks' dormitory was over the cattle stalls. He delighted in the intensive manual labour of the community—cotton-picking, stone-clearing, wood-cutting—but his superiors told him that he had to study theology. He says, 'I did not conceal my lack of attraction for this new vocation.' At the same time, the hunger for contemplation was overtaking him. He wrote in a letter to his cousin, 'I relish the charms of solitude more and more, and I am trying to find out how to enter into a deeper and deeper solitude.'

In 1896 he became convinced that his vocation lay outside the Trappists. The abbey, while primitive and poor, was secure. As Europeans, the monks were safe from the bloody upheavals which were going on throughout the Turkish Empire. They were even guarded. It was one of those moments when the army turned on the local Christians, and most savagely on the Armenians, and massacred them wholesale. At the gate of the monastery were men and women whose hold on life was very tenuous. Charles longed to be like them, in the 'lowest place' with Christ at Nazareth, identified with him, voiceless and powerless. He dreamed of founding an order of like-minded men, who would share his vision. He asked the Father General of the Trappists for a dispensation from his Cistercian vows. The Father General replied; you may be dispensed, but first of all you have to go to Rome and study theology for two years.

So Charles came to Rome. He lived in the Cistercian Generalate in Via S. Giovanni in Laterano, and he went to the Lateran. He describes himself in a letter: 'Old and ignorant, and unfamiliar with Latin, I find it very hard to follow the lectures ... I shall be as great an ass in theology as in everything else.' But he did it willingly and with a good grace. However, relief was at hand. In 1897 the authorities recognized his unusual vocation, and released him from his obligations, and he set out for Nazareth. There he got a job as a sacristan, odd-job man and errand-runner for the Poor Clares, and lived in a shed in their garden. He made do with a few crusts of bread to eat, and he was blissfully happy. The shed became his hermitage, and he divided his time between that and the nuns' chapel, spending many hours day and night in prayer. At night, in order to stay awake, he would write down his reflections. It was here that he came to the conclusion that he was called to be a priest, though how this would work out was by no means clear. The land which included the probable site of the Mount of Beatitudes became available for sale. He had a grandiose and at the same time humble dream, which was to use his family money to buy the land, and to set up a simple chapel at the top, where he could say Mass and adore the Blessed Sacrament all day long, but have an ever-open door for passing Bedouins and pilgrims. 'In desolation and isolation, surrounded by malevolent Arabs … there I shall be able to do infinitely more for my neighbour by the sole offering-up of the Holy Sacrifice.' He went to present his scheme to the Patriarch in Jerusalem, but either was, or felt, rejected, and in the rejection perceived God's will: the dream of the Mount of Beatitudes was over, but was about to be replaced by another.

We next find him back in Algeria, at a place called Beni-Abbes, near the Moroccan border. He has built himself a hermitage with the help of the French troops. The Bishop of Viviers in France has ordained him a priest, in theory a diocesan priest, but he will spend the rest of his life in the Sahara. He is still planning his new religious order: he is very exact and precise. He designs the habit. He traces the foundations of the building where they will live. He writes a holy rule and begins to live by it himself. All that is lacking is men: no-one will join him. It will be like this till his dying day. His self-discipline and asceticism are inspiring, but only from a distance: close up they are rather intimidating. He does not have the temperate patience of Benedict at Subiaco. He spends long hours during the day and night, kneeling and sitting before the monstrance in his makeshift chapel. He dreams that the conversion of the Sahara will come about by establishing the Blessed Sacrament in as many places as possible, so that the power and grace will radiate out to the Muslims. Charles is an affectionate and hospitable man. His house is always open, to the French soldiers and the Arabs alike. He is an unofficial chaplain to the forces. He will always interrupt his prayer to spend time with people. He does not preach: he aims to draw people to the Gospel by the way he lives and the way he is. 'I wish to proclaim the Gospel by my life,' he says.

In 1904 he experienced a desire to penetrate more and more deeply into the poorest parts of Algeria, and in particular to go and live among the Touareg, who were a primitive and savage network of tribes which still practised slavery. Still that dream to establish himself among the most abandoned and needy people on earth. In our day we would have found him, perhaps, in a slum suburb of Rio or Nairobi. He travelled south with a military column until they reached Tamanrasset. This was the settlement where he was to live for the next twelve years, and then to die. He built himself a house and set himself to learn the Touareg language, with a view to compiling a French-Touareg dictionary. Still, no converts and no colleagues: he was alone and, by worldly standards, supremely unsuccessful. Yet he was animated by such a burning love of Jesus that the statistics did not really matter. In 1907 he fell ill, and was nursed back to strength by the tribespeople. At this stage, Charles began to make fewer plans for the future and to trust God more: we can see his old impatience for the spread of the Gospel, the recruitment of missionaries, the building of chapels, evaporating. He had been brushed by death and had learned to fall backwards into the arms of God. He was always a ferocious letter-writer, firing great epistles off into the blue to a whole variety of people without knowing when they would arrive, or how long the reply would take to reach him. He wrote to the Vicar-Apostolic, Mgr Guerin; to Huvelin, who continued to be his spiritual director at a distance until his death in 1910; to old army friends, who understood him well. He kept a voluminous diary. You can detect the increasing spiritual maturity.

The outbreak of the First World War distressed him enormously, and stirred his soldier's blood. He wrote to a friend, 'You know what it costs me to be so far away from our soldiers and the frontier; but my duty is evidently to remain here, to help to keep the population calm....' but three months later he wrote 'Should I not do more good at the front as chaplain or stretcher-bearer? ... If you tell me to come, I shall set out on the spot.'

The War in Europe had a profound effect on colonial Africa. The withdrawal of troops inevitably gave free rein to rebels. Of particular concern were the Senussi, who were closely linked with the Turks of Tripoli and thus with the Germans. The Senussi in their turn befriended disaffected Touaregs and armed them. The Italians in Libya did not do as good a job of containment as the French in Algeria, and there was seepage across the border. Charles resolved to find some way of defending *his* Touaregs at Tamarasset in case of a raid. He fortified his hermitage and obtained arms for the able-bodied men of the village.

On 1 December 1916 he was murdered by a passing group of hostile Touaregs. We don't know the motivation. It may have been simple religious fanaticism, and there is a story that before they killed him they tried to make him renounce his Christianity and he refused. It may have been because of the guns. It may have been because of the profound moral effect he had on the people of the village. It may have been his connections with the French army. His body was buried in a shallow grave and his house was sacked. Three weeks later the French commander of the district, Captain de la Roche, arrived in Tamanrasset, heard the full story of the killing, found the body and buried it more fittingly. He went into the hermitage, one room which served as living room and chapel, which had been plundered. Lying on the floor were articles of worship and devotion and pious books: the famous dictionary, in four volumes: a colonial helmet, a camp bed, and a number of letters, sealed and stamped and ready to be posted. The young officer stirred up the sand on the floor of the room with his foot, and discovered a small monstrance with the Sacred Host still inside it. He picked it up respectfully, wiped it, and enveloped it in a linen cloth. 'I was very worried,' he said later, 'for I felt it was not for me thus to carry the good God.' He took it away, and discussed with his sergeant what should be done with it: they remembered what Charles had told them to do in case of emergency, and the sergeant made an act of contrition and the captain gave him communion.

What has someone like Charles de Foucauld to say to us? His experience is hugely different from our own, past, present or future. Yet there is gold to be found beneath the surface of his life, just as the Blessed Sacrament was there beneath the sand of his hermitage.

He combined hospitality and contemplation. I could wish you no greater grace in your lives as diocesan priests. To be patiently welcoming to all comers at all hours is so very, very important: but even more important is to underpin this kindness and this open door with prayer. Prayer centred on the Eucharist, prayer before the tabernacle or the monstrance. Hours spent with Jesus, even if at the time they feel dry and unproductive, energize the whole of our apostolate and all our relationships.

He was apparently a failure. He achieved neither of his goals. He didn't convert the Sahara. He didn't convert anyone. He didn't start a new religious order. It was only after his death that things began to happen. The seed fell into the ground and produced a rich harvest. Not one, but several religious orders. A voluntary association for diocesan priests which is worldwide, and which tries to incarnate his values. A philosophy of priesthood and of ministry which is at the present time the inspiration of the hard-pressed clergy in Algeria. A model of Church which finds its expression in the Christian-Muslim friendship groups in Algiers, in spite of all the horrors of recent years. You and I, too, have to be content with apparent unproductiveness. One sows, another reaps, but it is God who gives the increase. That's the rhythm of pastoral life.

He was eccentric, and extreme in his love of the Lord and his fellow-men. He was a man of his age, a military man to his dying day, an unashamed colonialist. He had the limitations of the soil from which he sprang. So do you and I. In years to come people will look at us and say, 'How could they possibly have been like that?' It doesn't matter. All this is part of providence. So is the particular character you have, with all its singularity. There is room for us all in the Church. We don't have to clones of one another.

He used to say, 'I wish to be a universal brother.' He saw fraternity as the supreme value. To relate to all others, not as a superior or as one having power, but with the fellow-feeling of a brother. How marvelous it is when we can make this the dominant theme of diocesan priesthood and of seminary life: loyalty to one another, a listening ear, sympathy and support whatever happens, a basic equality which overrides all differences of rank or title, and an ability to talk to one another about serious things without embarrassment. An American bishop said to me of the Priests' Fraternity (that voluntary association I mentioned earlier) 'Gee, Tony, I need this: I've got a crappy kind of a job.'

The Church has recognized Charles's heroic virtues, and he is now, like the College, a 'Venerable'. A miracle or two will push him over the edge into beatification. In the meantime, we can pray: 'Father Charles, pray for us, that we may be good priests for the modern world, as you were a good one for yours.' [Charles de Foucauld was beatified by Pope Benedict XVI on 13 November 2005.]

✠

The Conversion of England

Permit me a piece of nostalgia.

At five minutes to one every weekday, the students of this College used to pile thunderously into the Martyr's Chapel for what were known as Starvation Prayers, a series of Latin psalms which we used to recite for the Conversion of England. In summer they were often prayed in a damp and steamy atmosphere. If the last Greg lecture finished at 12:15, with a judicious turn of speed you could be back at College by 12:35, and in the pool by 12:36. If you were out of the water by 12:50 you still had time to get substantially dry and be on parade when the duty member of Top Year launched into the first psalm. It is hard for men of my generation to pray these psalms in the breviary even today without thinking of the Conversion of England, and of the hunger pains which followed a thin breakfast and four Greg lectures.

What psalms are they? Those of grievance and lament. You know them. Psalm 79:

> O God, the pagans have invaded your heritage,
> they have desecrated your holy temple ...
> We are now insulted by our neighbours,
> Butt and laughing-stock of all those around us.
> How much longer will you be angry, Yahweh? For ever?

And Psalm 80:

> Yahweh Sabaoth, how much longer
> will you smoulder at your people's prayer?
> Having fed us on the bread of tears,
> having made us drink them in such measure,
> you now let our neighbours quarrel over us,
> and our enemies deride us.

And Psalm 89:

> You have repudiated the covenant with your servant
> and flung his crown dishonoured to the ground.
> You have pierced all his defences
> and laid his forts in ruins.
> Anyone may go and loot him,
> his neighbours treat him with scorn.

And Psalm 74:

> The enemy have sacked everything in the sanctuary,
> They roared where your Assemblies used to take place,
> They stuck their enemy emblems over the entrance,
> emblems we had never seen before.
> Axes deep in the wood, hacking at the panels,
> they battered them down with mallet and hatchet;
> then, God, setting fire to your sanctuary,
> they profanely razed the house of your name to the ground.

In the 1950s we were still fighting, mentally and emotionally, the battles of the 1550s. We easily applied those psalms to the religious history of England: they seemed custom-built for the purpose. The Reformation in England had been, for the Catholic Church, like having a leg amputated on the field of battle without an anaesthetic. She survived it, but with massive surgical shock which was if anything worse than the original wound. In the 1950s we were still suffering from surgical shock.

The cult of the English and Welsh Martyrs, and of the College Martyrs, included a massive dose of hurt, offence and grievance. The psalms chosen for Starvation Prayers referred to mockery, taunts and derision. Look at the paintings in the Tribune.* Besides being horribly

---

* The Tribune is a gallery that runs around three walls of the English College Church. The walls are painted with a series of paintings that depict the history of the English Church, including graphic depictions of the martyrdom of priests who were seminarians at the English College.

graphic, they speak of an attitude, a mindset: 'Let these things not be forgotten, because they have not yet been acknowledged,' they say. We felt in those years that we were still a second-class minority, often pilloried in polite society as 'The Italian Mission to the Irish'. Most members of the College in those days were born Catholics, although there was a sprinkling of converts, from Oxford and Cambridge mainly. Some had broken with their families in order to join the Church. Of the born Catholics, the northerners tended to belong to all-Catholic families who lived among other Catholics, shopped at Catholic stores, supported Catholic football teams, went to Catholic schools. The southerners less so: many of us came from mixed and divided parents and had been to non-Catholic schools, and had felt the pain—and occasionally, the derision—involved in the Protestant–Catholic thing of the period.

Another source of hurt, offence and grievance concerned buildings. We look with astonishment at today's polemics in the Ukraine between the Orthodox and the Catholics over churches expropriated at the end of the Second World War. Surely, we think, this problem is soluble: they're only buildings. We forget how we felt about the great mediaeval cathedrals, confiscated in the sixteenth century and in some cases vandalized and gutted. The headless statues at Ely still speak of iconoclastic violence. We forget the ruins of the priories and abbeys up and down the country, Rievaulx, Fountains and the rest, 'bare ruined choirs', as David Knowles called them, quoting a Shakespeare sonnet. They were methodically depopulated and destroyed by a highly efficient and single-minded state machine. Listen to this lament:

> Bitter, bitter, O, to behold,
> the grass to grow
> where the walls of Walsingham
> so stately did show ...
> Level, level with the ground
> the towers do lie,
> which with their glittering golden tops
> pierced once to the sky ...
> Owls do shriek where the sweetest hymns
> lately were sung;

toads and serpents hold their dens
where the palmers did throng.

The author of that may have been St Philip Howard. It's not great
poetry, but it breathes out that sense of wound and profound regret
which was still part of the Catholic heritage when I was growing up.
Regret for buildings, symbolizing regret for a beautiful way of life and
a lost sacramental tradition, regret for so many families systematically
pauperized and exiled, for so much blood spilt.

Allied with this feeling was the whole story of Ireland. More regret,
more pain, more long memories. Many of the students here in the
1950s, especially the northerners, were of Irish extraction. The near-
genocide of the Irish was part of their family tradition. At the time of
Elizabeth I there were the plantations, with Scots Protestant farmers
fed into Ulster to push the natives out. A century later Cromwell led
a military expedition which involved exile and massacre, illiteracy for
the survivors, imprisonment for the priests: and this in the name of
pure bible religion. In the nineteenth century, the mismanagement of
the Potato Famine by the London government had brought death and
misery to the countryside and massive emigration—ironically, much
of it to England, contributing to the rebirth of the Catholic Church on
our side of the Irish Sea. Racial and religious resentment is a heady
mixture, and folk-memories last a long time. They certainly lasted into
my youth and early priesthood. Many of the things done by the Nazis,
the Communists, Fidel Castro, Saddam Hussein and so forth were also
done by the English: but they were done at an early date, before there
was any television to record them.

It isn't that these things no longer matter. They do. You can't unwrite
history. You can't wind the film backwards and have it otherwise. These
things really did happen, and the damage done was great. But our
perspective has altered and the context has changed, in ways I would
never have imagined possible. The hurt, offence and grievance have given
way to something much more objective, to a cooler way of discussing
and describing things. The Second Vatican Council began, for us, the
healing of the surgical shock. Gradually and cautiously, each side felt
able to face the shadow-side of their virtue. Catholics had to face up

to the less-than-heroic behaviour of the Henrician bishops, and the ghastly Spanish-type persecution carried out by Mary Tudor. They admitted that St Pius V's excommunication of Elizabeth was at least in part responsible for the manhunts which followed. They had to admit that their forebears under Elizabeth were not united, and that quite a number conformed, at least outwardly, to the established Church in order to avoid fines and imprisonment. They had to concede that at the height of the persecution there were bitter Catholic quarrels, even between the hunted and incarcerated priests. In other words the scene was less romantic and idealistic than we once thought. And the Anglicans began to concede, at least implicitly, that Roman Catholic history and that of their own village churches were intertwined, and that it would be good for us to borrow them for Sunday Mass instead of setting up portable altars in pubs and clubs. It is hard to express the excitement and the joy I felt at greeting a Catholic congregation, for the first time, in a mediaeval church. It was done after a most gracious welcome by the vicar. Times indeed were changing. We began to meet in fraternals, bible study groups, charismatic prayer groups, and to discover many points of convergence. We held joint services praying for Christian Unity—stilted things, very often, but such a massive turn of the tide after the coldness and the snarling of previous years. The International Commissions were set up after the Council, bringing Catholics together on a theological level for the first time with Anglicans, Methodists and Lutherans, to dismantle prejudice and misunderstanding. Deep personal friendships developed between bishops, and between parishioners and the clergy across the boundaries of Christian Churches, and they continue to develop. In the 1960s the violence, bitterness and the bigotry of Northern Ireland began to seem ridiculous. Now, to us, in the 2000s, they are clearly absolutely crazy. In the 1950s, I'm afraid, they seemed normal.

So what about the conversion of England? The Wiseman prayers we used to say at Benediction have fallen out of use, partly because they belong to the culture of those pre-Vatican years. 'O Blessed Virgin Mary, Mother of God, and our most gentle Queen and Mother, look down with mercy on England thy Dowry...' Do we not care any more? Do we no longer believe that the Catholic Church is the ancestral Church of our nation, and don't we long for all our friends to find their home in her? Of course we care, and of course we long. But as I said, the context has changed.

During the years since Vatican II, Europe has been swamped with secularism and materialism. All Churches, all Christian bodies have been undermined by this. We were not ready for it, and did not fully understand it, and maybe we still don't understand it. Where did it come from? Why is it so disdainful of all faith, of all religion? I recall sharing a broadcast on local radio about test-tube babies. I was invited because the first clinic in Britain was in our parish. Someone phoned in and asked the professor in charge of the clinic whether the opposition of the Catholic Church to his work was not a problem, and he just laughed contemptuously and said that no-one paid any attention any longer to the Catholic Church, that those days were over, and that the Pope was a geriatric celibate who really didn't know what he was talking about. He was not so much argumentative as dismissive. That's the flavour of our time.

Today's context helps to make sense of ecumenism. Modern Britain is ignorant and pagan, and finding other people who believe in Jesus, follow him and wish to preach him is significant, important and beautiful. They are not the enemy. It is silly to demonize them. We may still have unfinished business from the Reformation. But it is nothing like the challenge facing us all from a godless population. Christianity has never faced such a test as this, since Augustine was sent by Gregory to convert the King of Kent.

Our danger is that of listlessness. The Catholic-Protestant polemic kept us on our toes in the old days, and made us all crusaders: I am speaking now of my own generation. The opposition was identifiable, and it stood still while you hammered it. Hymns we sang, like 'Faith of Our Fathers', were a rallying-cry. We were brought up on apologetics, and we admired people like the Catholic Evidence Guild, Frank Sheed and Vincent McNabb, who stood on street corners in London and took on all comers. When Pius XII condemned communism, and the cardinals in Hungary and Poland were arrested, when the Archbishop of Zagreb was condemned to sixteen years in prison, we occupied the Albert Hall and defined ourselves very much by what we were against. Creed matched itself against anti-creed, Christ against anti-Christ.

Whatever we were, we were not listless.

Now things are subtler and harder to identify. Harder to identify because we cannot distance ourselves from them. The hedonistic, consumerist world has wormed its way into us, and we are children of our age. We find it hard to criticize our culture and our century. And so we become passive and placid in the face of things which are destroying the faith of our people.

Let me list a few of these. The list is not exhaustive.

I would put first the issue of justice. I would never want the Church to abandon her emphasis on God, in order to do social work, nationally or internationally. That would be stupid. No-one sensible advocates this. A Church which didn't preach prayer and sacrifice and the absolute priority of God simply wouldn't be the Church. But all the members of the Church should take the Beatitudes to heart, have a hunger and thirst for justice, and be affronted and ashamed if the Church, or their own nation, fails in matters of justice. St Thomas quotes Aristotle as saying 'The many forms of injustice make the many forms of justice quite clear.' A two-tier world, where the well-to-do defend themselves against the poor or exploit them but do nothing to help them, is unjust. Successive popes have condemned such attitudes, in encyclicals such as *Populorum Progressio* and *Sollicitudo Rei Socialis*. Justice is not just a negative thing: it is a positive virtue of great beauty, a value in its own right. Thomas again: 'Justice outshines the other moral virtues because the common good surpasses the individual good of one person. Accordingly Aristotle declares that justice is the most splendid virtue, and Morning or Evening Star are not so wonderful.'[†] *Neque est Hesperus neque Lucifer ita admirabilis.* We have to fill in the small print for ourselves, and work out what the implications are for today. The Code says 'Clerics are always to do their utmost to foster among people peace and harmony based on justice.'[‡] You cannot have a valid spiritual life and at the same time prescind from matters of justice. The world will judge us largely by this criterion. Hardness of heart destroys your faith.

---

*   St Thomas, *In Eth.*, 5.1. Quoted in Pieper, *The Four Cardinal Virtues*, p. 43.

†   St Thomas, *Summa Theologiae* 2a 2ae.58.12

‡   CIC 287.1

I would put next the arrogance with which governments and scientists dispose of human life. There is a craziness in this which takes your breath away if you reflect upon it. To kill a human foetus, or create and then dispose of an embryo, or snuff out an elderly life, and occupy the moral high ground in doing so, labelling the defenders of human life as 'evil', is surely the ultimate lunacy. John Paul II refers to this in *Evangelium Vitae* (18): 'The process which once led to the discovery of 'human rights'—rights inherent in every person and prior to any Constitution and State legislation—is today marked by a surprising contradiction. Precisely in an age when the inviolable rights of the person are solemnly proclaimed and the value of life is publicly affirmed, the very right to life is being denied or trampled upon, especially at the more significant moments of existence: the moment of birth and the moment of death.' No amount of women's rights, or the right to choose, or the right to die with dignity, or the right to comfort, convenience and a high quality of life, can prevail against the right of God to give life and the right to take it away. Delight in, and celebration of human life is not just a negative thing. It is an appreciation of the stunning generosity of God, who has made us like sparks from the great fire, made us in his own image. Our firmness in defending the sanctity of life may bring persecution back on our heads one day; but it is also the touchstone of our soundness and saneness. These are causes worth suffering for.

Next I would put the sexual fixation of our times. It is a fixation. All public means of communication are awash with sexual suggestion and invitation. You don't have to invite it or go in search of it. Your own computer, your friendly television set, your neighbourhood cinema, can in a moment turn pornographic and fill your brain with images and fantasies you never asked for. One spiritual director has recommended that men should pray prayers of deliverance over their computers, 'May this computer never be an occasion of sin for me, may it never be the means of my enslavement.' It sounds extreme but it makes sense. The Christ-less world bores its way into our hearts and minds more easily in this way than in any other. Another colleague of mine, an American, once said that internet pornography is the crack-cocaine of pornography, since it is instantly addictive and instantly accessible. People hooked on this stuff are not available for lives of faith. No wonder vocations have plummeted. We have to make sure, absolutely sure, that we ourselves are free from such addiction, in order that we may look critically and objectively at our culture, and speak the truth to our people about human sexuality.

An anything-goes society, where people sleep together almost from their first meeting, and where sexually explicit entertainment is the norm, looks free and enlightened; in fact it is narrow, less than fully human, and victim to a single-issue obsession. How easy it is to become passive in the face of all this, half-condoning, semi-accepting, children of our age. Erotic fantasy, stimulation and fixation have nothing to do with deep love for other human beings. On grounds of humanity, not just of religion, we must proclaim the truth about sexuality. Sexuality is beautiful, positive and good: properly lived, it effects a union of persons which is a rehearsal, so to speak, for the union of our souls with God in heaven. But to live sexuality deeply and positively demands reason and self-discipline, not surrender to every itch. In this context celibacy makes particular sense. It still shocks the man or woman in the street. It is about the only thing which does shock them, stop them in their tracks. It is the beginning of our *kerygma* about an unhooked society.

Our forefathers in the Faith put their lives on the line to defend their belief in the Blessed Sacrament, in the motherhood of Our Lady, in the primacy of the pope. In many cases they died for these truths. I would not want any of you to go away saying that I had listed these beliefs as not mattering any more. Of course they matter. They will always matter. But the point I am making tonight is about our own seriousness, fervour, ardour and energy. We must not become placid, simply because we are physically comfortable and secure. In the name of Christ, and for the salvation of our country, we now need to recognize in the context of these modern crises I've mentioned the Gospel we must live and preach, and do it with the same selflessness as that of our Martyrs. They *walked* home to engage in the conversion of England; it took them months. They were blessed by St Philip Neri before they set out, and by St Charles Borromeo on the way; they changed their names and their plans often to bewilder the spies, they separated on the French coast and bought passages in little fishing boats to cross the Channel, on their way to probable death. We take the afternoon Easyjet from Ciampino, on our

way home to the evening news on television. But as we touch down at
Stansted two hours later let us, like them, hear Our Lord in St Luke,
speaking to us from the Martyrs' Picture: 'I have come to bring fire to
the earth, and how I wish it were blazing already!' Fire. And may we
reply with all our hearts, like Christ in Hebrews 10:7: 'God, here I am.
I am coming to obey your will.'

✝

The Devil

It is said that when Voltaire was dying, the priest said to him, 'My son, renounce the Devil' and Voltaire replied, 'Father, this is no time for making new enemies.' We find it hard to believe in the Devil. So much unintelligent stuff has been written and imagined about him; so many sensational films about the so-called supernatural have been made by men and women of no faith. We have to cut through the pagan and superstitious trash to find the reality.

The reality is sobering. It is clearly laid out in the Scriptures and in the tradition of the Church. The Devil is far more formidable than a dark lord with a huge cloak and vampire teeth, for the Devil is spirit, he is intelligent, and wise with a perverted wisdom. The *Catechism of the Catholic Church* calls him 'a seductive voice, opposed to God.' Jesus, much more baldly, refers to him in John's Gospel (8:44) as 'a murderer from the beginning.' Marie-Dominique Philippe, the founder of the Community of St John, says that the Devil is 'cerebral, with a cold, purely metallic intellect, for he has lost love and contemplation.' The Devil knows how to bring defeat and sadness to the human race. He knows how to depress us and take away our hope. He knows how to sabotage our finest efforts and pollute our purest endeavours. He knows how to do this because he understands the other side, the good side, because he once belonged to the good side. In a dreadful parody of what the Gospel says concerning Jesus, the Devil knows what is in the heart of man, and this places him very well when it comes to tempting us. To quote Dostoevsky, in *The Brothers Karamazov* (III.iii) 'Beauty is mysterious as well as terrible. God and the Devil are fighting there, and the battlefield is the heart of man.'

The *Spiritual Exercises* of St Ignatius describe the battlefield most powerfully. On the fourth day of the second week of his thirty-day retreat, Ignatius invites us to reflect on the Two Standards, and to decide whose side we're fighting on, because no-one can stand aside. 'Standard' in this sense means 'flag'. Being an old soldier, and accustomed to static battlefields, he depicts the opposing armies drawn up against one another, that of Christ and that of Lucifer, with their banners waving in the breeze. In the preliminary prayer he tells the retreatant to 'ask for an understanding of the tricks of the wicked leader': this, clearly, is not going to be a clean fight. He invites us to imagine the Devil sitting on a throne of smoking flame, and dispatching his servants, with traps and fetters, into different cities, till the whole world is covered, forgetting no province or locality, no class or single individual. Their instructions are to undermine people by tempting them with money, position and pride. Once people have caved in to these inducements, all other sins are possible.

We can be put off by the imagery. The throne of smoking flame sounds fanciful, like a fairy-story. But don't bother about the details and above all don't discard the meditation. Note the truth in this reflection of Ignatius: Lucifer reaches out to every province and locality, every class and individual. Your soul and mine are in his awareness, in his sights, for we are prizes worth winning. And what he will dangle in front of us? Prosperity, power and pride. If we embrace these and make gods of them—and, ultimately, of ourselves—the sexual stuff can easily be slipped in later. On the other hand, the humble man who chooses a simple life-style will be much harder to topple. We must expect to be Dostoevsky's battleground. We are cockpits, each of us, in which this cosmic struggle is taking place. This world is not spiritually neutral. St Peter had this sense of stark drama and urgency, one which we have sadly lost. He wrote in his first letter (5:8): 'Be calm but vigilant, because your enemy the Devil is prowling round like a roaring lion, looking for someone to eat. Stand up to him, strong in faith and in the knowledge that your brothers all over the world are suffering the same things.'

Once you are alert to the way things are, so many items in the news begin to make greater sense. Do you ever get the sense, when bad news breaks, that there is a twisted intelligence behind it which infuses an extra, satirical horror into human misbehaviour? An example would be the massacre at Srebrenica, where the Serbs rounded up all the men and boys in the village and took them away to the woods to shoot them. Now the United Nations had a peace-keeping force in that village, provided by the Dutch army. The Dutch were undermanned and under-equipped, precisely because they were peacekeepers. They had to watch while this happened. An added twist. At the time they were not certain that the Serbs were going to kill the men. They obviously hoped that what was planned was some temporary internment. They even helped the Serbs put the Bosnian men and boys on the trucks. There is a photograph of the Dutch and Serb commanding officers shaking hands. It is likely, I think, that the Dutch were naïve rather than cowardly. It would be fairer, perhaps, to place the responsibility on those who deployed them in such a weak way. Yet they were there to guarantee the safe haven, as it was called. There's the cruel irony, the pathos, the terrible cynical tragedy of the affair. What went so wrong with human efforts to do the right thing? What robbed words like safe, defence, security, haven, of the meaning they should have had, and made them a mockery? Who was mocking, who was jeering, who was laughing? There was, I am convinced, a malevolent intelligence at work, crude racial hatred, yes, but also something more refined.

It is in the light of this realization, that the Devil is intelligent and the great Mocker, that we must see the phenomenon of clerical child abuse. This is something which I would much rather not discuss, but in honesty I must discuss it, and try to shed some spiritual sense upon it. The issue is peculiarly painful. It is painful above all because it destroys the lives of innocent children, which, as the Pope says, is an awful crime. It is painful because it humiliates all priests and bishops, not just the abusers. It is painful because it has polluted our relationship with children, cast a shadow on them. Our first concern must be for the children, that goes without saying. To be abused is a dreadful invasion of your human rights. The shame the Church experiences comes second. But it is painful for us. It is painful because it has made the whole Church less credible as a vehicle for God's word, and as moral guide. It has inflicted a quite unexpected and very deep wound on the whole of English-speaking Catholicism. When it all blew up, years ago, I thought in my simplicity that it was a localized problem in Newfoundland, and later in Ireland. Something which would be a nine-days wonder, and which would soon blow over. I, and others like me, have had to do a radical re-think. Granted that the majority of child-abuse is perpetrated by married people and family members, and not by the clergy at all, there have still been sufficient clerical cases for us to say that there has been a fault-line in the Catholic priesthood, in many countries, for many years. A small but constant minority among us have been abusing children. Let's admit it. The Devil has got in under our guard.

Why would he want to do this? It may seem a silly question to ask, but I still think it is worth asking. Put it another way. If you were the Devil, and you wanted to cause Christianity to collapse, what would you attack? I know what I would do. I would attack the word of God, and make it less credible. And I would attack the Eucharist, the Blessed Sacrament, so that people no longer wanted to celebrate it, receive it, adore it. If I could knock down these two pillars of faith, I would be well on the way to achieving my goal. And what would be the best way to do this? Surely, by attacking the priesthood. The priest is the expounder and explainer of the word of God—in a sense he is its guardian. The priest is the celebrator and protector of the Eucharist. If you devalue the priest, you devalue in the public eye what he preaches, celebrates and offers to the people.

The recent unveiling of priestly sinfulness and addiction has left these treasures exposed. The Letter attributed to Barnabas, all those years ago, says 'For these are evil days, with the Worker of Evil himself in the ascendant.' Thank God the damage is not terminal, not fatal. When you went home to your parishes in the summer you found that fundamentally things were all right. Your parish priest has retained the confidence of the majority of his people, who are astonishingly faithful. If he is a good preacher, they are still listening to him; they still believe what they have always believed about the Mass and about Holy Communion, and if they were practising before the scandals, by and large they are still practising. There have been some losses, among those for whom the pain has been too much to bear, but on the whole the parishes have held the line, unless the scandal has been right on their doorstep. But make no mistake: what is at risk here is far more than the reputation of a generation of clerics. It is the power of God's word, and it is the Bread of Life. The priest, as custodian of both, simply has to be a man of holiness and integrity. Nothing less will do. The two greatest gifts

Christ has given his people are scripture and sacrament. These are our greatest weapons in the fight with the power of evil. If the Worker of Evil can blunt those weapons, or make them less accessible, he is doing very nicely. By undermining, morally, the men pledged to the full-time service of the Lord, he strikes deeply into the heart of Christian religion. Your life-style and mine are like the tabernacle door, like the silver cover on the Book of the Gospels, they are symbolic protection for what is dearest and most precious to the Christian people.

That is why, during the six years of formation in seminary, it is vital for us to attend, daily, to the quality of our moral and spiritual life. We cannot afford to be laid-back about this, or to slacken off. There is so much at stake, for hundreds of thousands of people, not just for us. We are here not for us, but for them. When we become priests, we will be priests not for us, but for them. We will be men given over to the care of the people—it isn't just a job. The Pope [John Paul II] said in Korea, back in 1989, 'Pastoral charity is the virtue by which we imitate Christ in his self-giving and service. *It is not just what we do, but our gift of self*, which manifests Christ's love for his flock.' Let's think again about the three-pronged attack by the Devil against which Ignatius Loyola warns us. Money, power and pride.

It is easy for us to become obsessed with money—the making of it, the receiving of it, the spending of it. Occasionally at home you come across what you might call a fat-cat priest. He has the flair for playing the stock-market and feathering his own nest. He looks forward to the day when he can thumb his nose at the Bishop and say 'I'm self-sufficient, and now I'm retiring.' The parishioners are quietly scandalized at his opulent life-style, at the luxury holidays and the over-the-top cars and clothes. They feel, rightly, that they only have part of his attention. They also have the feeling that he is compensating for celibate priesthood by surrounding himself with creature comforts. Although we have no vow of poverty, as diocesan priests, we must still try to live by the evangelical virtues, and this is one of them. A certain simplicity of life befits us. It also gives strength to the soul. We can acquire that attitude here. It may take us six years. It is not easy. But it is worth the effort.

It is easy for us to become obsessed with power. Here in Rome we live on the fringe of a massive hierarchy with an involved and complicated pecking-order. We live in a College where every wall displays a portrait or a coat-of-arms of a bishop, an archbishop or a cardinal. One of the cracks people make at our expense at home is that the English College is the staff college of the Church, that we all have our eyes fixed on title and promotion. If this were so, it would indeed be tragic. It would make nonsense of the gospel we preach. Luke 22:25: 'Among the pagans it is the kings who lord it over them, and those who have authority over them are given the title Benefactor. This must not happen with you. No, the greatest among you must behave as if he were the youngest, the leader as if he were the one he serves.' Ambition is a cancer. During our six years here, we must confront it, name it, and try to root it out. It is not easy. But it matters enormously, and is worth the effort.

It is easy for us to be proud men. Pride shows itself in contempt and disdain for people who are less accomplished than ourselves, who belong to another class, race or culture, or who quite simply make mistakes. It shows itself in a refusal to accept criticism, and in great waves of resentment at even the gentlest correction. It shows itself when we put clear blue water between ourselves and the magisterium of the Church. 'They may say that, but I know better.' Or, on the other hand, clear blue water between our teachers and ourselves, too quickly labelling them as unsound and unorthodox. 'He has shown the power of his arm,' says the Magnificat, 'He has routed the proud of heart.' The Greek word for this kind of pride is *hyperephania*, and it crops up again in Mark 7:22 on Jesus's list of evil things, coming from within and making a man unclean. Pride comes from within, and makes us unclean. The one class of people who consistently got the rough side of Our Lord's tongue in the Gospel are the scribes and the Pharisees, not because they were correct, but because they were proud. Six years is not too long for us to begin, at least, the overcome our pride.

Many people have analysed the mind of the abuser, and you will often hear it said that many abusers were themselves once victims of abuse; or that they display a dreadful streak of immaturity; or that what they enjoy most is the exercise of power. I am not denying any of this. But the fact remains that at the heart of the abuse is lust. The abuser is a man who has given himself permission to act lustfully. A man who has persuaded himself that it doesn't count, or it doesn't matter, or that it is an issue of no importance, because everybody these days is sexually engaged in one way or another. An article in the Guardian thirteen years ago said 'Society drives people crazy with lust and calls it advertising.' How are we to reconcile these two things: that lust is a deadly sin, and that we are being bombarded every moment of the day with material intended to incite lust? It is very difficult.

But the principles are crystal clear. As Christians we take the Gospel as our rule of life, and in the Gospel Our Lord repeats the commandments, including the ones about adultery, and about coveting your neighbour's wife. And in St Matthew's Gospel (5:28) he also says 'If a man looks at a woman lustfully, he has already committed adultery with her in his heart.' We are expected to base our behaviour and our thoughts on this: it's part of the deal. We must not act lustfully, nor must we fill our minds with images which could cause us so to act. This is where the Church stands. Then, in addition to our vocation as Christians, you and I have a vocation as deacons and priests, and here, too, the principles are crystal clear. For the sake of the Kingdom I have committed myself to celibate chastity. At some point the abuser has allowed himself a holiday from this commitment. If you could play the film of his life backwards, there would be a moment you could identify: 'That's where it went wrong. That's where he settled for something less.' It might have been the Internet that started the rot; or a diet of late-night television. Humbly we have to implore God for the grace to remain clear-minded and totally faithful on this issue. We can't afford muddled thinking, and we can't afford self-indulgence. Nothing less than chastity will do.

The last word, however, is about mercy. I say this because I have floated for you a very high standard, one only achievable by grace, and one that goes far, far beyond the issue of child-abuse. Only by the mercy and grace of God can I be evangelically poor, unambitious, humble and completely pure of heart. And when I fail to be these things, which I often do, it is simply the mercy of God which welcomes me back. If I stay close to the mercy of God, the Devil can do precious little. Sure, he will try to persuade me that I don't need mercy, that I have grown out of that nonsense, that confession is a pointless routine, that I must break free from a superstitious and mediaeval picture of sin and so on. Or he may try to persuade me that I am irreformable, so why keep struggling?

'After all, compared with others you're not that bad,' he will say. He will do this because once I am enveloped in the Father's mercy, he cannot touch me. However often we fail, we must always keep before our minds that sublime picture of Rembrandt, of the Father welcoming the Prodigal Son back home, tilting his head with pity over the kneeling boy. What wise compassion and comprehension there is on his face, what limitless mercy: it is the diametrical opposite to the cold, metallic logic with which the Devil attacks us. St Peter writes (2:10): 'Once you were outside the mercy and now you have been given mercy.' *Kyrie eleison.* Lord Jesus Christ, Son of the living God, have mercy on me a sinner.

> Let us then have no fear
> in approaching the throne of grace
> to receive mercy
> and to find grace
> when we are in need of help.
> (Hebrews 4:16)

HOLES IN THE ROAD

I know it seems a long while ago, but while you were away this summer, some quite important things happened. They were to do with the infrastructure of your lives here in Rome. To be exact, two roads were dug up so that the electricity and the telephone services could be renewed, ready for your return in September. They were two pretty vital roads. In each case, a motorist had to be inventive at the last moment and pluck a detour out of thin air. There was the Via dei Farnesi, which normally enables you to get from the Giulia to the top of our street. This one, of course, is still closed. And then there was the Via dei Cartari, which as a rule takes you from the end of the Monserrato on to the Corso Vittorio Emanuele, from which, as every College driver knows, the world is your oyster.

The barred streets were hugely inconvenient and quite unexpected. The patch of paint you will see on the bumper of the staff car originally belonged to an unmarked white van which stopped just behind me at one of these blocked arteries. In general, it was a season of backing, filling and light crunching. It was rather like the bumper cars at a fun fair. The men actually working (I use the word lightly) on the roads also did a certain amount of leaning on their shovels, adjusting of their Gucci sunglasses and displaying of their tattoos. I do not blame them in the least. Digging up streets in a Roman August is a challenge to which no mortal should be subjected.

Now what fascinated me was the way they dealt with the cobbles. They stacked them up at the side of the trench they had dug in neat, orderly piles, so that they could be slotted back at a moment's notice. In the trench itself you could see the cables or the pipes, properly encased in tubes; and on top of the tubes went the cement. So to get at the actual business, there were three stages to be gone through—cobbles, cement, tube; and when the job was done, the whole thing in reverse: tube, cement, cobbles.

The holes in the road had, I realized, a parable-value. The electricity and the phone lines are what bring warmth, power, light and truth into our lives. They are not, however, on the surface. If you want to connect directly with them you have to dig, dig laboriously, and as you do so, dispose in an orderly way of what lies on top. Likewise, whenever I come to pray, I have to do some spadework. I do not pray in a vacuum. My mind is full of perfectly legitimate issues, which do not fade away when I say 'Fade'. Here are some examples.

I kneel down in church, and what floats to the surface? My self-respect has been dented, and I find myself rehearsing haughty speeches to put the adversary in his place. A friendship has turned sour and I feel partly to blame. I have money worries. My mother is unwell. I have sexual scenarios shooting round my imagination. I have a deadline for an essay or a seminar. I have philosophical or theological conundrums in my head which are blocking academic progress. These are like the cobble-stones which have to be picked out, acknowledged, identified, and stacked for later reference. Not denied or suppressed, but treated with respect. My interest at the present moment is, however, with the one underlying person who brings warmth, and light, and truth into my life; and this can only be the person of Christ. He is my cable, my lifeline. Way, truth and life. My way to the Father, the truth about the Father, life from the Father. Christ who died, and rose to new life, and is enthroned at his Father's right hand, and who is alive now, and available, and accessible to me, and awaiting my call. My job now is to establish that awareness of being-with, that eye-to-eye contact with, that meeting of minds with, him. It is a question of priorities. For the moment, nothing else matters. It is he who is power, and movement, and grace, and hope for my future. If I can draw on that power, movement, grace and hope, I can return later to all the other stuff with a new perspective, because I shall be a man enlivened and enlightened by Christ, a man transformed.

In practice, it means being brave enough to consecrate the time to what at first sight is an unproductive exercise. Consecrating the time is the equivalent of digging up the cobbles and drilling through the cement. A Jesuit father gave me a little leaflet describing the steps in the examination of consciousness at the end of the day. The first step is 'I become still, and remember that I am in the presence of God.'

Become still. What a wealth of meaning is packed into those two words. Become still. That is the spadework I mentioned earlier. You can't switch contemplative prayer on and off in the midst of a busy life. It may on some days, take you quite a long time to become still. It took the men in the Via dei Cartari the best part of a morning to reach the cables at the bottom of the trench.

The question is, have I the resolution and the strength of mind to shelve my preoccupations? To attend to what is deep down in the trench instead of constantly picking over the cobble-stones? It *is* deep in the trench, this mystery, so deep that you cannot see it clearly. Our relationship with Jesus is real, but fuzzy round the edges. We cannot see his face. Yes, the painting by Caravaggio of the disciples with Jesus at Emmaus, or the mosaic of the Pantokrator at Monreale may help the imagination, but that's as far as it goes. Karl Rahner, at the age of 80, said 'The real high point of my life is still to come. I mean the abyss of the mystery of God, into which one lets oneself fall in complete confidence of being caught up by God's love and mercy for ever.' The abyss of the mystery of God. Ultimately we have to say: he is present to me, and I to him, but it is like the presence of two people in a darkened room. Am I prepared to dwell at length in the darkened room with my Lord?

It is useful to ask, like St Ignatius Loyola, 'What do I really want?' Christ, through the Spirit, holds out to me the possibility of change, development, growth and increasing depth. I may say I want these things. But I wonder if I really do. Am I ready for the abyss of the mystery of God, for not being in control, for abandoning myself to him? In a way, embarking on an hour's silent prayer is a bit like lowering yourself into a chasm and letting someone else look after you. In parentheses, embarking on an eight-day silent retreat is even more like that. Maybe that is why we find it hard, for above all we like to be in charge. When change and growth are held out to us as a possibility, but on God's terms, not ours, we retreat on to safer ground. Churchill said to the Viceroy, Lord Halifax, 'I am quite satisfied with my views on India, and I don't want them disturbed by any bloody Indians.' Jesus in John 21, talking to Peter: 'When you were young, you put on your own belt and walked where you liked; but when you are old you will stretch out your hands and somebody else will put a belt round you and take you where you would rather not go.' Jesus was forecasting Peter's death. But he might just as well have been describing the contours of the contemplative prayer of a Christian. We stretch out our hands and somebody else puts a belt round us. Unlike Mr Churchill, we may be saying 'Yes' to being disturbed. It feels safer to stay on the surface, picking over the cobble stones, praying for defined and measurable intentions, than to descend into the trench, tangle with the source of power and submit ourselves to change.

Another modern-day parable from the summer, when I was here 'minding the shop' so to speak. I went into the Chiesa Nuova one morning to pray in the cool and the quiet. Well, 'quiet' is a relative term. After a few minutes there was the faint sound of a distant drill, not unpleasant: you might have thought that the Oratorians had let a faraway upstairs room to a dentist. But then the noise gathered strength, and became a full-throated, vibrating roar: clearly, someone was trying to break through the south wall of the Church, and the place began to shake. Whenever the drill stopped, the sacristan could be heard having a shrieked conversation with a lady who had dropped by. 'What price silence?' I thought. All that was missing was a pious group of people striking up the rosary. I wondered where you have to go to be sure of absolute silence. I wondered whether blokes with pneumatic drills turned up at Parkminster, sometimes, and entertained the Carthusian monks? Come to think of it, the only time in my life when I have been in absolute, 100% silence, is in the fog and the snow three-quarters of the way up the Gran Sasso: and clearly, you can't go to the Gran Sasso every time you want to talk to God. You have to make do with what's available.

In this case the question was, do I stay or do I go? It was a toss-up. I decided to stay because underneath the noise and the distraction, I knew, was the Lord. I felt like a man in a fast-flowing river who has found a fixed support, like a tree growing out from the bank. My job was to hang on to the tree at all costs, and not be swept away by the river. In prayer terms, my job was to maintain my focus on Christ, really present in the tabernacle, and let nothing dislodge me. The sheer effort of doing this would be my prayer. In spite of everything, Lord, I was saying, I am your man. I had something to react against, something to prescind from: my prayer that morning was ready-made for me.

Often this is all we can manage. We focus, briefly, on God truly present. Then we are distracted. After a minute or two we re-focus. And then we are distracted again. The act of focusing makes the prayer good. The secret is not to stop trying. It may be almost at the end of your prayer that the peace comes, the awareness that God has been there all the time, the sense of being loved by him. Some days the peace may not come at all. But we don't stop trying, giving him the time. Invisibly, we are progressing, coming closer to God.

Our great enemy is noise. Now we, living in Rome, are connoisseurs of noise. We live through indescribable racket. Helicopters whose sole whole aim in life is to persecute the English College, and take photographs of the fish in our pond. The magician across the road who is still shouting 'Nothing up my sleeve' at two on summer mornings. Phones that ring when there is nobody there. Bottle-shops which empty their empties into metal containers from a great height in the small hours. Fireworks. Oliver barking in the cortile. People slamming the gate. All this fits in with the dictionary definition of noise.

There are, however, other kinds of noise. They distract us at the level of our deepest self. They are things like grievances and resentments against individuals or institutions, internal grouses if you like, and they grind on like circular saws, day after day. You can't 'become still' with that goinig on. Anxiety about exams would be another noise. It may be silent, but it's still noise in your mind and your heart. Our sexual self pulls us about. I don't think anyone is immune from this. Keeping your balance can take up an awful lot of energy. That's a kind of noise, like a voice clamouring for attention, isn't it? News of school friends or college friends who have hit the big time, become rich, got super jobs, married beautiful girls, produced adorable twins, guys who say airily, 'We thought we might come and pay you a visit.' Of course you are delighted to see them, but it is still a sort of noise, an insidious reminder about what might have been. Then, sadness at the way world affairs are going. How much corruption there is, how much cynical cruelty and fanaticism there is, how much heartlessness towards the poor and hungry, how much emphasis on weapons, war and retaliation. The sense that things are going down rather than up, and there is so little we can do about it: that, too, is noise in our mind and heart. We may sometimes have similar feelings about the Church. The abuse business is a case in point. We are distressed when innocent youngsters are violated and exploited, and when the personnel of the Church get snarled up in stupid scandals, when the media target us: all this, too, is noise. Like the drill at the Chiesa Nuova, it can reduce our capacity to be still and concentrate on the pearl of great price, the treasure hidden in the field.

The story is told of the young disciples of St Francis, his novices, who eavesdropped on him praying in a cave at La Verna. All they heard him saying was 'You, you, you'—'Tu, tu, tu'. Here he was at the heart of things. He had discovered where the source of light and power and truth was—in Jesus, and only in Jesus. There was a lot of noise in the life of Francis—real noise and figurative noise. There was his abominable health, for a start: a lot of pain. Then there was his disappointment when his immediate successors began to dilute the true Franciscan charism, and acquire property for the Order. But he had discovered how to go behind the noise, and be in union with the one thing—the one Person— who really mattered. To say 'Tu' to Jesus, and to know that he is saying it to you: that's prayer. From this we gain the strength to deal with the pains and wounds of our poor world, with patience and bravery. It isn't that contemplative prayer is selfish and introverted. It enables us to be supremely unselfish and public-spirited. But there is no substitute for it. Short cuts end in disaster. Perseverance brings a rich prize.

✝

HUMILITY

St Francis de Sales, the Bishop of Geneva, had a younger brother, Jean-François, who was also a bishop. One day they were dining together, and Francis left the table to speak to a little servant-girl. Jean-François was surprised and a little offended. Francis, on returning to the table, looked silently at his brother. The following conversation then took place.

'What are you thinking about?' That's the younger brother. 'I was thinking that somewhere there must be a most happy woman. Can you guess who?' Jean-François guessed wrongly. 'You are not even close. This happy woman is the one you did not marry. Because you are so irascible that you would really have made her suffer. You see, my dear brother, we bishops have to be like those great watering-troughs where everyone has a right to draw water. Where not only men but beasts come to refresh themselves.'

This episcopal give-and-take is a good illustration of what, in practice, humility is all about. The saint is absolutely at home with people who are ignorant, and of a class far below his own. His esteem for them overcomes all incidental differences. He loves them as children of the Father, and does not feel himself demeaned if they ask him for help or take his time. The younger brother has yet to learn the humble patience which must accompany ordination: bishops, and priests too, should be like great watering-troughs, never feeling put-upon, never standing on their dignity, never responding with pride.

I must have done about sixty of these talks since I started this job, and it occurred to me the other night that I have never done one on humility. I ask myself why. After all, it is a virtue harped on by every saint, every religious tradition within the Church, every decent manual of spirituality. Why have I, unconsciously, avoided the issue? It is like those passages in the Gospel we never meditate on, because they are enigmatic and thorny. So perhaps it is because I personally find this virtue difficult, and discussing it is rather like climbing over barbed wire. I discover unexpected reservoirs of pride in myself, and find myself rehearsing haughty speeches which will cut people down to size. Even if I never actually deliver them. So, here goes: a challenge for me every bit as much as for you.

> His state was divine, yet he did not cling to equality with God, but emptied himself to assume the condition of a slave, and became as men are; and being as all men are, he was humbler yet, even to accepting death, death on a cross. But God raised him high and gave him the name which is above all other names so that all beings in the heavens, on earth and in the underworld, should bend the knee at the name of Jesus, and that every tongue should acclaim Jesus Christ as Lord, to the glory of God the Father. (Philippians 2:6, JB)

That, I suppose, is the classic biblical text on humility. Jesus is our model of humility. He gives it a wholly unexpected value. Why should the Incarnate God opt for the lowest place? Was it not sufficient for him just to become incarnate? That in itself was an act of infinite condescension. The Suffering Servant says in Isaiah, 'I made no resistance, neither did I turn away. I offered my back to those who struck me, my cheeks to those who tore at my beard, I did not cover my face against insult and spittle' (Isaiah 50:5–6, JB). That God should have chosen this mode of human existence is actually quite astonishing, and at first sight, quite gratuitous. It is as if he wished to ally himself explicitly with the lowest strata of people; not just the *anawim* [poor and humble/lowly] of the Palestine of his day, but with the down-and-outs of our great cities, the untouchables of India, the street children of Brazil. A deliberate choice, which makes the rest of us a bit uncomfortable. 'He who humbles himself will be exalted.' And this is what happens to Jesus. He submits to his lot as a humble Galilean workman, even to the point of accepting death on a cross, the death of a slave, shorn of every vestige of human dignity, an object of mockery, a thing. And God raises him high, and gives him the name which is above every other name. It's not an accident, all this. Christian Bobin, in his reflection on the life of Francis of Assisi which is called 'Le Très-Bas', says 'You can only know the All-highest through the All-lowest' and Jesus made himself the All-lowest.

If Jesus is outlining for you and me the path of salvation, of ultimate fulfilment, then the outline is this, in all its stark simplicity: you have to go down before you can come up. You have to let go before God can receive you into his powerful arms. Humility and trust are closely allied. See how, at his temptation in the desert, he refuses the un-humble ways of asserting himself as Messiah and Saviour: miraculous production of food, earthly might, power and authority, flamboyant demonstration of his special relationship with the Father (Luke 4:5–13). These were his for the having, and they would have made the job of preaching the Kingdom easier and more effective. Instead, he chooses the hard way of simplicity, and is sure that the Father will care for him. The Little Brothers and Little Sisters of Jesus talk a lot about 'poverty of means'— not opting for all the modern short-cuts to efficiency, but being content to live as the poor live, waiting in queues, straphanging, working in shops and factories with second-rate equipment, living in slum suburbs with precarious water supplies and electricity. It's the same thing. If Jesus lived in solidarity with humble people, he did it for a reason.

If you construct your own dignity and cling to it, insist upon it, you're like a drowning man who fights the lifesaver. 'I know best' he says; and so he drowns. It is the humble man who says 'You know best' and is saved. A priest-psychologist who helps families in Chile said to me that the poor can often save their marriage after two sessions of therapy; the well-to-do need twenty. The poor accept help, trusting the good sense of the professional. They know they don't have all the answers. How good am I, how good are you, at accepting help and advice, at not knowing best?

'His state was divine, yet he did not cling.' Neither you nor I can say that our state is divine. But we do cling. We have talents that others haven't got, and we have experiences that others haven't had, and we cling to our scraps of grandeur. How easy it is to assert superiority without actually saying 'I'm better than you.' At school we used to call it 'showing off'. To let someone more ignorant than you get away with an inaccurate statement, when you could so easily put him right, that is humility. Not to humiliate someone else is itself humility. Not constantly to grab the limelight in conversation by being the great comic or the great authority, that is humility. Be careful: we don't always know the effect we are having. A priest friend of mine, by no means a proud man, came home after five years in South America and spoke once too often at a deanery meeting about 'how they do things out there.' He was very taken aback, and quite hurt, when another priest exploded and said 'Damn bloody Bolivia.'

Francis of Assisi is a supreme example of humility. Not because he stripped himself naked in Assisi market-square to show that he was abandoning middle-class existence for ever. Not because he made a habit out of sackcloth and slept rough. But because he was a father rejected by his own sons. He was a victim of his own success. His inspiration was such that people flocked to him, and demanded to be admitted to his brotherhood. It grew quickly into hundreds, even thousands. Every little town in Italy had its friars preaching on market day, begging in the High Street, reminding the people of Gospel values. Francis had set an example which was quite tight: the Friars must possess no property, and have no fixed abode. As soon as he had handed over the government of the Friars Minor to his disciples, he saw his dearest principles betrayed. He saw the Franciscans being turned into just another order, with goods, houses, and the kind of stability which sapped at freedom and blunted witness. The *Legend of Perugia*, which is an account of his life by three of his faithful brothers, shows his mind:

> He founded himself and his order upon firm rock, namely upon the very great humility and the very great poverty of the Son of God ... When the order had just begun, after the brothers had commenced to increase in number, he directed the brothers to dwell in the lepers' hospitals and be at their service; in the time when both noblemen and men of humble condition were coming to the order, he told them, among other things, that they were expected to serve lepers and stay in their houses.

He would rather see his men deprived of the decencies of community living in a friary, so that they could put themselves alongside those who caused most disgust in contemporary society. This was subversive and revolutionary stuff. Strong meat for the wealthy churchmen of his time. Strong meat, too, for his more pedestrian followers: too strong, in the event. The soaring inspiration, the primitive charism, did not survive even Francis himself. His greatness stems from his willingness to submit to the betrayal of his dearest dream. He was never so humble as in this.

I lived for eight months in South America—I am a failed missionary, among other things. Let me tell you a tiny thing about Peru. (I hope it won't make you say 'Damn bloody Peru'.) There used to be an internal airline called Faucett. One of its idiosyncratic habits was to fly its planes up to 25,000 ft (this was the minimum for getting over the Andes) and then to invite you to play bingo for the price of your return ticket. The loudspeaking equipment in the cabin was not very good. The stewardess would pick numbered pingpong balls out of a basket and the microphone would crackle as she spoke into it. It was not rare for two passengers to be having a fierce row as the plane landed, as they had both shouted 'House' at the same moment. Another airline was called Satco, and their unusual feature was to fly planes with unpressurized cabins, but above a certain height they would provide oxygen for each passenger through a personal tube from the ceiling. The oxygen, from being an object of curiosity and speculation, became an absolute necessity for survival. The little plastic tube was, literally, a lifeline.

The oxygen analogy is useful. In spiritual and personal terms, where does yours come from? A happily married husband and father finds it largely in the love and company of his wife and children. Some people are buoyed up by doing a job well, whether it is liturgy, or painting and decorating, or a doctorate thesis rounded off. Some people are invigorated by climbing a mountain, or a good game of football, or planting the spuds for the coming year. Some people are restored by acquiring and understanding new bits of technology. Some people are a mixture of all these. What makes life worth living for you? Digital cameras? Symphony concerts? A good steak and a bottle of Burgundy?

Some people, in order to survive, need to be in charge of whatever they are doing, they need to be top dog. Even if the pond is small, they need to be Big Fish in Small Pond. Their lifeline is that feeling of being in command. Some people need frequent injections of praise and admiration from those around them, and particularly from those above them. Some people need to be in the public eye and on the public stage: obscurity, for them, is like oxygen-starvation, and out of the limelight they become restless. Some people need everyone to agree with them. I once knew a bishop who said 'I cannot tolerate a loyal opposition.'

None of these is sinful. But they are all observable. They demand of us a degree of self-knowledge. I must know where my oxygen comes from, and plan accordingly. For instance, if I know myself really well and am not deceiving myself, I can stop myself dropping into pits of jealousy when someone is promoted above me. I can be humorous when afflicted with a feeling of disregard and neglect—I can say 'There I go again' instead of 'Everybody hates me, nobody loves me.' I can discipline myself to be less of a show-off. I can dwell peacefully with dissent. In other words, I can learn to be humble. I can learn to live with less oxygen, or obtain it in other ways. Self-knowledge is a marvellous thing.

Eight months after his election the Holy Father [Pope St John Paul II] returned to Poland. One of his meetings was with the seminarians at Jasna Gora, the national shrine of Our Lady. He said this to them: 'We discover in ourselves the interior man with his qualities, talents, noble desires and ideals; but we also discover the weakness, the bad habits, the bad tendencies: selfishness, pride and sensuality. We are vividly aware how the first set of personality traits deserves developing and reinforcing, but how the second set have to be overcome, fought and transformed … the most sublime activity of man is his work on himself.'

A surprisingly modern observation, that. 'The most sublime activity of man is his work on himself.' To embark on this, of course, you have first to admit that work needs to be done, that you're not a finished article. Here's where the humility kicks in. If I am a priest, much of my oxygen should come from my love of the Lord and my awareness of being loved by him. This awareness gives me a safe space in which to do the work on myself. I can take criticism without being destroyed by it. There should be a mystical streak in me—a relationship of love and trust with the living God which goes beyond words, which provides me with my stability, so that I can accept the inevitable humiliations of life without being crushed by them. A truly humble man is rooted in God,

God is the ballast in his boat, so that the boat can never be capsized. The ultimate truth about me is not that I was successful, or perceived to be successful. It is that God loved, and loves me. I depend on God for affection, fatherly affection, brotherly affection. This is not humiliating; it makes me humbly grateful.

And in fact the Pope is a perfect example of a man with self-knowledge and humility. Think of how he was on the night of his election—fit, athletic, active, independent, a powerhouse of energy and intelligence, articulate and eloquent. See now what age has done to him, and the attempt on his life, and sickness. He is cut off from those sources of satisfaction which must have meant so much to him. For a man with such gifts to be so reduced: to being washed and dressed, to being wheeled about, to need someone to speak his homilies for him and to be at hand with a handkerchief … what a test, what a drama. You are tempted to say 'How are the mighty fallen!' But he is not fallen. He is respected and revered as much as he ever was, because he has humbly submitted to the will of God for him. His oxygen never came from his personal gifts, from skiing and canoeing, although he loved these things. It always came from his intimate relationship with Christ and Our Lady. So his woes have not destroyed him. He could have folded with fury as his incapacity increased. But he's made of greater stuff than that, because he is a humble man. He makes his own the words of Job, 'If we take happiness from God's hand, must we not take sorrow too?' (Job 2:10). And so we find him at Lourdes, earlier this year, saying to the sick, 'With you I share a time of life marked by physical suffering, yet not for that reason any less fruitful in God's wondrous plan.' And also, 'We wish to learn from the lowly handmaid of the Lord an attitude of docility and openness to the word of God.' Docility. At eighty-four. To be docile. That's the language of humility. Twenty-six years ago, at Jasna Gora, he said to the sick, 'I unite myself spiritually with all of you. I specially renew the spiritual bond which unites me with all who suffer, all sick people, everyone confined to a hospital bed or a wheelchair, everyone who, in whatever way, is meeting the Cross in his life.' Well, that union is now even closer for him: the acceptance of the Cross was the supreme act of humility on the part of Jesus, and so it is for John Paul, and so it is for us too.

There is something in this about bending as opposed to breaking. The green and pliable tree survives the greatest storms; the stiff and rigid one is uprooted. Pride makes us rigid, humility keeps us green. May you all be green wood.

✠

A Meditation
on the Martyrs' Picture

The Martyrs' Picture [shown on the front cover of this book] isn't about the Martyrs at all. It is theirs by association, because it was the focus of their devotion to the Lord when they lived here, and because their friends sang the Te Deum before it when the news of their martyrdom came. The picture does a very daring and highly theological thing: it discusses, in pictorial form, the Blessed Trinity. It is a charmed picture, since it has survived a twenty-year occupation by the French and a six-year exile of the College in the Second World War. It is precious to us, because it provided the backdrop to the spiritual lives of heroic men who sprang from the same soil as ourselves. It deserves half an hour of our attention.

The word 'power' comes very quickly to mind. It's a picture which radiates power. The focal point of the picture is Jesus, taken from the Cross. His saving power stems from his Passion. As we dwell on this image of him, it is clear that he has given his all: there is no more to give. In his life and his death he was sheer gift to the Apostles, to his contemporaries, to us. The scale of his self-offering is staggering. So is the scale of his self-abandonment to the Father. See how the Father sustains him, hold him up. This is a relationship we find it very hard to imagine, because our own relationship with God can be cool, distant and intermittent, and our relationship with our own parents can be flawed in one way or another. As you look at this picture, you begin to understand what Christ meant when he said, 'My teaching is not from myself: it comes from the one who sent me' (John 7:16, JB) and 'There is one who sent me and I really come from him, and you do not know him but I know him because I have come from him and it was he who sent me' (John 7:28–9, JB) and 'As the Father raises the dead and gives them life, so the Son gives life to anyone he chooses' (John 5:21, JB). The

Father gives power to his Son in his very self-abandonment, and that power comes through to us above all as saving power. The drama of this picture is that it's about saving you and me, coming to our rescue. We are familiar with rescue stories in the movies. John Wayne or Clint Eastwood rides into town, alone, realizes that there is real injustice going on and the mayor and the police chief are totally corrupt, and sets about putting things straight. As soon as the innocent have been vindicated and the guilty punished, and considerable blood has been shed, he rides out of town into the setting sun, still alone, and the titles roll and the music plays. The power the hero uses is his own power, his own bravery, his own skill with a gun, his own maverick sense of fairness.

When we look at the Martyrs' Picture we feel that we too should be on it somewhere, because this is all about us. We were the ones being rescued. But there are differences in the nature of the rescue. I am being saved not from wicked and corrupt men, but to a great extent from my own malice and weakness. The rescuer sheds a lot of blood, but it is his own. His power, by his own humble admission, is not simply his own, but is conferred on him by his Father. 'For the Father, who is the source of life, has made the Son the source of life' (John 5:26, JB). And he doesn't ride off into the setting sun. He is raised from the dead and ascends into heaven, but still remains among us. His saving power, which is immense, comes not from his macho dexterity with a pistol, but from his self-gift and self-abandonment, and his guaranteed continuing personal and individual care for us. 'It follows, then, that his power to save those who come to God through him is absolute, since he lives for ever to intercede for them' (Hebrews 7:25, NJB). His power to save is absolute. Morning by morning I am brought face to face with my own incredible good luck. I have such a Saviour.

At the time of the Counter-Reformation in Italy, there was a hugely influential order called the 'Barnabites'. They were based in Milan and took their name from the Church of St Barnabas. They are still around, though no longer among the major movers and stirrers of the Church. (They run the church of S. Carlo ai Catinari at the end of the Via dei Giubbonari, near the English College.) They were founded by Antonio Maria Zaccaria, a young doctor from Cremona who became a priest. They were great reformers, insisting on an educated and self-denying clergy who would preach well to the people, and were particular experts in the letters of St Paul. They were famous for their dramatic sermons, over the top by our standards and tastes, but really effective and absolutely right for their time. A Barnabite priest would arrive to preach in a church, for example, dragging a great cross behind him, and wearing a halter round his neck to show that he was a condemned criminal, destined for hell—but for the grace of God. It wouldn't do in Tunbridge Wells, or St James's Spanish Place. Yet behind the theatrical thrills lay a truth of substance.

My eternal life hung, and hangs, by a thread, but it is a thread of colossal strength. Here is a paradox: in one sense my salvation is sure, because I know the story of Calvary and the Resurrection, and unless I deliberately put myself outside the grace of God, the gates of heaven are open to me; but in another sense the whole thing is very precarious, since but for the goodwill of Christ, I was and am a dead duck. The mere fact of my human existence is not enough. I depend on the generosity of someone other than myself.

That generosity is clear from the Precious Blood of Christ, poured out upon the world in this picture. The College guide book says it is poured out upon the British Isles. I may be obtuse, but I have stared and stared at the picture and cannot personally see anything particularly British there. I would have expected, at the very least, to be able to detect the outline of East Anglia, but in honesty I can't. Still, it is enough for me that the planet, the globe, and the human race which inhabits it, is cleansed from the side and the hands of Jesus. The significance of blood for us is enormous, isn't it—it is the very essence of vitality. In this picture, our poor world is being irrigated with the Blood of Christ. Thus, and only thus, I am a saved man, purchased like a slave in a market. 'You are not your own property, then: you were bought at a price' (I Corinthians 6:20, NJB). That's Paul to the Corinthians. And Peter says the same in his First Letter: 'Remember, the ransom that was paid to free you from the useless way of life your ancestors handed down was not paid in anything corruptible, neither in silver nor gold, but in the precious blood of a lamb without spot or stain' (I Peter 1:18, JB). Morning by morning, then, as I look at this picture, I am brought face to face with the receipt for my purchase.

The Son is depicted here as lifeless, spent, derelict. Yet, as Peter says to the Sanhedrin, 'This is the stone rejected by you the builders, but which has proved to be the keystone' (Acts 4:11). I think of the depiction in stone of the Paschal Lamb at Palazzola, which for so many years, centuries perhaps, was a miscellaneous piece of masonry lying about in the garden, grimy and neglected, but is now properly enshrined in the altar of sacrifice, cleaned and floodlit. 'For of all the names in the world given to men, this is the only one by which we can be saved.'

If the Son's power is saving power, the Father's is sovereign power. He holds all things in being, just as he holds the Son up before our eyes here. There is all the difference in the world—literally—between the believer in God and the non-believer. If you don't believe, then you are the top of the tree: there is no-one more powerful than man, and he is accountable only to himself. That's a lonely place to be, even if you live in a book-lined house with a log fire in a tree-lined street, surrounded by your loving family, sustained by a lucrative and secure job, with frequent holidays, and enjoying the best of health. Even with all these advantages, there are moments when you realize they only amount to anaesthetics. Atheism is a lonely place to be. On the other hand, if you believe in the sovereign power of God, that power infiltrates everything you do. Your hopes, your plans, your family and professional relationships, your job, your feeling about yourself, your response to pain and disappointment ... all these take place under God, and with reference to him. Read Psalm 138/9: 'Yahweh, you examine me and you know me, you know if I am standing or sitting, you read my thoughts from far away, whether I walk or lie down, you are watching, you know every detail of my conduct.' I remember a day of retreat in a very hot country, sitting on a hillside and trying to keep out of the sun. I had the sudden and, I suppose correct intuition that I was being revolved under the sun, paraded past the sun, that it wasn't moving but I was; and that in the same way each day rolls me past God the Creator. I am nothing if I am not man under God, exposed to God.

Look at the expression on the Father's face in this picture. It isn't shallow emotional response. It is the wise compassion of the Ancient of Days. It reminds you of the Rembrandt picture of the Prodigal Son coming home, and being welcomed by his old father. In Rembrandt the father's head is slightly tipped to one side, and as he stoops down over the kneeling boy and blesses him you sense the huge empathy he has with the silly youth: it is as if he were saying 'I know. I know. I know.' He knows about sin, he knows about repentance, he knows how people screw up their courage to come in from the cold. He's seen it all before. He knows, and his paternal heart goes out to the boy with much love, and in that torrent of love all is forgiven. Well, in the Martyrs' Picture there is clearly nothing in the Son to forgive, and the situation is entirely different. The Father is looking straight ahead, not down. Yet he is not impassive, uncaring. There is suffering on his face, and comprehension. Some theologians reckon that, as part of our Redemption, not only God the Son suffered, but God the Father as well. How could the Father, who is pure relationship, not be caught up in the agony of his only Son? Suffering with other people, enduring the pain of others, is often the most acute kind of suffering. People with a parent dying of cancer, or with Alzheimer's, or whose child has leukemia, have this look upon their face. It is a preoccupied look. There is nothing I can do, they are saying, but how could I not care? However, because we humans are not pure relationship, we can to some extent switch off, distract ourselves, be ourselves; in the Trinity there is no switch. The Persons are in perfect and perpetual communion.

What is true in heaven from all eternity, takes place here on earth in time. In eternity the Father begets the Son. Because it's in eternity, this means that the Father is not older than the Son; it all takes place outside time. The Son and the Father, being purely 'for' one another, and having no identity outside this relationship, generate such wisdom, knowledge and love, that what they generate has personality of its own, personality taken from them and referring back to them, rather as children reflect the personality now of one parent, now of the other: and that is the Holy Spirit. As I said, it all happens outside time. We are tempted to say 'All that happened in the beginning, before God got round to creating the universe' but we might just as well say 'It's happening now.' Words like before and after and now have no meaning in this context, yet we have to use them because we have no other: we have not been issued with an eternal vocabulary. Anyway, in the Martyrs' Picture, the bright, intensely alive dove appears in that electric space between Father and Son. It reminds you of Michelangelo's painting on the roof of the Sistine Chapel, showing God touching Adam's finger with his own. You have the impression there that an immensely powerful current is being transmitted through those index fingers: and the clay man becomes a living soul. Communication with God must always be productive. Well, the communication within God is even more productive, it is supremely productive. We say the Spirit 'proceeds' from the Father and the Son; he is the product of their communication. The Spirit appears several times in the Gospel account, and you would expect him to. He speaks of the Father to the Son and the Son to the Father. He personifies their love for each other. He speaks of contact and conversation, as opposed to distance and separation.

I said that what happens in heaven in eternity happens on earth in time, and this is so. When the fullness of time had come (that is our time, not God's), God sent Gabriel to Mary, and spoke his Word into the world; in a way, it's a second begetting. And after the Resurrection and Ascension, the Father and the Son send the Spirit into the world, and he makes them present to us; in a way, it's a second proceeding. If Jesus came to set fire upon the earth, it is his Spirit who makes sure, now, that the fire is kindled and remains burning. Fire is drastic, and betokens energy. It is the Spirit who gives us the courage to make radical decisions for the sake of the Gospel, and the sticking-power to see them through. He is the burning zeal of the Martyrs. He is the lightning inspiration of men and women who found new congregations and new movements. He is the love and the knowledge which exists within the Trinity for ever and ever, and he enters into our puny world, and—if we let him—transforms it. *Ignem veni mittere in terram* [I have come to bring fire to the earth (Luke 12:49)—the motto of the English College, Rome]. Jesus returns to his Father so that he may send us the Paraclete. 'It is for your own good that I am going, because unless I go, the Advocate will not come to you. But if I do go, I will send him to you' (John 16:7).

It is interesting to reflect that the Spirit is suggested to us as a dove. A dove is a benign bird, a peaceful bird. Pius XII had as his crest a dove holding an olive branch in its mouth, and the olive branch was a sign of hope, because it showed Noah in Genesis (8:10) that the waters had receded from the earth. Pius XII was elected six months before the outbreak of the Second World War. He knew the hunger of the world for signs of hope. But of course, Noah's dove was also a homing pigeon, returning like a boomerang to the place from which it was sent out. The Holy Spirit does this too: he returns to the bosom of the Father, and he takes us with him, transformed and purified. Ephesians talks about 'the hidden plan he [the Father] so kindly made in Christ from the beginning, to act upon when the times had run their course to the end: that he would bring everything together under Christ as Head, everything in the heavens and everything on earth' (Ephesians 1:9). And in the Second Vatican Council, the document *Gaudium et Spes* has this paragraph: 'When we have spread on earth the fruits of our nature and our enterprise—human dignity, sisterly and brotherly communion, and freedom—according to the command of the Lord and in his Spirit, we will find them once again, cleansed this time from the stain of sin, illuminated and transfigured, when Christ presents to his Father an eternal and universal kingdom 'of truth and life, a kingdom of holiness and grace, a kingdom of justice, love and peace.'* In other words, the Spirit enables us to work according to the mind of Christ, so that at the final consummation we may be part of the Church purified and glorified.

I said at the beginning of this talk that you and I ought to be on the Martyrs' Picture. In a way we are. Thomas of Canterbury is there, and Edmund, King of East Anglia, with an angel peeping over the shoulder of each of them and carrying, rather like a caddie on a golf course, the weapons of their martyrdom, the sword and the arrows. Thomas, who was really a Norman, was assassinated in a grubby and murky plot, by four knights apparently obeying a king who had lost his temper. Edmund was cornered by the Danes in a Suffolk village, and was made the target for some archery practice before being beheaded. Both of them knew what they were risking. Thomas, who had already suffered six years' exile when he asserted the Church's rights against Henry II, was already a seasoned campaigner who knew the King well and had few illusions. Young Edmund, a Saxon, when he defended his Christian people against the invaders instead of collaborating, understood the probable consequences, because the Danes took few prisoners. They

---

* *Gaudium et Spes*, n. 39.

both went into what they did with their eyes open. Christian people recognized their heroism in the huge cult which grew up so quickly around their burial places, in Canterbury and Bury St Edmunds. The Spirit is powerful in men like these. He was powerful in Ralph Sherwin and the other forty-three.

May he be powerful in us as well.

✝

MATURITY

I want tonight to tackle quite a difficult subject, but I believe a very important one. It is the issue of personal and religious maturity. I have known more priests than I can count, in the course of forty-six years of ministry. Some have been towering figures, a real gift to their people. Their power to attract and lead has come principally from their holiness. But hot on the heels of holiness, I would rate their maturity. And conversely, I have known priests whose ministry was wounded and damaged by their lack of maturity.

Maturity is hard to define; easier to describe. Much of what I'm going to say applies to men and women in general. Clearly, in the present context, I am interested in you as priests and future priests. But the gift of maturity is needed just as much by husband and wives. Indeed, if we are afflicted with parishes full of immature adult laypeople, we are the most unfortunate of men. Edith Sitwell, in her book *English Eccentrics*, refers to Charles Waterton, the landed gentleman in the early nineteenth century, who would invite you to dinner, but then hide under the cloaks on the hat stand, growling, and fix his teeth in your leg while you were hanging up your overcoat. This lighthearted knockabout humour betrayed, perhaps, just a touch of arrested development. I would not care to have Mr Waterton on my parish council. Immaturity is unfortunate because you can't say to an immature person 'Be mature'. If he knew what you were talking about, he would be mature already. The drawback about the immature is that they don't know how immature they are.

A mature priest is one who has knowledge of himself. He knows his strengths. Some of us have musical talents, some of us are sportsmen, some of us are good with words, some of us are naturally charming and friendly and able to put people at their ease. Some of us are intelligent and able to marshal a good argument. If these things are true of us, the mature thing is not to pretend otherwise, it is to thank God for our gifts and use them well. It is also to avoid jealousy like the plague, because other men will surely have gifts not given to me. Paul is quite clear about this to the Corinthians, when he lists the charisms. Nobody has the lot.

The mature priest also knows his weaknesses, and has cast aside all self-deception concerning them. He knows if he has a short temper. He knows if he is too addicted to *la dolce vita.* He knows whether he has a cowardly side to him which makes him duck conflict. He knows whether he is too easily infatuated, if his heart is easily touched. He knows if he is periodically lazy. He knows whether he has a problem with authority, all authority. He has learned by experience, by his own mistakes, and by other people's as well. He has not lost hope of growth in the Spirit and in virtue, but neither is he under any illusions about lightning or magic solutions. He is soberly optimistic that with the grace and mercy of God, he can still change; equally, he is quietly humorous about his failures to do so.

The mature priest has too much sense to be vain, either about his appearance or his crowd-pulling potential. He knows that these things are the most ephemeral of qualities, and that public praise can quickly change to public contempt, or indifference. He knows the history of Holy Week, and the fickle crowd. And he can see what happens to politicians who manage to reach the top of the greasy pole of power, and what the media do to them. So his centre of gravity is somewhere else. His sense of self-worth flows from his prayer, or his daily attempt to pray, and the consciousness of having done his duty not perfectly, but reasonably well. He is too grown-up to be ambitious, or to nourish fantasies about preferment and promotion in the Church.

A mature man, knowing himself, knows what other people are like as well. He is not easily taken in, and doesn't canonize people while they're still alive: he has grown out of having unreasonable expectations of others. Nor does he demonize people: he knows that all of us are a mixture of good and evil, and manages to avoid crude blanket condemnations. He never writes anybody off. There is a sage wisdom in this, a deep understanding of human nature; part of this comes from the confessional, part is innate.

You will notice that lots of what I've already said is 'This, but on the other hand that,' a statement of balance. Balance is the sign of maturity:

a reluctance to rush to any extremes, except extreme love of God and neighbour. Cardinal Suenens was asked by a journalist during the Council whether he was a conservative or a progressive, and he replied, 'I belong to the extreme centre.' It is not the same as being lukewarm. It is more like staying on the highway and refusing to be enticed into the boggy fields to left and right, because on the highway you travel faster towards your target. Among the boggy fields which entice priests off the mature highway I would give first place to resentment. It is the boggiest. You see, there is always just reason to be resentful if you are so inclined. Other people *are* inconsiderate, and other people *do* walk on your face to get what they want; bishops *do* misjudge us, and give us unwise assignments, or get taken in by plausible rogues and bad advisers. Parishioners *can* hook us up in their neuroses, and their anger can generate anger in us—especially if they criticize our celebration of Mass and sacraments, or our preaching. How easy it is for us to get thrown on the defensive, and lose our peace of mind. Other priests can make us resentful, specially when we find we are doing their work for them because they are lazy or forgetful. The national rush to litigation is part of the boggy field of resentment. I remember a man, years ago, who ruined his family, lost his job and destroyed his health, all because his daughter had not been admitted to the training college he wanted for her: the ensuing court cases made him obsessive; he became more and more coldly angry and flinty-eyed till he died. He was in a very boggy field, and a long way from the highway. And, I would say, he suffered from a fatal lack of maturity. He had no sense of proportion. He could not see what was important and what was less important; what was reasonably possible, and what was downright impossible. He wasted all his energy and in the end, his life as well. A mature man will know if he has a temptation to resentment, to take offence, and he will take contrary action: he will say 'I do not choose to go down that route,' and find other strategies.

Our model of maturity is Christ himself. Here is the Letter to the Ephesians:

> The gifts he gave were that some would be apostles, some prophets, some evangelists, some pastors and teachers, to

equip the saints for the work of ministry, for building up the
body of Christ, until all of us come to the unity of the faith
and of the knowledge of the Son of God, to maturity, to the
measure of the full stature of Christ. (Ephesians 4:13, NRSV)

If we unpick this, we have a pretty good blueprint for action as mature
priests. *a.* We are given differing gifts. No-one has them all. The thing is
to develop the ones you have, not be envious of other people's skills and
talents. *b.* The point of your gifts is not self-indulgence; it is to equip your
people to minister to one another. *c.* Your long-term aim is to build up
the body of Christ, the Church; not to build yourself up in some kind of
ego-trip, and become a celebrity. *d.* Compared with Christ's trust of the
Father, his deep intimacy with the Father, our trust and our knowledge
are woefully threadbare: they always need deepening and intensifying.
e. Maturity lies at the end of this road; you're not there yet, and neither
am I. We'll be there when the full majesty and dignity of Jesus, Son of
Mary and Son of God, really bursts upon us, when we appreciate his real
stature, so that we don't just talk about him as an intellectual concept,
but live our union with him in wonder and adoration, and everything
else falls into place in the light of this union.

That passage in Ephesians is anticipating the day when the whole
Church will be mature with the maturity of Christ, it isn't primarily
about individuals. History, I'm afraid, shows us an immature Church:
burning people, sluggish about slavery, enriching her high officials,
getting embroiled in territorial wars. If you and I are mature men, we
shall help the whole Church to achieve the goal of Ephesians. Vatican II,
in the Document on the Church, said 'This messianic people, although it
does not, in fact, include everybody, and at times may seem to be a little
flock, is, however, a most certain seed of unity, hope and salvation for the
whole human race.'* Well, we ain't there yet, and the Council speaks in a
kind of prophetic present: that's what the Church is supposed to be, and
is becoming, and will be, when she achieves that maturity, the measure
of the full stature of Christ. We can contribute our sixpennyworth, or
six centesimi worth, by being mature, prudent, sage, wise priests.

---

* *Lumen Gentium*, n. 9.

And here is Paul to the Romans, saying the same thing in a different way.

> I appeal to you therefore, brothers and sisters, by the mercies of God, to present your bodies as a living sacrifice, holy and acceptable to God, which is your spiritual worship. Do not be conformed to this world, but be transformed by the renewal of your minds, so that you may discern what is the will of God—what is good and acceptable and perfect. (Romans 12:1–2)

Here is the agenda of a mature Christian, and thus of a mature priest as well. Let's unpick this one too. *a.* The process of becoming the kind of person God wants us to be cannot be achieved on our own; it's done by the mercy and the compassion of God. *b.* We are to present our bodies, indeed our whole selves to God, as a living sacrifice. The Greek for this is *thusia zosa,* and the first of those words is connected with our word 'thurible'. Our lives are to be like slow-burning incense, not fireworks, which are all bang and flash and leave nothing but a smell of gunpowder. This gift of self to God is a patient, daily offering: you want the charcoal to last for the whole of the Mass. *c.* And this constant slow-release devotion is our 'spiritual worship'. The Greek is *logike latreia,* which really means 'worship which is infused with reason'. Our love and service of God and neighbour are not sheer impulse or habit; they are deliberate, thought-out, worthy of human beings, a consciously adopted way of life, a lifestyle we have assumed on purpose. *d.* This common-sense, balanced devotion will stop us being conformed to our world, which has nothing to offer us in terms of values or attitudes. The mature man isn't taken in by the soap operas; he can distinguish fantasy from fact. The Greek doesn't say 'world' so much as 'age'; Paul is contrasting this passing slice of time with the eternity of life with God. *e.* 'Be transformed by the renewal of your minds': this is an interior change. By the grace of God your whole mindset is to shift so that you see everything in a new light, the light of heaven and of God's abiding presence. It's a conversion, not a road-to-Damascus experience, but still a real conversion. *f.* And the result will be that you can discern what

God wants of you. You will have a nose for what is good and acceptable and perfect. The word for 'perfect', *teleion*, really means 'fully grown', or mature. We're back where we started. If you are a mature man, with your religion fully integrated into your life, you will make mature judgments and mature choices. You won't be like the people described by St Jude in his letter: 'Waterless clouds carried along by the winds; autumn trees without fruit, twice-dead, uprooted; wild waves of the sea, casting up the foam of their own shame; wandering stars …' (Jude 12–13). You will be a man of level head and solid purpose.

It is good to have flesh-and-blood models of what I am describing. One would be St Thomas More. This highly mature Chancellor of the Realm and father of a family was also a man of infectious, and occasionally salacious, humour. He was pleasantly ironical. He once said of his wife, Alice, that she was 'a jolly master-woman, all bedecked in finery, with strait bracing in her body to make her middle small.' He did not seek confrontation, either with his wife or with the King who employed him. In the matter of the King's marriage, so long as he was not forced to swear to something he did not believe, he was willing to resign his job, retire into his own home, remain silent. He was not so rash as to court martyrdom. In the 'Dialogue of Comfort against Tribulation', which he wrote in prison, he recognized this as a temptation. He was aware of his own weakness, and apprehensive about his capacity to survive torture, what he called 'duress and hard handling' and 'violent forcible ways'. His beloved daughter visited him in the Tower and tried to persuade him to change his mind, and he told her that he had come to his fatal decision only after long consideration and after reflecting upon 'the very worst and the uttermost that can by possibility fall.'* Not a hothead, then. But he had arrived at a seasoned conclusion and would not be budged from it, even when Thomas Cromwell hinted to him that his bad example had rubbed off on the three Carthusian priors who were about to be executed, and he would be in part responsible for their death.

I do nobody harm, I say none harm, I think none harm, but

---

* Peter Ackroyd, *The Life of Thomas More*, ch. 30.

wish everybody good. And if this be not enough to keep a man alive, in good faith I long not to live. And I am dying already, and have since I came here, been divers times in the case that I thought to die within one hour, and I thank Our Lord I was never sorry for it, but rather sorry when I saw the pang past. And therefore my poor body is at the King's pleasure, would God my death might do him some good.[*]

He had tasted greatness, and weighed it in the balance, and he died with his wits about him. A mature man.

My other model was born thirty-two years after Thomas More died. He was St Francis de Sales, the Bishop of Geneva. He was a gentleman, a minor aristocrat by birth; but he was also a gentle man, who knew how to govern his temper as well as his diocese, and be unfailingly courteous. He was highly intelligent, but deeply pastoral with it: he applied his learning to the care of his flock. They made him the coadjutor bishop of Geneva at a very early age, but high office never went to his head. He was a ceaseless visitor of his outlying mountain parishes, climbing steep alpine paths in all weathers. The Calvinists had gained a lot of ground in his diocese. In fact he could not live in Geneva at all because of them, and when he became the Bishop he was a bishop in exile. He used sweet reason to counter their arguments, and on the personal level was unfailingly polite. Maybe it was because of his sweetness of temperament and his approachability that he was able to reclaim many thousands of people for the Catholic Church. The same qualities brought him an extraordinary number of correspondents. He was spiritual director by post to a huge number of clients. There are whole books of his letters, and they all breathe the same spirit. Implicit trust in God; an invitation to balanced, unceasing effort to please God; a conviction that anyone, in any walk of life, has sanctity within his or her grasp; a desire for people to live their present state of life to the full, with a spirituality suitable to that state of life. Here are a couple of lines from one of his sermons:

Do you want to know which is the best time for serving God?

[*] *ibid.,* ch. 31.

It's now, the time which is passing at this moment. Because the past is no longer ours, and the future is not yet here, and is uncertain. So the present time is really the best time, and we must faithfully employ it for the service of God.

That ability to focus on the present, that sort of time competence, is the hallmark of a mature man. Here is an excerpt from one of his letters:

Don't love anything to excess, I beg you, not even the virtues themselves—you can let them slip by loving them too much. Let's be what we are, and be it well, to give honour to the one who fashioned us. Let's be what God wants. The only thing is to be his. Don't let's bother ourselves with becoming what we want, at variance with God's intention. Even if we were the most excellent creatures under heaven, what would be the point, if it's not God's will which is being done?

This calm submission to the will of God, even when it means relaxing control of our life, is the hallmark of a mature man.

He used to teach catechism to the children in Annecy, where he lived, and their parents would come and listen in. One day his own mother appeared in the audience, and he said: 'Madame, you cause me some distraction when I see you at my catechism lesson to all our little children, because it was you yourself who taught it to me.' And on another occasion, when he was exhausted, he wrote in a letter, with complete self-knowledge:

I shall spend this Lent in residence in my Cathedral and in rehabilitating my soul, which is almost totally fragmented by so many worries it has suffered. It is a clock which is out of order. It must be dismantled piece by piece and after it has been cleaned and oiled it must be reassembled to make it chime more accurately.

To the King of France who wanted to make him Archbishop of Paris, and was offering him money:

Sire, I thank your Majesty with all my heart for the thoughtfulness you have condescended to bestow on me. I accept, yes, I accept with a very great affection for your royal liberality, but thanks to Our Lord, I am now in such a position that I have no need of this pension. Consequently I very humbly beg your Majesty that your present be kept within the safekeeping of your Treasurer, and I shall avail myself of it whenever I shall have need of it.

The King remarked 'Now that is the wittiest refusal I have ever heard.' It was the style of the man; he knew who he was, and where he wanted to go, and with the highest degree of politeness he would deter anyone who tried to deflect him from his purpose.

May God grant us the same gift of maturity, for our sake, and the sake of our people.

✛

No Free Lunch

This one is about the gratuity of God.

'Gratuity of God' sounds as if the Almighty were distributing tips in a restaurant or a taxi. 'Gratuity' in English has acquired this minimalist sense—an impulsive, transient act of goodwill, a detail, something benign but of little importance. And even this, in our functional setting, often gets ossified into an automatic ten-per-cent 'service charge'. It is as if we found the chanciness of a tip unbearable: let it be fixed.

But gratuity as an attribute of God is infinitely more than this. An allied word, grace, means literally 'something for nothing'. A breathtaking concept, if you rest your mind on it. So foreign to most of our experience. We are saying that God's goodness to us is unearned and un-earnable. That we have the incredible good luck to serve a God who doesn't calibrate his blessings or his forgiveness according to what we deserve. We *say* this, in articles and sermons. But do we really believe it?

There are days when I can come into the presence of the Blessed Sacrament, and kneel, and know instinctively that my prayer today is already planned out for me. I don't even have to work at it. I simply have to let myself be engulfed by the sheer benevolence, the charity of God. On those days I don't have to convince myself that his enfolding affection for his sons and daughters is real, unlimited and unconditioned. It's clear. 'Fear not, little flock, for it has pleased your father to give you a kingdom.' Not five per cent at the end of a meal well-cooked and well-served, or even ten per cent, but a kingdom. The breadth of it is staggering. Mostly I find it hard to believe because I'm not like this myself. My charity is calculated. My right hand always knows what my left is doing.

If my relationship with God is characterized by his gratuitous love and friendship, then when I pray it will always be God who takes the initiative. If prayer is like a conversation, then it is He who speaks first, and He who sets the agenda. For openers he says 'I love you.' Anything

I say will be by way of reply; I cannot ignore what he has just said. He says 'I love you without taking into account your performance or your track record. You don't have to prove anything to me, or bluff me, or pull the wool over my eyes. You are my creation, and I cannot behold you or perceive you without loving you. That's what I'm like.'

Deep down inside me there is a nagging, limiting voice which wants to say 'Of course, that doesn't apply to me.' or 'Philpot, you have failed to qualify, you're not part of the club of those God loves. Sorry.' This worm-like insidious whisper has its roots somewhere in my past, where I *did* fail to qualify for something, and my class-mates or colleagues succeeded. A moment when I knew myself to be an outsider while the others were insiders. Just by way of illustration ... 'Roman Catholics and Jews may now leave,' my headmaster used to intone, in the days when we Catholics didn't pray with anyone else. 'Roman Catholics and Jews may now leave,' said my form teacher at the beginning of a Bible lesson. I was always leaving. Fate, I felt, had marked me out as the boy who was different, who sat on the shoe-boxes in the passage and waited for the bell to go. Not part of the club.

A little excursus into the English school examination system. In 1950 my year group was the first to do the new-fangled exam which replaced the School Certificate, the staging-post which marked departure from school for many children, especially those who had no plans for college or university. The new invention was called the O-level, and is now the GCSE. No-one, least of all our teachers, knew what to expect from the examiners, so they prepared and coached us as though for the old exam. They were as surprised as we were when the examiners said, not 'These boys have not passed the exam' or even 'These boys did not know the answers', but 'These boys are disqualified because they are not yet sixteen.' We did not get even to square one. There was something constitutionally wrong with us. We had fallen outside the favour of our lords and masters. Bureaucracy had spat us out. We were not yet sixteen. Sorry. His Majesty's Government, speaking through the Secretary of State for Education, was short on gratuity that year. It wasn't their strong suit. The next year, I believe, they changed the rules.

Where God is concerned, you are an insider. This is true whatever your self-perception. If you are willing to let him love you, he will.

Even if you're not willing, he will. Remember Romans 5:7: one might be prepared to die for a really good man, but what proves that God loves us is that he died for us while we still sinners. In his letters Paul is always using expressions for us like 'citizens', 'first-born sons', 'heirs', the language of inclusion. Picked, favoured and privileged, that's what we are. God knows why. I mean that literally: God knows why. But let us bask in the fact. This time, as you say in America, you got lucky. You may be the kind of person who never wins lotteries or jackpots, who never gets upgraded on plane flights, never gets the prize for the crossword: but this time, you got lucky. Lucky is not a good word, because it suggests blind, impersonal chance. What I'm talking about is not blind or impersonal. It is the meant, aware, targeted, directed love and affection of Almighty God. 'And Jesus, looking upon him, loved him.' Everything that happens to you in the Church—baptism and confirmation, absolution and communion, your call to the priesthood— takes place in this context. And through you, Almighty God is going to make hundreds of other people aware of his gratuitous love.

If you have a streak of the Devil's advocate in you, at this point you probably want to say 'If all that is true, what about hell? There's plenty about hell in the Bible. Surely hell is the place where you are definitively cut off from the love of God? And what about the Church's tradition concerning mortal sin? It is called mortal precisely because it's a killer, it kills the life of God in the soul. All this talk about the gratuitous love of God is a wicked over-simplification, and wishful thinking. It is only too possible for us to put ourselves outside the love of God. So his love is not gratuitous. There is a price to be paid for it. Good behaviour. We have to cooperate with God's grace.'

Well, I stick to my guns. It is true that God respects our free will. He is not going to frogmarch us into heaven. We have within us the dark capacity for stubborn and terminal resistance. Just once or twice in your priestly life we do meet somebody who appears to be, literally, hell-bent. There is a huge mystery about this, how a person can opt for evil. Thank God that He is the one who does the judging, not me. The Church used to be very severe on suicides, denying them Christian burial. Now she has an intuition that there is nearly always something which drains the sin out of the act, or at least dilutes it. In the same way

God can read the heart of the most grace-resistant person on earth, and quite possibly find extenuating reasons. He judges—which lets us off the hook; we don't have to judge, and if we do, we shall almost certainly get it wrong. We don't actually know that there is anyone in hell at all. But even sustained evil will does not stop God loving us. 'For I am certain of this: neither death nor life, no angel or prince, nothing that exists, nothing still to come, not any power, or height or depth, nor any created thing, can ever come between us and the love of God made visible in Christ Jesus Our Lord' (Romans 8:38).

I think that, without meaning to, the Church has often propagated a doctrine of earned love. In pulpits and in classrooms we have given the impression that the Father is like some earthly fathers who say to their children, 'I will love you if you're good. I will love you if you get a good school report. [There used to be another exam which decided whether you would go to an ordinary school, and become a manual worker of some kind, or a superior place called a grammar school, from which you could easily get access to university. It was called the 11-plus. Parents used to bribe their children to pass this exam]. If you pass the 11-plus, or the common entrance, or jump through some other conventional hoop, you get a bicycle. No pass, no bike.' There is an area of outer darkness to which you are consigned if you don't measure up. But that is a human way of carrying on. Only humans say that they will be generous on condition that the other person is grateful. It is not God's way of carrying on. God defines what generosity really is. He can't not-be-generous. His cherishing love is not turned on and off as if by a tap. And this stands to reason if you reflect that God is, and must be, the totality of all that is positive. He can't graduate from no-love to love, or from less love to more. If he could, he wouldn't be God.

When you and I talk about the Good News, or the Gospel, this is the nub of it. The pillars that hold the roof up are these statements: God is there; God is good; Christ is risen; Christ is alive. And the corollary of these statements is another pillar—you are loved. Whoever you are, and whatever you have done, you are loved. At the start of Lent we say 'Repent and believe the Gospel.' For me to believe this bit of the Gospel, that I am loved, may indeed demand a kind of repentance, a *metanoia*, a change of heart. To credit God with the correct measure of goodness we have to stretch our hearts and minds, and stretch them again: otherwise they will never encompass the wonder of it, and we shall end up making God in our own image and likeness rather than the other way round. I have to repent of my penny-pinching imagination.

Some of the people we meet as priests have despaired. They have been born into unfortunate families and have been passed from pillar to post, made to know they are unwanted, an embarrassment. Or they were born handicapped in some way, and have realized what a disappointment they are to those whose approval they most value. Or they are incurable alcoholics of whom society has eventually washed its hands, and they sleep underneath bridges in cardboard boxes with the other fringe people who have received the same message: 'You have put yourself beyond love; you are too dirty, too smelly, too insanitary, too unreliable to fit in anywhere.' This is the anti-Gospel, the Bad News. There is no worse news than to say to someone 'You are not loved' or 'You are no longer loved.' The most important element in your ministry will be to convince such people that this is wrong, that on the contrary they are lovable, and they matter.

The Catholic Church, and Catholic people in general, are not always very good at converting the Bad News into Good News. One of my great regrets as I look back over my priestly life is that I did not do better at this myself. Out of a sense of helplessness and frustration I sometimes shouted at persistent beggars at the rectory door, at drunks I almost ran over because they had kipped down in my garage, at tramps who turned up at the start of a Bank Holiday weekend saying 'My giro has not come and the Social Security are closed till Tuesday.' And at sneak-thieves who got themselves locked into the church at the end of the day so that they could rifle the money-boxes and break *out* in the middle of the night. I did not always model Good News to these people. I may have given away more money than some other priests, but I spoiled the effect by doing it sarcastically or with a bad grace. Other priests could find time to chat with the down-and-outs, to joke with them, even to refuse their requests in ways that did not speak of total rejection. It's a bit late for me now. I think this is one of the greatest challenges of our priestly life. A grace to ask God for. 'May I be Good News. May I not be the mirror-image of a middle-class society which protects itself by only having time for PLU—that is, people like us.'

Paul says in Romans 5:15: 'If death came to many through the offence of one man, how much greater an effect the grace of God has had, coming to so many and so plentifully as a free gift through the one man Jesus Christ.' To so many and so plentifully. Think of some simple examples of the plentiful coming of the grace of God. Think of daily Mass at the Gesù in the centre of Rome: every half-hour the Paschal Mystery, every half-hour the Bread of Life distributed. Think of the long lines for confession at a Christmas Penance Service, even today, in a downtown parish at home. How many times in your life have you said 'I absolve you from your sins in the name of the Father and of the Son and of the Holy Spirit'? Each time God comes down to earth from heaven with forgiveness as a prodigal free gift. Think of the hospital chaplain who slips through the curtains round the bed in the early hours of the morning with the incredible comfort of the oil of the sick: 'May the Lord who frees you from sin save you and raise you up.' All this is God's language of gratuitous love.

Gratuitous love is at the heart of our Faith. If you read the references to the Resurrection in the New Testament it is fascinating to see how often the expression used is *egegertai* or some variation on it—I mean a passive verb: it was something done to Jesus by his Father, something bestowed on him by the Father: he was raised. Jesus knew, as we know, what it is to be a recipient of the Father's overwhelming love and favour.

We are supposed to ferry this love and favour onwards. I spoke a moment ago about being Good News to those society had discarded. Here is another aspect of the same thing. In II Corinthians 8:9 Paul says: 'You are well aware of the generosity which Our Lord Jesus Christ had, that, although he was rich, he became poor for your sake, so that you should become rich through his poverty.' Don't be a hoarder. To give away as easily as you receive makes you Good News, gratuitous Good News, to a world which has stopped believing that there are free gifts with no strings attached. The sour, sardonic caption which summed up the Depression in the United States in the 1930s was 'There's no free lunch.' You and I have to be a signal that, in fact, since the Incarnation, there *is* free lunch. Simply by our open-handedness we are prophetic, and the world has need of prophets. The Greek word for the generosity of Christ is *charis*, and *charis* means more than a cheque, it means a movement of the heart, it means kindness which does not count the cost and does not look backward.

There is an intriguing section in the *Catechism of the Catholic Church* on grace. The main thing to say about grace is that it is supernatural. It means that it is above any logical or reasonable demand of our nature, that we have no automatic affinity or entitlement to it. It is, as we say, 'out of a clear blue sky'. This is obviously true about grace. God alone can reveal and give himself. God alone can adopt new children. God alone can give out the key of his house. God alone can infuse new life into us. We are and always will be net debtors, sheer debtors. It is crystal clear that God's action in our regard is gratuitous. St Augustine says, 'God's mercy goes before us so that we may live devoutly, and follows us so that we may always live with God: for without Him we can do nothing.'

Our attitude to gratuity will decide the shape of Church we propagate. Is your shape like the rigging of a schooner, with the boy-sailors swarming up in competition to see who can get to the crows-nest first, and a rope's-end for the stragglers? This kind of Church is a meritocracy. The goodies in this world, and the next, go to the achievers. Another shape would be like a dancing circle at a Greek or Israeli wedding, where the dancers are always ready to loosen their hands and admit a latecomer, and the dance goes on, and the latecomer joins in and is accepted as an equal, immediately. That is a Church where the grace of God and the gratuitousness of God are taken seriously, and joyfully.

Scripture puts it beyond doubt that the act and work of creation are God's gratuitous act. Indeed it could not be otherwise. In the nature of the case, there was nobody round to temper that gratuitousness, to put God under an obligation. Such an idea is absurd. So, of all God's acts, creation is the most obviously sovereign and self-determined. What we forget is that in the knowledge and intention of God, creation and salvation are united. They must be. Everything we find in John's Prologue, and the hymn in Colossians 1, confirms this. The universe was created not only *through* the Second Person of the Trinity, Wisdom

* *De Natura et Gratia*, 31.

personified, the Logos: it was also created *for* him. The Incarnation was envisioned in the same contemplative act as creation itself. The world is a receptacle for the Incarnate God—that is its primary purpose and function, not an afterthought. A majestic one-sided decree of Almighty God, that the human race and its material setting should be both made and redeemed—redeemed globally, but also that each member of the human race should be redeemed individually. We, like Mary in the hymn, are 'chosen before the Creation began.'

This talk has tended to dwell on the uplands of abstract theology. I want to end it on a warmer and more familiar note. I would like to recall to your mind what it felt like to be a child. I know full well that for some of us family life has not been straightforward. Parental divorce, and stepmothers and stepfathers, have become more and more an everyday experience, and not exceptional. Sometimes the experience is not damaging to the children, but sometimes it is. If in your case it has been painful, you have my deepest sympathy. But even allowing for this, every one of us, at some stage, quietly appropriated the entitlements of a child in the house. We accepted love as a right, without much reflection or self-consciousness. We took it for granted that we would be given presents at Christmas and birthdays, and taken away on holiday. We accepted being nursed and fed and clothed and educated, being nourished intellectually and socially, because all this was as normal and natural as breathing in and out. We did not even feel particularly grateful for it. It was, quite simply, the law of things. Most people wake up to the debt they owe their parents quite late on, only in their twenties perhaps. Suddenly it dawns on them: it can't have been easy. With the income my parents had, with the problems of health from which they suffered, it can't have been easy. How do most people discharge that debt? Why, by looking after their own children well. Three generations are caught up in this drama of generosity and thankfulness. There is a gratuitousness in simply being alive. We are given life without asking for it. Our life is nurtured without our deserving it. Ideally, the gratuitousness gets passed down the generations. We receive gifts from above; we lavish gifts on those who come after us.

Our standing with God fits into this pattern. We are children with a providing Father. We accept existence from him, and spiritual life, and all that follows from this. We are pure receptiveness, pure being-filled by a generous God in a way that is beyond reason. What Our Lord did for us on the Cross is stupendous. Our appreciation of it gets blunted with habit, but it is still stupendous. How are we to express our sense of being beneficiaries of so much kindness? Surely, by making kindness the theme tune of our professional and private lives. We receive, fundamentally, without meriting: let us swim against the tide of our civilization by showing unmerited love.

☦

On being Dealt a Poor Hand

In middle years it became clear to me that things are never perfect and they never will be. When I was younger I pinned my hopes on my circumstances improving, so that I could mobilize all my talents and achieve all my ambitions. When I was young, I thought the future was infinite. Put yourself in the position of an assistant priest in a parish with a boss who feels petty and restrictive; but that will change, you comfort yourself, I shall soon be my own boss. At present you are plagued with sexual temptation and distraction, but that will change, you say, with the years I shall grow calmer and stronger, and then I'll be able to get on with my life better. Today you're hampered by lack of money, and you can't buy the equipment you feel you need to do your job, the right car, the right computer, a *telefonino* which can also do infra-red photos and takes the chihuahua for a walk; but that will change, you say to yourself, somewhere out there is a kind benefactor with a crock of gold who will help me out, and my luck will change. At present you can't ski, or swim, or speak Spanish, or ride a motorbike, or spend hours in contemplative prayer; but sometime soon you will be able to do all these things: I shall become proficient, you tell yourself. The future is a great consoler in that we can imagine the end result of our desires without having to put in the effort.

The fact is that things will never be perfect. You will shed the immediate petty and restrictive boss, but you will still be subject to authority, and you will feel equally critical of it, whether it's the bishop, the dean or the pope. The present source of sexual temptation will move away, but I promise you another will replace it. You will never have enough money to fulfil all your desires: even millionaires are restless, jealous people. And all those skills you dream of can be acquired, but at a cost which is mundane, persevering slog and practice. The writings of Ecclesiastes seem to us very pessimistic, and not very Christian, but in a downbeat way he had a good grasp of the way things are.

> So I became great and surpassed all who were before me in
> Jerusalem; also my wisdom remained with me. Whatever
> my eyes desired I did not keep from them; I kept my heart
> from no pleasure, for my heart found pleasure in all my toil,
> and this was my reward for all my toil. Then I considered all
> that my hands had done and the toil I had spent in doing it,
> and again, all was vanity and a chasing after wind, and there
> was nothing to be gained under the sun. (Ecclesiastes 2:9–11)

He's really saying that if you could change all the unfavourable circumstances of your life, you would not thereby make yourself happy. And the point of this talk is to say that our spiritual growth and depth will come not from the changes we bring about in our circumstances, but in our response to those circumstances as they are. To use the analogy of a poker game: you and I have been dealt different hands of cards, and your hand may be better than mine. The point of the game is not somehow to rewind the film so that you are dealt a different hand; it is to make the very best of the hand you have. What saves us from the pessimism of Ecclesiastes is the New Testament. It is our personal knowledge of Jesus, the just judge, and our awareness of the Holy Spirit, who does not come more grudgingly to people with poor hands of cards, but more generously and more kindly. Let's try to spell this out a bit tonight.

What cards are in your hand at the moment? I'm only guessing. All I know is that they will be different, in some respect, from those of your neighbour to the left and the right. Because when you were conceived God issued you with a character. It's been modified as the years have passed, but it is still your character, and it is unique. It is not all a question of heredity—otherwise brothers and sisters would have identical characters, and they don't. Similar, yes, but not identical. Each of us is unique.

I wonder, for example, whether you are a natural believer, or whether belief comes hard to you. Have you had to fight for your faith? Does doubt assail you from time to time? I remember as a teenager schooled in heavy rationalism, thinking that the whole of the Catholic Faith was a confidence trick worked by priests and nuns; and they did this to me because, of course, the confidence trick had been worked on them by other priests and nuns, and so on back *ad infinitum.* The problem was insoluble. It wasn't doubt about any particular doctrine that I suffered from, it was endemic doubt, suspicion and scepticism. It was inflamed by the kind of education I had received, but the tendency to doubt was in me anyway. When I got to the English College I remember looking wistfully at my fellow students who came from Catholic homes and schools, and wishing I was like them. The old catechism said 'Faith is a supernatural gift of God by which we believe without doubting whatever God has revealed.' That calm, serene possession of truth came hard to me. Perhaps it comes hard to you, and you feel in this respect you have been dealt a dud hand. Michael Paul Gallagher quotes Dante's *Paradiso* at the beginning of his book *Free to Believe.* Here is one of the verses.

> *Io veggio ben che giammai non si sazia*
> *Nostro intelletto, se il ver non lo illustra,*
> *Di fuor dal qual nessun vero si spazia.*

> I see it well; my mind will never be at peace
> Till that Truth dawn upon it which hides
> No further truth beyond itself.[*]

It's a certain kind of character, isn't it, which reacts instinctively and with hostility to any dogmatic statement. Once I visited a bereaved family before a funeral, and the son of the woman who had died said to me, 'In your sermon I don't want you to say anything definite.' He, too, it seems, was a congenital doubter. Doubt was in the hand he had been dealt. Newman would have understood him, Newman who said that the best you would ever get is a convergence of probabilities: the act of faith is always a generous thing on our part, by which we go beyond ourselves, exceed ourselves, and make a brave leap into the arms of God. It is never the QED answer to a mathematical problem; the conclusion is never self-evident. If doubt is in the hand you have been dealt, your

[*] Dante, *Paradiso,* IV.124

jump into the arms of God will be all the braver, all the more generous, and the stuff of which heaven is made for you. Don't despair. There is Providence even in your doubt.

For some people the whole sexual scene presents no great challenge, because they are not highly sexed. The whole business of fantasy and desire is pretty much under control, and doesn't interfere with the rest of life. Whether they opt for celibacy or enter a placid and harmonious marriage, faithfulness is never for them a massive hurdle. But there are others of us who are aware that being human is—at least for us—a bit like being a volcano. There is an elemental force and power in us which at intervals erupts, and so easily sweeps us away. When that happens we are sorry afterwards, but at the time the urge seems irresistible. There was an anonymous rhyme written about two English headmistresses, back in 1884, which sums it up neatly:

> Miss Buss and Miss Beale
> Cupid's darts do not feel;
> How different from us,
> Miss Beale and Miss Buss.

Think of the track record of people like Kennedy and Clinton, the most powerful men in the world, but without control over their own behaviour. Men of enormous charisma and intelligence, but dealt this very high sexual card. I am not saying that if you're highly sexed you are thereby excused from obeying the sixth commandment. Far from it. But I am saying that for some people it's much, much harder than for others. If it's hard for you, you may feel again that you've been dealt a dud hand. Well, what you have been dealt by God is an invitation to a kind of heroism of which others can only dream, a steep, hard road to sanctity. He will be with you to strengthen you every step of the climb. And if your failures keep you humble, that too is a grace. Proud people will have difficulty getting into heaven. If you persevere, you won't.

For some people, the main card they have been dealt is that they are homosexual. This is something they discovered in adolescence, and they have spent a lot of their lives concealing it from peers who they suspect would mock them and take advantage. It is the reason for a great deal of lonely suffering, this, and a lot of false guilt. How important it is to have someone to trust—one's enough—in whom to confide totally. And if you are the recipient of that kind of confidence, what a privilege it is. You hold your brother's life in your hand, because he knows that you will treat it gently and with compassion. Trust and compassion—there are vital Christian virtues at play here. Then, a certain measure of self-esteem is vital if we are to make our way through life, and some homosexual people struggle with self-esteem in a big way. Of course, you can deal with this by going down the route of pink power and the Mardi Gras parade, becoming flamboyant and provocatively gay, and some people opt for this. It isn't the Catholic way. On the other hand, a sincere Catholic can read the documents of the Church and interpret them as a kind of reproach, and the phrases like 'intrinsically disordered' strike home personally and are the cause of distress to him. It seems as though his sexuality is all loss, and at the same time it seems so unfair: he never asked to be homosexual. Here is a quotation from the *Catechism of the Catholic Church* which is relevant:

> The number of men and women who have deep-seated homosexual tendencies is not negligible. They do not choose their homosexual condition; for most of them it is a trial ... [they] are called to fulfil God's will in their lives, and if they are Christians to unite to the sacrifice of the Lord's Cross the difficulties they may encounter ... Homosexual persons are called to chastity. By the virtues of self-mastery that teach them inner freedom, at times by the support of disinterested friendship, by prayer and sacramental grace, they can and should gradually and resolutely approach Christian perfection.*

Statements in catechisms often sound a bit cold-blooded, and people may feel they are being discussed in their presence in a rather arms-lengthy and objective way. What is boils down to is this. How great it is when someone can see, and even more feel, that it is precisely through

---

* *Catechism of the Catholic Church*, nos. 2358–9.

being gay that he is going to save his soul. That his final judgment will actually revolve round the brave way in which he managed his homosexuality, the fact that he expressed it by being personally chaste in spite of everything, and empathetic and sensitive to the plight of others. When you're homosexual it is easy to fall in love, it can hit you like a Japanese bullet train. It can be a daily pain. To cope with that chastely, patiently, discreetly, and with dignity is heroism of the highest order. It is the stuff that heaven is made of. Not all loss, not at all.

For some people the dud card is pain. They are afflicted before their time with arthritis; or they have been asthmatic since they were kids, always having to get the puffer out and inhale something to help them breathe. They are subject to fierce migraines, which other people cannot even imagine. Or, worst of all, they are the victim of periodic depression which strikes really deep, emptying life of all hope and meaning. All these people say to God frequently in their prayers, 'Why me?' and there doesn't seem to be any answer coming back. The same is true of children born with a handicap. I have a niece who is deaf and dumb and now blind, but whose brain is sufficiently undamaged for her to experience the frustration of it all. What a huge mystery there is in her pain, and in that of her mother who can do so little for her. If you are subject to daily pain you must feel indeed that you have been dealt a poor hand, and that after a while there is no-one to talk to about it because no-one wants to know. Pain can lock you up in yourself, make you entirely self-centred. If, however, you can hear the daily invitation from God to love him and to love others in spite of it all, to refuse to be locked up in yourself, to take the risk of being other-centred, what a great reward will be yours. What seemed to be the loser's fistful of cards turns out to have the royal flush and the full house in it. In his book *The God of Surprises* Gerard Hughes says this:

> Those to whom Christ appears [after his resurrection] are portrayed as being in a negative mood of some kind or other; the women in Mark's Gospel are terrified out of their wits; the disciples on the road to Emmaus are sad and disillusioned; Mary Magdalen is distraught; the disciples in the Upper Room are afraid and living behind closed doors; Thomas is

in doubt. This suggests a truth which subsequent Christian experience confirms, that we can only come to know the Risen Christ when we have experienced some kind of death, some kind of disillusionment with ourselves and others, some loss, bereavement, sense of fear, hopelessness or meaninglessness, and have not tried to anaesthetize ourselves against it. The answer is in the pain.

Simply not being brilliant when you are living with a brilliant set of men can be a source of much suffering. It seems so unfair that really gifted people, really bright people can get where they are going without as much effort as the rest of us. I can remember men who in my time at the College fought their way through to the Licence in Philosophy and Theology (in those days we did both) but with what self-sacrifice, grappling with lectures and studying systematically, every spare minute till lights-out, only God knows. Others were chaotic and disorganized but had the compensating touch of genius which carried them through. The amount of hard graft demanded of us is not equal. If you are one of those who has to put in the time and sometimes gets quite exhausted in the process, there is a choice. You can either be bitter twisted and jealous; or you can welcome the way you are as God's dispensation for you, and therefore something to be embraced with good humour and patience. There is nothing you can do about it, or indeed about any of the things I have been describing. What you can do is adjust your response to them, so that the circumstances of your life become not a brick wall but an occasion of grace.

Have you ever heard of 'the sacrament of the present moment'? When we are at Mass, we receive the living Christ in Holy Communion: body, blood, soul and divinity. In the circumstances of our daily lives, if we are willing, we receive him again, for in accepting the will of God we accept God himself. 'Then Job arose, tore his robe, shaved his head, and fell on the ground and worshipped. He said 'Naked I came from my mother's womb and naked shall I return there; The Lord gave, and the Lord has taken away; blessed be the name of the Lord' (Job 1:20).

'Accepting the will of God' in this context means responding constructively and positively to the things we can't change. I'm not going into the question of whether God positively wills suffering, or only permits it. What I do say is that that God is present in the hand of cards you are dealt. As Gerry Hughes says in one of his books, I cannot recall which, 'God is in the facts'. Psalm 118, of which we recite a part every day in the breviary, enables us to greet God in the facts. It has all these different words for the will of God: statutes, law, commandments, decrees, ways, promise, ordinances, precepts, word. Every verse is an act of acceptance of the facts as they are: 'Lead me in the path of your commandments, for I delight in it ... Having sought your precepts, I shall walk in all freedom ... Your promise, how sweet to my palate! Sweeter than honey to my mouth! ... Your word is a lamp to my feet, a light on my path.'

I am setting before you now one of the great principles of the spiritual life. If you can take it to heart, and not just nod at it, you will have discovered the secret of spiritual growth and depth.

The question we all have to ask ourselves tonight is whether spiritual growth and depth really matter to us, whether we just give them lip-service or whether we actually take them very seriously, seeing them as the main goal of our time here. I say this deliberately. Spiritual growth and depth are the main goal of your time here.

If you are serious, then you will be conscientious about regular prayer-time, building the day around it and not just doing a bit on occasion. You will also be conscientious about turning up for spiritual direction, seeing it as an important way in which God steers you towards himself. In this context, I might say that I have had a lot of unprogrammed free time this year, and have got very good at playing that card-game FreeCell on the computer; perhaps we could organize a College championship? If you are in earnest about your spiritual life, you will also be keen, whatever your academic commitments, to have some good spiritual reading on the go.

So the question with which to start your journey towards priesthood is, 'Just how serious am I about my spiritual life?' If you are serious, you will see God present in all the things I've mentioned: prayer, spiritual direction, spiritual reading. More, you will detect his presence and his hand in all the circumstances of your daily lives, including the less agreeable ones, and you will joyfully go to meet him.

✝

PILGRIMAGE (2003)

To make a pilgrimage is a humble thing to do. Saxon and mediaeval kings, when they came to the tombs of the Apostles at Rome, or went the Shrine of Our Lady of Walsingham, were implicitly saying 'There is a higher power than me.' They were humbling themselves under the mighty hand of God. Henry II probably did not recognize his penitential trip to Canterbury as a formal pilgrimage, but that in fact is what it was. He was humbly admitting that there was a law higher than his law, and that he had breached it by having the Archbishop assassinated. The speed at which devotion to St Thomas spread throughout Europe was a sign of this, a kind of outrage among the common people that monarchs should arrogate to themselves the attributes of God. Both kings and commoners remembered what Jesus said before Pilate: 'You would have no power over me unless it had been given to you from above.' The most autocratic of Catholic monarchs would demonstrate from time to time that he knew he was not the ultimate authority. The policy of dismantling shrines and destroying them, in the sixteenth century, was apart from anything else an assertion of pride. There would be no more acts of abasement.

So, a humble thing. At the start of the year, you and I need to do a humble thing. We need to admit, in some external way, that our vocation is God-given, not of our own manufacture. It is profoundly mysterious. Why me? Why not others I know, who are holier, more courageous, wiser, more in touch with the Lord? By choosing to associate me with himself in this peculiarly intimate way, God has pulled me very clearly into the mystery of the Divine Will. It is almost as if I can hear him breathing. He is very close to me. My job is not to hold him accountable for his choice, or to try to explain it; it is, in all simplicity, to accept and to adore.

A pilgrimage is a good way of doing this. Because it is an act of self-displacement it concentrates attention where it needs to be concentrated—on God and not on ourselves. This is a good way of saying 'I am entirely dependent on the Lord. In the matter of this call to the priesthood, I am in unknown territory, and I am not in control.' Little Sister Madeleine, the foundress of the Little Sisters of Jesus, said of her own vocation, 'I slipped my hand into the hand of Jesus, and he led me where he wanted me to go.' So I go off my home ground and symbolically on to God's ground, in order to say to him, 'You're the boss.'

So let us begin the year as we mean to go on. Entrusting our spiritual and vocational life to God, asking urgently and humbly for his continuing grace and direction. The truth of the matter is that we have each, in one way or another, heard the voice of God calling us as he called Samuel and Paul. We told the Holy Roman Church that this was the case. And the Church said, 'Here are some professors who will teach you what you need to know. Here is a College staff who will help you discern your vocation more clearly.' That's how you ended up here. But professors and staff themselves must remain very humble before the miracle of grace which is taking place before their eyes. A man is being mysteriously and beautifully picked to speak and act *in persona Christi*. Our pilgrimage this autumn is a recognition of this. Into your hands, O Lord, I commend my spirit.

What is true individually is also true collectively. Our pilgrimage is also a way of entrusting our College to the Lord. We are all aware of the fragility of things these days. No institution, except the Universal Church itself, has the rocklike stability and guaranteed permanence of days gone by. All is gift. Our 425-year history, Martyrs included, is not what underpins us. The chequered history of the Venerabile, with its twenty-year exile at the time of the French Revolutionary and Napoleonic invasion, and the six-year exile during the Second World War, should teach us this. Our help is in the Name of the Lord. Only in the Name of the Lord. So we go, as a College, to meet him, and place our future in his lap.

We are going on Sunday afternoon to Tre Fontane. Tre Fontane is a shrine on the Via Laurentina, one of the old roads leading south out of Rome. It marks the spot where St Paul was beheaded, in the time of the Emperor Nero. It is of great antiquity. There was a monastic community from Asia living here by the middle of the seventh century, and Pope

Honorius I constructed the first abbey on this spot, although the place was mosquito-infested and malarial. It is always interesting to make connections. Honorius I was a pope after the model of St Gregory. He attended to the aqueducts bringing water into the City: he was a practical man. He was also, like Gregory, interested in us. He gets an honourable mention from the Venerable Bede, because he wrote a letter to King Edwin, sent missionaries to Wessex, and confirmed the primacy of Canterbury in English Church life. If you want to know what he looked like, go to S. Agnese fuori le Mura, which he rebuilt, and where he appears in mosaic. Anyway … the Cistercians moved into Tre Fontane, quite early in their existence, and rebuilt the church as it is today. Incidentally, Palazzola was their daughter-foundation. Immediately beside the abbey is an avenue, and at the end of this the chapel marking the spot of the martyrdom. Imagine: there has been a chapel on this site since the fifth century. You may know the legend: Paul's head was struck off with such violence that it rebounded three times, and fountains of water sprang up wherever it touched the ground. Legends like that make no claim on our belief, but they are fascinating if only for their antiquity. If you have a feeling for the communion of saints, not just geographically—the union of believers across the world—but also historically, the fact that we share faith, and the Faith, with our ancestors, such old legends have their own particular beauty. It is intriguing that after the execution, the Christians were allowed to take the body away, and it is said that a Roman matron called Lucina buried it in a vineyard a little way outside the walls of Rome: in time the vast and rich basilica of S. Paolo arose around the tomb. Tre Fontane on the other hand has remained simple, and quiet, and reflective.

Why is Paul such a good model for the diocesan priest? Let me list a few reasons. The first is his absolute and total commitment to the person of Jesus. The legend is that the last word he spoke was the Holy Name: Jesus. He knew from experience on the Road to Jerusalem, and he never stopped being utterly convinced, that Christ is alive, active, strong, constantly sending his Spirit into the hearts of the faithful. Paul teaches us that as priests we are not working purely off a historical base. We're not just saying to our people, 'Remember.' No, the drama continues, and we are part of it. 'I believe nothing can happen that will outweigh the supreme advantage of knowing Christ Jesus my Lord. For him I have accepted the loss of everything, and I look on everything as so much rubbish if only I can have Christ, and be given a place in him.' (Philippians 3:8) This is faith in a living and active Lord. We, in our own lives, and in our dioceses and parishes, need this faith.

Then Paul is a good model for us because of his endurance, his resilience. To quote II Corinthians 11:23: 'I have worked harder, I have been sent to prison more often, and whipped so many times more, often almost to death. Five times I had the thirty-nine lashed from the Jews; three times I have been beaten with sticks; once I was stoned; three times I have been shipwrecked and once adrift in the open sea for a night and a day. Constantly travelling, I have been in danger from rivers and in danger from brigands, in danger from my own people and in danger from pagans; in danger in the towns, in danger in the open country, danger at sea and danger from so-called brothers. I have worked and laboured, often without sleep; I have been hungry and thirsty and often starving; I have been in the cold without clothes. And, to leave out much more, there is my daily preoccupation: my anxiety for all the churches.' Paul bounces back, that's what it comes to. Whether his suffering is due to natural causes or human cruelty, whether it is physical or mental, he bounces back. He is full of hope. He seems subject neither to burn-out nor depression. He has long-term sticking-power. As he says in Romans 5:3: 'We can boast about our sufferings. These sufferings bring patience, as we know, and patience brings perseverance, and perseverance brings hope, and this hope is not deceptive, because the love of God has been poured into our hearts by the Holy Spirit, which has been given to us.' We, in our own lives, and in our dioceses and parishes, need this hope.

Paul is a good model for us because of the primacy he gives to love. That passage from I Corinthians 13 is profound, the one we use so often in weddings that it runs the risk of sounding hackneyed. 'If I have all the eloquence of men or of angels, but speak without love, I am simply a gong booming or a cymbal clashing ... If I give away all that I possess, piece by piece, and if I even let them take my body to burn it, but am without love, it will do me no good whatever ... Love is always patient and kind; it is never jealous; love is never boastful or conceited; it is never rude or selfish; it does not take offence, and is not resentful.' Clearly Paul lived by this standard, or tried to. He was not an easy man. At different times, his helpers and disciples found it necessary to have time away from him: Barnabas, and John Mark for instance. Single-minded men are hard to deal with. But this was a man full of affection, too. At the end of Romans he sends his love to a whole catalogue of people, people he calls by name. At the end of II Corinthians he says 'I am all prepared now to come to you for the third time, and I am not going to be a burden on you: it is you I want, not your possessions. Children are not expected to save up for their parents, but parents for children. I am perfectly willing to spend what I have, and to be expended, in the interests of your souls. Because I love you more, must I be loved the less?' To the Philippians he says 'You have a permanent place in my heart, and God knows how much I miss you all.' In I Thessalonians 2, he says 'Like a mother feeding and looking after her own children, we felt so devoted and protective towards you, and had come to love you so much, that we were eager to hand over to you not only the Good News but ourselves as well.' This is the language of a highly emotional man, who allowed himself not just to know, and to teach, but to feel, and to treasure friendship. Whether Paul personally wrote II Timothy or not, the sentiments in it are surely his: 'I remember your tears, and long to see you again to complete my happiness. Then I am reminded of the sincere faith you have; it came first to live in your grandmother Lois, and your mother Eunice, and I have no doubt that it is the same faith in you as well.' See again how he remembers names, and the faith-stories of whole families. It could be an old parish priest talking, a jagged character but fundamentally a deeply affectionate one.

I could wish no better for you than this—that you be indomitable, doggedly persistent, centred on the person of Jesus, and affectionate and faithful friends.

The second part of our afternoon lies up the hill behind the Abbey. When the Cistercians returned here in 1868 they drained the malarial marshes and planted a wood of eucalyptus trees. In the middle of this wood, at the top of the hill, is the mother house of the Little Sisters of Jesus. It is a village of timber huts, dating only from 1957, centred round a beautiful and simple chapel where the Blessed Sacrament is always exposed. You can find them there at any time of day, the Little

Sisters in their characteristic blue denim habits, sitting cross-legged on the floor in adoration. They are a contemplative order which lives in the world, and which has hospitality as a high priority. Wherever you go in the world, if you visit the Little Sisters of Jesus, you find they always have the neighbours in—often the most disadvantaged neighbours, immigrants, poor people and people with disabilities. When I found them in Turin many years ago they lived in a tiny flat in the middle of the red-light district, and had an open door for the prostitutes who sometimes hovered on the brink of despair. When I found them in Algeria, in a little village on the edge of the desert, I saw how they had built up relationships with the Arab women round about, relationships based on respect and affection. Every house has its tiny chapel, where the Eucharist has place of honour. They are extraordinary and inspiring women, and their special character comes from those hours of eucharistic adoration. They are content to be little, unassuming: when they have jobs, they often do things like working on the checkout in a supermarket. They are content to be the people at whose face nobody looks, because they want to identify themselves with Jesus in his hidden life at Nazareth. That is their style.

They were founded by Madeleine Hutin and René Voillaume, just after the Second World War, but their real founder is Charles de Foucauld. Their inspiration comes from the writings and the example of this extraordinary twentieth century French hermit, who lived in the Sahara for sixteen years, studied the Gospel minutely, and produced his own synthesis of the Christian life, a synthesis as original as that of St Francis. He has recently been declared 'Venerable', and if the present miracle due to his intercession and recently reported in Milan proves genuine, he may well be beatified. [Charles de Foucauld was beatified in 2005.]

There was a bitter war in Algeria at the beginning of the 1960s. De Gaulle decided to grant the Algerians their independence, but many people of French extraction were not so minded, and a lot of blood was spilt. It was decided to bring back to Europe the relics of Charles de Foucauld. Not his body, which is buried in the Sahara, but the relics of the two places where he lived: Beni-Abbes, near the Moroccan frontier, and Tamanrasset in the deep south of Algeria, among the Touareg.

They were in the possession of the White Fathers, who sent them to Tre Fontane. Charles made plans for a new religious order of brothers. He wrote a Rule, he sketched out the foundations of a monastery, he designed a habit, he built a chapel and decorated it with hangings of his own creation. He hammered out his own equipment, both for the chapel and to dig the patch of land which surrounded it. He wrote voluminously in a neat spidery hand, filling notebook after notebook with retreat reflections and meditations, corresponding with friends and family, with his spiritual director in Paris, with the Bishop of the Sahara. He learned the Touareg language and composed the first French-Touareg dictionary. The Little Sisters h;ave brought much of this material together in a little underground chapel at Tre Fontane which we can visit on Sunday. When I go there for Mass, I am often privileged to use his chalice; the tabernacle and the rough candlesticks come from his crude chapel in the desert.

Many diocesan priests around the world have taken Charles de Foucauld as their patron. They are struck by his humility, since he never strove for promotion or honour; they are struck by his deeply contemplative life, centred on the Eucharist; they are struck by his never-failing hospitality to Christians and Muslims alike; they are struck by the way he identified himself with the poorest and most abandoned people he could find, trying to be what he called a 'universal brother'. His style was different from that of Paul, down the hill. He shared Paul's zeal for souls, his longing to convert the world to Jesus. Unlike Paul, he tackled this not by preaching and arguing, but by being as Christlike as he possibly could, in his acceptance of suffering and in his meekness. Such meekness did not come easily to an old soldier and explorer: Charles had known other ways of being. But this was his way of incarnating the Gospel.

The church of the Little Sisters has become something of a spiritual home for me, and I hope that you too will discover it as a precious resource for your time in Rome. Sunday's pilgrimage will be a two-tone expedition. The first century and the twentieth. Paul would probably be surprised to see Charles de Foucauld's monstrance, and would need an explanation about what it was for! But the faith expressed by Paul and Charles de Foucauld is the same, and it is our faith too. May the

Lord bless us, individually and collectively, as we seek his face and his will for our lives.

✛

PILGRIMAGE

Ever since Jesus set foot on our planet, all land has been holy. When he took flesh, he took to himself the whole material world and sanctified it. He gave it a destiny. This is why Paul can say in Romans 8:21: 'Creation still retains the hope of being freed, like us, from its slavery to decadence, to enjoy the same freedom and glory as the children of God.' This is at the root of the Church's commitment to ecology. The physical world, too, has been brushed by the wing of the Spirit. It, too, deserves our respect.

All land is holy, yet we still speak of 'The Holy Land', meaning Israel and Palestine. We do this because human beings, in their search for God and their response to God, have always found certain places easier to pray in. And one of these is the actual spot on earth where Jesus lived, died and rose again. Somehow our spirit rises more easily to God in awe-inspiring places: Gethsemane and Calvary, and by the Sea of Galilee.

Why should this be? One explanation is this. God's way of being is eternity. In eternity, he does not have to wait for things to happen, or remember them—they are all present to him. In eternity he does not have to travel to be in one place rather than another—he is everywhere simultaneously. 'Time' and 'space' lose their sense. To us they seem inevitable and universal. In fact they are neither. To put it imaginatively, we live in a bubble where time and space rule our existence, where they are the iron rules which govern us. But outside the bubble, where God is, is normality, and another way of being. We, in our time/space bubble, are the eccentric ones, the abnormal ones. When we die, and go to God in eternity, our being will be regulated otherwise. It is hard to imagine, but it is true.

Let's return to that bubble. Like all the best bubbles it is at least partly transparent: we have inklings, blurred impressions, of what's going on on the other side of the membrane which encloses us. Deeply spiritual people have very strong impressions. Moreover, there are certain places on earth where the membrane is very thin, and you can see through it more clearly—see through it, that it, not with the eyes in your head or the eyes of the intellect, but with the eyes of the heart. These are the places of pilgrimage. Because seeing through the membrane is not an intellectual exercise but an exercise of the heart, pilgrimage is not only for intellectual people, but also for ordinary people. On pilgrimage they can bear witness to their intuition that God is real, and great, and good, and merciful, and to be trusted. It is an instinct which is more widespread than Christianity. See the Hindus who flock to the Ganges to wash, see the Muslims who go to Mecca on the 'hajj'. Remember the journeys made by the Jews, including the family of Jesus, to the Temple.

In the Catholic tradition it is Mary who has provided us with most of our pilgrimage places. When Bernadette came panting home to her family from the first encounter with Our Lady in the Grotto, she could have had no notion of the modern Lourdes, with its network of massive churches, its processions of the Blessed Sacrament, its deep significance for the sick, its network of hotels, its streets of holy shops, its pubs. Lourdes is the best example of pilgrimage as done by Catholics. Man has managed to do quite a lot to commercialize it, to pull it down, to make it banal. Remember Gerard Manley Hopkins in that poem 'God's Grandeur'? 'And all is seared with trade; bleared, smeared with toil; and wears man's smudge and shares man's smell.' Yet above the smear, the smudge, the smell and the banality there towers a spiritual reality which makes all the rest unimportant. This is a place where human beings can dialogue with God, and do dialogue with him, day after day, and spirits are lifted and hearts are changed. At Lourdes the membrane is thin.

Another place where the membrane is thin is Walsingham. The apparition of Our Lady in this little village in north Norfolk, just six miles from the North Sea, is seven hundred years older than that at Lourdes. As Catholics we are not required to believe in any apparitions of the Blessed Virgin; they are not an integral part of our faith. Somehow it is easier to believe in a modern apparition, though, than in an old one—it's quite illogical, but it's true. Things that happened a thousand years ago are easier to classify as 'legends'. What gives you pause for thought in this case is the devotion of mediaeval people to Our Lady of Walsingham. For them the apparition was no legend. They flocked there in their thousands, not only from English towns and villages but from the Continent as well. Through the thick forests of Norfolk there were well-trodden pathways for miles and miles, pilgrim pathways. People plodded across whole counties to Our Lady's shrine to pray. Often they prayed for very limited and personal things: for a healing, for the solution of a family problem. They sacrificed the time, and they made the sacrifice of discomfort and risk and they travelled. Time and space being used to do homage to the Lord who dwells beyond both. It is fascinating to see how God speaks to us in our own idiom. When the widow Richeldis saw the Blessed Virgin in 1061, Our Lady asked Richeldis to build a replica of the Holy House of Nazareth there in the fields, so that people would have a physical goal to their pilgrimage, an actual building. Of course, the Holy House was eventually encased in a vast monastery, rather like the tiny Portiuncola in Assisi being enclosed in S. Maria degli Angeli. For centuries it was a focal point for Christianity in England, until its destruction in 1538. Walsingham is sometimes called 'England's Nazareth'. Even now it has about it something of the calm and the ordinariness and the hiddenness of Nazareth. I love to go to Walsingham off-season, and to walk the winding Holy Mile by myself from the village to the Slipper Chapel, with the fallow fields on one side and the cold brook gurgling away behind the line of trees on the other, and to unite myself in spirit with the pilgrims who are my religious forefathers and foremothers.

On Sunday we are going, as a College, on pilgrimage. We are going to the Shrine of the Madonna del Divino Amore, just outside Rome on the Via Ardeatina. Here is a brief synopsis of the history of this shrine, so that you won't be visiting it cold, so to speak. In 1740 a man was crossing the Campagna by himself. The Campagna is the country district between Rome and the sea. In those days it was like a desert, largely uncultivated, inhabited by malarial mosquitos, brigands and feral dogs: not a good place to be on your own. The man was confronted by a band of these wild dogs on a lonely footpath. He thought his last hour had come, and he was terrified. He saw a simple painting of the Madonna fixed to a wall by the path, prayed to Our Lady for help, and the dogs went away. Simple as that: nothing spectacular. What made it spectacular was the reaction of the local people and of the people of Rome. A cardinal came and took away the picture, but appeals were made to the Rota, and two years later the people got it back again. They adopted the place as their place of prayer and pilgrimage, and a small church was erected in which the picture was enthroned. The pilgrimages got bigger and bigger. Eventually, halfway through the last century, a group of priests and sisters were formed—oblates of the Madonna del Divino Amore— simply to care for the shrine. Vocations flowed in, and they were able to spare clergy and nuns even for overseas missions. Their founder, Don Umberto Terenzi, is buried in a crypt just by the original church. During the last Holy Year, Pope John Paul II opened a vast underground basilica to accommodate the crowds. For years now there has been a huge hostel for pilgrims and retreatants. On Sunday afternoons the place is thronged with ordinary Romans. Formerly they came on foot from the Circus Maximus, walking all night, and sometimes they still do: but today the carpark, too, tells its own story. This is Rome's domestic shrine. They come here for weddings and baptisms and confessions. All religious life is here, a bit untidy sometimes, not as manicured and orderly as a British place of pilgrimage, but utterly genuine. You'll see. One of those places where the membrane wears thin.

During the Second World War Pope Pius XII prayed to the Madonna del Divino Amore that Rome would not be destroyed, and his prayer was heard. There were some bombs—in the area of S. Lorenzo, killing many people, and on the Vatican itself on one occasion—but nothing on the scale of Coventry or Dresden: the City was spared. As the Allies were advancing inland from Nettuno, the picture of the Madonna del Divin Amore was brought into Rome, to the Church of S. Ignazio, for safe keeping. In the Novena before Pentecost and in the following octave, Mass was offered every half hour in the morning, and in the afternoon the Rosary was recited several times. The people could hear the bombs falling on the Castelli, on Frascati and Albano, and they were terrified. The great climax of this prayer by a whole city was on Sunday evening, 4 June 1944, when at the end of his sermon the preacher besought Our Lady to ask her Son to save Rome. The people were encouraged to promise now to live faithful and moral lives. That very evening the Germans began, methodically, to requisition everything on wheels and to withdraw swiftly to the north. On the same evening, American troops moved into the southern suburbs. There was no fighting. The Romans honour Our Lady as the Saviour of their City, *Salus Populi Romani*, along with Pope Pius who ceaselessly badgered both the Germans and the Allies to leave Rome alone. A week after the liberation, the Pope went to S. Ignazio to give thanks. The pulpit from which he spoke is now in the new basilica we shall see. He said: 'Dear sons and daughters. Never did we feel so strongly as now that we are your spiritual father, because during four long years we have shared in common the sufferings and anxieties of a cruel war. Your sorrows have also been ours. But we have experienced also great consolation, when we watched your faith that brought you to the feet of Mary, the Mother of Divine Love. Our Immaculate Mother has saved Rome once more from the greatest danger.'

Incidentally, there was an echo of the transfer of that picture, in 1982, when John Paul II came to England. He wanted to make his own pilgrimage to Walsingham, but the infrastructure of Norfolk by-roads simply would not take a papal visit; so instead the statue was transferred to Wembley Stadium and placed on the altar during Mass.

So we start our year in the English College with an act of simple, but genuine and heartfelt piety, and in doing this we place ourselves right at the heart of Catholic tradition. Think of the hundreds of men who studied here during the years of persecution, and of the pilgrimages they made to local shrines. They prayed the Rosary. They prayed that their families would be safe. They prayed for their fellow-students who had been ordained and were working in secret. They prayed for the chance to practise their religion once again, unhampered, in their native land.

We too have things to pray for. We pray for the Conversion of England, no longer in a polemical anti-Anglican way, but thinking much more of the millions of people in our cities and countryside who have no faith at all, and who somehow seem to lack the mental machinery for faith. And we include in this number relatives of our own who have fallen away from the practice of their faith, or who seem never to have had the gift in the first place. We pray for our fellow-students who have been ordained and who are, each in his own way, working now to evangelize England and Wales. May they not get tired or discouraged, but be filled with grace of God, and be true and durable labourers in his vineyard, as we hope to be. We pray for the Church at home, for the whole complex, bishops priests and parishioners, that the Holy Spirit may be powerfully with them this Sunday. And we pray for the English College, for our corporate life, that this may be a place of charity, a truly Christian community, a microcosm of what the Church should be. May our Lady pray for us, as she must so often have prayed for the English College in the past, praying that it would produce good priests, men prepared to go right down the line for their people, even to shedding their blood. We are engaged upon a spiritual enterprise, you and I. God has called each of us personally and by name, and he has caused us to assemble here in Rome, in this house, for the accomplishment of his purpose. May Mary, by her prayers, make us flexible and responsive instruments in his hands. It is a spiritual enterprise; that is why we start it in a spiritual way.

It will be a simple pilgrimage. We'll leave the College by bus after lunch, and we have the Chapel of the Holy Spirit booked for three o'clock. We'll say the Rosary and Litany together, and dedicate ourselves and those we love to Our Lady's care. We cannot spend a great deal of time there because there are baptisms to follow: but we shall have time to explore the shrine, the great basilica, the original little church with the famous picture, the crypt ... and the Church built of living stones, which is the people of Rome unselfconsciously and devotedly at prayer in a place where the membrane between heaven and earth is very thin.

✛

Prayer of the Church

The Divine Office is the prayer of the Church. I find the concept of 'Church' in this statement rather unsatisfying. I can know it theologically—I know what the Church is. In the 1950s I did an interminable tract on the Church with Father Zapalena. His book was so big that if I had taken it home on the plane, I would have been done for excess baggage. And after all, I live in Rome, and I see the men who govern the Church— pope, cardinals; on the other hand I have worked overseas, and have seen poor Catholics who live in the slum suburbs of South American cities, the other extreme of the Church. I know *about* the Church. But I cannot know the whole thing experientially. It's too big. There is so much Church that I haven't got under my belt, so to speak.

What I *can* think about, though, in a global way and from experience, is the Church in my own country, in England. (If you are Maltese, or Danish, or Bolivian, or Lebanese, or Polish, or Italian, please make the requisite adjustment.) This Church, my home Church, is small enough to get my head round. This is where I have worked for most of my life, thirty-seven years of parish ministry. It is a Church with its strengths and weaknesses, with its peculiar character which is unlike any other. Some of its weaknesses are hitting the headlines this week. It is a Church which I love. Those of you who are priests with parish experience will know what I mean. When I pray the psalms of the breviary, I can easily pray them in the name of the Church I know, and for that Church. I think of it while I pray, and I find that this helps me concentrate. I believe that this is the authentic frame to put round the Office, and I want to offer it to you. Whatever psalms and readings have been selected for today, my dearest longing is that God will drench his Church with grace, that his power will compensate for all our human weakness, that the English Church may become what it is meant to be, a mighty agent of evangelization, a place where men and women are reconciled to God and to one another, and a beacon of light and hope for secular England. The Church at home needs our prayers. Psalm 20 says: 'O Lord, your strength gives joy to the king; how your saving help makes him glad! You have granted him his heart's desire; you have not refused the prayer of his lips.' Well, that's my heart's desire, that's the prayer of my lips—that the Church in my own country may be what it is supposed to be, and equipped to be, the light of the world and the salt of the earth.

I wrote this partly on a Sunday morning, about 9:30 Italian time, which is 8:30 English time. I thought: all over England, people are getting ready for Mass. Families are chivvying one another to get up, get washed, get dressed, have breakfast, get the car out or we'll be late again. Priests are working all out in sacristies, doing a host of things simultaneously, marking missals, preparing cruets, talking to readers and eucharistic ministers, finding people to do the offertory procession, adding last minute petitions to the bidding prayers, telling servers for heaven's sake to find an alb that fits them, with, at the back of their minds, the skeleton of the homily they mean to give. This is happening in the gaunt Gothic sacristies of huge Victorian churches, minute biscuit-tin sacristies at the side of graceless utility churches, and in the vestries of mediaeval village churches lent to us for an hour on Sunday mornings. Choirs are assembling, and organists and guitarists are finding somewhere to put their wet coats and making sure they have their music. It is a collective busy-ness, and it happens in an atmosphere of distraction, patience and relative good humour. The pattern is repeated in thousands of parishes, up and down the country. Tens of thousands of folk are involved. Psalm 15 says 'He has put into my heart a marvellous love for the faithful ones who dwell in his land', and that's right: how can we not have enormous affection for these people. What grand people they are. They are quite unselfconscious about it all: nobody is saying, reflectively, 'We are the Church'. But that's the fact. These tens of thousands of people come together in their idiosyncratic way to do what Psalm 148 says: 'Praise the Lord from the earth ... all earth's kings and peoples, earth's princes and rulers; young men and maidens, old men together with children.' Old men together with children. I want to say to grand-parents who take their grandchildren to Mass: You're mentioned in the Prayer of the Church. Hold up your heads: you are the Church.

When I join in Morning and Evening Prayer, here in the seminary, it is these people I'm thinking of. I pray that the liturgy in our parishes at home may be meaningful and effective, not just in the automatic way that all sacraments are effective, but humanly too. May the homilies preached in our churches touch hearts and change lives; I know and believe that only God can bring this about. 'O send forth your light and your truth,' says Psalm 42. Unless the Holy Spirit is involved, the most learned sermon will fall on deaf ears. That Canticle from Wisdom 9 can be a prayer for preachers: 'With you is wisdom, who knows your works ... Send her forth from the holy heavens, and from the throne of your glory send her, that she may be with me and toil.' If all the homilies delivered in England next Sunday were really good, there would be a sudden upward tilt in the Church's life. People would be glad they had come, and be able to say with Psalm 121, 'I rejoiced when I heard them say: 'Let us go to God's house.' Churchgoing would become, not a duty or a habit, but something exciting. You know the grand old metrical psalm 'O God our help in ages past'? It is based on Psalm 89, which meditates on the shortness of human life, and the inevitability of judgment, but ends on a high note: 'In the morning, fill us with your love ... give us joy to balance our affliction ... give success to the work of our hands, give success to the work of our hands.' As I say these words I have in mind the priests and deacons, who have mused on the scriptures of the day's Mass, and prayed for guidance, and tried to discern what really needs to be said, in this assembly and on this day, and have banged the thing out on their computers or typewriters. They have done it with industry and humility, maybe with no great faith in their own talent. May the Lord give success to the work of their hands. 'I did the planting, Apollos did the watering, but God made things grow' (I Corinthians 3:6). Lord, make things grow in England this Sunday morning. Make vocations grow, make conversions grow, make reconciliation a reality.

Going to Sunday Mass is a time for remembering. Most probably it was one or both of our parents who took us to church when we were infants. Faith is a gift of God, but allowing for that we owe a great deal to the mother or father who first gave us an inkling that this was serious stuff, serious enough to bring even parents to their knees. Often the semi-darkness and the peculiar smell of church, if ours is a Victorian one, makes us remember our parents. We recall, too, the way things were. 'I muse on what your hand has wrought, and to you I stretch out my hands', says Psalm 142. If we ourselves are knocking on now, we can recall full congregations where teenagers came with their parents and knelt patiently through the Latin Mass: we recall the Saturday queues outside the confessionals, and the May procession and the Corpus Christi procession, and the crowds at Benediction on a Sunday night, and the families waiting to light a candle to Our Lady before going home. 'I thought of the days of long ago and remembered the years long past. At night I mused within my heart. I pondered and my spirit questioned. 'Will the Lord reject us for ever? Will he show us his favour no more?' (Psalm 76) We are deeply distressed by the general lack of faith in our society. It isn't that we want to recreate, item by item, the Church of those days. There has been a Council in between. But we would dearly love to recreate the devotion, the seriousness of Catholic people fifty years ago. 'If the Lord does not build the house', says Psalm 126, 'in vain do its builders labour.' If it is to happen again, it will be the Lord's work. We rely overmuch on human effort, on schemes and projects, and quite simply pray too little.

Our Church is suffering at the moment from an unexpected pain, which is the scandal of clerical child-abuse. The abused children, many of them now adults, are the ones who suffer most. They must be first in our thoughts and prayers. 'May he defend the poor of the people and save the children of the needy' (Psalm 71). These things bring us, as a Church, into the critical, sardonic eye of the public. How, in the light of this, can we say convincingly that we care about children? We have a lot of leeway to make up, and we can only make it up by impeccable behaviour over a long period. Jeremiah 14, which we read in morning prayer on Friday in week 4, sums our feelings up so well: 'Let my eyes run down with tears night and day, and let them not cease, for the virgin daughter of my people is smitten with a great wound, with a very grievous blow.' We pray for the victims, and also for the Church in her affliction. 'With all my voice I cry to the Lord, with all my voice I entreat the Lord. I pour out my trouble before him; I tell him all my distress', says Psalm 141. Many of the psalms are this kind of prayer, that of the man who has discovered through hard experience that God is his only refuge and his only hope. How much more true is this of the Church, which is Christ's Body on earth. It is his Church, not ours. Out of the messes man has made comes, slowly, a true spirituality of humble dependence. 'Have mercy on me, God, in your kindness. In your compassion blot out my offence. O wash me more and more from my guilt and cleanse me from my sin' (Psalm 50). This is the kind of prayer that gets answered.

The Church has, in its foundation-deeds, the command to evangelize, to recruit. We can do no other. If you really believe in the Church as the sacrament of Christ on earth, how can you not long for everyone to belong to it? When the legal disabilities of English Catholics were removed in the nineteenth century, the converts began to flock in. Some of them, like Newman and Manning, were giants. Many more were humble people whose names are forgotten. The point is, it happened. In those days the polemic was between the Church of Rome and the Church of England. What Catholics did was not, for the most part, evangelization. After all, neither Newman nor Manning needed evangelizing, being convinced of the Gospel—quite the reverse. Today it's a different polemic, and *all* Christians are aware that we are face to face with a pagan and materialistic world, which desperately does need evangelizing, because it has not heard the Gospel of Jesus at all. Well, whenever conversion happens, it is a sign of authenticity: we are living up to our mission statement. Some people find this tendency in Catholics shocking. Well, we no longer resort to coercion or arm-twisting—joining the Catholic Church must and can only be a freely chosen thing, and we would not want people on any other terms. Conversion, however, is not a dirty word. It is a logical consequence of having the 'holy Catholic Church' as an article of faith in the Creed; we're not just an *ad hoc* assembly of worshippers. We long for this evangelization to continue, and prosper, and grow. 'Now the salvation and the power and the kingdom of our God and the authority of his Christ have come.' This verse from Revelation is a prophetic prayer: may it be so, and soon. On the second Friday of the month, in the morning, we read three verses from Ephesians, which begin, 'Now, in union with Christ Jesus, you who used to be far away have been brought near by the death of Christ.' I think of the RCIA [Rite of Christian Initiation of Adults] in our parishes, and I pray that thousands of people may be brought near by the death of Christ. The death of Christ is powerful enough to do it. I think of the vast unchurched housing estates on the edge of our cities, and I long for the inhabitants of those tower-blocks, again to quote and slightly adapt Ephesians, 'to be united into one body, and brought back to God.' On the third Monday of the month in the morning Isaiah says: 'It shall come to pass in the latter days that the mountain of the house of the Lord shall be established as the highest of the mountains, and shall be raised above the hills; and all the nations shall flow to it. And many peoples shall come, and say, 'Come, let us go up to the mountain of the Lord, to the house of the God of Jacob, that he may teach us his ways, and that we may walk in his paths.' It is within the gift of God to make this happen. O God, let it happen, make it happen. May people, seeing the Church, not be put off, but perceive it as their true and natural home, and come flocking home. How can we not pray for this?

What makes the Catholic Church in England so different from the Catholic Church, say, in France or Germany? One of the differences is our history. We have a big Irish element. It is no longer first generation, and most of the Irish families have taken on a British veneer, at least: the children and the grandchildren have been to British schools and universities, supported British football teams, learned to speak with British accents: yet the old loyalty remains, and thousands of our people are equally at home on both sides of the Irish Sea. The Irish element of our Church is aware of having been mauled, in the course of history, very badly. Governments in London have mistreated the Irish, either by colonial cruelty or by laziness and negligence, over a period not of years but of centuries. 'They have pressed me hard from my youth, this is Israel's song. They have pressed me hard from my youth, but have never destroyed me.' That's Psalm 128. Think of the brutal physical punishment inflicted on Irishmen transported to Australia: 'They ploughed my back like ploughmen, drawing long furrows.' The colossal influx of Irish people into Britain, in 1846 and the years following, would never have happened had the government in London handled the Famine in another way; and the history of the Catholic Church in England would therefore having been vastly different. 'Put not your trust in princes', says Psalm 146. The Catholic Church at home has always stood somewhat apart from the seat of power. In the past, because it was first persecuted, and then excluded. But even today, old folk-memories and habits die hard, and we look at civil authority quizzically and critically. This attitude is in our bones and our blood.

Another hallmark of English Catholicism is its attachment to the Holy See and the person of the pope. We take this so much for granted that we don't really reflect on it until we go, for example, to Belgium or to Holland. When we first meet Catholics who have turned their back on this ingredient of the faith, we are astonished. They explain to us the reasons: the Vatican has appointed this or that bishop, the Vatican has issued this or that document on sexual morality, the Vatican has adopted this stance concerning women priests. OK, we say, we can see this is difficult: but you really cannot construct Catholicism without the pope. It doesn't make sense. 'May your hand be on the man you have chosen, the man you have given your strength' (Psalm 118). Again, history comes into play. When European Churches were grappling with Gallicanism, or Josephism, or Jansenism, we in England were being squashed flat by punitive governments: we hadn't the puff or the energy to quarrel with the Holy See. In the 1500s, when we were proscribed and driven underground, it was because Catholics would not relinquish the pope. When, two hundred and fifty years later, we re-surfaced, this loyalty was still in place. There were exceptions, of course. At the time of the Restoration of the Hierarchy in 1850, and the arrival of Wiseman as the most ultramontane of cardinals, some of the old Catholic gentry who had borne the heat of the day gave vent to anti-papal sentiments. But by and large, the English Church has always been marked by a warm and reverent feeling towards the Holy Father. On the Fourth Thursday we say at morning prayer the Canticle from Isaiah: 'Rejoice with Jerusalem and be glad for her, all you who love her; rejoice with her in joy, all you who mourn over her ... For this says the Lord: Behold, I will extend prosperity to her like a river, and the wealth of the nations like an overflowing stream ... As one whom your mother comforts, so will I comfort you; you shall be comforted in Jerusalem, You shall see and your heart will rejoice.' The feeling the Jews had about the Holy City corresponds in some way to the way many ordinary English Catholics feel about the Holy Father. He is a focal point, a bearer of our corporate identity. And, of course, much more than this. We pray for him.

Every local Church has its catechetical programmes. Some of these are more successful than others. In England, recent syllabuses have come in for a great deal of criticism, some of it informed and intelligent, some of it vitriolic and unintelligent. The way the faith is taught is a delicate matter. The well-being of the whole of our national Church depends on its being well done. Teaching religious education is a specialized and expert job. We need to pray that the job be well done, in our schools and parishes; pray for religious-education teachers and catechists, and for the children. Psalm 118 is full of requests that God will teach us. 'Teach me judgment and knowledge, for I rely on your commandments.' I cannot rely on his commandments unless I know them. The Holy Spirit is as necessary here as in the work of evangelization. 'Come my children, listen to me, and I will teach you the fear of the Lord' (Psalm 33). Our prayer for teachers echoes the Canticle from Deuteronomy which we say on the Saturday of week 2: 'Listen, O heavens, and I will speak, let the earth hear the words on my lips. May my teaching fall like the rain, my speech descend like the dew, like rain drops on the young green, like showers falling on the grass.' Lord, strengthen the arm of the teacher in the classroom, of the catechist in the parish, and of those who provide the material for them.

You can see what I have done. I have applied the psalms and readings to a present reality and need, so that we may pray them with more conviction. You could do the same. I have found twenty-five quotations which answer the needs of the Church at home. You could find another, different twenty-five. If the psalms are the collective prayer of the people of God, it is right to use them *in the name of* the Church, speaking for those who find prayer difficult, putting ourselves in their skin, and also *for* the Church, that the Lord may bind up her wounds and fill her with energy and wisdom.

It is fashionable to look at the Catholic Church in England with sadness, and reproach for those who are seen as responsible for dismantling what was good. Pessimists preach inexorable decline. Every new initiative is lampooned. Mocking is easy. It is the flavour of our time. The media delight in debunking public figures and disillusioning viewers and readers; it's not only done to the Church, it's done to every other organization as well. But the Church isn't 'every other organization.' The Church is not a human enterprise, at root; it is a divine enterprise. We cannot see the shape or the size of it in the years to come, even in our own lifetime. But because of who God is and what he's like, we know for sure that there is no reason to despair. Things are tough at present, but we have joined the winning team. Most of the psalms end on a note of hope and trust. When we pray for the Catholic Church in England, so must we. 'So we shall not fear though the earth should rock, though the mountains fall into the depths of the sea ... God is within, it cannot be shaken, God will help it at the dawning of the day ... The Lord of hosts is with us, the God of Jacob is our stronghold' (Psalm 45). That has to be the last word.

✛

PRIESTHOOD—I

The first thing that strikes me on coming to the College [St John's College, Wonersh] is that it is the most astonishing place. What, I ask myself, can have induced so many highly intelligent and gifted men like you to abandon their careers, their plans for the future, their flats and cars, their decent incomes, their whole network of human contacts and company, to come up this hill out of Guildford and live for up to six years with a bunch of other guys in a secluded institution like this? Most of our contemporaries, if you suggested such a thing to them, would turn pale and say 'Wild horses on their bended knees would not get me there.' The existence of St John's Seminary, and indeed of any other seminary, is to me a source of constant wonder. They are, in purely human terms, such improbable places. They prove the power of the Spirit.

Because it is the Spirit who has given us a burning desire for something precious and beautiful beyond words, which is the Catholic priesthood. That's what's brought us here. Nothing else could have done it. Priesthood is the raison-d'etre of this place. This is true for you whatever your stage of formation: even if you've recently arrived, and ordination seems incredibly distant, you are quite right to dream of the day when you become a priest. In other words, Wonersh is not an end in itself, it is a means to an end. The end is you, conformed to the Good Shepherd, moving among your people, caring for them with a sure touch and much affection. Well. If everything here revolves around priesthood, it seems logical to spend some time thinking and talking about it.

The first thing to say is this: *priesthood is a mystery of faith*. It is part of the bigger mystery of faith which is our redemption by Christ. It is a continuation, a prolongation, of this mystery. This is the only proper light in which to view priesthood, and it is a theological and a spiritual light. This is the only context which makes sense. If you view being a priest as just a job, or as a profession conferring status, power and privilege, or as a means of combating the political and social ills of the present age, in other words if you view the priesthood as a purely horizontal reality, you are on the way to a big disappointment. The real reality is the vertical one. It's God who is powerful. It's God who acts, who is at work while we speak. It's God who became human out of love. It's God-made-man who died on the Cross, and rose from the dead. God desires to save his people. The priesthood is part of his chosen way of implementing that plan. When you are ordained, you will become God's instrument for achieving his purpose, nothing more and nothing less. It's *his* plan. 'Thy will be done' suddenly acquires an added edge. So it's God who calls the shots. It's God who decides what the priesthood shall be, and what it's for, not us.

In 1999 the Congregation for the Clergy published a reflection on the priesthood. Here is a paragraph from it.

> The goal of our efforts is the definitive Reign of Christ, the drawing together in him of every created thing. This goal will only be fully realized at the end of time,but it is already present through the life-giving Spirit,through whom Christ has set up his Body the Churchas universal sacrament of salvation.

There was an old Jesuit in Bedford years ago who said to the congregation on Sunday, 'Now today we have a letter from the Bishop, and I think what he's *trying* to say is this.' I would not be so impertinent with an important document from the Congregation. But if I might be permitted to highlight one aspect of it, it is that God chose to save his people *through the Church*. He didn't have to do it this way. He didn't have to saddle himself with a Church at all. The Church must have caused God unlimited grief, over the centuries. He must get fed up with the Church in the way that he used to get fed up with the People of Israel, in the way he used to get fed up with the Apostles. Think of the Crusades. Think of the Pope who said 'Since God has given us the papacy, let us enjoy it.' Think of the persecution of Jews, and of witches. Think of condoning slavery and castrating boy sopranos. Lord Halifax once delivered himself of this masterpiece of understatement: 'Some people found Our Lord very tiresome.' Well, it would be a similar understatement to say that Our Lord must sometimes have found the Church very tiresome. Nevertheless, there it is. It is humanly weak but theologically central to God's purpose—in this sense it is always 'holy'. It's formed by the Holy Spirit, it's the continuing Body of Christ on earth, and through it God applies the redemption won by Christ on the Cross to individual men and women, across the centuries and across the continents. This is a vast, magnificent, generous plan. It is cosmic and majestic in its dimensions. How merciful God is! He actually calls sinful men and women into partnership with himself, in this job of pulling round a whole planet full of people.

Now when the Church actually gets down to the job entrusted to her, she does this, not exclusively but largely, through priests. Eucharist and sacraments above all are what bring the death and resurrection of Jesus into the experience of ordinary men and women, twenty-one centuries after they actually happened. And for eucharist and sacraments priests are indispensable. Of course the whole assembly of Christian people is priestly, we know that. Already by baptism we enter into the paschal mystery and take on ourselves the mantle of Christ's self-gift and victory. But to help the whole people operate in a genuinely priestly way, the Church needs ministerial priests, ordained priests, and that's us. For better or worse, the Catholic Church is a priestly Church. And because the Catholic Church has no alternative shape, no other way of being, it becomes crucially important to make sure that the priests we have are good ones. Here is a paragraph from a papal encyclical:

> Be very careful in the choosing of the seminarians, since the salvation of the people principally depends on good pastors. Nothing contributes more to ruin of souls than impious, weak or uninformed clerics.

That was not John Paul II, but Pius VIII in 1829, addressing his brother bishops for the first time. It sounds rather negative, doesn't it? He was a rather alarmed pope, and he only reigned for a year. But there is a positive implied in it. If we do have good priests, then the salvation of the people will happen. The Catholic priesthood is indeed a part of the mystery of salvation.

A priestly Church is not the same as a clerical Church, where the clergy erect themselves into a caste rather like the Pharisees, with pharisaic perks and attitudes. We're not to be clerical in this negative, self-regarding way. In *Pastores Dabo Vobis* (n. 21) the Pope [John Paul II] sums it up precisely. He describes how Jesus came not to be served but to serve. He quotes St Augustine ordaining a new bishop and saying 'He who is the head of the people must in the first place realize that he is to be the servant of many.' And then the Pope says:

> The spiritual life of the ministers of the New Testament should therefore be marked by this fundamental attitude of service to the People of God, freed from all presumption or desire of 'lording it over' those in their charge.

'Fundamental attitude', he says. Priesthood and priestliness are essential to our Church, part of the mix. Clericalism is not.

Think of your own vocation. Each of you has his story to tell. God called you one day, and he did it uniquely, personally, knowing full well your heredity, talents, personal circumstances, strengths and fault-lines. Your story, whatever it is, has great beauty in it. You have been brushed by the wing of the Spirit, and you have said, in your own way, 'Speak, Lord, your servant is listening.' You may even be able to recall the moment. That is beautiful beyond words. It's also dramatic. Who's at the centre of this drama? Is your call a purely individual thing? The real vocation, surely, is to the whole Messianic people, to enter into the death and resurrection of Christ and be transformed by it. That's the longing of God's heart, that's what expresses his unspeakable tenderness for his children, that's the mystery of faith, his constant yearning for his sons and daughters. Remember Ephesians 1:8: 'With all wisdom and insight he has made known to us the mystery of his will, according to his good pleasure that he set forth in Christ, as a plan for the fullness of time, to gather up all things in him, things in heaven and things on earth.' You and I are part of that, and our priesthood is part of that, and our personal vocation is part of that. Gathering up all things in Christ.

Out there, unknown to you but already known to God, are the men and women who are destined to be saved, under God, by what you will do for them. You cannot yet see their faces, but they're there. It's your words, your example, your patience and availability, your selfless and intelligent and sensitive celebration of Mass and sacraments which is going to bring them home. And the heart of God will be glad when that happens, and you will have helped to make the heart of God glad. Can you see what I meant at the beginning, about the vertical context in which we must perceive priesthood? There is no other context.

The history of salvation is like the most masterly, majestic symphony, with its slow and fast movements, with its moments of pathos and sadness and its moments of triumph and glory. In the providence of God, the priest is part of that symphony, an integral part of it. When we think of ourselves as priests, our hearts should lighten. By God's grace, you are the men who will lead his people home. You are the men who will surprise them by joy. You are the men who will help them to 'lift up their eyes to the mountains, from which their salvation comes.' On any scale of personal fulfilment, this comes pretty high.

In symphonies, there comes now and then a coda to the principal theme. Here are two codas.

If my basic vocation is to take my place within God's cosmic plan, then for me to be ambitious is fatuous and counter-productive. The careerist priest is a contradiction in terms. Each of us is like a piece in God's jigsaw, and no-one else has our exact shape. To try and force the wrong piece into a space in the jigsaw is ridiculous and damaging to the big picture. 'Oh rebellious children, says the Lord, who carry our a plan, but not mine' (Isaiah 30:1). I mention this because jealousy about other people's advancement is a real temptation. Ambition and jealousy are clergy vices, however well they may be disguised. Let's recognize them for what they are and name it—this is the stuff of sin.

And here's the second coda. Ignatius used to talk about discovering the deepest desire of your life. If my deepest desire is that God's will be done and his Kingdom established, and I want that to remain my deepest desire, then I personally need to stay very close to God. This means daily prayer, over and above the prayer of the Church. The priest who does not pray is absurd. It should be possible to have him under the Trades Descriptions Act. The only way of making sure that we are men of single purpose, of purity of heart, is by spending reservoirs of time each day being present to the Lord and letting him be present to us. Contemplative prayer, silent time spent with the Beloved, is absolutely vital. Otherwise we lose sight of the vertical and become pure activists, exceeding our brief, and building our house on sand. It's God's plan. It's his big picture. It's his symphony. It's his world. Tim Radcliffe in his book *Sing a New Song* wrote: 'Contemplation of the only-begotten Son is the root of all mission; ... without this stillness there is no movement.' If we do this, refer constantly back to him who is the Master, then the sky's the limit, indeed there's no limit to what we can do for God, and we will be astonished at what he achieves through us. Let us end with profound joy at what the future holds for us, as we reflect on Ephesians 3:20:

> Now to him who by the power at work within us is able to accomplish abundantly far more than all we can ask or imagine, to him be glory in the Church and in Christ Jesus, to all generations, for ever and ever.

PRIESTHOOD—II

Many years ago, Cardinal Avery Dulles, then an original young Jesuit theologian, wrote a seminal work called *Models of the Church.* In it he offered this unusual insight: we could think of the Church according to a whole string of different analogies, and these analogies need not be mutually exclusive. The traditional category, those days, into which we put the Church was 'institution'. We thought first of all of the Church in terms of hierarchy, who's in charge, who owes obedience to whom. Dulles presented us with other categories: the Church as herald of the Gospel, for instance. Thinking of the Church as herald, however, didn't mean 'if this, then not that.' Herald and institution could co-exist.

It is hard to describe to you the opening-up effect the Vatican Council had on those of us who actually lived through it. I recall my old bishop, just before he got on the plane for Rome, delivering himself of this prophetic opinion: 'I wouldn't be at all surprised if, as a result of this Council, the Holy Father were to allow those priests who have to say Mass three times on a Sunday to say only three psalms at Matins instead of nine.' Sharp intake of breath: this was radical stuff. His horizons, and ours, were very limited. He must have found the speed at which things happened quite bewildering, a bewilderment which was increased when a heavy wardrobe fell on him in the Salone [Guest rooms at the English College]. He had to be plucked from the ruins of Mgr Tickle's prize piece of antique furniture, but he was a courageous and tenacious old man and, nothing daunted, he proceeded to go every morning to St Peter's. At Midnight Mass in the Cathedral at Northampton he said, 'We have just returned from the first session of the epoch-making Vatican Council. Many bishops spoke, and some of them were most intelligent men.' One of the things which must have stretched his mind most was the way, at the beginning of the Decree on the Church, *Lumen Gentium*, the Council does a similar thing to Dulles. It gives us scriptural word-pictures of the Church. The Church is vineyard, field, our mother, the heavenly Jerusalem, Spouse of the Lamb, God's building. They're all true, these word-pictures. There are others too. Chapter I of the decree devotes a lot of space to discussing the Church as Christ's Body. But then, in chapter II, the Council declares, so to speak, its preference, which is the Old Testament image of the messianic People of God, the New Testament equivalent of the Israelites on their journey to the Promised Land. 'People of God', however, doesn't knock out all the others. No question of 'if this, then not that.' It is simply that the Council is saying, 'At this time, we think the most fruitful and rich analogy for our purposes is this one—the messianic People of God.'

Thirty years later in *Pastores Dabo Vobis*, when he encapsulates just what priesthood is in the Catholic Church, the present Pope [John Paul II] does a similar thing. The document is really about the formation of priests, and naturally it begins with a reflection on just what a priest is, and what he's for. Now the Pope could have concentrated on the priest as the man of sacrifice, or as mediator, or as preacher to the nations; all these are adequate headings under which to view the priesthood. However, the Holy Father puts his main emphasis on none of these, but on the priest as Shepherd. We priests are, he says, 'configured' to Christ, the Head and Shepherd of the Church. 'Configured' is a word that packs a punch. He spins it out and makes it explicit with expressions like 'marked, moulded and characterized.' In other words, something happens to us when we are ordained. This is not just a public commissioning by the Church of a certain man to do a certain job, or series of jobs. There is an interior remodelling. By ordination we're given a new personal shape. Remember, this is an old philosophy professor from Lublin and Kraków: 'According to St Peter, he says, the whole people of the New Covenant is established as a 'spiritual house', 'a holy priesthood, to offer spiritual sacrifices acceptable to God through Jesus Christ.' ... The new priestly people not only has its authentic image in Christ, but also receives from him a real *ontological share* in his one eternal priesthood.' 'Ontological' is a professorial word, isn't it? It means 'in its deep-down being', or 'by its very nature.' When we become Christians, our share in Christ's priesthood is not a bolt-on afterthought, a pleasant little decoration to our baptism. Our share in Christ's priesthood is automatic and total.

There has never been a baptized person who was not committed to offering spiritual sacrifices acceptable to God. It's part of the deal. Now if the Pope uses this language of all the baptized faithful, let's look again at the way the Pope talks about ordained priests. *Configured* is his word, and he takes it from the Council Decree on the Life of Priests, which says 'Through that sacrament, priests by the anointing of the Holy Spirit are signed with a special character and so configured to Christ the Priest in such a way that they are able to act in the person of Christ the Head.' He's still using 'ontological' language. By ordination we are re-cast, like molten metal, and our being is in a certain way fused with the being of Jesus, Shepherd and Head of the flock. That's what he's saying. And that's going to be you, in a very short time.

Seminary is to prepare you for that fusion. We could put it in the form of a dramatic question: are you ready to become molten, like metal, so that you may be re-cast, not just in the image of Christ, but in his identity? If you are, six years is probably not too long for this process. We all know that seminary brings its share of suffering: it is not willed by anyone, not deliberately devised, but it's still there. If we can see the suffering in the light of the analogy of I Peter 1:6, it becomes the refining fire which makes us ready to be re-cast. It isn't wasted, in other words. Not a scrap of it is wasted. 'In this you rejoice, even if for a little while you have had to suffer various trials, so that the genuineness of your faith—being more precious than gold that, though perishable, is tested by fire—may be found to result in praise and glory and honour...'

And the Pope, still in *Pastores Dabo Vobis*, points out the quality which you will need above all as a priest, and he calls it *pastoral charity*. There is a danger here of our half-digesting a piece of jargon, specially if we were not brought up on Latin. 'Pastoral' really means 'shepherd-like'. And charity means love. At the heart of the mix must be love, that's what the Pope is saying. If you become a priest because you think it will give you power, or excite people's admiration, or give you status, or afford you security, you have missed the point. If you do any of this, you are thinking in the first place of yourself. Your centre of gravity is in the wrong place. In the first place, says the Pope, you should be thinking of the flock, thinking of the people you are asked to look after. To start with, I expect your flock will be people in a parish. Later it may be couples looking for the annulment of their marriages; or the staff and patients of an enormous hospital; or the teachers and catechists of your diocese; or even a group of seminarians. The question is, how will you treat them? What vibes will they pick up from you? Pastoral charity on our part is a share in Christ's own pastoral charity. It means loving the flock. This kind of love is not sentimental and does not consist in emotional attraction. It consists rather in a willingness to make a gift of myself, to be the man who serves, even when the people I serve are not always all that lovable. It consists in making the Church, and souls (quoting the Pope again) my first interest. I have to be person-centred rather than issue-centred. Pastoral charity will show, incidentally, in the way I preach: will I seek eye-contact with the congregation as I speak to them, because they are my first concern? Or will I have my eyes down on a text on the lectern, so as to get the words absolutely right, because *that* is my first concern? This is just a detail, but it may illustrate what my basic attitude is, where my interest lies. I hasten to add that I am not criticizing the homiletic style of anybody here. I know that when you are learning to preach you do feel tied to your text, it's like a prop until you have gained a bit of confidence. That's fine and perfectly understandable. But if in ten years' time you are still lecturing the congregation without looking at it, without in any way engaging with it, that's a different matter. Our love must be like a spark from the white-hot redemptive fire of Christ's love for ordinary folks. He liked people. Love isn't a generalized thing. It is destined for a concrete person or a concrete number of people. Even our body-language speaks out our love.

The Pope says that this love, this pastoral charity, is a gift freely bestowed by the Holy Spirit. That's nice. It's a comforting reflection. If I have not yet learned to love as Jesus loves, I might think, I can just lie back and wait for it to come, gift-wrapped, from heaven, with the other ordination presents. Not so! Alas, the Pope adds that pastoral charity isn't only a gift: it's also a task and a call. No lying back then. I have to do something about it. Here at the seminary I have to get into practice. It's my task. Pastoral charity won't develop miraculously when the bishop puts his hands on my head. Easy to be a bit theoretical about stuff in papal documents, do bits of exegesis on it, argue about precise meanings and so forth. We learn at the Greg and the Angelicum to be quite good at that. In this case, however, the call is not to scholarship, it is to action. The call is, here and now, to treat with courtesy, patience, good humour and self-sacrifice, all the members of the community in which I find myself. I am not here in Rome just to imbibe a certain quantity of information and three letters after my name. I am here to become molten metal, re-cast with Christ as my model, fused with him, my heart beating in tune with his Sacred Heart. It's now that I have the grow the spiritual muscles, not later. And the biggest spiritual muscle is the charity-muscle.

So now we know pretty much what a priest *is*: he is a Shepherd in union with Christ. And we know the dominant quality required for this: charity, love. But concretely, what does a priest *do*? How is he of use to the community? Why does the People of God on the march home to the Father's house need shepherding, and in what way? When you go to get your hair cut—whenever you go to get your hair cut—the barber will make conversation, and he will say 'I suppose this is your busy time of year, Sir' (snip, snip), and you will bite back and suppress a crushing response like 'Have you the slightest idea what you are talking about, you inane gnome, you putrid ignoramus, you empty-headed loon?' and instead will answer lamely, 'Well, always plenty to do, you know.' The barber thinks you spend all your time in church organizing hymn sandwiches, weddings and funerals and talking in a funny upbeat voice to temporarily captive audiences. The point where the secular world meets traditional religion is a *locus* for such misunderstandings. I remember doing the baptisms one hot Sunday afternoon in a tin chapel in Chile. Some thumb-sucking children stood and watched me as I climbed, sweating, into the correct gear for the occasion. When it got to the surplice, one girl took her thumb out of her mouth and said to her little sister, 'Now he's putting on his blouse.' What the priest *does*, essentially, is find ways of overcoming misunderstandings, of being the bridge, of making the Catholic Faith in all its beauty comprehensible to the barber and the girl with her thumb in her mouth. The priest, says the Pope in *Pastores Dabo Vobis*, is 'first of all a minister of the Word of God. He is consecrated and sent forth to proclaim the Good News of the Kingdom to all.' We are professional evangelizers, and this before all else. There are lots of other things that we do. For instance, we care for the faithful committed to us, by sacramental ministry and by teaching. We celebrate the Eucharist in union with our bishop and the universal Church. We are channels of Christ's forgiveness to countless souls, and especially to those on the point of death. God knows I would not want to downgrade any of these. In order of priority, however, evangelization must come first, because it is only by receiving the gift of faith that anyone comes into line for any of these other blessings. 'How can I (understand) unless I have someone to guide me?' said the Ethiopian eunuch to Philip (Acts 8:31). Your task will be making the Catholic Faith intelligible to countless thousands, in an idiom which is theirs, in thought-patterns which are theirs, in images which make sense to them. No wonder the Pope has been talking for the past ten years about the 'new evangelization'. Everything you do at the Greg and the Angelicum, everything you learn in your pastoral classes here in the College, has to feed into this. You are not just custodians of the flock. You are recruiters for the flock. You assure the continuity of the flock. This is shepherding. It is a thrilling and exciting prospect.

What I've done tonight is give you some points of reference. Forgive me if I have accentuated the obvious, repeated things you already know, and generally bored the pants off you. But these points of reference are like our mission-statement, and we need to hang on to them through thick and thin. Here they are again.

* What am I aiming to be? I am aiming to be a shepherd in union with Jesus the chief shepherd, the good shepherd.
* How am I going to do it? I am going to do it with love: I'm going to put myself on the line for my people, I am going to be their loving servant, and I'm going to get into training for this now.
* And, concretely, what will have priority in my life? Evangelizing will be my top priority, so that Isaiah 40:10 may come true, and the Lord, who is the real Shepherd, the Chief Shepherd, the Arch-shepherd, will have full scope for his love and his grace:

> Here is the Lord Yahweh coming with power
> His arm subduing all things to him.
> The prize of his victory is with him
> His trophies all go before him.

He is like a shepherd feeding his flock,
Gathering lambs in his arms,
Holding them against his breast
And leading to their rest the mother ewes.

✠

Purgatory

Last time I was home, my sister's parish priest, who is a deeply kind man, said to me in the sacristy, 'How are you off for Mass stipends?' and I replied that Rome did not abound in such commodities, and he said, 'I'll see what I can do.' A very Catholic conversation, resulting in a cheque for £50.

On the basis of not taking anything for granted, perhaps I should say a word now to explain Mass stipends, just in case there are some people here for whom the idea is novel. There is an age-old tradition in the Catholic Church that when people want a priest to offer Mass for their intention, or for the welfare of a friend or relative, or for someone who has died, they make him an offering in cash. There was a time when this provided a priest with the main part of his income. It was never seen as a quid-pro-quo payment: that would have been immoral, since you can't put a price on sacred things. It was, rather, a voluntary contribution to the maintenance of the clergy, made on the occasion of a request. Inevitably, it came to be misunderstood by simple people. I can recall immigrants from Naples coming into the sacristy at home and asking bluntly 'Quanto costa una Messa?' ['How much is a Mass?'] I would reply virtuously 'La Messa non costa niente, ma se Lei vuole fare qualche offerta ...' ['The Mass doesn't cost anything, but if you would like to make an offering ...'] and then I would catch them looking at me out pityingly of the corner of their eye as if to say 'We all know that everything has a price-tag. Just cut the crap and name a figure.' Sometimes the clergy do little to alleviate such misunderstanding. The shameful story is told of a priest on a fairly short fuse looking with dismay at the pile of coins in his hand, and saying to the lady who had produced them, 'Madam, that won't get me past the offertory.'

A lot of priests do not agree with the principle of Mass stipends. They say it sails uncomfortably close to the wind of simony, of selling what is holy for money. They say that it frightens away poor people. They say that the Mass should never even appear to be appropriated by individuals, or have anyone's name attached to it, because it is the sacrifice of all God's people. Now this is a defensible point of view. *You* may well feel like this, and when you are ordained you will have to decide—in consultation with your parish priest—where you stand. The argument on the other side is many-pronged. One prong is that people who ask you to pray for their special needs during Mass actually *want* a personal input into the sacrifice, in the way that centuries ago people supplied the bread and the wine. Another more pragmatic one is that if it were not for Mass stipends, many of our foreign missions would have to close. An Argentinian priest talked to a group of us the other day in some distress. Because of the financial collapse in his own country he had no money to pay his fare home after his Licence. Some kind Italians had come to his rescue and supplied the price of the ticket, but they had given him the money in Mass stipends, about two hundred of them. He was distressed because in Argentina they don't offer Mass for private intentions, and he foresaw that he would have no way of discharging his obligation. So a number of us volunteered to celebrate the Masses on his behalf. All of which goes to illustrate that Mass stipends are a way in which the people can help to maintain their clergy, something they actually want to do. And another argument, perhaps the clincher, is that the highest authority in the Church, in spite of all the objections, continues to approve of the idea. Personally, when I celebrate Mass for which a stipend has been offered, I always make a special effort to pray specifically for that intention and for the people whose intention it is, both during and after the Mass, so that it is not just a theoretical thing, but real.

So anyway, I returned to Rome from London in September with ten Masses for the Holy Souls. As I worked my way through them, day by day, I reflected on just what this means, to celebrate the Eucharist for all the people in Purgatory. And the more I thought about it, the richer the theme became. Tonight I would like to share my reflections with you.

Let's think aloud for a moment. Just what does it mean to be a Holy Soul, a soul in Purgatory? Is that going to happen to me? The answer is, quite probably, yes. I am conscious that when I die there will be a lot of unfinished business in my life. It is not so much a matter of major sins I have committed without repenting of them. Please God, there won't be any of those. So I am not talking here of the definitive rejection of God. That is something quite different. It is, much more, a matter of the sort of man I have gradually let myself become. I occasionally get glimpses of myself as hardened in pettiness, and blinkered, incurably small. I am like someone who is offered a lengthy cruise on a luxury liner, and who replies infuriatingly, 'If it is all the same to you, I would rather have a week at a bed-and-breakfast in the rainy season at Great Yarmouth.' God wants to bestow on me the actual vision of Himself. But how can I ever be fit and ready for this? Moses says to the people in Deuteronomy 4, 'Did ever a people hear the voice of the living God speaking from the heart of the fire, as you heard it, and remain alive?' Too much self-indulgence, too much smugness and self-satisfaction, have limited me, lowered my vision, lowered my capacity. The truth of God is a blinding clarity. The love of God is white heat. The intensity of all this, absolute truth and love without ambiguity, would be more than I could stand. I fear that if I had to absorb all this together, I would be demolished. 'The things that no eye has seen and no ear has heard, things beyond the mind of man, all that God has prepared for those who love him' (I Corinthians 2:9). ' says Paul. The mind of *this* man has not imagined the greatness of God, and *cannot* for the moment imagine it. I am constitutionally too small, and I have made myself smaller during my life by the no-go signs I have put up to God. How could I ever contain that vision? It would be like putting Niagara into a plastic bucket. If I am ever to be able to sustain the uninterrupted possession of Him who is the ground of all meaning and goodness, he will have to work on me first, that's what it comes to. He will have to change the shape and capacity of my soul.

And God working on me first, that's purgatory. Explanations of the penny catechism I learned in my youth were full of accounts of fire, purging the sinful soul to make it ready for, and worthy of, heaven. One of the saints is supposed to have had a privileged glimpse of the souls in the fire of purgatory, and to have received a drop of sweat from one such soul on his hand, which was actually scorched by the heat of it. The Council of Lyons in 1245, attempting convergence with the

Orthodox, talks of *ignis transitorius*, a passing fire. Pope Clement VI in 1351, dealing with the Armenians, uses almost identical language. The Council of Florence in 1439, again finding common ground with the Greeks, says *hoc Sacro universali approbante Florentino Concilio diffinimus... animas poenis purgatoriis post mortem purgari*, i.e. it talks about purgation, but doesn't speak explicitly of fire. The Council of Trent, in Session VI (1547) talks about *reatus poenae temporalis exsolvendae vel in hoc saeculo vel in futuro in purgatorio*, i.e. after forgiveness, there may well still be some penance to be done either in this world or the next; again, no mention of fire. In 1563 the same Council, still sitting, ordered bishops to teach a healthy doctrine about purgatory, the one handed down by the Fathers of the Church and the Councils, and to make sure that it was believed, held, taught and preached. The *rudis plebs*, the rude plebs, should be shielded from knotty questions, which did not contribute to their edification. Uncertain things, which smack of falsehood, superstition or filthy lucre were to be avoided, as scandal and a stumbling-block to the faithful. The present *Catechism of the Catholic Church* says, a little cautiously it is true, 'The tradition of the Church, by reference to certain texts of Scripture, speaks of a cleansing fire.' It refers us to an intriguing verse in I Corinthians 3:15 about the Final Judgment. Paul is talking about building up the Church on Jesus Christ as the only possible foundation. He says 'The work of each builder is going to be clearly revealed when the day comes. The day will begin with fire, and the fire will test the quality of each man's work. If his structure stands up to it, he will get his wages; if it is burnt down, he will be the loser, and though he is saved himself, it will be as one who has gone through fire.'

I have no private source of inspiration on this matter. But I have an intuition that the use of fire is metaphorical, and that what awaits us in purgatory is something much subtler but equally painful. It is self-knowledge. Not the glimpses of self that come this side of the grave, but the whole thing, my whole self relentlessly revealed in the clear daylight of God's truth, and nowhere to run, no alibi, no pretext, no way of shifting the blame. von Balthasar says in *Theodramatik*: 'The soul sees itself only in the Lord's mirror.' What does Paul say? 'The work of each builder is going to be clearly revealed when that day comes.' My life's work, my whole self revealed—to whom? Why, to me. When I signed the page about myself in the Liber Ruber, back in 1959, I wrote at the bottom, *Ita est*: that's how it is. When God reveals me to myself I shall have to say, again, *Ita est*, I admit it, I admit it without qualification. God gave me the opportunity to grow in holiness and justice, to be a saint, and he gave me seventy, eighty years in which to do it, and by and large I blew it. That's how it is. I recall deeply unpleasant moments in my adolescence, when I had pushed my poor father beyond the bounds of human endurance, and he sat me down and said, 'Let me tell you just how other people perceive you. Let me tell you exactly what you're like.' I would have done anything *not* to know exactly what I was like.

However, this is the price to be paid. In heaven, there is no place for people with illusions. Heaven is the place of truth. My preparation for heaven will be the shedding of my illusions. My illusions have sheltered and protected me all my life. When Jesus was stripped before being nailed to the Cross, he was telling us in a wordless way that in the cause of sanctity, the illusions have to go. They have to be stripped away, so that what is left is my naked character, with all its murky motivations and ingenious excuses disclosed. Ego-trips which masquerade as charity, that sort of thing. *Ita est.* This ultimate honesty gives, at last, an opening to God's mercy. von Balthasar again: 'Purgatory comes into existence on Holy Saturday, when the Son walks through 'hell' introducing the element of mercy into the condition of those who are justly lost. Purgatory arises as if under the Lord's striding feet; he brings comfort to this place of hopelessness, fire to this place of iciness.' You know how a plasterer needs to apply his plaster to a rough surface, so that it will have a key, something to dig into, something to hold on to. In the same way God's saving mercy needs the key of a humble and contrite heart, the key of someone who realizes that he is not stainless steel, but in fact tarnished goods. 'Lord Jesus Christ, Son of the living God, have mercy on me a sinner.' That's a powerful prayer precisely because it springs from an admission of vulnerability. This basic no-illusions honesty with ourselves is the preliminary. It enables us to say 'Of myself I am bankrupt and helpless. I depend on the grace of God. Spiritually I can never be self-sufficient.' I believe that Purgatory will bring me to the point of knowing this, and saying it, admitting that I am personally without resource or credit and that God is my only hope, and that this will cause the gates of heaven to swing open, and the choirs of angels to welcome me home.

So what about praying for the Holy Souls? How do our prayers and Masses help them? Innocent III, in 1208, sketched out a profession of faith for convert Waldensians, saying among other things that our almsgiving and sacrifice can be of benefit to the faithful departed. The First Council of Lyons says the same about the 'prayers of the Church'. The Second Council of Lyons adds to the list the celebration of Mass. So does the Council of Florence. So Mass for the dead has a long and very respectable pedigree. It is based, ultimately, on our belief in the Communion of Saints. In modern parlance, this means solidarity between all the people on earth, those in heaven, and those on their way there. Solidarity with Christ and his Mother; and solidarity among ourselves. We profit by the prayers of the saints; we offer our prayers for those who have gone before us, and who will one day themselves be uncanonized saints. I say 'one day' because *we* have to reduce things to time and space, it is the only way we can think; but as Ratzinger says in his book *Eschatologie*, 'Man is drawn into the eschatological fire. The transforming 'moment' of this encounter is beyond the earthly calculation of time.' Even if *we* cannot penetrate the frontier between time and eternity, the Sacrifice of Calvary can and does penetrate it, enabling Christ who walked among the dead and liberated Adam to walk among our beloved dead also, keying his mercy to their self-acknowledged sinfulness.

What the theologians and the Councils say chimes in with a deep intuition of the faithful. When you are priests you will discover how people's deceased relatives play a major role in their religious life. Anniversaries are hugely important, and we must take them very seriously. If you neglect to put the name of someone's granny in the news-sheet, or mention it before or during the celebration of the Eucharist, the reaction can be quite sobering. You may discover that the person died many, many years ago, but it makes no difference. It is as though your parishioners had found a way of spanning the gap between this world and the next, and sending their dear ones the regular assurance of their love, and that way is you. You must never take this lightly—it is deep in the psyche of our folk. Once you are ordained and appointed to a parish you will find that one of the wall-boxes which fills up most quickly is the one labelled 'Holy Souls', and sometimes people will ask you to offer Mass for the most neglected soul in Purgatory; it is as if there were a poor prisoner in a prisoner-of-war camp who never got a food parcel, and these people want to be sure that no-one is left out. It is easy for us to laugh at this sort of thing. The expression of the instinct may be a bit gauche on occasion. But the instinct is sound, and according to the mind of the Church. Your diocese will circulate regularly the names of priests in a thing called 'The Pact': these are the men who have died in your group of dioceses or province, and you are asked to offer Mass for them, with the assurance that when you die, other men will do the same for you. It is a fraternal thing to do. Even if the names mean nothing to you, these are your brothers. That's how the Communion of Saints works.

The doctrine of Purgatory reconciles two gut-certainties that I, like any Christian, must have. One is that God is incredibly, vibrantly, staggeringly, good, and true. The other is that I am neither of those things. To put God and me together, with me in my present state, would not work. We used to say that, accepting evolution as the most likely origin of humanity, and putting it crudely, God must have modified the body of the chosen ape before it was fit and ready to receive a human soul, and that's where Adam came from. In an analogous way, I shall need some attention from God before I am fit and ready for the Beatific Vision. It isn't just a question of forgiveness. God can forgive in the twinkling of an eye. It's a matter of equipping me for the supreme experience, one for which I long with all my heart. One day I shall be able to say 'My heart is ready, O God, my heart is ready.' If my friends pray for me, that day will come all the sooner.

✝

'TI EMOI KAI SOI?'

This quaint Greek expression crops up twice in the Gospels. Once in the account of the Marriage Feast at Cana, in John. On this occasion it is Jesus himself who uses this figure of speech, to his mother. And once in Mark, when Jesus confronts the legion of devils in the possessed man in the graveyard, and sends the devils into a herd of pigs. On this occasion, it is the evil spirit who says it to Jesus.

It takes a bit of unpacking. In Latin it would be 'Quid mihi et tibi?' In English, literally, 'What to me and to you?' Most commentators take it to mean 'What is there between us?' or 'What have we in common?' If this is so, in the context of the marriage feast, and the wine running out, Jesus was saying to Mary, 'In what way does this concern us both?' We know how the story works out, in terms of the love and affection between Jesus and Mary, and their compassion for the newly married couple. So it was not a hostile question. But still a question. The account of the devils and the pigs is rather different. In this case the demon, or demons infesting the poor lunatic in the cemetery recognize Jesus and react: 'What have you got to do with us?' If they had been English demons they would probably have said, in these or similar words, 'We want nothing to do with you, buzz off and leave us alone'.

The question, for us, hangs in the air. *Ti emoi kai soi?* 'What is it that links us?' we say to God. And in this sense it can form the basis for some very profitable prayer. It is interesting how you can take the complaints of evil spirits and turn them into prayers. Demons are intelligent and perceptive, above all when it comes to spiritual realities. Do you recall the time when Jesus approached a possessed man and the spirit shouted, 'I know who you are, the holy one of God!' That, in however perverted a way, was an act of faith in Our Lord. We could do worse than repeat this. In the same way 'What have we got in common?' is a good beginning to a conversation with Christ, what St Ignatius would call a 'colloquy'.

Well, what we have in common is a link, a channel by which he feeds power and meaning into our lives. When *Humanae Vitae* was published, the English translation was called 'The Transmission of Life'. Well, Jesus transmits life to us, every day of our lives. Remember the account of the woman with the issue of blood, in the Gospel (Mark 5:25). She had exhausted all human avenues to a cure. Then she touched the hem of Jesus's cloak, and was healed on the spot: and Jesus said 'Who touched me?' because he was immediately aware that the power had gone out from him. You get the impression that Our Lord is so brimful of power that the slightest contact will cause it to flow out into us. Our relationship to him is one of intimacy and dependency, of touch and need. I want to explore this further in the course of this talk.

Old friends, when they meet, reminisce. They say to one another, 'We go back a long way.' You and I can say that to Our Lord, and through him to the Father. We go back a long way. The creation of each one of us took place in the mind and heart of God before and beyond time, somewhere in eternity. It was done out of love, out of expansiveness. I can say of myself (and you can say this of yourself) that from the first moment of my existence God has taken an interest in me. No, in fact that is far too weak a statement. God is not like a wealthy patron or a rich godfather who occasionally asks the parents 'How's the lad doing?' and sends a cheque for birthdays. God has loved me throughout with a focused, passionate and enduring love. When I was baptized a new phase of this relationship began. The saving effect of the Crucifixion and Resurrection of Jesus was applied directly to me, not like a poultice or a plaster, more like a massive and continuous blood transfusion. 'I live, now not with my own life, but with the life of Christ who lives in me' (Galatians 2:20). And so it has gone on. God's active intervention in my life. And all this started long before I became conscious of it. It started at my baptism.

Then, somewhere about First Communion time, came the earliest awareness. I am not about to inflict on you large doses of autobiography. I mention these details only to encourage you to substitute your own, which are much more important, so that you may be able to see the silken thread with which God has been drawing you all these years. In the 1940s, French and Irish nuns who taught me had more than a suspicion of Jansenism in their spirituality, and they generously shared this with me. So I became aware of a God who loves me, yes, and is on the receiving end of my prayers, but who is hurt and offended by my sins. I learned out of a nineteenth-century Old Testament, with etchings of a bearded and ferocious God, peering out of a cloud, potentially volcanic and unpredictable: the God who told Abraham to sacrifice Isaac, a God to be feared. God always had me on the wrong foot. But he was real, he was a fixture, he was an item in my life. It was the beginning of a conscious relationship, even if distorted on my side. However fitfully, I began to respond to God. Yes, we go back a long way. Then the nuns taught us about the Sacred Heart of Jesus, a suffering heart, suffering because of his cruel enemies and unfaithful disciples, but also suffering because of me, my childish peccadilloes, because I did not do my work as neatly and correctly as I should. Jesus, too, had me on the wrong foot. But again, Jesus became a fixture, a reality, an item in my life. It was the beginning of a conscious relationship, even if on my side it was skewed. In a childish way I began to respond: Jesus and I go back a long way.

Since then the relationship has gone through all sorts of vicissitudes. Again, I won't bore you with personal data. I spoke of a silken thread. A fishing line would be a better metaphor. From God's side it must have been rather like playing a fish. Maybe it still is. He has had me on the end of a very, very long line, and every now and then he sees his chance, gives it a twitch, and in spite of my resistance reels me in a little. In spite of myself I come closer to him. He has reeled me in like this through confirmation, vocation and ordination, through a shoal of misunderstandings and mixed motives. He has reeled me in through a chequered history of priestly ministry. He has reeled me in through four parish priests, five bishops, sixteen assistants, and now five seminary rectors. He has reeled me in through successive depths of self-knowledge, which were painfully acquired, and humbling. He has empowered me to surrender myself to him. I have done this only in instalments and not all at once, and the job is not done yet, but he has been patient, incredibly patient. When I think of some of the things I have said and done, and some of the things I have omitted to do, I am appalled, and find it hard to love or even like myself. He is much kinder to me than I am to myself. He still thinks me worth reeling in, worth saving. His tenderness for me has never ceased, his forgiveness of me penetrates the deepest recesses of my heart and restores me, re-creates me. *Ti emoi kai soi?* What is there between us? That's what's between us. All that history of faithfulness on his side, fickleness on mine, over more than half a century. We go back a long time. *Ti emoi kai soi?* What is there between us? An intimate friendship which is not ruined by my failures because God is not at all neurotic and does not take offence. More than a friendship. A symbiotic relationship, in which I draw power and strength from him, day by day, and he lets me. What links us is grace.

From the heart of this relationship, which over the years has become more and more precious to me, I can look at God and see someone quite other than the God I saw as an eight-year-old boy. I see the Father as the ground of my being, the supplier of the is-ness of things and the is-ness of me, who made me out of sheer benevolence and who overflows with a love which is so uncalculated and unrationed that I in my meanness and paltriness cannot conceive it. That un-rationed love he expresses concretely in Jesus. God loved the world so much that he gave his only Son (John 3:16). I see Jesus as the one whose heart beats with that of the Father, in perfect time. He lived and died for me, to prove to me that I am precious in the Father's eyes. However, like the Apostles right up to the moment of Pentecost, I am unresponsive and uncomprehending. So the Father and the Son scoop me up, in spite of myself, by soaking me in their Spirit, so that I can believe and so that I can pray. So that in this continuing relationship, this continuing conversation between us, I can at least reply, if only with a puny and squeaky voice, and say 'Lord, you know everything. You know that I love you.' God puts the words into my mouth. In Isaiah we find the Suffering Servant saying 'The Lord Yahweh has given me a disciple's tongue' (Isaiah 50:4). It's a gift. All is gift. The Pope [John Paul II], in *Novo Millennio Ineunte*, says 'We cannot come to the fullness of contemplation of the Lord's face by our own efforts alone, but by allowing grace to take us by the hand.'* Without the grace of God, I could not be on God's wavelength at all. God is like a parent who gives his children money so that they can buy him a birthday present. And in his time this parent has put up

---

*   *Novo Millennio Ineunte*, n. 20.

with some pretty limp presents from me, in terms of belief and prayer. *Ti emoi kai soi?* What do I share with the Father and the Son? I share the Spirit. The Spirit is God's abiding and active presence in my life, divinizing me so that I can respond to his kindness and his promises with the divine currency of faith and hope. That's how I see God; that's how it looks from this side of the relationship. And it's still going on. Day by day God proves in my life that he's a hands-on God, constantly providing me with the grace I need.

But how does it look from the other side? What does God see when he looks at me? A beloved son, certainly, baptized into Christ, so that he looks on me with undisguised affection. But also, I suspect, with a degree of disappointment. It happens, doesn't it, that fathers have sons who don't inherit their talents, their gift for concentration, application and hard work? Fathers don't stop loving their sons because they aren't intelligent or because they are lazy. But they do wish they were different. For instance, when God looks at me, he must wish that I took my spiritual life more seriously. How much time I have wasted, time I could have spent knowing him better, like the Apostles after Pentecost, like the Fathers of the Church, like the great saints who are masters and mistresses of prayer: how could and can I be so offhand about my spiritual life, as though it were an optional extra to the business of living? Knowing what I know, I should have been much more determined and single-minded in the way I tackled prayer, seeing it not as a duty, as homework, but as a lifegiving encounter with the only one who deserves my undivided love, and who can really help me. God must say to himself, 'How can he fail to see it?' like Jesus weeping over Jerusalem, 'If you, even you, had only known on this day what would bring you peace ...' (Luke 19:41, NIV).

And God's love is un-rationed, as we said before. In the way Jesus gave away his life for love, we see this plainly. But in my case, God has adopted a son who lacks that generous and courageous heart. Why am I not more generous to the poor, who are the apple of God's eye? Why am I so parsimonious in the way I use my energy for others? Why do I make such heavy weather of sharing what I have? Why have I not been more courageous in going after the lost sheep, courageous in standing up for justice, courageous in tackling my moral weaknesses and addictions? There is something penny-pinching about my efforts. When God looks at me he must wonder, 'How did I manage to adopt a son who is so incurably small-minded, who misses the big issues and gets obsessed with details, who guards his little independent no-go corner, nurses petty grudges, and is frightened of commitment?' Surely if Jesus teaches us anything it is wholesale self-gift, self-gift without a backward look. He teaches us this by the way he lives and the way he dies. Why do I, who claim to be his disciple, fail to pick up the signal? God says to us through the prophet Jeremiah 'You will seek me and find me when you seek me with all your heart' (Jeremiah 29:13). It is the divided heart which keeps me small. It is the divided heart which means I lack nobility of soul. *Ti emoi kai soi?* could well be a question God asks of me. 'What on earth have we in common?'

Unexpectedly, God produces an answer to his own question. We have Mary in common. The virgin he chose to be the mother of his Son belongs to us as well. She has a mother's empathy for the ugly duckling in the brood, for the backward child, for the awkward son, for me. She who is spiritually the highest of high-flyers was given to us at the foot of the Cross to be not only a model, but a mother. Here is the wisdom of God working at full throttle, appreciating our need: a mother who will coax, who will encourage, who will never say to us 'You are a definitive mess and I wash my hands of you', a mother who will intercede for us effectively, as Abraham interceded for Sodom, daring to beat God down, bargaining with him like an Arab in the market for the lives of the people, even when God seems to have run out of patience (Genesis 18:22). We need such a mother. She, above all others, had the gift of contemplation, contemplating the face of Jesus day by day. She was generous and courageous, she had the gift of self-sacrifice to the highest degree, and we can see this from the moment of the Annunciation to the moment of Jesus's burial. In her God was never disappointed. What better ally could we have? Without doubt she is God's. But he has shared her with us. *Ti emoi kai soi?* Holy Mary, Mother of God, show us how to do it, show us how to fulfil the potential the Father has put into us, show us how to be children who gladden his heart when he looks at us.

So there you have it. God, had he wished it, could have been the God of the Deists, the God of Voltaire and Rousseau, the clockmaker, who having created us sat back and watched, with cold and detached interest, our futile struggles. This God would have been unattainable, uncontactable. The whole concept of a personal spiritual life would have been a nonsense. The fact that intelligent men could ever have imagined such a God makes us realize, in the light of the Gospel and the Church's teaching, how lucky we are that God *isn't* like that. The reverse is true. *Ti emoi kai soi?* has a positive answer. God builds bridges between us and him. God even comes to dwell in my heart. My faith should be expectant, because God is responsive. Moses says it better than I can. Here is God caring for Jacob, for the people he has adopted by covenant (Deuteronomy 32:10). We know that we can substitute ourselves for Jacob in this passage, both as individuals and as Church.

> In the waste lands he adopts him,
> in the howling desert of the wilderness.
> He protects him, rears him, guards him
> as the pupil of his eye.
> Like an eagle watching its nest
> hovering over its young,
> he spreads out his wings to hold him,
> he supports him on his pinions.

✝

The Hands of Men

In Luke 9:44, Jesus says to his apostles that he will be 'handed over into the power of men'. In this particular passage, incidentally, there is no mention of scourging, or mocking, or crucifying, nor for that matter of resurrection. (Earlier in Luke (9:22) it's more explicit, as it is in Mark (8:31; 9:31; 10:33) and Matthew (16:21; 17:22)). But no, here we have simply that ominous little phrase 'handed over into the power of men'.

And in fact the Greek for this phrase doesn't say 'the power of men'; it says 'the hands of men', *cheiras anthropon*. And it is preceded by a command which the modern translations tone down and make cosmetically acceptable—for instance, the Jerusalem Bible says 'for your part, you must have these words constantly in your minds'—but the Greek is much more dramatic, *thesthe humeis eis ta ota*; it is as though Jesus were saying, roughly and explicitly, 'Stick this once and for all in your ears'. The apostles had the gift of only hearing what they wanted to hear, and his forecasts of arrest and death were not welcome to them. He knew this from experience, and wanted badly to gain their attention.

That phrase, 'the hands of men'. It is graphic, it has a chilly concreteness about it. Must 'to be put into the hands of men' always have a sinister meaning? Are the hands of men primarily destined to tear, to destroy, to inflict pain? Jesus uses this shorthand phrase to forecast his entire Passion. The arrest in the Garden, the blow in the face in the High Priest's house, the tying-up, the stripping, the scourging, the crucifying: all, to use a phrase well-known to all of us, the work of human hands. So, 'stick this once and for all in your ears', says Jesus. For God's sake, get real. It sounds crude. But this is what men are like. The truth about man's ruthlessness is crude. Left to themselves, without the grace of God, men are cruel, and sadistic, and ingenious in the inflicting of suffering. Animals hunt one another, and kill, for food. Cats kill birds out of a kind of fascination. But only men do large-scale ethnic cleansing, racial pogroms; only men use their hands to build concentration camps and gas chambers, and dig mass graves. Only men have perfected systems of torture. We bring our manual dexterity, our incredible giftedness, as well as our genius for planning and our technical know-how, to bear on making our brother suffer, and die.

This ingeniousness, I hardly need to say, resides not in the hands themselves, but in the heart and mind which control the hands. I need to ask myself what difference there is between myself and Osama bin Laden. What trigger would it take for me to organize a 9/11? Obviously, the trigger has not yet been activated, or I wouldn't be here today, subscribing to a religion which has pardon, patience and non-violence at its heart. But we are brothers under the skin. I am a brother under the skin to Pol Pot, who massacred millions of Cambodians because they had professions, or wore glasses. I am a brother under the skin to the Hutu militia who disposed of hundreds of thousands of Tutsis in 1994, as often as not mowing them down in their village churches. I am a brother under the skin to the Chilean security services, who, thirty years ago, set up the centre for torture and interrogation on a prison ship in Valparaiso Harbour. I am a brother under the skin to the Bosnian Serbs who coolly loaded all the men at Srebrenica into lorries, granddads, fathers and teenage boys, and drove them away to murder them in the woods. I am a brother under the skin to the Catholics in Paris who organized the Massacre of St Bartholomew, in 1572. Is it simply, I wonder, that that bit of me has not been accessed?

We need to be very humble. To be human is an ambiguous thing, and all of us are only too human. Only the power and goodness of God can permeate us in such a way that we can, in the words of the Benedictus, 'serve him in holiness and justice all the days of our life in his presence'. Only the power and goodness of God can enable us to climb free, in a permanent way, from the things which disgrace humanity. And if we achieve this, it will be pure gift, sheer grace. Nothing to boast about.

In chapter 7 of the Decree of Justification, in the sixth session of the Council of Trent, the Fathers described 'justification' as not just the remission of sins, but the sanctification and renewal of the interior man through his willing acceptance of grace and of God's gifts, so that from being unjust he becomes just, and from being an enemy he becomes a friend. They were of course fighting the classical Protestant notion that the Passion of Christ cloaks our sins, and that under this cloak the Father lets us into Paradise. No, said the Catholic Church, we can do better than that. The grace of God even here on earth changes us and penetrates us so that we become intrinsically good, and lovable. Remember the context of this decree: it was published on 13 Jan. 1547, the year in which Henry VIII was to die and leave the throne to his baby son and some radically reforming regents, who would invite the Calvinists to move in on the English religious scene. Calvinism was the background to this session of Trent, Calvinism with all its craggy pessimism and apparent virtuous simplicity. Ronald Knox once contrasted different Christian pictures of salvation. The classical Protestant picture, he said, was of the shipwrecked sailor washed ashore, clinging to a piece of driftwood, but still by the grace of God alive. The Catholic image was of the fine schooner sailing proudly and peacefully into port, by the grace of God, and furling her sails. Indeed, said Trent in chapter 10 of the same decree, we can not only be interiorly justified by the grace of God, and become friends of God and members of his household, we can also grow in that state of justification. The Church prays for this in one of her collects—'Give us, Lord, an increase of faith, hope and charity.' So the Catholic view of the work of grace is basically very optimistic. We can be saved in style.

Chapter 13 of the same decree, however, is about perseverance in goodness. It quotes St Paul when he says to the Corinthians, 'So if you think you are standing, watch out that you do not fall' (I Corinthians 10:12, NRSV) and the Philippians 'Work out your own salvation with fear and trembling' (Philippians 2:12). Presumption is a terrible thing. The first Protestants spoke a lot about their absolute certainty of being saved, their assurance that all their sins were forgiven: Trent was reacting against this. Trent could not foresee that in the twenty-first century the danger threatening us would be not an overwhelming feeling of being predestined to heaven, but an excessively placid, contented and vague notion about the fatherly goodness of God, along with a very diluted idea of personal sin. It won't do, the Council Fathers would have said. Indeed, they would have given us a decree all to ourselves. Sin is a reality, and none of us is immune. Under God we work out our salvation in labours, in vigils, in almsgiving, in prayers and offerings, in fasting and chastity, says Trent. We cannot presume on that fine schooner sailing into port without any effort on our part. We must always be aware that the opposite of eternal salvation remains a possibility. You would need a special and private revelation. said Trent, to know the names of those whom God has chosen and predestined.*

So our moral and spiritual life is a serious and whole-time business, and it deserves our attention. Not in a way which renders us scrupulous and narcissistic, obsessed with details. Not in a way which distracts us from the spiritual and material help we owe our neighbour. No. But it's still a major issue. I want to go to heaven, and it is not yet a done deal. If we are complacent about bad habits which pull us away from God, or about longstanding refusals to forgive which infest our souls like dormant cancers, or about fatally easy lumps of self-indulgence, addiction and greediness, then we are in grave danger. This is as true today as it was in the sixteenth century. Labours and vigils, almsgiving, prayers and offerings, fasting and chastity. It's a language our Martyrs would have understood without any hesitation, and it was because they had these elements in their lives as students here that they could face the scaffold at Tyburn. This was the school in which they had learned to serve God in holiness and justice.

What I am describing is the difference between appearance and substance. The difference becomes crucial after ordination. We arrive in our first parish with money already in the bank, in the sense that many of our parishioners believe that because we are priests we are holy men. We may know that it is not true, but in order not to scandalize the customers we play up to the notion. It is not difficult, after all, to look holy, or to sound holy. The mother asks her daughter on her return from church 'What was the new curate like?' and the daughter replies, 'Oh Mum, he's lovely, he closes his eyes upwards, just like a chicken.' But in our hearts we know that play-acting will not get us through. At the heart of our ministry there must be a relationship with God which is deep and personal, and to which we are faithful, through thick and thin. If I am to be basically a generous man, keeping my temper with

* *Trid.* VI.12.

aggressive tramps, turning out for hospital calls at two in the morning, dealing patiently with aggressively feminist teachers, sitting quietly in the confessional waiting for penitents who do not come, eating the prunes served up by the housekeeper for the fifth time this week, chairing parish or school meetings which go on for ever, preaching homilies which inspire and move my people, being a good confrère in the presbytery and the deanery, then I need to have been transformed from the inside out.

Let's spell it out, this being transformed. Only God can do it. But to give him an entry to my soul, I need to pray every day, in addition to the Breviary, whether the Lord feels easily accessed or not. I need to go to confession frequently and humbly, because this is one of the ways in which I stay close to Our Lord, remain in intimate touch with him. I need to reveal the true state of my soul to another person—a spiritual director, a priest in confession; I need, in other words, to be accountable. This will certainly include my motivation for the things I do; and my sexuality and how I live it; it will involve turning over some stones I would rather like to leave undisturbed. I need to do some serious spiritual reading on a regular basis, not always going for the latest paperback but immersing myself in the masters and mistresses of the spiritual life: Augustine, Bernard, Francis of Assisi, Francis de Sales, John of the Cross, the two Teresas, the Cloud of Unknowing, de Caussade, Catherine of Siena. These writers provide a sort of perpetual current in the Church, like a ring-main, into which we can all plug from time to time. And modern writers too, like Cantalamessa, Martini, Jean Vanier, Jean Lafrance, Thomas Green, Ruth Burrows, can feed our prayer, give it body and direction. I need to have a habit of asceticism, of mortification, of self-sacrifice, of saying 'No' to myself. In this way my life will have a vertical dimension to it as well as a horizontal one.

Gradually the substance of me will be transformed. That's what I long for, that's what I pray for. Gradually I shall become less selfish, less vain, less lustful, less greedy. I shall put clear blue water between me and the horrors with which we started this talk. You might say 'Oh but there's clear blue water already—I would never dream of behaving like that.' Perfectly true. But is the clear blue water due simply to convention and upbringing, or is it because you are an integrally holy and just man? There used to be an acronym to describe certain word-processing fonts—WYSIWYG: what you see is what you get. When the parishioners ascribe holiness to me, when they say 'He is a spiritual man', are they getting what they see? Real holiness involves a certain transparency.

When Jesus talked about being handed over into the hands of men, he had particular men in mind. He had Judas Iscariot in mind, who was an arch-example of not being transparent. His apparent intimacy with Jesus, his apparent affection masked an icy heart and a willingness to betray. 'So when he came, he went up to him at once and said 'Rabbi' and kissed him' (Mark 14:45, NRSV). Jesus had the Pharisees in mind, religious leaders of the greatest propriety, upright and respected men, pillars of the parish, enthusiasts for the religion of their forefathers, who were yet capable of the most cynical contempt for ordinary people: 'But this crowd, which does not know the law—they are accursed' (John 7:49, NRSV). He had Annas and Caiaphas in mind, venerable men looked up to by all true lovers of the Jewish Law, examples of rectitude, but beneath it all clerical politicians: 'You know nothing at all! You do not understand that it is better for you to have one man die for the people than to have the whole nation destroyed' (John 11:49–50, NRSV). He had Pilate in mind, Pilate the ultimate sceptic who didn't believe that truth could be found or pinned down, who was willing in the end to sacrifice a Galilean carpenter to keep his own job and save his own skin. He had the Roman mercenary soldiers in mind, brutalized characters, for whom the slow death of slaves and natives was a commonplace.

How did Jesus feel as the shape of his approaching passion became gradually clearer? The crucifixion of a criminal who had been rejected by the multitude was, for his executioners, carte blanche to be sadistic. No-one would object, no-one would complain. To bring a perfectly healthy man of 33 to the point of death, in the space of fifteen hours, not with a clean bullet but by stages, pounding and whipping and bleeding the life out of him, breaking his spirit with mockery, insult and threat, this would give satisfaction to a certain type of soldier. 'The Son of Man will be handed over into the hands of men.' That is indeed a pregnant phrase.

We begin Holy Week with this two-day recollection, and it has a dual purpose. One is, to quote the old version of the Stations of the Cross, that we may contemplate 'compassionate our Saviour, thus cruelly treated'. The great heart which accepted these awful sufferings for the salvation of the world deserves that our hearts speak out in answer. He deserves that the world march beside him on the Way of the Cross. For these purposes, you and I are the world. We do it with a sorrow and a sympathy which is to a large extent wordless. No words suffice to express our admiration, our gratitude, our sorrow for sin, our desire to show our loyalty and our steadfastness even when others run away. So one function of this mini-retreat is that we have the chance to reflect on the details of Our Lord's Passion, and to let them move us. This is classic Catholic spirituality. Ignatius in the *Spiritual Exercises* would recognize it as authentic.

The other purpose is that we actively seek holiness and justice. Trent talks in a rather ungainly sentence about 'the justice of God, which doesn't mean him being just, but the quality by which he makes us just, so that when we receive it we are not merely thought to be just, but we really are.'* 'Just' in this sense doesn't mean equity in the legal sense, having a finely tuned feeling for what is fair, although of course it includes this; it means rather that, by the gift of the Spirit, we are transformed and become pleasing to God, in ourselves. Colossians 1 says 'He has rescued us from the power of darkness and transferred us into the kingdom of his beloved Son in whom we have redemption' (Colossians 1:14, NRSV). I must actively seek to be transferred, to be renewed, to be converted in my heart. I must realize how vital this is. I must pray for the gift of the Spirit that this may happen. If it has happened, or is happening, I must pray for the grace of perseverance. And in the meantime I must resolve to take my spiritual life seriously— negatively, through calling sin by its proper name, and detesting it and resisting it; and positively, by the quality and the quantity of my prayer, and by my unselfish service of others.

So the burden of this talk is not something creamy-sweet and consoling, nor would you expect it at the start of Holy Week. I would be selling you short if I dished you out a load of platitudes. This is the real stuff of religion. To mix betting and sporting metaphors, we are in the big league, and the stakes are high. We can't keep our faith 'out there', a subject for endless intellectual speculation and discussion;

---

* *Trid.* VI.7.

eventually it has to come 'in here', and the vulnerable, private part of me has to be turned over by it as the soil of a garden is turned over by the spade. Only God can do this. This week, I beg him to do it. Jesus handed himself over into the hands of men, for them to do with him as they wished. Today, I hand myself over into the hands of God, that he may do with me as he wishes.

✥

Passover and Eucharist

The Jews saw the Exodus as the defining moment in their history. It was what made them a nation. The fact that this bunch of people, and no other, was spared when the Angel of the Lord passed over the cities of Egypt; the fact that this bunch of people and no other was led by Moses across the Red Sea dry-shod, and on into the desert—this fact united them and drew them together, in a permanent way. It meant that their children and their children's children, who had not themselves experienced the Exodus, would also have this sense of belonging to a chosen people.

This defining moment they re-lived over the centuries, and still re-live. God's instructions were quite explicit.

> The Lord said to Moses and Aaron: This is the ordinance for the Passover ... It shall be eaten in one house; you shall not take any of the animal outside the house, and you shall not break any of its bones. The whole congregation of Israel shall celebrate it ... If an alien who resides with you wants to celebrate the Passover to the Lord, all his males shall be circumcised; then he may draw near to celebrate it. (Exodus 12:43, NRSV)

> The Lord spoke to Moses in the wilderness of Sinai, in the first month of the second year after they had come out of the land of Egypt, saying: Let the Israelites keep the Passover at the appointed time. On the fourteenth day of this month, at twilight, you shall keep it at its appointed time: according to all its statutes and all its regulations you shall keep it. So Moses told the Israelites that they should keep the Passover. They kept the Passover in the first month, on the fourteenth

239

day of the month, at twilight, in the wilderness of Sinai.
(Numbers 9:1 ff., NRSV)

And then, in Deuteronomy, a development: the Passover is to be kept
not in family groups or private houses, but 'at the place the Lord will
choose as a dwelling for his name' (Deuteronomy 16:1, NRSV). In other
words, the Temple. But the Temple was destined to be destroyed, and in
the year AD 70 Titus destroyed it once and for all: the record is on the
carved arch which marks the entrance to the Forum here in Rome. So
again, the Jews began to keep the Passover at home—in a modified form,
but still recognizably the Passover. When they did so, they believed that
they were re-living the rescue effected by God, all those years ago, when
he brought the people out with Moses at their head. They believed that
the Passover meal, however humbly celebrated, was more than a simple
commemoration. It was an act of thanksgiving, by a whole nation. And
it made the drama present, with them as participants. It made present
the act of sovereign power which made them a people. And so it has
been now for twenty centuries: a durable observance indeed.

The Passover enters our Christian experience too. The Synoptic
Gospels present the Last Supper as the Passover meal, celebrated by Jesus
and his disciples as though they were a family group. St John's Gospel,
on the other hand, puts the Crucifixion on 'the day of preparation for
the Passover' (John 19:14). Whichever chronology you favour, it is clear
that the Last Supper, and Our Lord's Passion and death, both took place
within the period of the Passover feast, and this was why there were so
many people in town when Pilate brought Our Lord out in front of his
palace to say 'Ecce homo'. The Passover is the context for the sufferings
of Christ both historically and theologically.

The animal which, in that paragraph from Exodus I quoted at the
start of this talk, was not to be taken outside the house, and whose bones
were not to be broken, was the Lamb. It was to be slaughtered on the
fourteenth day of the month at twilight, so that its blood could be put
on the doorposts against the hour when the angel of the Lord passed
over Egypt; and it was to be eaten by the family when they were packed
up and ready for the road: they were to eat it in haste, and standing up.
The eating of the Lamb marked the moment of escape, of rescue. When

Moses gave the order to move out, there would be no time to waste.

St John claims that Jesus was crucified at the hour when, across in the city of Jerusalem, fourteen hundred years after Moses and the Exodus, the lambs were being slaughtered. Thus Our Lord is dramatically identified as 'the Lamb of God', just as the Baptist said when he pointed him out to Andrew and the other disciple at the beginning of John's Gospel. Even today at Mass we say, as we hold up the Sacred Host, '*Ecce Agnus Dei*, Behold the Lamb of God.'

Our Mass is grafted into the Passover experience and Passover feast as entirely and totally as, for instance, the Church of S. Maria ad Martyres is grafted into the Pantheon. The same elements are all there. The sacrifice of the Paschal Lamb is there, the Lamb whose blood saves us, and whose flesh feeds us, as he saved and fed the Israelites. The rescue is there. Through the Passion and death of Christ, the Father rescues us as surely as he rescued the Israelites: 'he has rescued us from the power of darkness and transferred us into the kingdom of his beloved Son, in whom we have redemption, the forgiveness of sins' (Colossians 1:13). The thanksgiving meal is there, just as it was—and is—for the Israelites: 'Father, all-powerful and ever-living God, we do well always and everywhere to give you thanks.' 'Eucharist' is simply the Hellenization of the word for 'thanks'. And the past-made-present is there. The *Catechism of the Catholic Church* says:

> When the Church celebrates the Eucharist, she commemorates Christ's Passover, and it is made present: the sacrifice Christ offered once for all on the Cross remains ever present. 'As often as the sacrifice of the Cross by which 'Christ our Pasch has been sacrificed' is celebrated on the altar, the work of our redemption is carried out.'*

There is another way in which the Mass is grafted into the Passover. Remember how in the Exodus instructions there was that one about who qualified to celebrate the Passover: you had to be circumcised. It was, in other words, a domestic feast, one for the household of the faith.

---

* *Catechism of the Catholic Church*, 1364.

We have a similar requirement—you have to be baptized, and you have to be in communion with the rest of the Catholic Church, which for practical purposes means the local bishop, and the pope. Justin Martyr, in the middle of the second century, writes:

> And this food is called among us Eucharistia, of which no-one is allowed to partake but the man who believes that the things we teach are true, and who has been washed by the washing that is for the remission of sins and unto regeneration, and who is so living as Christ has enjoined.*

If you want to concelebrate, well, it's a domestic feast. John Paul II devotes chapter 4 of *Ecclesia de Eucharistia* to the theme of 'The Eucharist and Ecclesial Communion' and he is crystal clear on this point He quotes St Ignatius to the Church of Smyrna:

> That Eucharist which is celebrated under the bishop, or under one to whom the bishop has given this charge, may be considered certain.

And also the 1992 document of the Congregation for the Doctrine of the Faith *Communionis Notio*:

> Every celebration of the Eucharist is performed in union not only with the proper Bishop, but also with the Pope, with the episcopal order, with all the clergy, and with the entire people. Every valid celebration of the Eucharist expresses this universal communion with Peter and with the whole Church ...

In other words, there is an intrinsic link between communion as a sacrament, and communion as a lived experience. When you arrive in your first parish and attend your first clergy fraternal, you will find this belief of the Church is met with blank incomprehension, or is

---

* *First Apology*, LXVI.

seen as deliberate rudeness and insensitivity on the part of the Church of Rome. The other Christians will say to you, 'But we have an open table—why don't you? Isn't this elementary Christian charity?' and you will have a hard job convincing them otherwise. You know and I know that we cannot jettison antique and venerable principle to avoid hurting people's feelings. The principle is that when we celebrate Mass we are celebrating our unity in belief, in doctrine and in moral conduct, and that we hold this belief in common with the whole Church. The importance of ecumenism in the context of modern Christianity and the modern world is enormous. Not being able to invite Anglicans and Methodists to share the Eucharist is for me a constant source of pain and sadness. Being true to principle hurts. Especially when I like and respect the people involved.

We celebrate our belief and our belonging—really celebrate it, not just admit it grudgingly. Along with the death and resurrection of the Lord we celebrate our incredible good luck: we have been blessed by God far beyond our merits, for he has made us members of his Holy Catholic Church. By parental faith handed on, or by a tortuous and lonely road of conversion he has done it. There is motive here for rejoicing. The Church is a mystery of faith, an article of the Creed, life-giving and deep, a potent channel of grace. Why should God have chosen me for the astonishing privilege of being part of it? I don't know, but I humbly celebrate his goodness whenever I put on the vestments or kneel in the benches.

Old men are liable to reminisce. P. G. Wodehouse writes about a golf club where there is a character called 'the Oldest Member', who loves to buttonhole unsuspecting victims and deluge them with memories. Wise members beat a swift retreat when they see him coming, or hear him clearing his throat. But there are times when remembering is good for all of us. In recalling our common heritage we are drawn together. The Eucharist is our common heritage, the vein of gold which runs through twenty centuries of our common history, pulls us together like a draw-string. Young Tarcisius, carrying the Blessed Sacrament to some Christian prisoners in the persecution of Decius or Valerius, was killed because he would not surrender the sacred Host. He was buried initially at the Catacomb of S. Callisto, and then later at S. Silvestro. That's third-century Rome. About the same time Pope Sixtus II was executed for presiding over a liturgy inside the Catacomb: was it Mass? The history does not say. The Catacombs certainly have frescoes depicting, allegorically but surely, eucharistic faith—the fish with the basket of loaves, and red wine in the basket with the loaves; the dove feeding on the grapes. This was their belief and their practice, and these people are our people, even if they preceded us by eighteen hundred years. Irenaeus, the Bishop of Lyons, writing shortly after Justin in the second century, puts up a spirited defence of the resurrection of the body, drawing on eucharistic practice. Listen to him:

> When therefore the mingled cup and the manufactured bread receives the Word of God, and the Eucharist of the body and blood of Christ is made, from which the substance of our flesh is increased and supported, how can they [the heretics] affirm that the flesh is incapable of receiving the gift of God, which is life eternal, which flesh is nourished from the body and blood of the Lord and is a member of him?*

At Ecton Bridge in Yorkshire, they found a secret room in a farmhouse. It had been bricked up and concealed in a terrible hurry with all the equipment for Mass set out inside it, because word had come that old Fr Nicholas Postgate had been arrested on his way across the moors: this was the seventeenth century, and the Catholics were terrified. In spite of his age, the priest was publicly executed, a martyr for the Mass to which he had devoted his long life. He too belongs to us, is part of our ecclesiastical family, shares our faith. As does Archbishop Romero, shot at Mass in San Salvador in1980. The Eucharist gathers us all into a very special family, and our place in time does not matter. Listen to the present Pope [John Paul II], reminiscing:

> For over half a century, every day, beginning on 2 November 1946, when I celebrated my first Mass in the Crypt of St Leonard in Wawel Cathedral in Krakow, my eyes have

---

* *Adversus Haereses* V.2.

gazed in recollection upon the host and the chalice, where time and space in some way 'merge' and the drama of Golgotha is re-presented in a living way, thus revealing its mysterious 'contemporaneity'. Each day my faith has been able to recognize in the consecrated bread and wine the divine Wayfarer who joined the two disciples on the way to Emmaus and opened their eyes to the light and their hearts to new hope.*

W. B. Yeats, in his poem 'Easter 1916', talks of one of the Irish patriots who died in the uprising in Dublin, and says

> He, too, has been changed in his turn,
> Transformed utterly:
> A terrible beauty is born.

We could borrow those words and apply them to the Crucifixion and Resurrection, and their re-presentation in the Mass. Truly, at the Last Supper, a terrible beauty was born. Truly, every time we celebrate the Eucharist, a terrible beauty is enacted, heroism and unselfishness at an unbelievable price. How easy it is for the Mass to become routine, or for us to be caught up in the details of celebration, and ignore the broad sweep of it. Every celebration of the Mass is truly an event of cosmic significance. The kindness and generosity of God is carried to its extreme. We try in our halting words, in our childish word-pictures, to describe the importance of Jesus's death and resurrection. We say that through his death 'the gates of heaven were opened for us'. And we think how long they had been closed: ever since the sin of Adam. What a picture! The news arrives in heaven: 'Christ has died in agony for the sins of all people'. And the great portals, so long hermetically sealed, begin to swing back on their hinges, and the angels look down at this tiny faraway planet spinning on its axis and circling the sun, and nudge one another, and say, 'That's where it happened'. And down here on earth, the great stone in front of

* *Ecclesia de Eucharistia*, n. 59.

the tomb, so close to Calvary, too large for the women to move, is also rolled back. It must have made quite a noise as it rolled back, that Sunday morning. Was there an echo of that noise in heaven? It certainly had heavenly repercussions. Father, Son and Spirit were all involved, all committed. 'Blessed be the Lord, the God of Israel; he has visited his people and redeemed them.' The whole status of humanity is irrevocably altered as we look, in our imagination, into the dark tomb, and detect a movement, and then another, and hear a sound, and suddenly Our Lord is here at the mouth of the cave, coming out into the light, not just a resuscitated corpse, but strong, immortal, commanding, vindicated. The Paschal Lamb was slaughtered at twilight, Christ rises at dawn. Fear not, I have overcome the world. Truly we are the most blessed of people to have such a Saviour.

I have painted the events in naïve and primary colours. But you know, and I know, that the substance is right. And this substance is preserved for us, renewed for us, every time the priest stands at the altar. That terrible beauty is there. The beauty stems from the fact that Christ is light in thick darkness; he is hope when otherwise we would surely despair. He is light and hope because he is truly risen. Ignatius writes to the Church at Smyrna:

> All this he submitted to for our sakes, that salvation might
> be ours. And suffer he did, verily and indeed; just as he did
> verily and indeed raise himself again.

That 'verily and indeed' is there at a pontifical Mass where the pope presides, in panoply and splendour. It is there at a Mass said in a field for the scouts. It is there at the very private Mass of a retired priest in the sitting-room of his tiny flat. And it is there in the chapel of the Venerable English College at 6:45 on an ordinary, a very ordinary morning. John Paul II says in *Ecclesia de Eucharistia*:

> Christ's Passover includes not only his passion and death,
> but also his resurrection ... The Eucharistic Sacrifice makes
> present not only the mystery of the Saviour's passion and
> death, but also the mystery of the resurrection which crowned

his sacrifice. It is as the living and risen One that Christ can become in the Eucharist the bread of life.[*]

Sometimes we come down to Mass with a heavy heart, with anxieties already grinding away apparently with a life and momentum of their own; the darkness of a winter morning seems to have wormed its way into our feelings and our prospects, we have the sense that we have woken up tired and a morning's menu of four lectures does little to raise our spirits. Then we receive communion, the Body and Blood of the resurrected Christ, and as we make our way back to our place we can say 'Lord, you change everything. You are the bubbling source of hope in my life. In spite of all this stuff, which can be deeply depressing, I know now with absolute certainty that the balance is positive, because you are with me and in me, and you give me life.' And thus the stone is rolled back for us, too. The Pope, in the same letter, quotes St Ambrose: 'Today Christ is yours, yet each day he rises again for you.' The Mass puts me fairly and squarely with Mary Magdalen in the garden recognizing the Lord when he says her name: 'Mary!' At Mass he says my name. Let us acclaim the mystery of faith.

[*] *Ecclesia de Eucharistia*, n. 14.

✝

The Seed that Dies

The people of Galilee who came to hear Jesus were, initially, wide-eyed and simple peasants, the sort of people the Pharisees despised because of their illiteracy. 'This crowd, which does not know the law—they are accursed' (John 7:49). So Jesus did not teach the people by expounding the Old Testament, at least not directly. Instead, he spoke to them in word-pictures arising from their own experience. He was a fine example of an inductive teacher, who started from the known and proceeded into the unknown. So we get parables arising from farming and fishery and shepherding and family relationships. Familiar stuff. Familiar to them, that is.

Thus there are several sowing-and-reaping references. 'Listen, a sower went out to sow; and as he sowed, some seed fell on the path ...' (Mark 4:3 ff.). 'The Kingdom of God is as if someone would scatter seed on the ground, and would sleep and rise night and day, and the seed would sprout and grow, he does not know how' (Mark 4:26). 'The Kingdom of God ... is like a mustard seed which, when sown upon the ground, is the smallest of all the seeds on earth ...' (Mark 4:30). 'The Kingdom of heaven may be compared to someone who sowed good seed in his field; but while everybody was asleep, and enemy came and sowed weeds among the wheat ...' (Matthew 13:24).

These parables stand perfectly well by themselves. They acquire, however, a richer meaning in the light of the ultimate destiny of Jesus. In John's Gospel, as his Passion approaches, we find the same sowing-and-reaping analogy enriched.

Now among those who sent up to worship at the festival were some Greeks. They came to Philip, who was from Bethsaida in Galilee, and said to him, 'Sir, we wish to see Jesus.' Philip went and told Andrew; then Andrew and Philip went and told Jesus. Jesus answered them, 'The hour has come for the Son of Man to be glorified. Very truly, I tell you, unless a grain of wheat falls into the earth and dies, it remains just a single grain; but if it dies, it bears much fruit. Those who love their life lose it, and those who hate their life in this world will keep it for eternal life. Whoever serves me must follow me, and where I am, there will my servant be also. Whoever serves me, the Father will honour. (John 12:20–6)

The whole pattern of self-abandonment, of annihilation, of disappearance and of copious reward is there. Jesus gives up his life in order that others may have life. He does not just pretend, go through the motions. He actually allows other men to do away with him, elbow him violently off the surface of this planet, so that he isn't here any more. And in the process of being annihilated, he is glorified. This, the greatest of all paradoxes, needs to be teased out. It needs to be teased out if only because it's going to apply to you and me as well. 'Whoever serves me must follow me'. It is an old gospel tradition that the servant treads in his master's footsteps, like the slave of Good King Wenceslas, and he shares his master's lot. What, then, awaits us if we are faithful disciples? Glory awaits us.

When I was the International Responsible for Jesus Caritas, I had two Rwandan priest friends. One of them was a Tutsi. He was a joyful, quick-witted, highly talented young man of enormous potential. He was very useful in assemblies where we needed to use several languages at once, because while being a native French-speaker he was fluent in English. He had spent two years in a parish in north London and was good enough to do even simultaneous translation for us. (I don't know if you've ever tried this—it is a real skill, being able to take things in through your ears, process them, and speak them into a microphone while listening at the same time to the next instalment). His name was Justin, and he was a great favourite with everyone. His bishop put him in charge of one of the oldest parishes in the country, and they were lucky to have him. When the ethnic upheaval began in 1994, the Hutus came for him, arrested him, and took him down to the police station. He was interrogated there over the weekend, but on the Monday morning, 31

August, they said 'You can go.' As he walked home through the forest with another priest, they came after him and shot him.

The other was a Hutu. His name was Denis. He was the Director of Catechetics for the diocese of Butare, in the south of the country, an older man than Justin, a man of wisdom and considerable organizing skill. During the civil war the Hutus were very much on top, at least to start with. The dangerous people were what they called the Interahamwe militias, the extremist Hutu groups who were bent on genocide, on getting rid of the Tutsis once and for all, because the Tutsis had been favoured by the Belgians in colonial times, as being more intelligent and more able. The moderates were unable to control the Interahamwe, who torched churches full of people and set up road-blocks at which Tutsis were liable to disappear. One of these road-blocks was set up outside Denis's house in Butare. From his window he could see them operating, and one day he went out into the road to persuade them to let some Tutsis pass through. However he was seen from a distance talking to the commander of the road-block, and when the Tutsis finally gained power, he was arrested for collaboration with the killers and put in a prison camp, where it looked as if he would remain indefinitely, probably to die there. As conditions in the camp marginally improved, he became the unofficial chaplain to the other prisoners, in fact a father-figure for thousands of people. After four years he was put on trial and Tutsis actually came forward to witness on his behalf, that far from being a killer he had saved their lives, and even hidden them in his house at grave risk to himself. He was found innocent and discharged. He came to our meeting in Cairo in 2000, and described the whole experience to us. He was like a man who had come back from the dead.

Both of these men were seeds who fell into the ground and died, one literally, one equivalently. They were pastoral priests of great ability and great goodness. Had they been less visible persons, perhaps their story would have been different. They were servants whom Our Lord took seriously, and whom he invited to follow him and to be with him right up to the point of glory. That's the Christian perspective on what otherwise is unendurable pain.

In the John text I quoted a moment ago, the Greeks come to Philip and say, 'Sir, we wish to see Jesus.' And when at length the request reaches the Lord himself, the response seems enigmatic. 'The hour has come for the Son of Man to be glorified.' It is as if Our Lord were saying, 'Tell your Greek friends that if they want to speak to me, they'll find me on the Cross. From now on that is where I belong. The time for consoling tête-à-têtes is over, that was all very well in Galilee, but now my mind is set on my identity as the seed which falls into the ground ... from now on, that's who I am.' And it's true. We can have all kinds of images of Christ, and all of us have our favourite ones: at Cana, at the Samaritan well, raising Jairus's daughter, healing the man born blind. But all these images have a shadow slanting back across them, which is the shadow of the Cross. We can no longer think about Jesus without adverting to the fact that he is the Crucified. That's how he ended up, and all the other things were a preparation for this, and must be interpreted in the light of this.

Just as I can no longer think of Justin without reflecting on his sudden, violent and unfair death.

The seed which dies produces an abundant harvest. The first, and spectacular, element in this harvest is the Resurrection.

> Forth he came at Easter, like the risen grain,
> He that for three days in the grave had lain,
> Quick from the dead my risen Lord is seen,
> Love is come again like wheat that springeth green.

Mark's Gospel describes the women going to the tomb on Easter Sunday morning, and relays to us the words of the young man in the white robe. 'Do not be alarmed; you are looking for Jesus of Nazareth, who was crucified. He has been raised; he is not here.' That's the NRSV version, and when it says 'he has been raised' that's a faithful rendering of the Greek, *egerthe*. Matthew uses the same passive verb. The Father did it, he is saying. Jesus has been raised by his Father. This is a harvest which is pulled out of the ground by the sovereign power of God. If you lay down your life for your friends, your Father will look after you, make you 'quick from the dead', vindicate you, justify you. You can leave it up to him.

I confess that maybe my emphasizing the passive verb is making too much of it, because in Mark 8, 9 and 10, when Jesus forecasts his death and resurrection, he uses an active verb—the Son of Man will rise again, as though he were doing it by his own energy. And in John 10, he says 'For this reason the Father loves me, because I lay down my life in order to take it up again ... I have power to lay it down, and I have power to take it up again' (John 10:17–18, NRSV). This is quite explicit. Christ is in charge. On the other hand, when the primitive kerygma is relayed in the Acts of the Apostles, in chapters 2:3,4:5,10 and 13, the message is always the same: God raised him to life. It's the same when Paul preaches to the sceptical Athenians in the Areopagus: 'He [the Father] has given assurance to all by raising him from the dead' (Acts 17:31). I suppose the contrast is resolved in the sublime relationship of Father and Son in the heart of the Trinity, which is a place you and I cannot penetrate: we are left thrashing about in the semantic undergrowth. Not, then, a thing to get worked up about.

If we go with the idea of the Father as the prime mover in the Resurrection, there is a symmetry. The Resurrection matches the self-abandonment of Our Lord. He is handed over into the hands of men; he is raised by his Father. Philippians says:

> He humbled himself and became obedient to the point of death even death on a cross. Therefore God also highly exalted him. (Philippians 2:8–9)

You see, in each case Jesus gives up control over his own life—to the men who kill him; and then to the Father who raises him. How hard it is not to be in the driving seat!

Now it certainly appears, from the forecasts in Mark 8, 9 and 10, that Jesus knew in advance about the Resurrection—in other words, that even beyond death he would have a life, and identity, that he wasn't going to be simply blotted out. However, from his prayer on the Cross—'My God, my God, why have you abandoned me?' you have the impression that at the culminating point of the Passion this certainty was taken away from him. What we all fear most of all is ceasing to exist: no longer being the subject of feeling or of understanding, because we're simply not there any more. The Constitution *Gaudium et Spes* of the Second Vatican Council expresses this so well.

The enigma of the human condition becomes greatest when we contemplate death. Man suffers not only from pain or the slow breaking-down of his body, but also from the terror of perpetual extinction. It is a sound instinct which makes him recoil and revolt at the thought of this total destruction, of being snuffed out. He is more than matter, and the seed of eternity he bears within him rebels against death. All technical undertakings, however valuable, are powerless to allay man's anxiety; prolonging his span of life here cannot satisfy the desire for a future life inescapably rooted in him.*

I think of the rich people in California who pay to have themselves deep-frozen after death, so that advancing medical science can resurrect them when the research is perfected. These are people who suffer from the fear of perpetual extinction. A large part of the agony of human death is this. At this point we are certainly like seeds that fall into the ground and die. In fact, there is a grim humour which refers to the burial of a body as 'planting': 'We planted old Bill last Tuesday.' If Jesus 'had to become like his brothers and sisters in every respect, so that he might be a merciful and faithful high priest in the service of God' (Hebrews 2:17, NRSV) this anguish concerning death would seem to be an appropriate part of his sacrifice. It would certainly have increased his sense of passivity and helplessness, and it would certainly make sense of all those passages in the Acts of the Apostles where Paul and others proclaim: 'God raised him.' It makes the nobility of his sacrifice all the greater, because what he actually experienced was annihilation that others might live. Seen from this perspective, the Resurrection would have felt like a gratuitous act of generosity on the part of the Father.

An interesting coda to this discussion isn't in fact a coda at all, because the text of it was in fact written before John's Gospel. It is in I Corinthians 15. Paul is reasoning from the Resurrection of Christ to our Resurrection. 'If Christ is proclaimed as raised from the dead, how can some of you say there is no resurrection from the dead?' And then he goes on, 'What you sow does not come to life unless it dies. And as for

---

* *Gaudium et Spes*, n. 18.

what you sow, you do not sow the body that is to be, but a bare seed, perhaps of wheat or of some other grain. But God gives it a body as he has chosen, and to each kind of seed its own body.' And then, a few verses later, 'So it is with the resurrection of the dead. What is sown is perishable, what is raised is imperishable. It is sown in dishonour, it is raised in glory. It is sown in weakness, it is raised in power.'

The bare seed being sown makes me remember old Alfredo at Palazzola, very early on a spring morning, sowing tiny zucchini seeds in a shallow trench. They looked desiccated, light as a feather, and very dead. But he knew that within a matter of weeks there would be a massive result, quite out of proportion to the size of the seed. He would harvest vast zucchini, day after day, and bring them into the kitchen in bucket-loads: the cooks used to roll their eyes heavenwards, and the diet risked becoming monotonous—how many different ways are there of cooking courgettes? It was as if God had brought a prodigal crop out of man's puny sowing. Paul is saying the same about our resurrection. What is buried may be an old and broken body, a worn-out, used body. What rises again is quite different. We talk about the Risen Christ as having a glorified body, and this explains how he, who had been broken upon the Cross, could appear in rooms whose doors were closed, and disappear from the dinner-table at Emmaus. Paul's implication is that we too will share the glory.

Holy Week is a bitter-sweet time. We remember that Jesus had come to Jerusalem aware of the danger. Luke 9:51 introduces this phase of his life in the most solemn way. 'When the days drew near for him to be taken up, he set his face to go to Jerusalem.' The Greek word for 'being taken up' suggests that Luke is looking back on the events that everybody knows by now, and is adding an editorial comment: Jesus was going to be crucified, but of course he rose from the dead and was taken up into heaven. It makes the account more bearable. 'And they all lived happily ever after.' It is *il senno di poi*, being wise after the event. But Luke also tells us that Jesus 'set his face'. The resolve needed to start the journey south, to certain death, expressed itself in a grim determination which spread even to the muscles of the face. The journey south, in Luke, takes a considerable time, and is packed with teaching and with miracles. But the shadow of the Cross stretches back over it. Every step was a step nearer Gethsemani and Golgotha, a step nearer Holy Week. All is done that he may be a seed that dies.

We attempt in this retreat to re-live the events of Holy Week with Jesus. We share in the false hope of Palm Sunday. How fickle the crowd is. How fickle it still is. The young people who turn out, sometimes in a kind of loving frenzy, to see the Holy Father [John Paul II], still have a distance to travel before they can internalize his teachings and accept his moral authority. It is twenty-five years since he went to Galway [in 1979], and said 'Young people of Ireland, I love you!' and they cheered him for a solid twenty minutes. It would be good to know if they are still living their faith in their mid-forties, or whether the tsunami of materialism has swept them away. I have no right to wring my hands in a patronizing way. I share in this fickleness. Cardinal Hume used to say that the Catholic Faith is not an à-la-carte religion, you can't pick and choose what you will accept and what not.

Meanwhile, we see the antagonism between Our Lord and his enemies getting sharper. During the week, between Palm Sunday and Holy Thursday, the scribes and chief priests, stung by his parable about the wicked tenants of the vineyard, 'watched him and sent spies who pretended to be honest, in order to trap him by what he said, so as to hand him over to the jurisdiction and authority of the governor' (Luke 20:20, NRSV). During these days there are verbal fencing matches about the divine origin of John the Baptist's baptism, the tribute due to Caesar, and the wife who marries the seven brothers, and in all these Jesus acquits himself well, he is a match for the hecklers. But this won't save him. The Cross stretches its shadow back over all these things. He may win the arguments, but that's how it's going to finish. The religious authorities have had enough of him, and they have decided to dispose of him. All that remains to be decided is the 'how' of the disposal. That feeling of other people determining our fate and our future, over our heads, as though we were things and not persons, is a bad feeling. We try to share it with Jesus this week. And if it sometimes happens to us in our present life, we offer it to the Father in union with him.

The bitter-sweetness of the Last Supper is so powerful that you can almost touch it. Jesus had real and deep affection for these twelve friends of his. The betrayal by Judas was a true heartbreak. 'Do quickly what you are going to do,' says Jesus to him (John 13:27, NRSV). But the Greek is 'What you *are* doing, do quickly.' Judas has already begun to betray him, in intention, because 'After he received the piece of bread, Satan entered him.' What depth of pain there is in the loss of a friend. Where there was once mutual understanding to a deep degree, now there is cold incomprehension, irritation, offence. It must have shown in the eyes of Judas. 'What you are doing, do quickly.' So, there is a note of deep sadness at the heart of a joyful meal shared by close comrades, by master and disciples. 'I have eagerly desired to eat this Passover with you before I suffer' (Luke 22:15, NRSV). If the Son of God eagerly desires something, it must be very special. Well, we share the meal with him at Mass. It is intensely personal. He desires eagerly to share it with us, really share it, not just go through the motions. How do we acquit ourselves as disciples? In terms of fidelity to him? When I go to Mass, am I prepared to be a seed that dies? Some of them were jostling for position at the Last Supper, Luke tells us—'a dispute ... as to which one of them was to be regarded as the greatest.' Not yet ready, then, to be a seed that dies.

The preliminaries to the Crucifixion are well-known to us. If you saw the film *The Passion of the Christ* they will still be vividly in your mind and imagination. But there is a point at which a frontier is passed, a frontier before which Jesus is seen by the priestly authorities and the Roman governor as a person, but after which he becomes a thing. Until Pilate washes his hands of him, he is still someone you can listen to, ask questions, take into account. A soon as Pilate, to quote Luke, 'hands him over to their will' he becomes a thing, destined for death, whose feelings and sufferings are no longer relevant or interesting. The crowning with thorns, the mocking on the Cross, the casting of lots to divide his clothing, are ways of emphasizing this. To the soldiers he is of no more consequence than an animal bound for the abattoir. Only Mary and the other women, and John, at the foot of the Cross, continue to see him as he really is. Here too, in having his personhood stripped off him just as his clothes were stripped off him, he is the seed that falls into the ground and dies. Do I ever do this to people? Deprive them of their singular dignity by regarding them as statistics? It is fascinating to see how the recent disaster in South-East Asia hit the headlines because so many Europeans lost their lives. If only Indonesians had been drowned, we would be tempted to see them as statistics and not as victims to be pitied.

But the big question I ask myself, as I read John 12, is whether my centre of gravity has shifted, or is shifting, so that I am prepared to give my life in order that others may live. This should be the hallmark of the priest. Am I content to be inconspicuous, unadmired, unpromoted; am I content to live with fatigue and disappointment; am I willing to be in a perpetual minority, and sometimes to be a minority of one ... if it will lead to my people to life, that they may have it more abundantly, that they may have it to the full? This is, if one ever dared to attempt such a thing, a character-description of Jesus himself. This kind of self-denial in this footsteps takes a long time to acquire, but the effort starts here, at seminary ... and maybe here at this retreat.

✝

Stewardship: Personality and Spiritual Formation

Every good bishop and every good pastor dreams of a Church where all the members are committed to true stewardship. The bishops and priests may not actually use the word 'stewardship' for the thing they are dreaming of: but this is what it amounts to. It's a vision of diocese or parish where the laypeople are not passive consumers, or privileged and carping critics, but real colleagues in the work of spreading the Gospel. A diocese or a parish where the members commit themselves, not on a passing whim, but in a serious, dedicated and lasting way, to the common good. A diocese or parish where the members are not on an ego-trip, seeking limelight and honour, but are prepared to share their faith without expecting any glory. A diocese or parish where people are not into false modesty, disclaiming their skills, but are prepared to own their gifts and see them as precisely this—gifts of God, to be invested in his Kingdom. A diocese or parish where the stewards are not jealous of one another, giving and taking offence to and at one another, being unduly sensitive; and where they do not try to collar all the action for themselves.

And the bishop or priest, having dreamed this dream and glimpsed this vision, must say, humbly, that he hopes this for himself, too: that he too may be a good steward. For in this respect he is in no way superior to the men and women in his diocese or parish, and the kind of leadership he displays needs to have all these characteristics if he is to call forth stewardship from the body of the faithful.

My task this morning is to discuss with you the spiritual underpinning of genuine stewardship. And because of what I've just said, I am talking to myself as much as to you. My ministry needs underpinning just as yours does. What I am going to say is born of deep conviction, stemming from five different experiences as pastor, in urban, suburban and rural parishes. When I talk of 'spiritual underpinning' I may leave you a little perplexed. Let me unpack that expression for you.

Our life as Christians and Catholics has a recognizable pattern to it. We are brought up, first of all, to go to Mass on Sundays. I remember an occasion, twenty-five years ago, when the clergy in our ecumenical fraternal got on to what is always a dangerous subject, the question of numbers. Comparing statistics is best avoided—it is not a very ecumenical pursuit—but at any rate on this occasion we fell into the trap. (By the way, the Americans among you may be surprised that in England so few people go to church at all, but that's the case, and these were the levels reported.) The Methodist said that on a good Sunday, out of a town of 20,000 or so, he had a hundred worshippers in his church. The United Reformed minister said he could count on seventy-five. The two Anglican Vicars said they could expect about a hundred each. And they looked at me, and I had to say that I celebrated Mass for a regular six hundred on a Sunday. There was a startled silence, and then one of the Vicars said, 'Well, of course, your people are obliged to come.'

Well, I know what he meant. Catholics are taught to go to Mass, really, as a condition of serious belonging to the Church. It does not depend on how we are feeling or whether it is convenient. It does not depend on the choir singing in tune or the priest preaching a halfway decent sermon. We have a sense of obligation. This has a down side. It means that not all the people in our benches are there out of enthusiasm, bursting to support the parish with their resources and their energy. Just being there may be as much as they can manage. And being there may be more of an outward thing than a deeply felt thing. I go to Mass because I was taught to do this when I was a child. I go because my parents went. I go because I want my children to acquire the same habit. I go because I have always gone, and there is a law of inertia which says it is easier to carry on doing a thing than to change. If we are honest, we have to say that this would describe at least a proportion of our parishioners. Sunday Mass is for them an outward observance; it does not have a lot to do with what is going on inside, in a person's heart.

The same could be said of other traditional Catholic practices, like sending your children to a Catholic school. Parents may do this from a deeply felt certainty that this is the only way of educating their sons and daughters in the love and fear of God. They may, on the other hand, do it out of a vague sense of tribal belonging, and nothing more: rather as people in big cities might support a Catholic football team without ever darkening the door of a church.

So what I am describing is the 'outwardness' of religion. For a certain number of our people (and you will see that I am diplomatically not even guessing at the percentage) this is as far as their commitment goes—they are committed to the visible signs of religion. But the things that move them in their hearts, the things that really matter to them, their real enthusiasms, the ambitions and visions that make their lives worth living, are not religious at all. There is a hollowness about this kind of Church membership, isn't there? Maybe in our days we encounter it less often, for the simple reason that in Europe at least the Catholic 'tribe' has to a high degree disintegrated, and the people who used to conform out of habit have largely faded out of the picture completely.

Well, for a steward, clearly it won't do! If I am going to be a genuine disciple of Jesus, he asks me first of all for my heart. As a disciple I am sold, not on a cause or an institution or a tradition, but on a person, and that person is Jesus Christ, son of Mary and son of God. If I am to be a disciple I must know and love the Master, and my prime motivation must be a burning desire to follow him wherever he goes. I can't throw the responsibility for my faith on to my parents or the pastor or the chairman of the parish council. No-one else can do it for me. My relationship with Jesus is mine, and no-one else's. It is this relationship which will be the motor of my life, the engine which will motivate me and drive me and colour all my decision-making. My skill may lie in one of many directions. I may be a superb money-raiser. I may be a highly competent administrator of parish or diocesan finance. I may be a gifted organizer of the RCIA [Rite of Christian Initiation of Adults], and the means of many people finding their way to the Church. I may be the Choirmaster the parish has been crying out for. But if my heart is not in the right place, none of it amounts to a row of beans, and sooner or later my stewardship will falter.

So what am I talking about now? I'm talking about the 'inwardness' of religion. I'm talking about the spiritual underpinning of men and women who have a practical ministry in the Church. I'm talking about having a proper spiritual life. This means, first of all, being a man or woman of prayer. By prayer I do not mean the recitation by rote of certain formulae. I mean serious, sincere, heartfelt, personal prayer. Personal prayer is not always easy. In order to avoid it we dodge and weave. I know this from experience. I go into the church to pray, and I notice that the altar cloth is crooked, so I fix it. I settle down, and I realize that the sanctuary light has gone out, so I replace it. Then there is a window banging because it isn't properly closed, or a hymn book left out on a seat. It takes discipline to put all these issues on one side and say, 'No, my prime task here is to enter into a loving relationship with Christ: everything else can wait.' There is a hymn which begins 'Be still and know that I am God.' Being still is the hardest part. We are so geared to activity, to achieving, to getting jobs done, to being diligent. Do you remember the story of Martha and Mary in Luke 10:38? Jesus has gone to their house in Bethany. Mary sits at his feet and listens to him. Martha, says Luke, was 'burdened with much serving', and she gets angry at the inactivity of Mary. Doesn't that describe the conflict which goes on inside us when we try to be still and pray? The Martha within us gets restless and says, 'That's enough time wasted—there are jobs to be done here,' and tries to pull the Mary in us out of reflection and listening, back into hard work with measurable results.

If you want your stewardship to be of lasting worth in the Church, you have to learn to be still, to listen, and to waste time with your Creator and your Saviour. You can do it in church; you can do it in your own home. You can do it before the Blessed Sacrament; you can do it in your own study or office or sitting-room with the New Testament open on your lap. The 'how' and the 'where' are unimportant. What matters is ring-fencing the time. The mediaeval monks have a great deal to teach us. Their prayer was composed of what was called, in technical terms, *lectio divina*. This means, literally, 'divine reading.' Reading of scripture, yes, but slow, ruminative reading, repetitive reading. We don't read scripture for information, as we would read a newspaper. We read it because it is God's word for us, because he is present here in his word, waiting to be found. We chew over his word until it is familiar to us, until we have extracted from it every atom of meaning it contains. We imagine the scenes of the Gospel, we place ourselves in those scenes. And then we apply what we have found to our own lives, pleading for the Lord's help in the words we have found. 'Lord, if you choose, you can make me clean.' 'You are the Son of God!' 'Lord, to whom can we go? You have the words of eternal life.' 'Lord, save us, we are perishing.' There are hundreds more texts, one-liners which can carry the burden of our hearts, and express exactly what it is we need to say to the Lord. We bring to him our weak faith, our spotted track-record, our chronic anxiety, our low self-esteem; we bring our families and colleagues who cause us so much concern; and the Church we love, but which can sometimes behave in such an exasperating and scandalous a way. We unroll these and display them to the Lord. And we hear him speaking to us in phrases which are familiar, and which now pack a new punch. 'Follow me.' 'You are not far from the kingdom of God.' 'Peace be with you.' 'Unbind him, and let him go.' If we are faithful to this kind of prayer, we shall mature in prayer. Gradually our prayers of petition will turn into prayers of adoration. Gradually the presence of the Lord will become more important to us than the granting of our requests. This is what I meant by 'spiritual underpinning'. We shall be in a vital, life-giving relationship with Christ.

If we want our stewardship to be of lasting value to the Church, we have to learn forgiveness. Failure to forgive is so often at the root of botched stewardship. How many parishes have been brought to a juddering halt by a quarrel between two leading lights, during which one of them says, in British cricketing parlance, 'If I can't be captain, I shall take my bat and ball and stumps home, and then nobody can play.' We have to learn the charity of Christ himself if resentment is not to poison our ministry. So often there are, humanly speaking, good reasons for resentment. Other people *are* stupid, and lazy, and they *do* fail to keep appointments and promises, and they *do* say unjust and wounding things. Just being a humanly nice guy (of either sex) won't save us from bitterness; it might drive it underground, but somewhere that bitterness will spill over and pollute the work we are doing for God. If however, as Paul writes to the Philippians we 'have that same mind in us which was in Christ Jesus' we shall become good at forgiving, and the old acid will be dissipated. To have Jesus's mind in us means absorbing his word and making it our own. It means forgiving people not because they deserve it, but because they are there. It means forgiving not once, but seventy times seven. It means something else, too. It means having experience ourselves of being forgiven.

The Sacrament of Reconciliation has undergone something of an eclipse, at least here in Europe. One of the reasons, paradoxically, may be that it was too well taught in past decades. Children acquired a rigid, cast-iron set of rules for going to confession, and a rigid, cast-iron set of sins. The list was never their own: it had been handed to them by somebody else, by Sister or Father or a teacher. As they turned into adults they found it hard to escape from that list they had been given at the age of seven or eight, and truly to examine their conscience, with no holds barred. I am not attacking the catechetical methods of past generations—on this I do not adopt any political stance—but I do know from my own experience that they sometimes inhibited spontaneous reflection. The outcome was that when people reached adolescence they began to question the value of the whole operation. They began to question it, too, because what the Church described to them as sinful did not feel sinful at all. In families children had always said to their parents 'Why shouldn't I?' and now, having grown up, they began to say it to the Church as well. And the Church was not always very good at coping with this new phenomenon. She was not used to independent thinkers. So often it was the most inventive and creative people who stopped going to confession, the kind of people, ironically, who make superb stewards.

You and I have to face this problem head-on. The Sacrament of Reconciliation is not just for primary-school, grade-school kids. It is a 'must' in our lives if our Catholicism is going to be the profound, inwardly healthy thing we want it to be. We should never become obsessed by sin, or scrupulous and anxious about it; but we should be aware of it as an ever-present reality, and one which needs periodically bringing to the feet of Christ. 'Lord, if you will, you can make me clean.' We must know from our own experience what it is to have the healing hand of Jesus on us, and to hear him say 'Your sins are forgiven.' We must know the life-giving potential of forgiveness. Then we shall be good at pardoning ourselves.

To make maximum use of this sacrament we need to know how to examine our conscience. Not just to have a hit-list of recurrent sins, but to look back over the past month (or whatever the interval is), remember the events of it, and remember too our reactions. Did I let the circumstances of my life drive me into depression, fury, exclusion of others? Or did I use them to open me to God, as a springboard for prayer, to make me more generous with my patience and our time? The things that happened to me this month—did they draw me away from God, or bring me closer to him? We need to survey not just staccato incidents but also the contours of our life, the geography of it. We believe in a hands-on God. How has he dealt with me this month? What inspirations has he sent me? Did I take any notice of them? Did the Spirit bang on my door unheard, because I was so busy with my own agenda? And are there recurrent traps I fall into when I'm tired or hurt, patterns of behaviour which are destructive and which have wormed their way into my deepest way of being? All this I need to pull out of the bag, like the man in the Gospel who brings out from his storeroom new things as well as old, so that the Lord may bring the laser-beam of his powerful and healing forgiveness to bear on them. If I use this sacrament well, and in an adult way, the consequences for my life and my stewardship will be incalculable. The sensible thing to do is to find a priest who is also a friend, but whose friendship does not block off his priesthood, so that I can talk to him with transparency about anything and everything; and make a monthly appointment with him. Which is exactly the advice I would give to priests themselves, and exactly what I try to do myself.

There is another reason, of course, why this Sacrament is important for a steward. Stewards are supposed to be accountable. They are supposed to report to their employer on the use they have made of his resources. Confession is just this—reporting in, being honest about the minuses, being grateful for the pluses. There is a superficial level on which we revolve through our minds a list of do's and dont's. There is a deeper level on which we read the Master's mind and assess whether we have done, out of love, what he's asking us to do, even if it isn't in any book. When St Paul writes about Christ supplanting the Mosaic Law with the law of love, and changing us from slaves into children of his family, he is really saying to us: 'Slaves carry out the letter of their instructions, and they do it our of fear; children know the mind of their Father, and they do out of love what they know he would want, even if it is not down in black and white.' I need to ask myself on a regular basis whether I have acted out of love rather than fear; whether I have simply kept a shopping list of rules, or whether I have tried to read the heart of God and act on my reading. The Sacrament of Reconciliation, intelligently used, helps me to do all this.

And the final plank in this spiritual underpinning is the universality of your welcome. How easy it is to reserve our greeting for people like yourselves, people of the same race, people of the same nationality or language, people of the same income bracket, people of the same tastes, people who shower every day and change their clothes as frequently as you do. There are enough of these to make you feel good. But they are only a fraction of the human race. The vast majority are not people like us. The vast majority are what we would describe, bluntly, as poor. A vital element in our spiritual life is our attitude to the poor.

I'm talking about how good we are at sharing our resources. We have acquired, over the centuries, the conviction that our property is inalienably ours, and that we must defend it against others even to the shedding of blood. It is not so very long since destitute people in England were hanged for stealing a sheep.

And I'm talking about something even deeper than sharing resources. I am talking about human dignity. Do I accord to the beggar on the street or the alcoholic who sleeps under the bridge the same courtesy that I offer my business colleagues or fellow-parishioners? There may be times when I have no resources to share. But there are never times when I have no smile to share, or no word of greeting to offer. Something of a revolution is called for in my attitudes and my life-style, something counter-cultural and astonishing to my friends. They will not expect to see or hear me dealing respectfully with those they regard as derelicts. I shall not always succeed, especially when I am pressed for time or concerned with other things. But I can try, and whenever I fail I can pick myself up and try again. This too is part of the spiritual underpinning of the steward.

Let me do a bit of summing up. There is a lake in South America called Titicaca. It is between Peru and Bolivia. It is unbelievably high. One of its features is a series of islands, made of reeds: these islands actually float. In the same way, our stewardship, if it is genuine, must float on our spiritual life. It must float on something which is sincere and inward, not just a matter of outward observance. The love of the Lord for us, and ours for him, is the spiritual underpinning of all that we do and all we commit ourselves to. In practice this means a habit of prayer, personal contact with Jesus, sometimes prolonged personal contact. It means forgiveness, given and received, including the Sacrament of Reconciliation. And it includes a heart for the no-hopers, for life's invalids. Our criterion for good work is not just efficiency. It is, as Paul wrote to the Philippians, having that same mind in us that was in Christ Jesus our Lord.

The Venerable Bede tells the story of the conversion of King Edwin in the north of England. Paulinus, the great missionary, arrived at court to preach the Gospel to him, and the king listened attentively. Then he turned to one of his courtiers and said, 'What do you think of all this?' and the courtier replied with a parable. 'Imagine, your Majesty,' he said, 'a banqueting hall, in which the king and his friends are rejoicing together. Inside the hall it is warm, the fires are lit, the oil lamps are flickering round the walls, there is singing and feasting. A sparrow flies out of the dark and the cold into the hall. He stays for a little while, flying round in circles up near the ceiling. Then he disappears again at the far end of the hall, out into the night, and he's gone. That is what our life is like: we come out of mystery into a warm, companionable life, and we spend a short time here, but in no time we are gone again, like that bird, back into the mystery.' The point was, of course, that Paulinus was giving a sense to that mystery of where we come from and where we're bound for. The Gospel makes sense where nothing else can. Stewardship is the Gospel in action, the Gospel lived. It is the word of God lived out, for our bewildered world.

✠

WATER

If you go today to Algeria, you have a sense first of all of danger; then of stagnation. Danger because fanatics may try to kill you simply because you are European. Stagnation because so many people have lived in Algeria and have left behind them signs of creative genius: the Romans, the early Christians, the French colonizers. But the Arabs seem to have generated nothing but a kind of listlessness, and peevish goats, and megatons of uncollected rubbish.

The Arabs are not—or were not—always like this. The height of their civilization was in Spain, before Ferdinand and Isabella drove them out. They had thinkers of towering stature. And an eye for beauty which still takes your breath away. If you go to the Alhambra in Granada, you will see what I mean.

The Alhambra is really a palace, but not a palace as we would expect one to be. The buildings are grouped around gardens, and their dominant motif is *water*. This in Andalucia, which is parched and dry as no other part of Europe: their superb engineers and architects got together, and produced what is truly a poem in water. Delicate Moorish arcades in perfect proportion, flanking tranquil pools of water: pools you could sit beside, and dream. The Caliph, wherever he lived in this vast collection of buildings, was never more than a stone's throw away from exquisite, calm water. At the heart of his estate, where Englishmen might put a croquet lawn, or a tennis court—something where people could amuse themselves and be active and competitive—the Caliph put tiny manmade lakes, with depths you could look into. This at the time of the first building of our great Cathedrals, which are and were poems in stone, and an aid to contemplating the greatness and the glory of God. But it never occurred to our ancestors to construct poems in water.

To have a pool of calm water at the heart of your house is an allegory of the spiritual life. Teresa of Avila is talking about this when she talks of the Interior Castle, and the keep of the castle where the Lord dwells in tranquillity, and to which he invites us. The Castle is made of concentric circles, and in the outer circles there is racket, noise, confusion. The journey inwards is a journey in self-knowledge, and also a test. Are we capable of leaving the racket behind? We resent the racket and complain about it, but are we also in a certain way dependent upon it? I always recall the story of the poor family from the East End of London who won a free holiday to the country, but after three days pleaded to be allowed back home again, because they couldn't stand the silence.

My faith teaches me that God dwells in me. From my baptism on, Father, Son and Spirit have inhabited me. 'It is no longer I who live, but it is Christ who lives in me' (Galations 2:20). 'God has set the Spirit of his Son into our hearts crying "Abba, Father"' (Galations 4:6). 'Those who love me will keep my word, and my Father will love them, and we will come to them and make our home with them' (John 14:23). 'If you hear my voice and open the door, I will come in to you and eat with you, and you with me' (Revelation 3:20). It has been an instinct of Christianity from the very beginning that our relationship with the Lord is not just one of admiration and example, but of symbiosis, of a shared life. From my baptism on I have been, as Peter, says, bought and paid for . I am occupied territory. God lives in me. St Bernard said in one of his sermons: 'God recalls sinners to the heart, and he reproaches them for the errors of the heart, because that is where he lives and that is where he speaks.'

And God is infinitely deep. I never exhaust the meaning of him, the truth of him or the freshness of him. He dwells in the centre of men and women who are limited in all senses. But he is not limited. It is, to return to the analogy, as if in the courtyard of my house I discover a well, and this well has no bottom; you can draw from it all day and all night, and there is always water there, clear and fresh. You can return to it whenever you want. It is an infinite resource. If you wish you can simply sit by it and let your attention dwell on it, dwell on the depth and the richness and the purity which is there at the heart of your house. I wonder if the old Caliphs in Spain did this, sat by their calm, clear pools and meditated on God. Water, in Semitic thought, means life; after all, it is the only thing that makes the desert bloom. And limitless water would be a reminder of eternal life.

When we are taught to pray, we are taught about the Blessed Sacrament as a focus for our prayer. I think this is the most incomparable gift of God to the Catholic Church. The old Curé of Ars would break off in the middle of his Sunday sermon, and turn to the tabernacle, and point to it, and say to his parishioners, 'Il est là!' as if to say 'Why do I go rabbiting on about God, when God himself has pitched his tent among us.' The simplicity of the vehicle of God's presence—a tiny wafer of bread—is like the simplicity of water. And it is an enduring presence, running through our lives in a totally dependable way. I may turn away, do other things, be grossly distracted, live a life of dissipation and sin; but push open the door of the church, and I am back in his company, even after many years' absence. When we started reordering churches after the Vatican Council, some churches moved the tabernacle to a new position, and the priests were surprised at the uproar this produced among the people. In my own case, I moved the Blessed Sacrament to a side altar, and put the tabernacle on a beautiful, specially commissioned pillar of Portland Stone. I did all this with the approval of the diocesan authorities. But within weeks of my leaving, my successor had restored it to the middle of the church, behind the high altar. When you interfere with the situation of the tabernacle, you touch a nerve. Rational explanations are not enough. I wasn't mature enough to appreciate this.

We are also taught to pray with Scripture. Either in a disciplined, Ignatian way, with three points to engage our imagination, intellect and will; or in a less structured way, with a form of *lectio divina* which allows us to read the Gospel and stop where a phrase or word strikes us, and base our prayer on that. We have come to realize that you don't just read the Bible for information. It is a word you make your own, so that the incarnate Word of God will speak to you, make you his friend and his disciple. Rather like the bottomless well, Scripture abounds in meaning for us, and we never wear it out.

Both these forms of prayer—prayer before the Blessed Sacrament, and prayer with Scripture, are provisional things, and means to an end. The end is that that God should dwell in us in all his fullness, and that we should recognize him, and adore and praise him. After all, in heaven there will be Blessed Sacrament and no Scripture—the Reality will replace the sign, and the Author will supplant the book—but the life I share with the living God will continue to be a reality. As we say, grace is the beginning of glory. The divine indwelling in my soul, now, will an enhanced reality in Paradise.

Seen from the garden of Palazzola, Lake Albano is many-faceted. Sometimes it's quite calm. Sometimes it has a gentle ripple on its surface. In storms it has whitecapped waves on it. It is, I know from experience as a student, very deep; you can dive off the bank into many fathoms of water. It is enigmatic, and powerful, and always there, and not always predictable, and it seems to me, cupped as it is by the rim of hills around it, like a parable of God's presence at the heart of me. A much bigger version of the Caliph's pools at Granada. Water is a permanent trigger for prayer.

Experience again convinces me of this. If there is one resolution you need to make as priests it is: that you will have the self-discipline and the maturity to pray, every day, to the living God who dwells both outside you and within you. Make yourself like Mary, Martha's sister. Coil yourself up at the Lord's feet and listen to his voice. Don't let anything pre-empt your right to do this. No amount of work, no number of duties, are entitled to muscle in on your life and stop you praying. If it means going to bed earlier and getting up earlier, so be it. I remember how, at the start of my priestly life, a mixture of anxiety and laziness sapped at my intention to pray daily, apart from the Mass and the Office. The principle had been firm enough at seminary, but then it was buttressed by compulsion. It didn't stand the test of the bracing atmosphere of parish life, and it took me many years to find my way back.

Whether you spend your time working as doctors of canon law; whether you end up teaching in a seminary, or annulling marriages in a tribunal, or serving in a huge parish somewhere, it makes no difference. This element of reflective, contemplative prayer needs to be at the heart of your life, if you are to do any lasting good. All kinds of things will happen to stop you doing this. Fatigue, sometimes. A desire to break with the rigidities of seminary life, understandably. The sheer materiality of life and of people's lives may tempt you to doubt the usefulness of prayer. The transition from seminary to diocese may be quite an emotional jump for you, as it was for most of us. You may be living in a house where nobody else prays. One of the pits which yawns in front of every priest is cynicism. You need to be brave enough and self-directed enough for your faith to overarch all this. If you haven't, grow the muscles now! Make it your habit to open your heart daily to God, until it becomes an indispensable part of your being. When you can't do it in the morning, do it after lunch or in the evening. 'Be elastic' might well be the motto of every diocesan priest. There is a sense in which it doesn't matter much how you do it, or whether you feel you are doing it successfully. Just to make to God the gift of your time is itself valuable prayer: never doubt the worth of it. It will make you a different kind of priest for the people, and they will know instinctively that they are dealing with a man who is reflective, and compassionate, and who knows the heart of God and can articulate it: the best kind of priest.

✝

Indwelling

When a new country comes into the European Union there is a lot of talk about its infrastructure. Are the roads and railways sufficiently developed and in sufficently good repair to take the strain of a twenty-first-century economy growing at full speed? What about the distribution of water, and of electricity? These basics are the things that must be there to underpin any kind of lasting economic success. Well, this talk is really about our infrastructure as diocesan priests. Some things are showy, and attract favourable comment: our organizing ability, our skill at preaching fine sermons at short notice, our sure touch in the school and the hospital. But what lies beneath? Are the foundations solid?

After feeding the four thousand in Mark 8, the Gospel tells us, Jesus 'immediately got into the boat with his disciples and went to the district of Dalmanutha'. Such a simple statement. And yet with such a wealth of meaning.

I wonder what sort of boat it was. Certainly, it was bigger than a little rowing boat from which one might dangle a line; this was a working fishing boat capable of taking a crew, certainly of three or four, maybe of half a dozen. I remember seeing on the coast of Peru the sea-going balsa rafts used by the fishermen there. They were terribly dangerous, and had to be poled through the high seas with a kind of home-made oar. It was not rare for the fishermen to be lost without trace: those rafts were notoriously unstable in the rollers of the Pacific. One of the best enterprises of my diocese in the 1980s was to provide a Peruvian village with twelve tough, safe, serviceable boats, equipped with both sails and engines, which put twenty-four families to work and kick-started the economy on that bit of the coast. These boats were built on the shore itself by local carpenters. I am sure you could have seen the same scene on the lakefront at Capernaum and Bethsaida, minus, of course, the engines. Very probably the boat in St Mark was the same one that Jesus had used for preaching to the crowds on the shore, and from which Peter had then caught the miraculous draught of fish. The disciples, once they had attached themselves to Jesus, seem to have used it constantly to ferry him—and themselves—backwards and forwards across the Sea of Galilee.

The point is that Jesus got into the boat with his friends, and then cast off from the shore: so there he was with this small number of men, un-get-at-able by the crowds, for the time it took to cross the water. They had him to themselves. These must have been the moments of greatest intimacy. We know that sometimes he went to sleep; but there must have been times when they were able to talk, in that easy and casual way which is possible when you're engaged in doing something practical but not too complicated. You can imagine the slap of the water on the planks, the creaking of the timbers, the easy pull on the oars, the desultory conversation which in fact was charged with meaning, and which they would remember until their dying days in Rome, or India, or Armenia, all those years later. They must have been the hours which the apostles cherished above all others. To have Jesus in your boat was really special. I recall when I first meditated on this passage, thinking to myself with a kind of wistfulness, 'I wish I could do that; I wish I could have Our Lord in my boat, so that I could listen to him, let his words sink into me; so that I could express my love and devotion to him without fear of interruption.'

And then it dawned on me that I do have him in my boat. 'I will not leave you orphaned,' says Jesus in the discourse after the Last Supper, 'I am coming to you. In a little while the world will no longer see me, but you will see me; because I live, you also will live. On that day you will know that I am in my Father, and you in me and I in you.' It has been the instinct and creed of the Catholic Church since the beginning that our relationship with the Risen Christ is not one just of imitation, but of symbiosis, of shared life. Here is St Leo the Great, in one of his Christmas sermons—probably in St Peter's—in the fifth century. 'For if we are the temple of God and the Spirit of God dwells within us, what each of the faithful has in his soul is greater than what can be seen in the heavens.' The Jesus lying in the straw in Bethlehem is the same as the Lord who inhabits the human heart. We can find him a surely there as the shepherds found him in the stable. The circumstances of the world we live in, and the shape and style of the Church we serve will change in the next few years, but the indwelling of God will not change. It will be the one constant.

We talk about Christ living in us. That word 'in' can be a distraction. It really belongs to the world of physical objects, where one object can contain and surround another. We use it when speaking of spiritual realities because it's the only language we have. Strictly speaking, Christ is no more 'in' my soul than my soul is 'in' my body. Sometimes we speak of the soul as animating the body, of impregnating the body, of being the life-principle of the body; we could use the same language of Christ's presence to the soul. Pope John Paul [II], in his encyclical on the Holy Spirit, says 'God is present in the intimacy of man's being, in his mind, conscience and heart: an ontological and psychological reality, in considering which Augustine said of God that he was "closer than my inmost being"'. An ontological and psychological reality: in other words, it's objectively true, this intimacy, this shared life. From the moment of baptism, his life and mine are intertwined, so that God is closer to me than I am to myself.

Our understanding of the Blessed Trinity is only fragmentary. In particular, we find it next-door to impossible to comprehend the union and the interaction of the Divine Persons—a union and an interaction so necessary that all the Persons are in fact defined and named in terms of one another. The Father and the Son are known by no other names but those which denote their relationship. The Spirit is, literally, the one ex-spired, breathed out in love, by Father and Son. None of the three is private and apart, although the Persons are distinct. Athanasius could say all this far more eloquently and correctly than I can. My point is that we speak quite loosely of the indwelling of God in the human soul: sometimes we refer to the Holy Spirit, sometimes to Christ; Christ himself tells us that he and the Father together will love us, and come to us, make their home with us. The truth must be that no Divine Person acts or dwells anywhere without the other two. Christ is the sacrament of the Father, and the Spirit is Christ's way of continuing his presence in our world. 'The Advocate, the Holy Spirit, whom the Father will send in my name.' When we try to separate them, earthly-style, we are blinded by the light. So let's not be too worried by what seems like imprecision. It's all right.

> Christ be beside me, Christ be before me,
> Christ be behind me, King of my heart,
> Christ be within me, Christ be below me,
> Christ be above me, never to part.

The indwelling of God in the human soul is something which stems from the Paschal Mystery of Christ, in other words from the first Holy Week and Easter. Paul says to the Galatians, 'I have been crucified with Christ, and I live now not with my own life but with the life of Christ who lives in me.' When we are baptized into the death and resurrection of Jesus there is a quantum shift in our identity. If the sacrament is celebrated by a weary priest at half past two on a wet Sunday afternoon with a congregation more interested in photography than sacraments, that's hard to believe, isn't it? Yet it's true. We are made over to the one who redeemed us. Signed, sealed and delivered. St Paul says 'Your body, you know, is the temple of the Holy Spirit, who is in you since you received him from God. You are not your own property; you have been bought and paid for.' We have to rethink the whole idea of distance. We do not communicate with God across space; he is the medium in which we exist. Spatial similes are therefore bound to be inadequate, but still carry some meaning. He surrounds us as the sea surrounds the fish. Paul to the Athenians: 'Yet in fact he is not far from any of us, since it is in him that we live, and move, and exist.' He is in us, and we in him. Ambrose says 'We must be in God, and live in him and cling to him, for he is beyond all human thought and understanding and he dwells in endless peace and tranquillity' and in the same treatise he says 'We have risen with Christ; we must live in Christ; we must ascend in Christ, so that the serpent can no longer find our heel on earth to wound.' There is in fact no difference between our dwelling in God and his dwelling in us. The important thing is that we have a common life with him. That God should deign to involve himself to this degree with our wayward and insolent race is utterly mind-blowing. It can only be explained in terms of the New Covenant. God is always faithful to his covenant even when we do not keep our side of the bargain. He has given his word, and he will keep it.

Nicholas Cabasilas, the Orthodox theologian who was writing just a few years after Aquinas, is quite dramatic in the way he describes the effect of the sacraments of baptism and the eucharist.

> It is clear that Christ infuses himself into us and mingles himself with us. He changes and transforms us into himself as a small drop of water is changed by being poured into a vast sea of perfume . . . Blending and mingling himself with us in this way throughout our whole being, he makes us his own body, and becomes to us what a head is to the members . . .

> He dwells in us and he is the house itself. How blessed are we in having such a house! How blessed we are that we have become a house for such an occupant . . . Christ is thus actually with us, and penetrates the whole of our being, and occupies all our inward parts and surrounds us.

Prayer, therefore, is not the chancy business we sometimes think. We are not contacting someone far away via a temperamental radio link. He is closer to us than we are to ourselves. That's what baptism does to us. Cyprian says:

> When we pray, may the Father recognize his Son's own words. He who dwells in our breast should also be our voice. We have him as our advocate with the Father to plead for our sins and so, when we ask God's pardon for our sins, let us put forward our advocate's own words.

It's the same idea as the one in Romans: 'For when we cannot choose words in order to pray properly, the Spirit himself expresses our plea in a way that could never be put into words' (Romans 8:27).

Christ is present to us in many different ways. The most obvious one, for a Catholic, is his real presence in the Eucharist, in Holy Communion, in the monstrance, in the tabernacle. We also believe that he is present in the Church, which is his Body; and in scripture. But all these ways of being present are at the service of the one we have been describing, the indwelling of God in the human heart. In heaven there will be no more Blessed Sacrament, because the sign will be superseded by the face-to-face vision; no more need of signs. Similarly, the book will be superseded by the author: no more need of words, if we have the Word himself. The Church which is the People of God on pilgrimage will be the People at its destination, still the Body of Christ, but in the presence now of its Head. However, the presence by indwelling in the human heart will not be superseded. If on earth we have succeeded in living in union and communion with the Lord who has 'taken possession of our souls and made them all his own', the life of glory will be a continuation of the same. The object and purpose of our life on earth is to deepen our awareness of that presence at the centre of our being, and to make everything else subordinate to it. Does this sound selfish? We will find that in the doing of it we are called to care for our neighbour in ways we never dreamed of before. Apart from anything else, we shall see our neighbours in a new light, as people who themselves are Christ-carriers and temples of the Holy Spirit; we shall wish to serve the Lord we find in them. 'Anyone who wants to save his life will lose it; but anyone who loses his life for my sake, will find it.'

St Teresa of Avila wrote in 'The Interior Castle' (*The Seventh Mansion*, ch. 1):

> When Our Lord is pleased to have pity upon this soul, which suffers and has suffered so much out of desire for him, and which he has now taken spiritually to be his bride, he brings her into this mansion of his, which is the seventh, before consummating the spiritual marriage. For he must needs have an abiding-place in the soul, just as he has one in heaven, where His Majesty alone dwells: so let us call this a second heaven.

and again:

> A king is living in his palace: many wars are waged in his

kingdom and many other distressing things happen there,
be he remains where he is despite them all.

That's your soul she's talking about!

I believe that many of our sins stem from our underestimation
of ourselves. Sometimes a priest can undersell his congregation by
preaching homilies which are not just humorous, but also flippant and
shallow, because he thinks he is no good at preaching. Similarly we can
undersell ourselves in our own appreciation. We can feel spiritually
defective, and in consequence lose our self-respect. We can become
cynical about our chance of pleasing God. We can come to regard
ourselves as frauds and hypocrites. A dangerous moment. That's when
sexual temptation can be strongest. That's when we can most easily lose
our temper at real or imagined slights. That's when we can compensate
by accumulating expensive property, or bulging bank accounts. If I think
I am rubbish, I shall not be concerned as I should with spiritual or moral
standards. Well, bad self-image is one of the endemic problems of many
Catholic clergy. This is one of the discoveries of the Ministry to Priests
programme, back in the 'eighties, when we began, in controlled and
confidential circumstances, to share our deeper feelings. Where does it
all come from? From parental influence? From school? From seminary?
From bishops and Church authority in general? I don't know. But it is
an observable fact, and quite honestly an unhealthy one. Somewhere
along the line, not a few priests have received the message that they
aren't worth much.

It isn't only unhealthy, it is also untrue. If the living Lord has come to
inhabit me, as I believe he has, I am worthy of the greatest respect, and
I can walk tall. Out of all the people in the world he has selected me for
this, that I should be his Temple and his Tabernacle. He has intermingled
his person with mine. He has, in a sense, already deified me, so that I
live with one foot in heaven. Baptism, communion, confirmation and
ordination have profoundly changed me. If I could see with physical eyes
the sacredness of myself, it would astonish me, it would take my breath
away. When I find myself descending into despair out of self-dislike or
self-contempt, I need urgently to remind myself that I have permanent
value, and from a source far greater than myself. It may be that in the

years to come some of you will be asked to become bishops, archbishops, cardinals. You will glow in the warmth and the honour of being chosen, however hard the job turns out to be afterwards. But the choice of you for these jobs will be of minor importance compared with the choice which has already been made. You have been picked for intimacy with Jesus, with his Father, with the Spirit; for a friendship and a love and a shared life which goes beyond words. This is the infrastructure of your pastoral and spiritual life. Let me give the last word in this reflection to Jean Vanier, the founder of l'Arche:

> God is not just a power, and energy or a light. God is a person with whom we can communicate and live in communion, a person who can satisfy our thirst to love and be loved; a person with whom we can enter into an intimate relationship. God hides quietly inside each of us. God does not want to force himself upon us or to curtail our freedom. He waits for us to turn towards him opening our hearts to hear him say, 'You are beautiful but you do not know it, or you have forgotten how beautiful you are.'

✠

Thin Cables, Strong Currents

In theology there are some obvious targets. Like Athanasius, we are good at slagging off old Arius. How can he have been so stupid, we think. How could he possibly miss the whole point of Christianity, God really did become man, that is that God has committed himself to the human race by becoming one of us, so that the death Christ died is the turning point for all of us? Surely it is obvious. Silly old Arius.

And yet the Christian belief in the Incarnation is, in the strict sense, scandalous. It is scandalous in that it subjects our faith to strain. The more we learn about the hugeness and the age of the universe, the less probable, *prima facie*, it seems that God the Creator of all this should pick our planet, and our race, for this stupendous advantage. The proportions seem somehow wrong. God is so great, timeless, total, filling all that is has been, is, will be: and humanity on planet Earth is so recent, small, fragile, puny. It isn't obvious at all.

It is the scandal, the stumbling-block, the tripwire which has toppled a lot of people. Religion in general, yes. But to say that God has actually personally become man, without any hedging … that's taking it a bit far. Lots of genial Christians are in fact crypto-Arians and crypto-Pelagians, willing to admit that Jesus is the most sublime of all God's creatures, a really fine chap, and that we should by all means follow his example—within limits, of course—but drawing the line at dogmatic assertions like that of the Incarnation. A bereaved son, realizing that I was down to preach at his mother's funeral, said 'I don't want you to say anything definite.'

It is scandal for many but it is also miraculous, and beautiful, and true. It is in fact God's style, to feed strong current through thin cables. He feeds divinity into the world through the thinnest of cables, through this single man. The relative frailty of Jesus astonishes us. How often things could have gone wrong. The account of Herod's attack on the babies is an example. Life was so cheap and so expendable. Health in the Holy Land was precarious, and there was relatively no medicine. Simply being human, two thousand years ago, was a dangerous affair. And then, the Holy Family was poor, and they belonged to an underprivileged class in an underprivileged province of the Empire, and this increased the precariousness of Jesus's life. The free will of so many human beings could have scuppered the whole enterprise. And yet he was the one who carried our fate in his hands.

God brought about the salvation of the whole human race through this one man, a divine Person with a human nature. All the spiritual gifts we take for granted: forgiveness, grace, the possibility of faith, the repeated inpouring of the Holy Spirit, the Church, the sacraments, the Eucharist ... all these flow through the narrowest of channels, the man Jesus. That's a frail pair of shoulders to carry so huge a load.

Halfway through the Second World War Mr Churchill flew to Canada and made a famous speech, which included these words. 'Mr Hitler says he is going to come to Britain and wring my neck like a chicken.' He paused. 'Some chicken! Some neck!' We say to Our Lord 'Lamb of God who takes away the sins of the world,' and we might add in the same spirit, 'Some Lamb!' The depth and volume of suffering that Jesus must have undergone in his Passion, when you think of what and who needed redeeming, beggars description. The sinfulness of the world is gross. The killing and injustice and the cruelty from the beginning of time, and it's still going on. The sexual depravity since the beginning of time, and it's still going on. The dishonesty and deception, the envy and the spite and the hatred, the enslaving and discriminating, the exploitation of the young and the innocent, and it's still going on. The only one to descend into this cauldron of horror and overcome it, is Jesus. A man alone. The dimensions of the evil he conquered have not yet been fully revealed. Oh, Lamb of God.

And that is God's style. He shares his only-begotten Son with us, gives him humanity so that he can shoulder the whole load, past present and future. It tells us a lot about what Christ is like—the sublimity of his character, the sheer courage of the man, the nobility of his Sacred Heart. But it also tells us so much about the Father. That's the kind of God we've got. When we say 'I believe in God' we're not just saying that on balance we incline to be theists, and to maintain that the universe is created by a supreme intelligence. That's the arms-lengthy religion of the British governing classes and public schools. We are saying on the other hand that we have come to recognize a Father who is so full of compassion and desire to save that he will go these extreme, extravagant lengths to rescue us. God makes himself a thin human cable and carries so much current, precisely in order to convince us how passionately he loves us. The pathos and heroism of Christ on the Cross, his utter humiliation, is the index of the love of the Father for us. If we were speaking of anyone else, we would say this love goes beyond reason, that is love to the point of folly. In the same breath as saying, 'I believe in God', *Dio c'è*, I am adding that God is as unlike me as he can be. Where we are calculating and careful about our love, he is the Prodigal Father, and the human idiom by which he describes himself to me is the Crucifix. The Crucifix tells me as much about the Father as it does about the Son.

And once you have come to recognize the style of God, you can see other examples of it. Take, for example, the selection of Mary to be the Mother of the Lord. The Church teaches us that Mary was a free agent in the Incarnation. In other words, when the Angel came to her at the Annunciation she could have said No. St Bernard has a dramatic couple of paragraphs in which he depicts the whole of creation holding its breath, waiting for her to say 'Let it be done to me according to your word.' If she had said No, we don't know what would have happened. You could, of course, say that she was predestined to say Yes, that God would not have subjected himself to that kind of rebuff, that she was conceived immaculate precisely in order that she would say Yes, because the Incarnation and the Redemption had to happen. You then get into the old arguments about how free will fits in with God's foreknowledge, and compared with descending into that tangle, hacking your way through the virgin jungles of Borneo is an afternoon saunter. Clement VIII discovered this, and tried to stop the argument between the theologians with his document *De Auxiliis*' We have his portrait on the stairs. If you think he looks slightly bemused, now you know why.

Leaving all that aside, the fact remains that Mary's part in our salvation was freely consented to, and that God channelled that huge, vast responsibility through the generous heart of a teenage Jewish girl.

A thin cable to take so great a current. But that is his style. And that is the measure of Mary's greatness, and that is why we love her so much.

Here is another case of God working through what at first sight seems insufficient for the job and incapable of it. It is the 'remnant'. The People of God is built up to an imposing size, but it becomes slack, and sits lightly to its duties. Suddenly it is zapped and decimated, exiled or proscribed by law, and only a faithful remnant is left. From this faithful remnant, poor, obscure, and without resources, God rebuilds his people. You find it in the Old Testament and you find it in the history of the Church.

> Then I myself will gather the remnant of my flock out of all the lands where I have driven them, and I will bring them back to their fold, and they shall be fruitful and multiply. I will raise up shepherds over them who will shepherd them, and they shall not fear any longer, or be dismayed, nor shall any be missing, says the Lord. (Jeremiah 23:3)

And Paul writes to the Romans, quoting twice from Isaiah:

> Though the number of the children of Israel were like the sand of the sea, only a remnant of them will be saved, for the Lord will execute his sentence on the earth quickly and decisively. If the Lord of hosts had not left survivors to us, we would have fared like Sodom and been made like Gomorrah. (Romans 9:27–9)

This capacity of God to work through a tiny rump-end of his flock is part of the mindset of the Jewish people. And we can see the same thing in Christianity. In the early days of the Church, the areas of present-day Turkey, Egypt, Tunisia, Algeria were strongholds of the faith. Giants like Cyprian, Athanasius, Augustine flourished there. Islam has changed all that. Now you have a tiny remnant, largely made up of expatriates. But the Church lives with hope. Charles de Foucauld devoted his life to the dream of converting the Sahara not by preaching but by being Christlike in the midst of the Islamic millions. He lived with hope. The tiny Church in Algeria today, which has recently seen the massacre of a bishop and a whole community of monks, still lives with vibrant hope. It is the Christian way.

In the seventeenth and eighteenth centuries the Catholic community in England sank to an all-time low, as much because of financial laws and social exclusion as anything else. Old Challoner stuck it out in London for forty years, serving a minute and divided flock, being bishop and parish priest at the same time, hearing confessions in his house and celebrating Mass over a pub, managing to survive events like the Gordon Riots, and living in hope. Because he did that, Catholic Emancipation actually meant something when it came in 1829, and the influx of the Irish after the Potato Famine from 1846 on found the framework of a Church on to which to graft itself. The remnant had held the fort. God had worked through a handful of people. It is his style, it is his way. And when we look at the state of the Catholics at home in our own day we have to ask ourselves questions about a leaner, stronger Church to come. Is it going to be a remnant of faithful believers? Are we going to lose hundreds of thousands to the consumer society, or to the sheer inconvenience of practising the faith at a distance because of the shortage of priests? It is quite possible. But even if we become a tenth of our present size, the power and the life of the Risen Lord will be at work in the community, and will in its own time radiate out again. Strong current, thin cable.

And there is a fourth example of a strong current passing through a thin cable, and that is you. As a priest, you are going to preach homilies which will cause people to change the direction of their lives. You are going to grant absolution to people in confession and flood their souls with the renewing grace of God. You are going to come to the bedside of the dying and be the midwife who ushers them into eternal life. You are going to re-present the sacrifice of Calvary on the altar of your parish church. You are going to do incredible things, and you are a very frail and thin cable, but God has chosen you, and he will enable you to sustain the charge. None of this will be of your own making, and if you try to take the credit for it you will pollute the results. The greater the work God accomplishes through us, the humbler we should be. All of us with a few years under our belts have had odd occasions of success, where we have had to say in all honesty, 'I don't know how that happened.' Or, like the psalm, *Non nobis Domine, non nobis, sed nomini tuo da gloriam.* 'Not to us, O Lord, not to us, but to your name give glory' (Psalm 113B/115).

> We have this treasure in clay jars, so that it may be made clear that this extraordinary power belongs to God and does not come from us. (II Corinthians 4:7)

The older versions of the New Testament talk about 'earthenware vessels'. The longer I live, the more earthenware I feel, and paradoxically the more aware I am of the good God does through me.

When we go on pastoral placements, and when we turn up at pastoral classes on Monday nights, we are, so to speak, learning the tricks of the trade, and that's important and not to be despised. But the main body of preparation, for being a thin but reliable cable, takes place over the whole of the six or seven years we spend here, not just in the summer or on Mondays. During these years we learn patience, for example with the early time for rising. During these years we learn how to cope with the uphill trudge of study, and with the frustration that comes from doing it in a foreign language and being examined by foreign professors. During these years we learn how to do house jobs with patience and humour, we learn in other words how to deacon. During these years we learn to know ourselves, our fault-lines, our sinfulness, and begin at least to lay the axe to the root of the sinful tree within us. Here we are honed and sharpened, shaped and stretched. We learn humility, and the value of kindness. Think of all this as the forging of a cable which, while slender, is immensely strong, and ready for the job it will have to do. The Divine Craftsman is beavering away, reconstructing you for his own purposes. None of it is wasted—the boring bits, the dramatic bits, even the despairing bits.

There is a paradox about our training. We are pretty brainy when we arrive. We spend six or seven years becoming brainier. All that stuff we learn at the Greg and the Angelicum, all the finesse of philosophical and theological thinking. But all the time we are aware that this will not, by itself, equip us to energize the People of God. Here is Paul to the Corinthians.

> When I came to you, brothers and sisters, I did not come to you claiming the mystery of God to you in lofty words or wisdom. For I decided to know nothing among you but Jesus Christ, and him crucified. And I came to you in weakness and in fear and in much trembling. My speech and my proclamation were not with plausible words of wisdom, but with a demonstration of the Spirit and of power, so that your faith might rest not on human wisdom but on the power of God. (I Corinthians 2:1–5)

If my evangelization and my catechesis rest solely on my own acquired expertise or on the undoubted charm of my character, if I am smug, I shall be a lousy cable, and the current will not get through. If God is to use me I must be a pliant tool in his hand, not asserting myself, not pushing myself. As I never tire of saying, this is not a p.l.c. we are running, it is the People of God once more trekking through the desert, relying not on what Moses could provide, which was nothing, but on the manna and the water from the rock which came directly from God. That People was a thin enough cable, and at times it looked as if it had come apart: think of the episode of the Golden Calf, when even Aaron faltered. You wouldn't have put your money on the Jews at that point. And yet the cable held, they made the Promised Land, and they wrote the scriptures, and produced the family tree from which, in the fullness of time, Christ would spring, and through them immeasurable blessing has come down to us. The same will be true of your work, if you remain stable and faithful, and put your trust in the living God.

✛

CELIBACY

You sometimes come across priests of long standing who say to you, with a kind of savage relish, 'Celibacy was never mentioned in my seminary'.

What are they implying? First, that the people who ran my seminary were so lily-livered, or so unintelligent, that they couldn't tackle the subject, didn't know how to do it. Silly old Catholic Church, they're saying, muddling through as usual without any planning, hoping that things would be all right. And secondly, they're saying 'I had to discover and work it all out for myself, because there was no help available. Aren't I good?'

I can't remember whether Fr Alfred, the Passionist who came here to talk to us on Fridays in the fifties, ever talked about this. I presume he must have done so. But overall, in my time, the tendency was not to repeat what everyone knew. It was presumed that everyone knew that priests couldn't get married, and that they were not supposed to have affairs, and that all this was morally binding in a grave way. But we were inhibited by embarrassment, and it could all have done with a bit of spinning-out. If everything is left to Greg lecturers and Vatican documents, what is propagated will be a lofty and inspiring formula, but will it touch the reality of how we feel and live?
So let's have a crack at this tonight.

Celibacy makes no sense unless you see it in the context of poverty and obedience. It is more than just switching off the tap of sexuality. It is part of our discipleship, and thus a very personal thing, centred on and dedicated to the person of Jesus, whose disciples we are. We model ourselves on him in his single-mindedness. Just as he was single-mindedly devoted to his Father and to his Father's will (let this chalice depart from me, but not my will but thine be done), just as he had no place to sleep while the foxes and birds had dens and nests, we too try to live obedience and poverty. The fact that Jesus lived a life of virginity was connected to his obedience and his poverty. So will ours be. Celibacy looks odd if a priest is compensating for it by a lavish lifestyle, and it also looks odd if he is conducting campaigns against his parish priest or his bishop. It may be worse than odd, it may be paper-thin, or even a pretence. Our attempt at holiness is a seamless robe, and the bits are interdependent. So when we embrace obedience, we are protecting our celibacy. When we align ourselves with those who live simply, we are protecting our celibacy.

For a very long time now it has been demanded of deacons and priests in the Latin Rite that they remain celibate. The main reason is a spiritual one. We believe that if a man guards his heart from earthly commitment, it will be freer to turn to God. We say this without any prejudice, and we fully recognize the excellence of the ministry of clergy in reformed churches who are married, and of course of Greek Catholic priests as well, not to speak of our own men who came from the Church of England in the 1990s. I imply no criticism of any of them. Indeed, there is an unspoken affinity between the two types of faithfulness, faithfulness in marriage and faithfulness to a celibate commitment: each certainly understands what the other is about. But virginity is a liberating thing, enabling us to centre our affective life on the Lord. Just as Jesus lived his earthly life without taking a partner, and was thus able to place his heavenly Father at the very centre of his life, pouring out his heart to him, sensitive to his Father's will, so it is with a man who is celibate for the sake of the Kingdom. And it is important, in fact vital, that a priest have this relationship with God. Our task is to lead men and women to God. To do this, we need to place God unambiguously in the first place, to make him the Beloved of our youth, of our middle years and of our old age. *Dio c'è*, say the graffiti on the bridges, God is there, God is real, you can't have a religion or an apostolate without God at the heart of it. Priesthood at the end of the day is not calm or cool, it is passionate, both in its love of God and its care for the people. Celibacy and virginity are passionate commitments, positive things, not just doing-without.

The Church does not demand of us that we seal off our loving capacity, that we become dry and crusty bachelors. Listen to John Paul II in his first encyclical.

Man cannot live without love. He remains a being that is incomprehensible for himself, his life is senseless, if love is not revealed to him, if he does not encounter love, if he does not experience it and make it his own, if he does not participate intimately in it.*

Celibacy frees me to love, to devotion, to self-gift. Read the poems of St John of the Cross, and appreciate how deeply the heart can be involved with God. The translation I'm about to quote does not succeed in conveying totally the vibrancy and depth of the original Spanish, which has all the abandonment of the Song of Songs in the Old Testament.

> O living flame of love
> Most tenderly you prove
> The hidden depths of meaning in my heart.
> Since you continue still,
> Then finish, if you will,
> And break the threads which keep us now apart.
>
> Where secretly you rest
> Alone within my breast,
> What gentleness and love you bring to me!
> What spirit of sweet pleasure
> You give in fullest measure
> Goodness and glory fill me joyfully!†

While our love of God is not a physical relationship, it is still a deeply affective one, an affair of the heart.

We live out our love of God by praying. There is an intimate connection between our prayer and our love. Our constancy in prayer, our determination to be there for God, is in exact parallel to the faithfulness of a husband. Our patience in prayer, when we feel we are in a bit of a desert, is in exact parallel to the patience and comprehension

---

* *Redemptor Hominis*, n. 10.
† *Poems of St John of the Cross*, tr. Kathleen Jones: 'Songs of the Soul', III.

of a husband whose wife is not, for the moment, responding to him. Our trust in God, when we pray, is the exact parallel of the implicit confidence husbands and wives in good marriages place in one another. Our contentment to dwell in silence with God is the exact parallel of the contentment of elderly married couples who can sit by the fire together and not talk, and still be supremely happy. The late Pope [John Paul II] used to talk about the 'spousal relationship' which exists between the Church and Christ, and between the individual soul and the Lord who made us and saved us.* As a priest I am, so to speak, married to the Church, which is the Body of Christ, the living Jesus. And I live and work in the Church which is the Spouse of Christ, personifying her presence in the world. It is hard to imagine a celibate priest who does not pray, over and above the Divine Office and the celebration of Mass. When we pray we are exercising the loving part of us. There is a direct connection.

Now the implication of celibacy is that it means celibate *chastity*. Some might say that celibacy simply means that priests don't get married, don't have marriage certificates, haven't contracted a legal bond. This is entirely to miss the point. The point is that we renounce sexual intimacy in order to relate more intimately to God. We make what seems a prodigal, crazy sacrifice, the sacrifice of sexual union, as a sign that we really care about God to the depths of our being. It is one of the few powerful signs left, in a world which has become largely deaf and blind to symbol. Our celibacy, honestly lived, is still an affront to the civilization we belong to, it brings men up short. That's why people attack it. There is no more potent way of showing the world we believe what we say, that God is the God of love, and supremely lovable in himself. Your celibacy and mine are signposts to another world, the world of the Kingdom.

We know about the recent Vatican document on homosexuals in formation. There are two issues here. One is the Church's belief that homosexuality cannot be accorded the same dignity or legitimacy as heterosexuality. The other is the beauty and importance of celibacy, but yes, also its imperative importance for us—and for some people,

* *Pastores Dabo Vobis*, n. 22.

its extreme difficulty. It is right and proper that the Holy See should draw the lines in the way it has. The present secular climate in Western Europe is so deceptive. It tends more and more to depict sexual activity, of whatever orientation, as normal, and a human right. Well, when we are ordained, we renounce that right. In the face of this, the Church needs to state unambiguously where the lines of acceptability and non-acceptability lie. It is an unworthy wriggle to claim that celibacy doesn't apply to homosexuals—of course it does. And if our inclinations, straight or gay, tend to be overwhelming, or if they are going to colour the way we deal with our people, then priesthood is not going to be our thing. It is fair to point out, at the same time, that there are many men whose feelings might incline them to people of the same sex who live chaste, honourable and fruitful lives as priests. This is the truth as it is on the ground. To live the spirit of celibacy we have to be generous, and this is true whether we are straight or gay. If we say 'yes' to celibate chastity, whoever we are, we are with a whole and generous heart renouncing the prospect of physical intimacy. When the document talks about 'deep-seated tendencies' it is asking the question and launching the challenge: can a particular person, with a whole and generous heart, live a chaste and continent life, honestly and peacefully?

By embracing celibacy we are also renouncing the things which are a caricature and a debasement of human sexuality. When it comes to keeping your mind and your heart unpolluted, these are difficult days. It isn't that we go out in search of stimulation, but rather that it comes in search of us. If our great-grandfathers were gravely disturbed at the sight of a chorus-girl's ankle, they would have apoplectic fits at what's on display in 2006. It sometimes helps to imagine yourself swimming in a very dirty canal. If you have to do it, you do it; but you keep your mouth shut and swallow as little of the water as possible. These days the canal *is* very dirty. We get accustomed to it because this is the world we have grown up in. I think our modern childhood and adolescence coarsens us, hardens us, makes us unconscious of the sort of world we're living in. Everything—billboards, television humour, advertisements of all kinds, so-called quality newspapers—everything has this erotic overload. Sex is part of the air we breathe. The aim of the propagators is not to help you relate better to someone you love deeply. The aim is to make you a fantasist, living your sex life inside your skull. It's aimed at giving you habits you would rather not have. Listen to Raniero Cantalamessa on habits.

> A habit is like a vampire. The vampire—at least according to what is believed—attacks people who are asleep, and, while it sucks their blood, at the same time injects a soporific substance which makes sleep even lovelier.*

The internet has thousands of degraded and degrading sites, and they are designed to make us habitual and compulsive clients. There is no point in getting twitchy about it, but we should recognize what has been done to our world, and to our people.

You and I, as priest or priests-in the making, do need to reflect on all this objectively, because it is going to be a major factor in the spiritual life, or lack of it, of the youngsters we care for. Contemporary society has fallen into an unhealthy way-of-being, and we don't have to accept it passively or uncritically. It doesn't have to be like this. I think about myself, in the sense that I have to model purity and chastity for my people. For their sake I stay on my guard. If I were to surrender to this wretched culture of artificial stimulus and kneejerk reaction, I would be immeasurably a poorer man. I'd be allowing myself to be controlled from outside myself, to have my strings pulled like a marionette. I'd be permitting myself to be tied hand and foot, by agencies who, to say the least, do not have my best interests at heart. That's not the pattern to portray.

You see, real freedom is not freedom to do whatever I feel like; that kind of freedom can land me up in the deepest dungeon, spiritual and physical. Child abusers claim this spurious kind of freedom. It is in fact a short cut to captivity. No, real freedom is freedom to grow to true greatness, to reach my full potential as a child of God and a self-respecting human being. The present Pope [Benedict XVI], in a recent homily, spoke eloquently about freedom. He described original sin like this:

---

* Commentary on Mark 13:33–7.

Man lives with the suspicion that, if he loves God, that will create a dependence, and he feels that if he is to be truly himself he must get rid of this dependence. Man does not wish to receive his existence and the fullness of his life from God ... Man does not want to trust love, which seems unreliable. He counts only on knowledge, because knowledge brings power, and he is intent upon power rather than love, since if he has power he can independently take charge of his own life.[*]

Only love, he says, can lead you to true freedom. Here's this old university professor, Benedict, actually telling us that love is more important than knowledge. Knowledge brings power, or the hope of power. Think of original sin. The fatal tree was the tree of knowledge, of good and evil. It'll make you like God, said Satan. But taking the fruit didn't bring freedom to poor Adam. Nor will satisfying curiosity throughout internet porn help the youngsters in my parish.

So yes, we need to reflect on the situation as it affects our people, our parishioners. The decency and the innocence of lots of our teenagers is being destroyed by unscrupulous merchants of what is degraded and subhuman. It is a spiritual challenge to us. We wonder why people stop coming to Mass, why vocations are so few and far between. Here, in part at least, is an explanation. Things of the spirit lose their taste and flavour when our senses are assaulted by heavy doses of in-your-face sexuality. We need to be fearless in identifying for our folk where the spiritual dangers lie. The incitement to act badly is enormously strong. Without seeming prudish or old-fashioned, it is vital that we help them recognize their right to personal freedom, just as we would if people came peddling drugs in the playground of our school.

All this is stirring stuff. The fact remains that the sexual battle is notoriously hard, and we must be prepared for repeated falls and disappointments, in ourselves and in others. Celibate chastity is a gift bestowed by God on some, a grace, not just an obligation; and in the spirit of gift and grace it is vital for us to be merciful to ourselves, to

* Homily for the Immaculate Conception, 8.12.05

encourage ourselves as one day we will encourage those who come to us in confession. It would be wrong if this talk were to send you away with a heavier heart than you had when it began. That is far from my intention. God is so kind, so understanding, and we must be kind and understanding in his name, both to others and to ourselves. We must have great and intuitive fellow-feeling for one another in our fragility. Our sexual story is not a thing we easily share with other people, and sometimes it becomes a very private misery. Our growth into mature celibacy, our response to and acceptance of the gift, may be slow. From this point of view, simply being alive is like dwelling on the top of a volcano, with all its violence and unpredictability. It reminds me of the limerick about the young lady from Riga who went for a ride on a tiger. But God is ultimately stronger than the volcano, and stronger than the tiger. You can be sure that no-one remains untouched by temptation, and no-one can say with his hand on his heart that he has never felt lonely, never longed for the intimacy of sexual union. It doesn't all have to be spelled out. If we can live fraternity, which means a loyal, unsentimental and deep support for one another, we make one another's cross easier to bear. Yes, we have to be morally sure before we offer ourselves for ordination that we can live a continent life. But we share the human condition, and it is right that we should show care for a brother, especially when he is clearly feeling low. One of the ways in which the Devil depresses us is by making us feel alone.

Here is John Paul II in his post-Synodal document *Ecclesia in Europa*, back in 2003. He sums up everything I've been trying to say.

> Priestly celibacy ... stands out as the sign of hope put totally in the Lord. Celibacy is not merely an ecclesiastical discipline imposed by authority; rather it is first and foremost a grace, a priceless gift of God for his Church, a prophetic value for the contemporary world, a source of intense spiritual life and pastoral fruitfulness, a witness to the eschatological Kingdom, a sign of God's love for this world, as well as a sign of the priest's undivided love for God and for his people.[*]

---

[*] *Ecclesia in Europa*, n. 35.

✠

Choosing Christ

Such a title for a reflection suggests the worst excesses of the evangelical movement. But the theme is pure Catholicism, and is lifted from the *Spiritual Exercises* of Ignatius Loyola.

Infant baptism has been the mind and policy of the Church for many centuries. It has many advantages. But one of its disadvantages is what you might call 'going through on the nod.' Someone who is introduced automatically to the sacramental life of the Church may never have been evangelized. This was notoriously the case in South America, where the Spanish and Portuguese Friars christened hundreds of thousands of babies, but never had the manpower to educate them in the Faith. Think of Francis Xavier in India ...

Everybody should have the chance to choose Christ, so that their Christian life is more than lip service or tribal adherence. Each man and woman needs to realize: Christ is alive, and active, and responsive, and he is close to me. He invites my loyalty and love. This need not be sentimental or frothy. It can be quiet, dogged and undemonstrative. English people recoil from fuss, and are easily embarrassed, and have a finely tuned sense of the ridiculous. But it must be deep and non-negotiable. Charles de Foucauld, describing the moment of his conversion, said:

> As soon as I believed that there was a God, I understood that I could do no other than to live solely for him: my religious vocation dates from the same moment as my faith: God is so great! There is such a difference between God and all that is not him.

And Adrienne von Speyr, in *They Followed His Call*, said:

That which is superfluous is excised and the essential is chiselled to a clean shape. In this process, a person may experience his existence in a new way, from the bottom up. Because of God, revaluations may now take place that are fundamental for all human life. The essential is separated from the unimportant in a way which is God's and which a person would never have attained on his own.

Ignatius in the *Spiritual Exercises* draws on his military experience and allows us to view a field of battle, with the exposing armies drawn up: the smoke and the din and the stench of Satan's army, and the calm, confident courage of the followers of Christ. The flags (the 'standards') are unfurled, and you have to decide: which army will I join? Being neutral is not an option. Joining one army or the other involves swearing fealty to your commander, and being prepared to fight on his behalf. It may not be a walkover. It may be tough. But the first step is committing yourself. It would be tragic to go all through life without ever having made a commitment.

Ignatius is saying, 'It's time to choose!' Maybe you have never chosen explicitly before, but have simply been swept along by events and preferences. But now I choose Christ, with all that this entails.

He said to him the third time, 'Simon, son of John, do you love me?' Peter felt hurt because he said to him the third time 'Do you love me?'. And he said to him, 'Lord, you know everything. You know that I love you' (John 21:17).

I am old enough to work out the implications for myself. I choose him not just because I am spoiling for a fight, but because he offers me more than leadership. He offers me himself, in intimate love and friendship. I am not just saying 'I like his style' (although I do) as if the Christian life were simply a question of good example to be followed. I choose him because he will be power and life in my life.

Intimacy is on offer if we opt for Christ. John Paul II said in one of his first encyclicals 'Man cannot live without love'. Here is a quotation from Bl. Elizabeth of the Trinity, a Carmelite who lived at the same time as Thérèse of Lisieux and who, like her, died young:

Let us live with God as with a friend, let's make our faith living so that we communicate with him whatever happens, that's what makes people saints. We carry our heaven within us, because he who satisfies those who are glorified in the light of the (Beatific) Vision, gives himself to us in faith and mystery: it is the same Lord.

In the context of priesthood-in-view, the Two Standards could well be two ways of living out our vocation. We have seen them both. We have seen laid-back and cynical priests, who have had a standard of living much above that of their people, who have not bothered to preach with conviction, who have kept office hours, who have been frankly lazy and unhelpful. They have been like the bad shepherds in Ezekiel and St Augustine, exploiting their sheep for their own advantage. And we have seen (thank God) priests who have been caught up by the Gospel, who have been unselfish, whose celebrations of Mass have been an inspiration, who have been constantly good-tempered, humble and approachable. They have lived not in abject poverty, but with a certain simplicity of life which left no room for jealousy or criticism. Which style of priesthood do I plan to make my own? If this December I am offering myself to the Church as a serious candidate for priesthood, the Church might say to me 'What sort of priesthood?' And the reply, stemming from this retreat, should be 'The kind of priesthood which makes me an *alter Christus*, devoted to God and my people, and forgetful of my own selfish interests.'

Scripture for reflection
    Deuteronomy 30:19–20
    Psalm 15/16
    John 6:66–9
    Acts 2:37–42

✠

Dawning Realization

We have an expression in English, 'dawning realization'. It can be a sinister thing. It can mean that in stages I come to realize how badly I have behaved, what damage I have done, what I have to repair. Or it can have a joyful sense: gradually I come to appreciate how lucky I have been, what a narrow escape I have had, what happiness the future now holds. If you look at the small group of Christ's followers after the Resurrection, this is what you see—dawning realization. Even for the most pessimistic and depressed. Jesus is actually alive again. It goes against all probability. No-one could have been more dead than he was on the Cross. No-one could have been more buried than he was in the tomb, with the rock rolled over the entrance. And yet, against all probability, here he is.

So we join the eleven disciples in the Upper Room. What is going through their minds? First, apprehension that the High Priests and the Roman army may come for them as well. So they are living on their nerves. Second, total confusion about what has happened to Jesus. These incredible reports keep coming. The women who went to the tomb and met Jesus. Mary Magdalen who says she has met Jesus. The two men on the road to Emmaus who say they spent the day with him, and recognized him at the evening meal. Surely they must all be hysterical, imagining things. Thomas in particular is the down-to-earth, commonsense disciple. Of course he has not risen from the tomb. Whatever he may have promised while he was still alive, that is simply impossible. It would be nice if it were true, but … come on, we must face facts. We can imagine ourselves in the same situation.

And now, suddenly, he is here. No sound of a door opening or closing, no advance warning. The simple fact. He is here in the midst of them. And here with words of reassurance. The disciples all have uneasy consciences, especially Peter. But Jesus's first words are so reassuring:

'Peace be with you!' and 'Why are you so agitated, and why are these doubts rising in your hearts? Look at my hands and my feet. Yes, it is I indeed. Touch me and see for yourselves.' Not a word of blame or reproach. 'You let me down. You abandoned me when I needed you most.' None of that. Simply renewing the old, intimate relationship. The Gospel says 'They stood there dumbfounded.' And yet it is of these eleven dumbfounded men that Jesus plans to make apostles for the conversion of the world.

Jesus is like that with us as well. We too have uneasy consciences from time to time. We too can be full of doubt: we let the unbelieving world get to us. When it comes to our religion we can be dumbfounded and confused. But he comes to us, and takes the initiative, again and again, in renewing the old, intimate relationship. He comes to us in communion, and binds us to himself with so much affection. He overlooks our bad track record and says 'I am the vine, you are the branches. Abide in me, and I in you.' He comes to us in confession and says 'I absolve you from your sins.' As we listen to the Gospel on Sundays, or open our Bible at home, he does for us what he did for the Eleven—he opens our minds to understand the scriptures. He takes the initiative, with affection and understanding. He knows what we are like. He knows the stuff we are made of. And yet he returns to us, again and again, with words of love and friendship which are deeply personal.

Our dawning realization this morning is simply this: how blessed we are, the most blessed people on earth.

✠

HEALING THE WOUND

I don't think we appreciate how deeply wounded our human nature is. We are born walking-wounded. 'Indeed I was born guilty, a sinner when my mother conceived me' (Psalm 51:4).

Nowhere is this more apparent than in the sensitive area of our sexuality. One of the reasons we talk about this so reluctantly is that the wound is tender, and pressure on it is painful. That's why we want to leave it alone.

Yet as priests, or priests-in-the-making, we realize how across-the-board is human suffering from this wound. You don't need to hear confessions to know this. You need only read the newspapers or watch the television. It is the common lot of men, and women, to be morally weak, and their weakness will most probably find a sexual expression, a sexual outlet.

It is when you realize the fatal ease with which we commit sexual sin, and the abominable difficulty of breaking sexual relationships and addictions, that it dawns on you: Original Sin must have been very, very bad, because it is Original Sin which wounded our humanity in this way. We are born, it seems, with a handicap, an ambiguity of will, a fatal lack of resistance; even our baptism does not abolish this, although it does give us the grace to fight, to repent and to improve. What exactly was it that Adam got up to? We may never know, but he certainly succeeded in crippling us. So much so that we cannot imagine what life would be like if the Sixth Commandment were not a problem. We live in the middle of the problem, and can only see a part of it, not the thing in its total dimensions, we can't see the way disordered sexuality has coloured the world we live in, the air we breathe.

At this stage it is important to say two things. The first is that moral weakness is not confined to sex. Too often we allow the sexual element in life to blunt our conscience to everything else: lack of charity, lack of justice, lack of trust. The world criticizes the Catholic Church for talking too much, and too often, about sex. Well, it needs talking about, because sexual misunderstanding, and still more sexual depravity, can poison us. But there are other things going on in the world which merit just as much attention: gross exploitation of human beings, hard-heartedness on a global scale, refusal to forgive and a thirst for revenge, cynical trafficking in arms, selfishness and self-indulgence which sometimes take your breath away. So we mustn't get tip-tilted into obsession about sex.

The other thing that needs saying is that overall the news is good. If the start of this talk seems a bit gloomy, I hope that it will brighten up for you very soon. Because the Passion, Death and Resurrection of Jesus, the Paschal Mystery, is stronger than all the evil in the world put together, including the evil in my life. The power and strength accessible to us is enormous. There is no wound in human nature which doesn't give God a chance to enter us, and to heal us, to penetrate to the heart of the problem and solve it, if we really want him to do that. This isn't just revivalist talk, it is straight Catholic teaching. As Catholics we are certainly no more virtuous than anyone else. But we are fortunate above the average, because in the Eucharist and the sacraments, the Mother of God, and in the clear teaching of the Church, we have a potent help for our weakness, and a clear indication of where we should be aiming.

Over time I have got into the habit of praying the Rosary for the gift of purity. I pray it as I would take a pill for blood pressure, for its long-term trickle effect. I pray it so that it may be clear not only to God but also to myself that I am single-minded in what I want. I pray it because it transports me into a world where the principal protagonists—Jesus and Mary—are people of huge strength of character, and unlike myself unshackled by any compromise with the erotic world in which I live. I pray it because it reminds me that there is another way to be: I don't have to be immersed in the innuendo and the grime of the entertainment industry, or the advertising industry, or the perversions of information technology. Let me add that I am not at all Manichee about sex: I don't regard it as evil, on the contrary I perceive it as the most beautiful gift of God, the vehicle for the deepest and most unspeakable love. I think the human body is beautiful. It is simply that people have managed to cheapen it, twist it and make it shallow.

Let me take you into some of the detail of this kind of prayer. You may find it useful. Each mystery of the Rosary lends itself to a different kind of reflection.

Take for instance the Mystery of the Scourging. I don't know if you saw the Mel Gibson film, I expect you did. People responded variously to it. I think the scene of the scourging was the most controversial, for its explicitness and for its sheer length. What it brought home to me was the sheer physicalness of the Passion. God took a body that he might suffer in his body, and suffer he did. Ephraem the Syrian puts it dramatically:

> And so, since death could not devour him without a body and the world of the flesh could not swallow him up without flesh, he came to the Virgin, so that he might receive from her a chariot on which to ride to the underworld.[*]

Human flesh and blood are capable of soaking up an infinite amount of punishment, and this is what was done to Jesus. He acquired flesh that he might be punished in the flesh. It is with my body that I have offended God and other people in the course of my life. The malice and the weakness, of course, weren't in the body, they were in my heart: but the body has been the instrument of sin. The body is ambiguous, it can be used for tremendous good: but it is also capable of sinking pretty low. I have used mine as a chariot to take me to some pretty bad places. Violence, drunkenness and gluttony, sins of speech, all these are performed by the body; and so is sexual sin. This Mystery of the Scourging is one in which I can implore God's help and blessing on my body, this apparently untameable thing, this sweet-and-sour thing, that he will purify it and bring it back into line. And Mary, who gave Jesus the chariot on which he was to ride to the underworld—her association with the body of Christ was not an ethereal one, she knew his flesh and loved it. I can talk to her about my wayward flesh and beg her prayers that my body may not be my undoing. Practically, concretely, today: may I not sin with my body: that is my prayer.

---

[*] Sermon on Our Lord, 3 (Breviary, Easter III, Friday)

Paul is quite blunt about this.

> Therefore, do not let sin exercise dominion in your mortal
> bodies, to make you obey their passions. No longer present
> your members to sin as instruments of wickedness, but
> present yourselves to God as those who have been brought
> from death to life, and present your members to God as
> instruments of righteousness. (Romans 6:12–13)

Paul knew about the body, only too well. And he knew that even after
the Resurrection it is only the grace of God that can stop us getting
stuck in sin.

> For I delight in the law of God in my inmost self, but I see
> in my members another law at war with the law of my
> mind, making me captive to the law of sin that dwells in my
> members. Wretched man that I am! Who will rescue me from
> this body of death? Thanks be to God, through Jesus Christ
> Our Lord. (Romans 7:22–5)

Another example. When I pray the Mystery of the Annunciation I am
contemplating a girl who is both wholly wise, wise beyond her years,
and also wholly innocent. Throughout her life Mary must have been
bewildered by sin, because she had never experienced it. To be conceived
immaculate—I cannot imagine what it feels like. Her character, her
spirit, were free to soar to God in unaffected and direct simplicity.
Again, I wonder what it feels like. My spirit has got cluttered over the
years with all sorts of irrelevant stuff. It has got cluttered with pride and
conceit, and with ambition, a longing for personal glory, recognition
and admiration. And it has got cluttered with fantasy.

What a strange thing fantasy is. Just as the internet is capable of
infinite expansion, so is my imagination. I can stock it like a library, with
images to which I have instant access. The more sexual imagery I pack
in there, the more spontaneously the ready-made pictures and scenarios
will come to mind. They will come uninvited, like the unwanted pop-
up on your laptop screen: suddenly it is there. In the long term, then,

I am the architect of my own downfall. If the library of my mind is a pornographic library, those are the books which fall into my lap and will clutter my life.

The sex of fantasy-and-masturbation is shallow and ultimately disappointing. Each feeds the other: the picture feeds the act, the act digs a groove which makes the picture come more easily next time. Sex was given to us so that we could love other people: but no-one gets loved when I go in for internet or television pornography, it is sad and loveless, and I am filling my mind with material which puts me into a vicious circle from which the only escape is the grace of God. To escape from it I need, too, a divine anger and impatience. I need to see myself from above, and dislike what I see, and say 'That's enough! I refuse to be a puppet manipulated by a bastard culture. This is slavery, other people are pressing my buttons, and with the grace of God I propose to escape from it.' And then to throw myself single-mindedly on the mercy of God. *Da robur, fer auxilium* we pray at Benediction. 'Give the strength of the oak tree, bring aid.' Or more colloquially, 'God, help me, and put backbone into me.' It is here that the tranquil image of Our Lady at the Annunciation is so great a help. I want her mindset. I want to rediscover innocence. The conception of the Word of God let loose a colossal power in the world, like a tidal wave. I ask Our Lady by her prayers to divert some of that power my way, so that I may be swept out of my unhealthy addictions, that I may not settle for them any more.

When I pray the Mystery of the Visitation I rest my mind on friendliness and love. Here are two women who unreservedly delight in one another's good fortune, and want to be of service. Elizabeth receives Mary into her home with wonder and pleasure. 'How is it that the mother of my Lord should come to me?' Mary is nowhere more fulfilled than when she comes to the aid of her older cousin. 'She arose with haste.' The affection even reaches the unborn sons of the two women, and John leaps for joy at the approach of Jesus. All this is profoundly and authentically human, it is the way humans are supposed to be. We're meant to have time for one another, to esteem and value one another. Mary leaves at Elizabeth's door the world of bitterness, of cynicism, of unkindness and injustice. She brings something else, something much more wholesome, into the home of her cousin.

I contrast this with the hardness and the exploitative nature of casual sex, promiscuous sex, sex without any profound regard or respect, sex for kicks. This kind of sex has a sharp edge to it, it carries a built-in risk of disappointment and let-down. The mere fact that it is not the expression of a lifelong commitment makes sure of this. Insecurity is an intrinsic part of it, and with it the chance of heartbreak. The end of a relationship, these days, is so much more painful than once it was. Once you have slept with someone you have made yourself vulnerable to them, and the more liable to hurt. How wise the Church is to say that sex belongs inside marriage, how caring and solicitous for people's feelings. It makes your heart bleed to see people being used, being exploited, and this is so often the way of it. The Mystery of the Visitation is the very opposite of exploitation, it is faithful, loving, unselfish and sympathetic. It reminds us that real and deep affection is possible outside the realm of sex. I pray that this kind of self-gift may characterize my life, self-gift which paradoxically means abstention, because premature and dislocated sex hurts people. On the other hand, a priest in a parish who is genuinely affectionate towards his flock and always has a welcome for them is loved by thousands of people with a gratitude beyond words.

✠

HOPE

The great danger of our times is despair. I don't just mean despair with its narrow catechism definition, losing trust in God, thinking we cannot be saved. I think it is a far more diffuse problem, that it affects non-religious people as well as religious ones, and that it shows in things like a dissipated life, even a self-destructive life, and a reluctance to cast a vote at election time. 'It's not worth it,' we say, 'because in the end nothing's worth it.' It shows in a bitter, cynical, sceptical brand of humour which has invaded all our media. Too many people feel, in their gut, that the world in all its aspects is beyond redemption. No-one is pure. No-one has integrity. Everyone has their price. You only need scratch in the right place to find the dirt. So why bother to struggle for a better world? The inexorable tendency of everything is downwards. Let's all go to hell together.

By contrast, Paul writes to the Romans: 'Do not be overcome by evil, but overcome evil with good' (Romans 12:21). And to the Ephesians:

> I pray that the God of Our Lord Jesus Christ, the Father
> of glory, may give you a spirit of wisdom and revelation as
> you come to know him, so that with the eyes of your heart
> enlightened, you may know what is the hope to which he has
> called you, what are the riches of his glorious inheritance
> among the saints. (Ephesians 1:17–18)

This couple of verses repays a bit of rumination. St Bernard said to the early Cistercians 'I want you to become ruminants'. They were, of course, expert farmers, and they would have known all about cattle, and the reflective way that cows have of chewing; what Bernard wanted was for his men to chew the Bible, to extract every last atom of meaning from it, to digest it and make it their own. So let's do our own bit of *lectio divina* on Ephesians.

'The God of Our Lord Jesus Christ' must mean God the Father. God the Father, in Paul's eyes, is active and interested in us, not a remote and arms-folded God. He doesn't leave all the action to the Son and the Spirit. May this fatherly, interested God give you new Christians the grace of coming to know him, he prays . So, that's the first thing, there is progress to be made. You are not stuck. Religion is not a static thing where you accept the package and then get on with your life. On the contrary there are new experiences to be had along the way, and one of these is the progressive deepening of your friendship with God 'as you come to know him'. This is true for priests and laity alike. It's not a done deal once you are baptized, or even once you're ordained. Baptism is only the beginning, and ordination is only the beginning.

Paul describes this new experience as 'a spirit of wisdom and revelation'. God is going to bestow friendship on us, and as he does, we shall feel that the scales are being removed from our eyes, that we have a new wisdom; that we understand things in a way we never thought possible before. Did you know you had eyes in your heart? You thought that the heart was for loving, and eyes were to do with knowing. Well, says Paul, God is going to illumine the eyes of your heart; from an unfocused love you will move to a focused one, you will have a much clearer idea of who you are and who it is you are loving. You are not stuck. Did you think that you would never again have a moment of truth, a sudden and exciting realization about anything? God says the opposite. That's wisdom and revelation.

If we are faithful to mental prayer, we shall experience these moments of consolation. Not every day, but they will come.

But then comes the surprising bit. Paul talks of 'hope' and 'inheritance'. It isn't just our faith which is going to be reinforced. It's also our hope. There's something to look forward to. The old Act of Hope used to say 'O my God I hope in you, for grace and for glory, because of your mercy, your promises and your power.' Grace and glory sounded vague enough and dry enough to a five-year-old boy, which was what I was when I learned to chant this. Well, says Paul, the gift of God is that you will develop a much clearer picture of his mercy, promises and power, and then your longing for him will become more acute. That clear picture is what he means by 'revelation'. You will, as he says in another place 'strain forward' (Philippians 3:13). Because it will dawn on you that you have an inheritance. You have expectations. God is like a very rich relative who says to you one day 'Oh, and in passing, I've remembered you in my will.' He has actually called you to be full of hope. Hope is your vocation. As a Christian hope is your vocation. *A fortiori* as a priest hope is your vocation. This isn't just talk. We live for the future, of which we have had a glimpse, and it's great. A permanently depressed, pessimistic, cynical priest is a contradiction in terms. We are to be full of hope, and we are to radiate hope to our people. However bad the present may be, we have a glorious inheritance among the saints, and it is rich, rich, rich. So hang on in there, that's the message, and above all, don't despair.

I'd like to give you an example of this, and it is the Church in Algeria. When I was the International Responsible of Jesus Caritas I visited Algeria, and got an idea of what is was like to be a Catholic and a Christian in an overwhelmingly Muslim country. When the French were in the saddle, of course, Christianity was privileged. Most little market towns have their church, with its neat steeple, very much as it would have been in the square of a Norman or a Breton village. These churches were built in colonial times, although the French hotly maintain that Algeria was never a colony, it was a department of metropolitan France. However, in 1962, when Algeria became independent, the number of Christians shrank to a few hundred, all expatriates. Churches were handed over to the State, and in many cases became mosques. The nature of Church life changed radically: the old structure of dioceses and parishes no longer had any meaning. Spiritual life tended to concentrate on the few religious communities which remained to serve the poor: now, the convent chapel would be the place for Sunday Mass. Male religious were not permitted to work or dress as priests, and got jobs as nurses in hospitals, agricultural advisers, librarians, university administrators. Conversions were forbidden. Female religious continued to run schools and clinics, and were much appreciated by the local people, but there were very few of them.

The Holy See maintained bishops in the main cities. One of these was a Dominican called Pierre Claverie, and he was the Bishop of Oran, on the coast. He had been born in Algeria, and in his youth had briefly flirted with the right-wing defenders of French power; but long before joining the Dominicans he had realized that his vocation was to side with the poor of the country, and they were Muslims to a man. As a priest, and as a bishop, he devoted himself to Islamic-Christian dialogue. He learned perfect Arabic. He fostered the movement called Ribat-es-Salaam, Bond of Peace, which sought to share spiritual riches through prayer and silence. At his ordination as bishop in 1981 he talked about being 'a minority in the House of Islam'. He made the Cathedral into a cultural centre, where Muslim lecturers, among others, could explain their culture. From 1987 till 1996, the year of his death, he was applying unsuccessfully for Algerian citizenship. In other words he wanted to identify himself entirely, and in complete charity, with the people of the country. Statistically there was no future for the Christians of Algeria. He used to say that Christians in Algeria were at the right place, at the foot of the Cross. But God's ways are not our ways, and Claverie was above all a man of hope.

He was blown up outside his own front door on 1 August 1996. His Muslim driver died with him. Commentators said there was something prophetic about their blood being mingled at the end. Because he was such a loving man, and such an intelligent man, and such an inspiring man, Claverie was rightly seen as a threat by the fundamentalists, and he had to go. He in his turn was deeply inspired by the example of Dietrich Bonhoeffer, the Protestant pastor killed by Hitler in a concentration camp at the end of the War. Bonhoeffer said 'The Kingdom comes for us in our death.' That ought to be written on Claverie's tomb.

His murder followed closely on that of the Cistercian monks at Tibhirine, in the diocese of Algiers. There were seven of them. Like Claverie, they had thrown in their lot with the local people. Their monastery had divested itself of its property, gave almost all its land to the State, shared its large garden with the local village. The monks chose a very literal poverty at the heart of a poor country. But of course, they were French, and that was enough to put them at risk. The 1990s were a decade of civil war, with the FLN [National Liberation Front], the ruling party, being seen as the fat cats, and the FIS [Islamic Salvation Front], the fundamentalists, being the defenders of the peasants. In 1992 the FIS won the general election, but the FLN annulled the results and imposed martial law. The result was a bloodbath, with indiscriminate massacres of whole villages, and the Cistercians were victims of this. It has even been suggested that they were accidentally killed by the French army, which had troops on the ground in defence of what they saw as democracy, and that their death was dressed up to look like a terrorist atrocity.

One of their friends, a priest from Oran who used to stay with them, said that theirs was 'a message of poverty, of abandonment in the hands of God and men, sharing in all the fragility, vulnerability and condition of forgiven sinners, in the conviction that only by being disarmed will we be able to meet Islam and discover in Muslims a part of the total face of Christ.' Christian de Chergé, their prior, used to say 'We are worshippers in the midst of a land of worshippers.'

They were warned to get out, and the Bishop of Algiers, Mgr Teissier, came to visit them and discuss the future. He was worried that if they departed suddenly, the tiny local Christian community would suffer a wound from which it would never recover. So the Prior invited the monks to come and see him, one by one, to open their mind about whether to stay or to go. They opted to stay. After their death, an Algerian poet wrote of them 'They stayed and we asked why. There was no answer. It was a long fidelity.' There is a tiny shrine of Our Lady above the monastery, known locally as Lalla Mariam. The statue has now lost both its arms and her stomach has been gouged with a chisel. This image provided a place of prayer and refuge for the women of the village, especially when they were pregnant. The peaceful witness of the monks registered with the ordinary villagers; it was the fanatics who could not abide them.

On the night of 26 March 1996, twenty gunmen kidnapped the monks and took them away. On 21 May the kidnappers published a statement: 'We have slit the monks' throats.' Their bodies were found nine days later.

On Pentecost Sunday, the day his body was found, his friends opened Father Christian's spiritual testament. It is profoundly moving. Here are some excerpts from it:

> If it should happen one day—and it could be today—that I
> become a victim of the terrorism which now seems ready

to engulf all the foreigners living in Algeria, I would like my community, my Church and my family to remember that my life was given to God and to this country. I ask them to accept the fact that the One Master of all life was not a stranger to this brutal departure. ... My life has no more value than any other. Nor any less value. In any case, it has not the innocence of childhood. I have lived long enough to know that I am an accomplice in the evil which seems to prevail so terribly in the world, even in the evil which might blindly strike me down. I should like, when the time comes, to have a moment of spiritual clarity which would allow me to beg forgiveness of God and of my fellow human beings, and at the same time forgive with all my heart the one who would strike me down.

It would be too high a price to pay for what will perhaps be called 'the grace of martyrdom' to owe it to an Algerian, whoever he might be, especially if he says he is acting in fidelity to what he believes to be Islam. I am aware of the scorn which can be heaped on the Algerians indiscriminately. ... For me Algeria and Islam are something different: it is a body and a soul.

Obviously my death will appear to confirm those who hastily judged me naive or idealistic: 'Let him tell us now what he thinks of his ideals!' But these persons should know that finally my most avid curiosity will be set free. This is what I shall be able to do, God willing: immerse my gaze in that of the Father to contemplate with him his children of Islam just as he sees them, all shining with the glory of Christ, the fruit of his Passion, filled with the gift of the Spirit whose secret joy will always be to establish communion and restore the likeness, playing with the differences. ... For this life lost, totally mine and totally theirs, I thank God, who seems to have willed it entirely for the sake of that joy in everything and in spite of everything.

And also you, my last-minute friend, who will not have known what you were doing: yes, I want to thank you and this

goodbye to be a 'God bless' for you too, because in God's face
I see yours. May we meet again as happy thieves in Paradise,
if it please God, the Father of us both. Amen. Inshallah.

It makes sense of the Act of Hope. O my God I hope in you for grace
and for glory, because of your mercy, your promises and your power.
God grant that in similar circumstances I too would be a limpid example
of Christian hope.

It always strikes me most forcibly that when the Church is at its most
corrupt, it manages to throw up supremely good people. St Francis de
Sales, with his gentleness and clarity of vision, with his superb skills
of preaching and writing, with his deep, deep prayer life—St Francis
de Sales lived at a time when the Church was dreadfully corrupt, but
he lived a life uncontaminated by the corruption. St Francis Borgia
was a member of one of the worst families which has ever afflicted the
Church, but became a great Jesuit general with unflinching spiritual
standards. St Thomas More and St John Fisher died for their loyalty to
a very unedifying papacy. St Francis Xavier and Bartolomé de las Casas
lived at a time when missionary activity was inextricably linked with
military colonial power, with slavery, forced labour and exploitation.
Yet these were spiritual giants, towering above their contemporaries. I
know for sure that there are men and women of outstanding holiness
today, who are walking saints even if they belong to a Church of scandals
and mediocrity.

> God tested them and found them worthy of himself; like
> gold in the furnace he tried them, and like a sacrificial burnt
> offering he accepted them. In the time of their visitation they
> will shine forth, and will run like sparks through the stubble.
> (Wisdom 3:5–7)

The Letter to the Hebrews is clear on this point.

> Now faith is the assurance of things hoped for, the conviction
> of things not seen. Indeed, by faith our ancestors received
> approval.

Then the author cites Abel, Enoch, Noah, Abraham, Moses and countless others of our ancestors who were men and women of hope. Then he says

> Therefore, since we are surrounded by so great a crowd of witnesses, let us also lay aside every weight and the sin that clings so closely, and let us run with perseverance the race that is set before us, looking to Jesus he pioneer and perfecter of our faith, who for the sake of the joy that was set before him endured the Cross, disregarding its shame, and has now taken his place at the right hand of the throne of God.

Run with perseverance. It's a clear command to hope. Hope is our vocation. As a priest my vocation is to keep hope alive in the hearts of my people.

Thinking now of Ireland, and of Western Europe generally, and of the situation of the Church in public esteem, it is clear that things are changing even as we speak. We are going to see a different shape of Catholicism emerging, probably in our lifetime. Our communities will have to find patterns of spirituality which depend less on having a priest. The Eucharist will be much less accessible. Lazy and offhand Catholics are going to sink without trace: to practise your faith will require some muscular determination in the years to come. This is not all bad. It will not happen outside God's providence. He won't have lost control. And indeed, it has happened before, in the centuries of the Mass-rock in Ireland and the priests' hole in England. The vital thing is for us, and for our people, to be able to see beyond the incidental difficulties to the prize. We are called to hope. Hope is our call.

> What no eye has seen, nor ear heard, nor the human heart conceived, what God has prepared for those who love him.
> (I Corinthians 2:9)

Then the saying which is written will be fulfilled: Death has been swallowed up in victory. Where, O death, is your victory? Where, O death, is your sting? The sting of death is sin, and the power of sin is the law. But thanks be to God, who gives us victory through Our Lord Jesus Christ (I Corinthians 15:54).

✜

I DO NOT KNOW THE MAN

In the four Gospels, the account of Peter's denial is chilling. It's there by the way, with incidental differences, in all four. Chilling because it is so eminently understandable, from the standpoint of our own weakness: we can put ourselves in Peter's shoes.

Peter really believed that he loved Our Lord above all things. Earlier on that same evening he had declared that he was ready to go to prison and to death with Jesus. Peter could have described his love in the words of his remote successor Benedict XVI in *Deus Caritas Est*:

> It is characteristic of mature love that it calls into play all man's potentialities; it engages the whole man, so to speak. Contact with the visible manifestations of God's love can awaken within us a feeling of joy born of the experience of being loved. But this encounter also engages our will and our intellect.*

Yes, Peter would have said, my love for Jesus is entire. When he washed my feet and I began to experience with joy how deeply he loved me, I was filled with love for him. And it wasn't a passing sentiment, a bit of emotion. My whole will and my mind were, and are, utterly given over to him. He is the heart and centre of my being.

Yet the experience of Gethsemane unbalanced Peter. He was not ready for the crudity and the cynicism of Judas's kiss, the roughness of the temple guards, the marching away of the prisoner. He was not ready for the total ruthlessness of the civil or religious authorities. He was not ready for the thinly veiled racialism which coloured Judaeans' attitude to Galileans. For all his fine words he was a vulnerable chap, Peter, and

* *Deus Caritas Est*, n. 17.

a simple one. A countryman out of his depth in the City. He panicked. He followed at a distance down the hill to the high priest's house. 'At a distance' is a pregnant phrase. He was already realizing that his love of Jesus was not as total as he had honestly thought. As yet, no denials, but self-protection was already coming first.

St John's Gospel says that John was able to follow Jesus into the courtyard of Caiaphas's house, because John was 'known to the high priest'. Presumably the relationship was friendly. Anyway, Peter was stopped at the gate, because he had no friends in high places, and there he stayed until John rescued him and engineered his admission. Already, before the triple denial, he was feeling inadequate. He took his place by the fire, among the guards, as Matthew says, 'to see how this would end.' An ominous phrase. He must have been depressed beyond words, and bewildered.

To the girl on the gate, the crowd by the fire, and the relative of the man whose ear he had cut off ... to all of these he then pretended that he had nothing to do with Our Lord. He must have felt that with each denial he was moving farther and farther away from Jesus, although he had started the evening so close to him, and yet the momentum was too much for him. Three denials. Each denial was stronger than the one before. St Mark is the one who shows this most graphically—the first denial is private and evasive; the second is public and evasive; the third is public and explicit. Then the cock crew, and then, says Luke, the Lord turned and looked at Peter. Luke says that Peter 'remembered' what Jesus had said about the cock crowing, and in Luke 'remember' is a word with a special meaning. It doesn't just mean recalling to mind. It means bringing the past event to bear powerfully upon the present. Peter finds himself in the heart of a drama which Jesus had delineated for him a few hours before, he has dropped right into it, and the part he is playing in the drama—faithlessness—contrasts painfully with the faithfulness of Jesus before his accusers. John makes a similar point when he contrasts Jesus's truthfulness about himself before the High Priest with the simultaneous denial by Peter. Peter cowers while Jesus stands up, says Raymond Brown in his commentary on John. When Luke says 'He went out and wept bitterly' that's surely an understatement.

So where *was* Jesus during all this? You see, Mark gives the impression that his interro-gation by the high priest took place on the first floor of the high priest's house, because, he says 'Peter was below in the courtyard'. How then could Jesus look at Peter? Mark says, furthermore, that after the first denial Peter left the fire and went out into the forecourt of the house. One explanation is that Our Lord, after the initial onslaught by the chief priests, the elders and the scribes, was being led away—perhaps to some sort of imprisonment in another part of the house. (After all, in later centuries, Anglican bishops would imprison Catholic recusants in their houses.) On his way from the makeshift courtroom to the lock-up, he could have caught sight of Peter, and their eyes would have met, however briefly. It's one possibility. Scripture scholars might disapprove of attempts to reconcile biblical accounts, but here the four evangelists are very concrete and apparently literal in the way they describe things.

There are differences in detail between the evangelists. Mark suggests that two of the denials were to the same serving girl. Matthew suggests that they were different girls. For the third denial, they agree that it's a surly crowd turning on the man with the regional accent, Peter, and taking that as proof of association with Jesus. John, on the other hand, says that the third time it was to the cousin of the man who had lost the ear that Peter made his last and most emphatic denial. But all these small discrepancies only serve to throw into relief the reliability of the main story.

Jesus has fallen into the hands of his enemies, and this time they are not about to let him go. There is only one possible conclusion to this drama. And Peter, the great standby, the great spokesman, is a broken reed, and finds himself humiliated and helpless. He warms himself by the brazier in the courtyard, but a cold terror and despair begins to grip him. Had he been born in the twentieth century instead of the first, he would be saying to himself, 'I've blown it'. Things have changed so quickly, and so radically.

And now it is as if Peter has been thrown out of the story entirely, rather as you could be flung off a wheel revolving at speed, by centrifugal force. He plays no further part in the story of the Passion. Indeed, Matthew and Mark do not mention him by name at all in the rest of the Gospel. When Jesus is taken to Pilate, he is taken alone. From the early hours of Good Friday until halfway through Easter Sunday, Peter is alone with his thoughts. Whether or not he found the other disciples and stayed with them for comfort, we don't know. He seems to have been with John when Mary Magdalene came with the news of the Resurrection. Whether or not he was with the others, his shame and loneliness must have been intense. That kind of self-loathing is a very great suffering. On Good Friday, when Our Lord met Pilate before the hysterical crowd, when he carried his Cross to Calvary, when he was crucified, where was Peter? How did he feel? Did he recall his brave profession of faith? Did he try to justify to himself what he had done, and what he had not done?

If Peter was missing for the Passion, logically he should also have been missing for the Resurrection. That, however, is human logic and not divine logic. In fact, Peter is chosen to be one of the first, after Mary Magdalene, to witness to the Resurrection, running to the tomb with John. He is there in the evening as one of the Eleven when Jesus comes to the disciples in the Upper Room and says 'Peace be with you', a salutation full of meaning in the circumstances. He is there by the Lake when Our Lord asks him three times 'Do you love me' and gives him the chance to mend his three denials. Christ takes him back into his full favour and friendship as if nothing had happened. The keys of the kingdom haven't been taken away from him. When God forgives, he does a total job: you don't have to slave away to re-earn his love.

Perhaps you can see where I am going with this. Peter stands for the Church, whom Christ has taken as his spouse. Because the Church is filled with the Spirit, she is infallible, indefectible. She is all the things the first two chapters of *Lumen Gentium* says she is. The sheepfold; God's field; God's building; Christ's Mystical Body; God's Holy People. She is what Paul says of her in Ephesians: glorious, with no speck of wrinkle or anything like that, but holy and faultless (Ephesians 5:27). God doesn't ditch her. But there are times when, in the face of the world, the Church fails to live up to her vocation. We have to be careful here. I am not conducting an assault on proper ecclesiology. I am saying that in the eyes of the secular world, there isn't a distinction between the claims the Church makes for herself and the misbehaviour of her members. And this misbehaviour is a way of denying the Lord. That's why Pope John Paul [II] said in *Ut Unum Sint*, quoting the Council:

> The pilgrim Church is called by Christ to this continual reform which, as a human and earthly institution, she always needs.*

And Cardinal Sodano, in an official pronouncement on the fourth centenary of the burning of Giordano Bruno in the Campo de' Fiori in Rome, said:

> Objectively, however, some aspects of those proceedings, and in particular their violent outcome at the hands of the civil power, cannot fail to constitute for the Church, in this and in similar cases, a motive for profound regret.[†]

Because we serve a God of forgiveness, the Father of the Prodigal Son, the Church can risk profound regret, to this extent can humble herself, and still continue to be what Peter was after the Resurrection, the chief witness to the Resurrection of Christ and the channel by which his Gospel reaches the world. For instance, we can take a new and honest look at the way the Crusades were conducted and the way Latin America was Christianized. We can acknowledge that the Church was involved, through the civil authorities, in torture and public executions. To say 'that was the culture of the time' and 'everybody was doing it' is not enough by way of an excuse. The Church should be shaping culture, not submitting to it. No, we can and must admit to greed and cruelty, and repent, and turn our back on all that, and know that we are still accepted by Christ as his Spouse and the love of his life.

Now what is true of the Church is true of us as individuals. You and I can risk facing up to our sins, because forgiveness is so close at

---

* *Ut Unum Sint*, n. 15; *Unitatis Redintegratio*, n. 6.
† Secretariat of State, 14.2.2000

hand, and with forgiveness comes reinstatement in the favour of God. Paul says in II Corinthians, 'We are only the earthenware jars that hold this treasure, to make it clear that such overwhelming power comes from God and not from us' (II Corinthians 4:7). Earthenware is very base material. We insist on precious metal for the sacred vessels at the altar, but you and I, carriers of the word of God and celebrators of the sacraments, are earthenware vessels. Earthenware cracks easily, it's brittle stuff; and when the potter is at work, he can easily throw a flawed pot, and if we are honest we have to admit ourselves to be flawed. In our case, when the potter did his stuff we were all right, but since then we have let ourselves be distorted by the recurrent sin in our lives. Yet God uses us to convey his glory to the world. We don't have to pretend to be stainless steel, or solid gold. The power is his.

I am not making out a case for taking sin lightly, or saying that it doesn't matter very much. On the contrary, it is the greatest disaster thinkable. Anything that offends God is appalling and to be avoided at all costs. Moreover, the scandal caused by the sins of Christians, whether collectively or personally, is the main reason why the world is not converted. To cause scandal, to be a stumbling-block for people who might otherwise have found their way from the darkness to the light, is something we should avoid at all costs. If we lived the Gospel to the hilt, the message we carry would be irresistible; but we don't. So sin is a major problem and a major sadness. Sin is the reason why God became incarnate. Sin caused the Cross. Sin is at the heart of the Eucharist—'so that sins may be forgiven'. Only God would know how to turn a disaster into a triumph and a blessing. So it is absurd to conduct our religious life as though sin did not exist. God's pardon is even greater, and he prides himself on using imperfect instruments to achieve, in the long run, a perfect result. So we can safely align ourselves with Peter at his darkest moment, and feel his shame, and receive forgiveness with him.

The point I am making is a serious one. The Church is, or should be, the home of repentant and fragile sinners, not the association of the faultless. At some stage we have inherited a good dose—or a bad dose—of the righteousness of various psalmists, like the one in Psalm 25/6, who says

Yahweh, be my judge!, I go my way in innocence ... I live my life in loyalty to you ... I hate the society of evil men, I refuse to sit down with the wicked ... I wash my hands in innocence and join the procession round your altar ... Do not let my soul share the fate of sinners ... My foot is set on the right path.

Our old Brummy housekeeper in Bedford would have taken a look at that psalmist and said 'He's got a bob on hisself, "asn't he?' A stance more in keeping with the Gospel would be that of Psalm 31/2:

At last I admitted to you that I had sinned; no longer concealing my guilt, I said 'I will go to Yahweh and confess my fault.' And you, you have forgiven the wrong I did, have pardoned my sin ... Many torments await the wicked, but grace enfolds the man who trusts in Yahweh.

If the people in our parishes think that we are immaculate and subject to the none of the temptations they encounter, and if they perceive the Church as the society of the saved, they will be frightened away. (These days there is less danger of this, of course: recent scandals have seen to that.) If they think, on the other hand, that the Church is the family of those who have experienced God's mercy (and, implicitly, stood and still stand in need of such mercy) they will be attracted. There's such a thing as being too good to be true.

As Catholics we have incredible good luck. We have received from the Lord the Sacrament of Reconciliation. Let me quote for you the *Catechism of the Catholic Church*.

The human heart is heavy and hardened. God must give man a new heart. Conversion is first of all a work of the grace of God who makes our hearts return to him: 'Restore us to thyself, O Lord, that we may be restored' (Lamentations 5:21). God gives us the strength to begin anew. It is in discovering the greatness of God's love that our heart is shaken by the horror and weight of sin and begins to fear offending God by sin and being separated from him. The

human heart is converted by looking upon him whom our
sins have pierced.*

It is when we go to confession that Christ steps in with a grace more
powerful than we shall ever know, and makes our tentative repentance
absolute, makes us capable of changing course, changing direction. He
gives us a new heart. He gives us a licence to be honest about ourselves,
because this is a sacrament of healing. In the past twenty or thirty years,
confession has taken a hammering, and there are countries in Europe
where it has all but disappeared. Admittedly, in the past it has not always
been used intelligently. But to reduce Catholicism to a six-sacrament
Church is a grave error. If we jettison confession, we are on the way to
jettisoning any examination of conscience, and any awareness of sin,
and this is catastrophic. Paradoxically, it is our sins which bring Jesus
close to us. They are the raison-d'etre of Christmas, Good Friday and
Easter Sunday. And they are the raison-d'etre of the Mass as well.

'This is the cup of my blood, the blood of the new and everlasting
covenant, which will be shed for you and for all, so that sins may be
forgiven.'

---

* *Catechism of the Catholic Church*, 1432.

✝

ADVENT

Advent is depicted by the Church as a time of breathless expectation. It is a time of waiting.

For most people in the world, waiting is a way of life. We all get used to standing in line. We queue at shops for food, at government offices for permissions, at post offices for pensions, at consulates for visas. We queue at supermarket checkouts, airport check-ins and at the counters of banks. We get stuck in traffic jams on the GRA [Grande Raccordo Anulare—the orbital motorway that encircles Rome] and on the Lungotevere. We wait patiently to get into St Peter's. Some of us waited for eleven hours when the Pope died. Highly developed countries try to eliminate waiting. They see it as undesirable, a strain on the patience. In poorer countries it is expected and taken for granted, it is a way of life. Poor people are used to waiting. They have a monumental, philosophical patience. It is the well-to-do people who get blood pressure when they are told to wait.

When the Angel came to Mary at Nazareth he told her, in effect, that she was to be the mother of the Saviour, but that she would have to wait. The power of the Most High would overshadow her now, yes, but then there would be a nine-month interval, and during this she would have to wait. She would have to wait to see what Joseph said, and how her parents reacted to her pregnancy. She would have to wait to see what this mysterious and wonderful baby was like. She would have to wait to discover what her future was, and indeed whether she had a future: if it all went wrong, the penalties for pregnancy out of wedlock could be severe. But there was no quick answer, no quick fix. Wait, Mary. And because Mary was a poor girl, she knew how to wait, how to contain her soul in patience.

The Angel brought astonishing news, but there must have been times in the ensuing years when Mary wondered what it was all about. For thirty years Jesus lived an ordinary life at home in Nazareth, concealing his godhead and the fact that he was the Messiah. When Mary looked at him, she looked at him with tremendous love; but she must sometimes have wondered whether the Annunciation was all a dream, and whether those promises of Gabriel would ever come true. Son of the Most High ... the throne of his father David ... he will reign over the house of Jacob for ever ... of his kingdom there will be no end. Grandiose, rolling promises, but there was no sign of their ever being fulfilled. She mulled over all these words in her mind, as she did the shepherds' message and the episode of the Finding in the Temple, she stored these things up in her heart, but as she did so she could hear the hammer from the workshop, and the saw, and the comfortable noises of a young artisan at work, and the sheer normality of it all must have perplexed her. And still she waited. Maybe she had no-one with whom she could share, no-one to whom she could talk. She had to contain her soul in patience. And she waited.

When Jesus left home and started his public life she no longer saw him every day. And sometimes when she did go to see him, she was apparently dismissed. 'Who are my mother and brothers? Those who do the will of my Father ...' And while Mary was wise enough and un-neurotic enough not to be offended by this, still she had to wait for the chance of a moment of intimacy with her son. And that moment did not really come until the grim experience of the Cross. Again, Mary, woman of faith, had to wait while the appalling sequence of suffering unfolded. People who wait feel powerless to do anything to help themselves or anyone else. So it was on the Way of the Cross and at the foot of the Cross. Did Our Lady think back, at this point, to the Annunciation and the Angel's message, and those promises? Did she continue to believe that the promises would be kept, would come true? Again, she would have to wait, wait for the Resurrection and the Ascension of her son in glory, to see that God does keep his promises.

With the Apostles she waited in the Upper Room for the coming of the Spirit, and at Pentecost she finally understood how things fitted together, how the death and rising of Jesus enabled the Spirit to come and transform these friends of her son, changing them from timid and confused men into clear and brave preachers of the Gospel. Perhaps she thought, in her heart of hearts 'About time.' Like all mothers, she may have been critical of her son's choice of companions, wondering whether they were worthy of him. She must have realized that they were conspicuous by their absence on Good Friday. She must have felt she had been waiting for ever for Peter, Andrew, James and John to come good ... But come good they did, and she was still at their side, a patient woman.

The idea of waiting patiently is tied up with contemplation. The true contemplative does not count the minutes and the hours when he is praying. He allows his mind and heart to rest in a constant way on the Persons of the Trinity and the truths of the Faith, rather as a ladder leans against a wall, exerting a constant, gentle pressure upon it. As the wall is present to the ladder, sustaining it, and the ladder is present to the wall, depending on it, so am I with God when I settle in to prayer. I don't resent the time I am going to spend in the company of the Lord, but I relish it, valuing the silence and the uninterrupted solitude as though it were a bath of water at exactly the right temperature. I lower myself into it with the same sentiment of relief and gratitude. To be present to God, with God present to me, is in itself a prayer, I am praying before I open a breviary or a New Testament. I am await and alert to the living God.

> As the eyes of servants
> Look to the hand of their master,
> As the eyes of a maid
> To the hand of her mistress,
> So our eyes look to the Lord our God
> Until he has mercy upon us. (Psalm 122/123)

I don't expect my prayer to deliver measurable results. While I am at prayer I go through long dry periods, like someone crossing a desert, and there is nothing to show for my prayer. But I still know, deep down inside myself, that I am in the right place, that I am doing the right thing, and that my job is to wait on the Lord with patience. When I come out of prayer, I may be changed, and others may notice this, but almost certainly I shan't. To see the long-term results of a life of prayer I shall have to wait. Again, waiting.

> I wait for the Lord, my soul waits,
> And in his word I hope;
> My soul waits for the Lord
> More than those who watch for the morning.
>   (Psalm 129/130)

It is the vocation of the disciple to wait for the master. The reward for waiting is incalculable. Listen to Jesus in St Luke's Gospel.

> Be dressed for action and have your lamps lit; be like those who are waiting for their master to return from the wedding banquet, so that they may open the door for him as soon as he comes and knocks. Blessed are those slaves whom the master finds alert when he comes; truly I tell you, he will fasten his belt and have them sit down to eat, and he will come and serve them. If he comes during the middle of the night, or near dawn, and finds them so, blessed are those slaves. (Luke 12:35–8)

That's a good Advent reading because it refers exactly to the frame of mind we should now be entering into. A willingness for the long haul: a peaceful, sustained waiting for the Lord to appear. And Advent is a microcosm of the whole of the Christian life, isn't it? The whole of our life is a living on trust, and knowing neither the day nor the hour when our trust will be rewarded.

Advent is a waiting for Christmas. The secular commercial machine has seized on this with great glee and perverted it, making it a time of febrile excitement for children, as they desire more and more consumer goods and badger their parents to buy them. In a way, the religious sense of waiting for Christmas is a lost cause. It is a hijacked feast. The commercial world even begins Christmas in October, because it cannot wait. Carols in the supermarket, decorations. But what the materialist world has not yet got hold of, and probably never will, because it can't manipulate it, is the Second Coming.

It seems that the early Christians expected the Second Coming to happen very soon, and that they were most disturbed when it did not take place. Now we have settled down to a Second Coming which may be unimaginably remote, coterminous with the end of the world which is as remote as the beginning of the world. Just as the Big Bang is a subject for theoretical speculation, so are the Last Judgment and the Last Day. It doesn't enter our serious and practical reckoning in any way. But what must enter into our serious and practical reckoning is the day of our own death, and this is going to arrive in the most unspectacular and matter-of-fact way, and we shall disappear from the surface of this planet leaving scarcely a ripple. This is a moment for which we are waiting, for which we are in perpetual Advent: the moment when we meet God face to face. Some people will be sorry and sad when we go; our colleagues will say Mass for us; our names will go into the diocesan calendar ... for a generation, at the most, there will be people who remember us with love. Ultimately, however, our only security is in the Lord. We are waiting to meet Him who is our only enduring and eternal security. Maranatha, Come Lord Jesus, as a friend and a compassionate brother, come, as a merciful judge, come.

When I was a young priest in Northampton there was a man in the parish called Danny McAuley. Danny was a writer of great distinction. He wrote in Irish, on an old stand-up typewriter, in the living-room of the little terrace house where he lived with his wife and children. He wrote, most movingly, of his life as an Irish emigrant, and some of his books were translated into English. Danny worked as a labourer; you would often find him down a hole in the road. I said to him 'Danny, why do you do these jobs? You are such a fine writer that you could make your living by writing.' And he replied, 'Sure, Father, if I didn't work on the roads, I'd have nothing to write about.' I vividly remember one passage in his biography, where he says that one year when he was very young he had decided not to go home for Christmas. But the time grew closer, and he felt more and more homesick. And in the end, on 23 December, he threw down his pick and shovel, walked down to the station, bought a ticket to Euston station in London, and from there caught the night train up to Holyhead. He had to waste some time there waiting for what they called a 'sailing ticket', a place on the boat (quite apart from the cost of the journey) but he was successful, crossed the Irish Sea during the next night, arrived in Dun Laoghaire, caught a train

across the middle of Ireland, then a bus, and walked in through the door
of his mother's farmhouse at lunchtime on Christmas morning, to find
the whole family seated there, and he said 'God bless all here' and sat
down with them as though he had never been away. The waiting had
been worth it; the hard work on the roads, the tedious and tiring hours
of travelling, with their discomfort and uncertainty, all had been worth
it: his patience was rewarded, and he was blissfully happy.

I sometimes have a fantasy of Purgatory as like that, a long and
lonely journey. You have just died, and you set out towards the Father's
house, but it is a long and wearisome way, walking in the heat of the
day and through the starlit night, walking through forest and scrubland,
marshland and bog, across hills and past farms shrouded in darkness,
with no apparent result except fatigue, and great sadness and loneliness.
As you walk you reflect on the mistakes of your life, and see them in
their true stupidity and shame, and regret them more than you can ever
say. It is indeed a profoundly lonely journey. But at length you breast
the last rise, one evening at dusk, and below you in the valley you see
the house. It is a big house, the lights are on, and from the open door
a shaft of light falls across the road; and there is the sound of laughter,
and of music. And you know intuitively that the road goes no farther,
and this is your journey's end. As you draw closer you recognize with
delight some of the voices you can hear. They belong to your mother,
your father, some of your oldest friends. And as you cross the threshold,
nervous yet hopeful, you suddenly find yourself face to face with Jesus,
Jesus whom you have adored so often in the Eucharist but never seen
face to face. You remember Aquinas's

> *Jesu quem velatum nunc aspicio, Oro fiat illud quod tam*
> *sitio, Ut te revelata cernes facie, Visu sim beatus tuae gloriae.*

> Jesus, whom now I see veiled, I pray you to grant me what
> I thirst for, to see you with the veil drawn back, and to be
> blessed by the sight of your glory.

And you realize with tears in your eyes that this is it: no more journeying,
no more loneliness. By God's grace and sovereign forgiveness your life

has been—incredibly—an ultimate success, you've made it home, and the embrace of your loving Lord is the proof of it. The Advent of your life has dawned into Christmas, the waiting was worthwhile, and nothing else matters, or will ever matter again.

✠

Our Lady and the Rosary

At the beginning of this talk I acknowledge my debt to Fr Tim Radcliffe, and what he wrote in his book 'Sing a New Song'. It may well be that I should acknowledge other authorities too, but that I have forgotten their effect on me. Thus it is that we accumulate the inspirations of others and make them our own, we make an original synthesis of other people's revelations, and the show goes on. Very little of our raw material is completely original. The old spiritual director of the seminary in Sydney used to say to me 'There is no copyright on spiritual ideas' but I think that even he was quoting another bloke he had met in America.

Some people in the Church catch the popular imagination, and are enshrined in the folk-memory of Catholics everywhere. Mother Teresa is one example. Pope John Paul [II] is another. It is hard to say exactly what the clutch of qualities is which hits the spot. There have been other priests and sisters, other popes and missionaries, who have done incredible things. But these two had a crucial blend of personal magnetism and self-sacrifice which proved irresistible. The public at large is not accountable for its preferences. It's the same with canonized saints. St Francis and the Little Flower are enthroned in the affection of Catholics everywhere. The calendar is stuffed with other saints, but these two hit the spot. Who can say why?

As with saints, so with devotions. And the devotion which far and away outstrips all others is the Rosary. It is via the Rosary that millions of ordinary Catholics in five continents have been able to short-circuit the hazards of doctrinal formulations and theological niceties, and fly to the arms of their Mother. We are like children coming home after a hard day at school, where there have been some lessons we didn't altogether grasp. Our instinctive relationship with our mother has nothing to do with fine-tuning, it is simpler and deeper and impossible to articulate, it is intense and instinctive and profoundly satisfying.

The Church marks out October as the month of the Rosary. Not that it really needs a month, since those of us who have the habit say the Rosary, or part of it, every day of the year. But maybe a special month will encourage us to meditate and reflect, and to appreciate just what it is that the Church has put into our hands: the size of the gift. It is at first sight deceptive. It would be easy to sneer at the Rosary from an intellectual height, as if it were all right for peasants, but not to be taken seriously by thinking people. What a mistake that would be.

A feeling for Mary is in the bones and the gut of the Church, Eastern and Western. It is a prime example of how tradition works. Our theology says to us that the norm of faith is not just scripture, but scripture intertwined with tradition; and tradition is the series of faith-discoveries the Church has made in the course of the centuries. These discoveries have normative value because we are sure that the Spirit of God was given to the Church, right from the beginning, to guide it. The Church doesn't make her faith-discoveries in conflict with scripture, or independently of it, because, after all, the Spirit is the principal author of the scriptures too. But in the spirit of the Gospel she—the Church—brings old things and new out of her store, emphasizes things, highlights things, deduces things. Because, way back, it was the Church who edited and published the Bible, and established the canon, this movement of the Spirit is not really two but one; you can't really wrench the Church and the word of God apart.

The importance of Mary is a faith-discovery. We know, but sometimes forget, how crucial motherhood is. It is the biggest formative influence of all, physically and psychologically. Many of us owe the fact that we are practising Catholics to our mothers. The link that binds us to our mothers, whether they are still living or whether they have long since gone to heaven, is so deep that it defies description. Sometimes it is complex, because original sin comes into play and the chemistry goes wrong. But you can never discount it. The Church's faith-discovery is that Jesus had this kind of intense relationship with Mary, and because original sin didn't enter the picture for either of them, the relationship was unsullied by any shadow of hurt or bitterness, it was a straightforward bond of the greatest love and trust.

I sometimes think that when people downgrade the place of Mary in the Church or popular devotion, or point out how little reference there is to her in the Gospel, and try therefore to marginalize her, it is because they have lost this human appreciation of just what motherhood means: the emotion that binds a mother to her son, for example … can men really comprehend this? I doubt it: a man cannot feel with a woman's heart, he's never been pregnant or in labour, and a man can forget, when he becomes an adult, just how formative his mother was in his development, how she poured her whole self into his well-being. We forget because of original sin, because we are tilted in the direction of self-centredness, a male growing-away, a male callousness even. But Jesus didn't forget, because he was immune from all that. He knew what, humanly speaking, he owed to his mother, and he loved her uncomplicatedly and intensely, as she loved him. This is the Church's faith-discovery, the closeness of Jesus to Mary. And this is what we re-live when we say the Rosary.

Most of the mysteries of the Rosary do not concern Mary directly, in the sense of our being able to say 'She was there'. The Joyful Mysteries do, of course, because they are taken from Luke's infancy narrative. But the Mysteries of Light … the Baptism, the setting forth to preach the Gospel, the Transfiguration, the Eucharist, do not at first sight have anything to do with Our Lady. Nor do the first two glorious ones, the Resurrection and the Ascension. The Sorrowful Mysteries involve her presence her only in so far as she was at the foot of the Cross at the Crucifixion (which is enormously significant) and that tradition tells us that Jesus met his Mother on the Way of the Cross.

That she wasn't present doesn't matter. When we pray the Rosary, we share our contemplation of these events with Mary. Even if she was not physically present at them all, they concern her Son, and thus are supremely important to her, even now We are sharing a recollection with her. When you go visiting, as a priest, you will realize that what gives greatest comfort to elderly people is to be able to talk about their children, remember occasions, tell stories, repeat what happened. To talk to people about their sons and daughters, and to listen to the reminiscences, is often a great kindness. When we say the Rosary, we talk to Mary about her Son, and we invite her to talk to us, to bring us on to the inside of that relationship which unites her with him. She knows his ways, she can predict his reactions. He lived with her until he was thirty, after all. She knew him as a child, as an adolescent and as an adult. Like us, she worships and adores him in his divinity, she comprehends now just who it was she conceived at Nazareth and brought forth at Bethlehem. But still, in spite of his divinity, we can say with confidence that she knows what he's like.

Every one of these events, the ones in the mysteries of the Rosary, is a source of grace for God's people living today. When we pray the Rosary we are asking Mary, by her intercession, to make sure that some of that grace comes our way, that it may benefit those we love and care for. You see, very often we offer the Rosary for an intention, or for a person. I always used to find it hard to concentrate on three things at once. The person I was praying for, the words of the Hail Mary, and the Mystery I was supposed to be contemplating. Typical of the Catholic Church, I used to think, expecting you to do three things at the same time. It's only later that it dawned on me that the Rosary is a kind of licensed distraction. You can let your mind wander between these three—mystery, words, intention—sometimes tying them together neatly, but more often not. And that's OK. This isn't a *tesina* [minor thesis] we are handing in, where it will be marked on the accuracy of its footnotes and general presentation. This is a prayer which wells up untidily from the roots of our being, and we're saying to God, 'Here are three things I care about tremendously, and I dump them all in your lap, you sort them out.' I love and trust Mary as my mother, because she took me on at the foot of the Cross. On the other hand, these Gospel events are the raw material of my spiritual life, my constant inspiration. And around me there are people in need of every kind, and my heart goes out to them. I knit these things into one, not at all in an up-together way, but in a way that leaves lots of loose ends, and with much love. That's all that matters.

The Hail Mary is the word of God addressed to us. God is breaking the silence of the centuries. He is taking the initiative. Prayer is not just us yelling at God, very loudly and repetitively in case he's got a bit deaf since the days of the Bible. Prayer is principally listening. We listen, then, as God breaks through into our individual and corporate life.

And what is the first thing he says to the one of us he has picked for his special confidence, Mary of Nazareth? He says 'You are full of grace, *kecharitomene*'. Words of enormous affirmation and reassurance. 'In this is love,' says St John, 'not that we loved God but that he loved us, and sent his Son' (I John 4:10). Part of prayer is sitting back and letting ourselves be loved.

When we do reply, we do so in a way which echoes what we have just heard. 'Hail Mary' says the angel. 'Holy Mary' we respond. 'Blessed is the fruit of thy womb', says Elizabeth. 'Holy Mary Mother of God' we respond. Our words are a reverberation, a prolongation of what has been said to us. Paul says to the Romans 'When we cry Abba, Father, it is that very Spirit bearing witness with our spirit that we are children of God' (Romans 8:15–16). The prayer is given to us, prays itself within us. Those who make advance in the contemplative life say that the day comes when their prayer is like a constant murmur going on in the depth of the soul. Meister Eckhart said 'We do not pray, we are prayed'. And John Paul II wrote in his Letter for the Millennium, 'Prayer can progress, as a genuine dialogue of love, to the point of rendering the person wholly possessed by the divine Beloved, vibrating at the Spirit's touch, resting filially within the Father's heart.'* If we say the Hail Mary with full attention, we are vibrating at the Spirit's touch. And we are remembering one who did this, constantly and superbly, in her day, Mary, who rested filially within the Father's heart.

The Rosary starts at home. It starts in Mary's house in Nazareth. Was this also the house of her parents Joachim and Anne? It surely must have been. This is the domestic place, the place of roots and belonging. And this is a vital bit of our make-up. We want to know where we belong, where we can retreat to and recoup our forces, where our base is. Irish parishioners will ask you when they first meet you, 'Where are you from, Father?' And secretly they hope that you'll say 'County Limerick' or County Kerry'. But even if you're entirely English, they cannot imagine that anyone would find that question hard to answer. You must be 'from' somewhere. But the news the angel brings Mary is going to shatter this security, this from-ness. It is going to take her over

---

* *Novo Millennio Ineunte*, n. 33.

the mountains to visit Elizabeth, to Bethlehem, to Egypt, to Jerusalem, to Calvary, to the Upper Room; it is going to launch her on a journey to some dark and perplexing places, until she reaches her real home in heaven. The mysteries of the Rosary reflect this. I once knew a priest who took liberties with the text of the Mass and said 'May the peace of the Lord disturb you profoundly'. I don't recommend his liturgical style. But what he said contained an uncomfortable truth, which is that living the Gospel is going to put us on the road, in one way or another, until our dying day, and that God has not promised us earthly security, and that if we look for static peace and quiet at any cost we are probably hiding from God. For this reason, the Rosary is a good prayer for planes and trains and buses. A good prayer for the departure lounge at Ciampino, when you have just heard the announcement which begins 'Due to the late arrival of the incoming flight ...'.

The Hail Mary brackets our life very neatly. It deals with conception and birth. Each of us issued from a womb blessed by God. It deals with the present. Pray for us sinners now. And it deals with our last moments. Now and at the hour of our death. Within these brackets we are to meet God, we do meet God. Within these brackets our salvation is worked out. I spend the time between these brackets as a funny amalgam of flesh and spirit, I am a rational animal, I reach out to God and he can touch my heart and yet there are volcanic instincts in me which are so hard to dominate. At times I am a mystery to myself. When I say the Hail Mary I am inviting the Lord into the heart of this enigma which is me; submitting the whole thing to him; expressing my trust in his mercy and forgiveness. In the Last Judgment of Michelangelo, after all, there is someone being pulled up out of Purgatory by his Rosary.

The Hail Mary, and thus the Rosary, is to do with fertility. Mary conceives and brings forth the Lord of Creation. It makes us reflect on our own fertility, which is clearly not physical, but of another order. It is still real fertility. By our preaching and by our example, as well as by the power of the sacraments we celebrate with our people, we engender souls for the Kingdom. Some of the Fathers of the Church would even assert that in this way we too become mothers. The Church brings forth new life at the font. One of the happiest evenings of your year will be Holy Saturday, when those you have prepared and nurtured in the

Faith come forward for baptism, to be transferred from the kingdom of darkness into the Kingdom of God's beloved Son. As members and ministers of the Church we are chosen to transmit faith. In years to come you will have the disconcerting experience of someone saying to you 'I shall never forget what you said at Mass one day,' and you think desperately 'What was it? Would I say the same today?' How many vocations, how many conversions of mind and heart, stem from a youngster knowing and admiring a really good priest? By God's grace Mary became the Mother of the Saviour. The same Spirit is going to give you the gift of spiritual fertility.

Then, G. K. Chesterton reflected, in his book *Orthodoxy*, how little children love to play repetitive games with adults. If you pull a face which makes a child laugh, she says 'Again!' and you have to do it a hundred times before she is tired of it. The Rosary is a repetitive prayer, and underlines how we are indeed children in the sight of God, the children for whom there is a place in the Kingdom. 'Let the little children come to me. Do not stop them, for it is to such as these that the kingdom of God belongs' (Mark 10:13). Chesterton muses aloud: Does God say to the sun, just before dawn, 'Do it again' and to the moon at dusk 'Do it again'? God understands about repetition and the need for repetition. 'Listen to what the unjust judge says. And will God not grant justice to his chosen ones who cry out to him day and night?' (Luke 18:6–7). The Rosary is an excellent way of crying out to God day and night. In 2002 Pope John Paul II wrote a letter about the Rosary in which he said 'insistent request and the corresponding reply are expressed in terms familiar from the universal experience of human love. To understand the Rosary, one has to enter the psychological dynamic proper to love.'* Which is another way of saying that when you love somebody you tell them, 'I love you' and they don't complain that you've said it before. The same words do very nicely. They never wear out.

The reflection in the Rosary is not linear but circular. This is what makes it hard for some people. It isn't full of consequences, like mathematical calculations at the end of which you can say 'QED.' The Rosary is more like the action of a drill, which by going round and round

---

* *Rosarium Virginis Mariae*, n. 26.

penetrates the surface of things and reaches the reality beneath. We
rest our minds on the great truths of religion, exert constant pressure
on them, until at length they give way and yield up their joint treasure.
'Every individual event in the life of Christ, as narrated by the Evangelists,
is resplendent with the Mystery that passes understanding.' That's the
Pope again, in the same Letter.* In the end, he's saying, there is only
one great Mystery, God's salvation of us. But there's no deadline: this
is an are eternal truth, after all, and these events have eternal meaning.
The Rosary enables us to come at them from different angles, to circle
round them and gradually penetrate them, but in our own time, and in
God's good time as well.

Dante Alighieri, in the third volume of the *Divine Comedy*, the
Paradiso, has St Bernard say

> *Riguarda omai nella faccia ch'a Cristo*
> *Più si somiglia, chè la sua chiarezza*
> *Sola ti può disporre a veder Cristo*

Look now upon that face which is most like the face of Christ,
because only this radiance can prepare you to see Christ
himself.

and

> *Vergine Madre, figlia del tuo figlio,*
> *umile ed alta più che creatura,*
> *termine fisso d'eterno consiglio*

Maiden yet a Mother, daughter of thy Son, High beyond all
other—lowlier is none; Thou the consummation, Planned by
God's decree, When our lost creation Nobler rose in thee.[†]

---

* *ibid.*, n. 24.
† R. A. Knox trans.

✜

PRIEST AS SERVANT

In Luke 12 we find an astonishing metaphor. Jesus says that if we are dressed for action and have our lamps lit, like slaves who are waiting for their master to return from the wedding banquet, the master when he comes will fasten his belt and have us sit down to eat, and he will come and serve us.

It is deliberately shocking. It is subversive. It is actually outrageous. The idea of a master waiting upon slaves turns the secure universe upside down. Which is, of course, what Jesus is very good at doing. From a safe distance we admire his technique, and we take pleasure in seeing him disconcert the rich, the correct, the learned, and rattle the bars of their cages. He did it with the parable of the employer who paid everyone the same, no matter how long they had worked. He did it when he reminded the people at Nazareth how in the time of the prophets God had cured and fed not card-carrying Jews, but a Sidonian widow and a Syrian army officer. He did it when he forgave the sins of the paralysed man on the stretcher. He did it when he went out to dinner with the tax-collectors. He did it when he healed the man with the withered hand on the Sabbath. So many of his miracles and teachings had a sharp, abrasive edge to them. He was provocative. He broke the rules and flouted the conventions. No wonder the scribes, Pharisees and high priests loathed his guts. He was a threat to the established order.

It's when Jesus rattles the bars of *our* cages that it stops being a matter of academic interest, and we feel uneasy. Well, he does it here. He presents us with the image of a servant-Lord. The Son of Man, he says, is coming at an unexpected hour, but if you are on the watch for him and prepared, he will invite you to sit down at his table and he will attend to all your needs. Do I really want that? Will it make me feel uncomfortable?

I am supposed to identify myself with the alert slaves in the parable. But as a priest I am also supposed to identify myself with the master, who is Jesus. At the altar we act *in persona Christi.* In our pastoral lives we try our feeble best to be icons of the living Christ, configured to the Good Shepherd. Talk like this sometimes exasperates laypeople. They see it as clericalism. They point sarcastically at the child-abusers, or at priests who have misappropriated parish funds. 'Don't make out that you are better than the rest of us,' they say. And patiently we have to reply that we don't claim that for a moment. What we do believe is that ordination does something irrevocable to us, whether we deserve it or not, just as baptism and confirmation do something irrevocable to you; and we have to spend the rest of our life trying to live up to that something. It is in this context that this parable summons you and me not only to be awake like the slaves, but also to be like this master of the household.

In other words we have to try to live up to the servant-status of Christ. Christ being a servant seems over-the-top. Yet it should not surprise us. Five centuries previously, Isaiah had described the mysterious Suffering Servant (Isaiah 50, 53) like this:

> The Lord God has given me the tongue of a teacher, that I may know how to sustain the weary with a word ... Surely he has borne our infirmities and carried our diseases ... He was wounded for our transgressions, crushed for our iniquities ... He was oppressed, and he was afflicted, yet he did not open his mouth; like a lamb that is led to the slaughter, and like a sheep that before its shearers is silent, so he did not open his mouth. By a perversion of justice he was taken away.

Being a servant is not so much being a butler as being a poor man unjustly victimized. Secular English masculinity is tempted to say to this shadowy Isaiah figure, only later identified with Jesus, 'Wimp! Stand up for yourself!' The picture is that of a slave who is treated like a thing, a piece of disposable property, someone whose job is to be of service, and to put up with harsh treatment when it comes his way. What a word-picture of the redeemer of the world. Had you or I been planning the redemption of the world, the Saviour would have had a different profile, more commanding, more powerful, more awe-inspiring, more dignified. Not a servant-Lord.

Look at the Jesus of the Last Supper. At the heart of this most sacred meal, Luke places the dispute over who was to be the greatest, right after Our Lord had taken the bread, blessed it, broken it and distributed it saying 'This is my body, which is given for you,' and had spoken the words of consecration over the cup. Now in our book these are actions of unbearable solemnity. To be greeted with a reverent and contemplative hush. The Apostles, however, jump into the hush with the old argument about who is best and who is greatest. We know how weary Jesus used to get with this theme. So Luke tells us his verbal response:

> The Kings of the Gentiles lord it over them; and those in authority over them are called benefactors. But not so with you; rather the greatest among you must become like the youngest, and the leader like one who serves. For who is the greater, the one who is at table or the one who serves? Is it not the one at table? But I am among you as one who serves. (Luke 22:24–7)

That's stark enough. But it's John who gives us the acting-out of the teaching (John 13:3–14). You have the impression that Our Lord despaired of ever getting this doctrine into the heads of his friends, so he decided to give them a mute object lesson. First John makes a statement about Jesus's sovereign power and sublime destiny: 'Jesus, knowing that the Father had given all things into his hands, and that he had come from God and was going to God ...' So you're all keyed-up for some demonstration of kingly power. But what follows? 'He got up from table, took off his outer robe, and tied a towel around himself.' Hear the deliberate detail of John's account. The Apostles would have known the Old Testament story of David's wooing of Abigail, and of the messengers he sent to Carmel to fetch her after her husband's death. 'She rose and bowed down, with her face to the ground, and said 'Your servant is a slave to wash the feet of the servants of my lord' (I Samuel 25:41). So what Jesus was doing at the Last Supper was a servile action.

Providing water for people to wash their hands at the start of a meal was one thing: washing their feet during the meal quite another, it was servile. The washing of the feet at the Last Supper was a long drawn-out affair, causing extreme embarrassment to the Apostles. After the first two they must have wanted to say 'All right, we get the message, you don't need to keep on.' But Jesus does keep on, and we with the Twelve have to bear the insistent power of the object-lesson, the duration of it: hear the clink of the jug and the basin, hear the repeated splashing of the water. Jesus chooses to act in a menial way, he chooses to be servant, he chooses to do something for which people, as a rule, are not praised or even thanked. It is only after he has finished that he articulates the meaning of it all.

> Do you know what I have done to you? You call me Teacher and Lord—and you are right, for that is what I am. So if I, your Lord and Teacher, have washed your feet, you also ought to wash one another's feet. For I have set you an example, that you also should do as I have done to you.

I wonder if it was this gesture of humility that tipped Judas over the edge. It is true that, according to John, even at the beginning of the Last Supper the devil had put it into the heart of Judas to betray him. But maybe this was the last straw. If he had conventional pictures of the Messiah, of a character rather like Aragorn in the third part of 'The Lord of the Rings', fighting a valiant battle and claiming his kingdom, this spectacle of Jesus shuffling round the room on his knees with a bowl of water and a towel may have disgusted him, caused him to despise Our Lord, made him want to teach Christ a lesson, lick him into shape. He had, after all, invested his whole life in this man: to see him behaving in this outrageous way was unendurable. Humility is hard not only for the humble person, but sometimes for the spectators too.

It's all of a piece with the whole strategy of the Incarnation. This has been dressed up by Fra Angelico and by the painters of the Nativity and by pious images of the Holy House at Nazareth, so that we miss the scandal of it, the scandal has been blunted by devotion. But the Incarnation was, and is, in the strict sense scandalous. The choice of

Mary, and of Joseph, and of Nazareth, and of the carpenter's shop, was scandalous. In the eyes of intelligent and successful people, this humble home in this nondescript village, and this humble couple, were not only poor, they were uninteresting, they were even boring. 'Can anything good come out of Nazareth?' asked Nathanael (John 1:46). God's entry into his world was, so to speak, by the back door. A deliberate strategy. It is as though he were saying to us 'Value and worth do not lie where you think they lie. They lie under the surface of what you dismiss as beneath contempt.'

I knew a couple of priests, years ago, in the Arundel & Brighton diocese. They were the best of friends, but one used to criticize the other unmercifully. 'Of course,' he'd say, 'he's got no brains.' Or 'He hasn't got the faintest idea of how to run a parish. Look how he wastes his time. The other day he spent the entire morning cooking a meal for an old lady across the road, and most of the afternoon feeding it to her.' One sees the force of the criticism. I tremble to think of what was being neglected in the parish while the second priest was peeling the potatoes. A bit of 'appraisal' would have done him no harm. But on the other hand he had discovered something unbelievably precious, which was the joy of being a servant. He was acting in a supremely Christlike way, with great tenderness and consideration. He was waiting on the old lady as Christ will wait on us on the last day, if we are awake when he comes. It ought to be added, out of fairness, that the critical priest, the first one, was also a great servant: I have known him sit for a long period beside a dying person, propping them up in bed, wiping the sweat from their forehead, truly caring for them. There is so much difference between getting your hands dirty, and standing at a distance and pontificating. I have to confess that I find it easier to stand at a distance, but this isn't because I don't want to get involved, it's because I am a clumsy and unpractical person with a fear of getting it wrong. If I cooked the old lady's dinner I would probably poison her.

I suppose the question is not just what we do. It's also who we mix with. If you only visit the houses of comfortable middle-class people, or intellectual people, or people who are going to do something for you, then that's sad. In the name of the Gospel, we need to visit people who would not normally be our close friends. It may not even be productive visiting: we may end up in listening to some pretty trivial small-talk, or watching some gruesomely mindless television. But in coming and knocking on those doors you show yourself to be a servant. That's what matters.

Anything is worthwhile which makes Christ present to us and to others. The great temptation is to see him as someone in the past, and simply to remember him, with a sort of nostalgia, a romantic and stylized figure. Even Christians often forget that he is with us, and close, and active, here and now. It is the corollary of the Resurrection. The *kerygma* is not just 'Christ is risen' but 'Christ is risen and is alive.' In Italian there is a word—*attuale*—which we don't have in English. It means 'here and now.' The here-and-nowness of Christ is obvious when we celebrate the sacraments, when we receive communion or are forgiven in confession. But he is also personally present, and *attuale*, when I act as servant to others, not in order to attract attention to myself, but out of love. The smallest act of service brings his mysterious presence into the room where I am, brings his distinctive footfall and the sound of his voice. For a moment I am in communion with him, because I am doing what he does, I am acting *in persona Christi*. Jobs which from the outside look tedious and pointless suddenly acquire a gigantic meaning: they put me in touch with the Lord whom I love, and his power and his life flow into me, and through me to others. All the more so if these acts remain unrecognized. 'The Son of Man came not to be served but to serve, and to give his life as a ransom for many' (Matthew 20:28). Well, he gives his life as a ransom for many whenever we celebrate Mass, and will do so till the end of time. Likewise the serving of others didn't stop at the Resurrection, or the Ascension, or when the last canonical book of the Bible was completed. It continues to the end of time, all through history, and you and I are part of history. Through you and me, God still humbly puts himself at the service of his world, and saves it not from above, but from below.

Cantalamessa, in his book *L'Eucaristia nostra santificazione* (1983) sounds a cautionary note. It is a false service, he says, when a priest neglects what he owes the people, above all decent preaching, in order to immerse himself in a pile of material occupations. That's not service, that's just distraction. The best way of being a servant is to do the reading and praying I know I need to do to produce a proper homily on Sunday. He quotes Gregory the Great's lament that

> the world is full of priests but it is rare to find them in the Lord's vineyard. We have taken on the priestly office but don't do the work that goes with it. We have immersed ourselves in earthly affairs, and while what we have committed ourselves to is one thing, what the facts display is quite another.

We have all known Parish Priests who used buildings and administration, or the counting of the collection, as an escape-hatch from the spiritual heart of priesthood, and I suppose that at root their problem is one of faith. If you're not sure what you believe in, it is fatally easy to distract yourself with programmes, blueprints, systems, equipment. So I am not recommending to you this kind of dissipation. Dissipation doesn't make you a Christlike servant. I am recommending an instinct which always prompts you to lend a hand when you could more easily not bother: quite another thing.

All this does great violence to the way we are brought up and the way we think. In the old public school system, it was the small boy who had to act as fag for the bigger one, polish his boots and make his tea. In the army it is the private on fatigues who has to clean the latrines. In western society it is the illegal-immigrant Filipino maid on half-pay who sweeps the floor of your flat. The middle-class mother hires a baby-sitter and then a nanny. We think instinctively that with age and promotion we should rightly grow away from a life of doing service and employ others to do this, that it's one of the perks of seniority. But how tragic it would be if at the same time we grew away from Jesus. Listen to Charles de Foucauld's plan for his first religious foundation in Algeria, a plan which, incidentally, was never realized quite in this form. However, it shows us the mind of a man who was a minor aristocrat, an officer in the army, but above all a saint.

> to found on the Moroccan frontier not a Trappist monastery, not a big or rich monastery, not an agricultural development programme, but a kind of small and humble hermitage

where a few poor monks could live on a bit of fruit and some barley, which they would harvest with their own hands, in a strict cloister, in penance and adoration of the Blessed Sacrament, not leaving their enclosure, and not preaching, but offering hospitality to all comers, good or bad, friend or enemy, Moslem or Christian. This is evangelization not by word but by the presence of the Blessed Sacrament, by the offering of the divine sacrifice, by prayer and penance, and by the practice of the evangelical virtues, especially charity, a brotherly and universal charity, sharing down to the last mouthful with every poor person, every guest, every unknown person who turns up; receiving every human being as a beloved brother ...

There's a lesson here on poverty, and that could be for another time. But there is also this element of service, being *disponibile* which is so attractive and so challenging. How does it translate into our life, the life which is *attuale*? Well, I suppose in things like offering a lift to the airport, lending a hand to make a single-handed job easier and quicker, a half-hour spent untying a theological knot for someone, a willingness to crack another man's computer problem. ('Aha!' you will say, 'I see what he's up to. This whole talk has been a crafty way of getting someone to fix his computer.' With my hand on my heart I swear it is not so.) They don't have to be huge dramatic things. I think many of you are already very good at this sort of generosity. Tonight we see it in its bigger, spiritual, christocentric context, and realize how beautiful it is when our whole existence is shot through with this instinct of service.

When we are ordained deacons, the accent is on service. But of course, none of us here has a vocation to be a permanent deacon. We are ordained deacons because this is the way to priesthood the Church has determined. Our eyes are already on the chasuble and the chalice. That's the experiential truth. Well, they should also be on the apron, the basin, the jar of water, whatever symbolizes service in our context. I remember overhearing a shouting match between one of my young assistants and a lady who worked in the parish. 'Do you realize who you're talking to?' he bellowed, 'I'm a priest.' 'I'm perfectly aware who

I'm talking to,' she said, raising her voice just a little bit. She was saying, implicitly, that she could hardly help appreciating he was a priest because he was throwing his weight about in the most awful way. Wouldn't it have been great if she had realized he must be a priest because he was humble, and patient, and of service. Alas, that was not what she meant. When we become priests (or, heaven help us, bishops) we don't stop being deacons. One step does not blot the other out. That commitment to loving service is for life, and it is in priesthood that the opportunities become so much richer.

✝

Secular Priests

Now here's an odd thing.

We are priests, or we're going to be. Our friends and relatives take it for granted that we are religious men. Our main motive for doing what we do, they suppose, is God. Somehow or other, sometime, we have picked up a special relationship with God that we can retreat into, that resources us and energizes us. They take it for granted that we do a lot of praying, and that in some mysterious way we make prayer work. That's why they ask us, very humbly, to pray for them and their sick relatives. They think that priests have a hot line. Their notion of what takes place in seminaries is very hazy, but it includes this idea of strengthening bonds with God, of becoming God's men in a way which is not open to mere laypeople. They think, in a word, that we are religious.

They would be surprised to learn that there is a distinction between religious, strictly speaking, and diocesan priests; that diocesan priests are not, technically, religious at all. Religious, as a word, has a double meaning: it can either be a personal quality or a canonical definition. Canonically, religious are those who belong to religious orders. Their main allegiance is to their order, while ours is to a bishop and a slice of territory. Indeed, if any technical term can be applied to us it is 'secular'. We are the secular clergy. Secular means 'of the world'. It is a label we are given not because of our personal character, not because we are lounge lizards and *bons viveurs*, but because of our sphere of activity. We are the ones that move about in civil society, who know its ways, who are at ease in it, and are therefore best equipped to evangelize it. That's the theory anyway. In practice, in recent years, there has been a tendency for everyone to do everything, so that you get religious running parishes and secular priests becoming missionaries. But the roots are still there, in that distinction.

It is useful for us to probe this adjective 'secular'. It has a benign and a malign meaning. Its benign meaning is that we are the ones who are not afraid of the world. *Saeculum* is the world. John, in his first letter, takes an almighty swipe at the world, warns his faithful people against the world. It is full of rot and corruption, he says, and our only hope is to flee the world, to seal ourselves away from the world.

> Do not love the world or the things in the world. If anyone
> loves the world, love for the Father is not in him. For all that
> is in the world, the lust of the flesh and the lust of the eyes
> and the pride of life, is not of the Father but of the world.
> (I John 2:15–16)

One can see what he means. The court cases where public men are prosecuted for corruption, the dawn arrests for child pornography, the appalling civil wars in Africa where warlords commit genocide, the coldheartedness of people in the face of earthquake and tidal wave, all these things show that human beings are very weak in the face of worldly desires and values. We easily cave in when tempted. The world is a dangerous place, and we are spiritually fragile. You can lose your soul in the world.

And yet if we all retreated into monasteries and shut the door, who would evangelize the *saeculum*, the world? Someone's got to chance it. With a realistic assessment of the temptations, stresses and strains involved, someone has got to venture out into the human jungle, be at home in the human jungle, and, while adhering faithfully to his own principles, know its language and its habits. There is a precedent for this. The Son of God, at the Annunciation and Christmas, stepped out into this ambiguous conglomeration called the human race, and embraced it, warts and all. He evangelized it not from afar, but from inside. In the process the was vilified by the authorities for bending religious regulations, mixing with sinners and consorting with foreigners—for being, if you like, too secular. In the process he got tempted, misunderstood, terribly mauled, and eventually killed. That's an occupational hazard of trying to bring the Gospel into the heart of the world. It will never be a pushover, this world. It's got sharp, cruel teeth. Yet it is not all negative. Even in its sharpness and cruelty it offers us an avenue to heaven. It was Ignatius of Antioch who said 'To be in front of the wild animals is to be in front of God'.* So being a secular priest is not an inferior way of being a priest, but it is a different one. The benign meaning of 'secular' when applied to us is that we are the men at the coalface, the ones most in touch with the everyday lives of ordinary wage-earning and unemployed people, the ones who know the idiom the world will understand. We are sure-footed, even when the ground is treacherous. It is sometimes thought that any old priest can run a parish, that it is the default place to be when you stop being a canonist or a professor or a missionary or a contemplative monk. It is not so. We are not just GPs, we are specialists, with a whole gamut of special skills we develop over the years. It is a beautiful and heroic vocation. That's the theory anyway, and often it is the practice too.

The malign meaning of 'secular', the sinister one, is that we are priests who have quietly sold out to the world. That our faith has worn so thin that we actually belong to the world. That we are no longer the knife which cuts the butter; we have become butter ourselves. That the values of the world have become, bit by bit, our values too. We wear the collar during the week and the vestments on Sundays, we make the right noises and present the right appearances, but underneath the fire has gone out. So that the assumptions of the laypeople are belied. We are as worldly as they are, maybe even more worldly. Our faith has died. We set more store by the regular income and the consumer goods, the plushy holidays and the entertainment culture, than they do. Our language and thought-patterns are those of the television soaps. Basically we are no more committed to unselfishness and service than they are, very possibly less. Beneath the façade of the celibate for the love of God is entrenched a bachelor with a love of the discreetly good life, and no family commitments.

The malign meaning of 'secular' is also that somewhere along the line we have stopped praying. The breviary goes west quite soon after ordination. 'It doesn't suit my personality,' we say, 'I prefer to talk to God in my own words and in my own way.' But private and personal prayer

---

* *Ad Smyrn.* IV.

soon disappears from our agenda too, and we are left with nothing, no anchor, nothing to ally us to the praying people of God. Into the void, as I hinted a moment ago, steps doubt. It is fed perhaps by half-digested scripture scholarship or immersion in some angry theologians; it seems more sophisticated and educated than naked doubt, but at root it's the kind of doubt which saps at faith. Disillusion with diocesan authorities, crossness with the Vatican, a noble-savage kind of churchmanship, can mask a detachment also from God. What appears is a mindset which owes more to the broadsheet British or Irish press than to the Gospel. The style of our national media is that no dogmatic assertion must ever be allowed to carry the day. It must immediately be confronted with an assertion of the opposite, so that the end-product, as the credits roll, is a misty-eyed 'Who knows?' You find priests who recoil from certainty.

These freethinking assumptions of the media easily became our own, and also the freewheeling condemnations, specially those of Church authority. Clearly, sometimes Church authority deserves condemnation because it makes stupid decisions or does things in stupid ways; to be critical on those occasions is quite different from an *a priori* assumption that everyone, from the pope in Rome down to the vicar general round the corner, is a permanent and inevitable disaster. Relentlessly contemptuous priests, always sarcastic and carping, are a pain. When we reach that point, it's the *Independent* and the *Guardian* talking, not the Gospel. At what point does the iron enter the soul? For some sooner, for others later. The real sadness is that being switched-off from the concrete, identifiable Church can lead to being switched-off God too. Then we really become, in the grimmest sense, secular priests.

Most dioceses offer something in the way of in-service training. But the most sensible form of in-service is self-imposed. I am a secular priest and proud of it. But I need to take all prudent means to be sure that the *saeculum* does not drown me, and that—to use an old translation of Paul—I who set out to preach to others do not myself become a castaway.

I need to construct my own pattern of prayer. I say 'pattern' advisedly. This is one of the contexts in which routine is good. When you are a bit off-colour routine can carry you through. Normally speaking I need to have regular times for the Office, and for my private and personal prayer. I need to do a deal with a friendly neighbouring priest about confession. And I need, if possible, to equip myself with a spiritual director, however non-directive he may be in practice. Just as all modern computer programmes have spell-checks as a matter of course, so I should have, as a matter of course, a man who is licensed to pull me into line if I am getting silly. I may be self-deceiving in sexual matters. I may be neurotic about taking offence where none is intended. I may become single-issue and allow an enthusiasm to skew my judgment. I may be thinking horizontally, meaning in terms of achievement and statistically verifiable results, instead of vertically, where all the power is God's, and where my job is simply to open up the channels of grace. I may be a workaholic, and need to hear the old adage 'God exists, and you're not him, so just relax.' A mate who can look at the broad structure of my life and who will give a touch on the tiller is precious beyond words.

A parenthesis here. It is hard to find a good spiritual director. Some religious do it superlatively well, but some of them don't really understand the life we lead; and in any case, there aren't all that many religious about these days. Occasionally there is a religious sister who is really gifted in this direction. But is it not time that our dioceses set about training some spiritual directors themselves? Why should each diocese not have two or three of the brethren who are able and willing to provide this service to the presbyterate? It is simply a matter of a few men being willing to offer their time to their brothers, without any suggestion about it of being holier-than-thou.

On a national or even international basis it would be quite possible to run an annual course to prepare men for this work. We did it in Rome in 1999, and twelve men signed up, but the Jesuit who ran the month—and it was a superb month—proceeded to have a heart attack, so that we could not repeat it. I have recently been jogging the elbow of the English in-service directors, trying to get them to set something going again. *Quis custodiet ipsos custodes?* Quite possibly the English Irish and Scots could combine forces, and mount something really good, maybe at Salamanca, or at Palazzola near Rome, or somewhere here in Ireland or in the UK, where we could all learn some expertise and garner a bit of confidence. The beneficial effect at grass-roots level could be enormous. I recall spending some time in a parish in Peru, back in the 1980s. One of the local businessmen had a fleet of taxis, brand-new Toyota people-carriers. I watched him drive them into the ground by pushing them at breakneck speeds over unmade roads, not pumping up the tyres, and not putting oil in the engines. One by one they seized up: what a criminal waste of money and resources. There is a lovely Latin American expression for 'It's broken down'. They say *Està descompuesto*, it is decomposed. Well, I, as a secular priest, need oil in my engine and I need my tyres pumping up if I am not to become decomposed. That's what a spiritual director would do for me. Maybe that's something I could do for a friend. Even in a month I could learn a lot about the theory and the practice. Spirituality isn't a *disciplina arcani*, a mysterious Gnostic affair into which some are initiated and others never will be. It is something much more workaday than that. It is learning to recognize and welcome the finger of God in the most banal human situations. I quote Rowan Williams:

> The Church is the place where selfless service is learned, in the daily rub of communal life.[*]

> Fleshly life is not a burden to be borne nor a prison to be escaped from, but a task to be perfected in grace.[†]

> Salvation, then, is in no sense a flight to God *from* what is human, but the realizing of God's 'likeness', and so the sharing of his life, in what *is* human.[‡]

Perfection doesn't lie in operating in a disembodied way. Christians often have this Platonist streak in them. But ever since the Incarnation, the material world as it comes to hand, which means our own ensouled bodies to start with, along with our possessions and relationships, are the raw material of the spiritual life. If we can grasp this, and live it with patience, we have the stuff of sanctity within us. It's about using

---

[*] Rowan Williams, *The Wound of Knowledge*, ch. entitled 'The Passion of My God'.
[†] *ibid.*
[‡] *ibid.*

the *saeculum* instead of being enslaved by it. But in the recognizing and the using of it, we need company. A result-at-a tangent of this week might be that one day, as a young priest, you will seek out this kind of company for yourself, and be this kind of company for a friend.

The Eucharist is at the heart of this. Jesus deliberately descends into the arena of the *saeculum* when he institutes the Eucharist. You need only look at the hands of the people who come to communion to appreciate that. Jesus confronts the world with all its ugliness, he penetrates it and loves it from the inside. When we expose the Blessed Sacrament in the monstrance, the frontier between what is sacred and what is worldly becomes porous. God comes down into his world, right into the middle of it, to sanctify it. Sometimes this can scandalize us. The sheer fleshly proximity of God can make us want to put up barriers. It is not so long since people were told never to go to communion without going to confession first. Quite apart from mortal sin, they felt, we needed to be sanitized before letting God in the Eucharist anywhere near us. 'Depart from me, for I am a sinful man, O Lord.' It is not so long since people were told not to touch the host with their teeth. The uproar when communion-in-the-hand was introduced was part of this; and indeed, many people still prefer to receive communion on the tongue. Anything which enhances reverence for Christ truly present in the Blessed Sacrament is to be praised. But equally we must never forget his reason for giving us his flesh to eat and his blood to drink. It was to sanctify the sheer ordinariness of our lives, to sanctify what is secular. I, secular priest, receive the Eucharist so that God may empower me to enter the *saeculum* with confidence, daring to embrace what is banal and everyday. 'Nihil alienum a me puto' said Paul; a loose translation might be 'Nothing is beneath my dignity.'

✛

SORROWFUL MYSTERIES

On Tuesday evenings long ago, as the main course for supper made its appearance in the refectory, a corporate groan could be heard. 'It's sorrowful mysteries again.' A sorrowful mystery was a peculiarly ambiguous post-war hamburger which was part of our staple diet. It was well named.

But the real sorrowful mysteries are enormously fruitful, enormously nourishing, if we spend time with them. I would like to do this with you tonight. There is an entire school for life here, a framework of personal asceticism and self-discipline which is perfectly attainable, and hugely helpful.

Because it's the Rosary, we do it in the company of Mary, asking her motherly help. Mothers know their sons intimately, in ways that can be quite embarrassing. They can see through our motives and know our hearts. They can puncture us when we start posturing, and encourage us when we are depressed. A good mother has her son taped. That's why, incidentally, Mary could say at the Marriage Feast 'Do whatever he tells you.' Mary, for us, is a good mother. She can help us take exactly what we need from these mysteries, exactly what will be for our spiritual good.

The tone tonight may be a bit sombre. I think we have to settle for that in Lent. I was interested the other day to read C. S. Lewis's *The Problem of Pain*, and to see that quite apart from the subject matter, which is rather dark in itself, there is in his writing a certain carbolic-soap-and-cold-showers air which belongs to the year of authorship—1940. It also belongs to my childhood. I will try not to inflict too much of that on you tonight.

So, off we go. We begin by contemplating Jesus in Gethsemane. As we finger our way through the Hail Marys, we watch him in the garden. Put yourself with Peter, James and John. Alarmingly, Our Lord who has always been in command of the situation, our total inspiration, is clearly undermined. He is terrified. And he is wrestling with demons which I, as a humble disciple, cannot even imagine. Within a stone's throw of me this man, in whom I have invested all my trust, thinking him unshakable, seems to be crumbling. Surely my instinct will be to stay alert, on the lookout for whatever I can do or say to be of service, to comfort. But what do I do? I go to sleep. The fact that Jesus chose to go a hundred yards up the hillside and do his own thing makes me feel, in my childish way, that I am off duty, off the hook: I can go to sleep. On the whole children simply take from their parents, they give nothing, they contribute only by what they are, by just being lovable, but they don't deliberately contribute anything—at least not until they are well on the way to being grown-up. You might expect a teenage boy to do a lot to support his widowed mother. You wouldn't expect the same of a lad of 8. Peter, James and John are not even spiritual teenagers. They are spiritual eight-year-olds. So they sleep. So do I.

Sleeping is a metaphor for switching off when there is nothing in it for me. So much of what I do is, on the surface, good. If I preach well, if I get good marks in exams, if I have a way of being pleasant and obliging to my colleagues, if I put the time in for meditative prayer, I can feel pretty virtuous. Things are going well, I say: my spiritual life is in order, it is progressing. Reality demands a periodic dose of cold water. How much of this am I doing because it *looks* good? How much am I worshipping my own image? I am the child of a utilitarian age, and tend to do things only if they are useful. My acts of charity, the time I put into study, my proclamation of the Gospel, I tend to gauge the value of these things in terms of their usefulness. In 'Yes Minister' the Paul Eddington character has one criterion of things being worthwhile: will they win votes? If I look deep into myself, is my criterion 'Will this make me look good, sound good?' Do I not bother to do things if they fail to improve the *persona* I try to project? If so, I am still a spiritual 8-year-old, and I snore away with Peter James and John until another little piece of self-aggrandizement becomes possible. You can see how selfishness is a wizard at disguises. I don't do it on purpose. It is simply the motive which worms its way into everything.

The test of all this, for me, is to resolve, this Lent, to do something every day which cannot possibly gain me any credit, any kudos. An act of kindness, a contribution to the common good, which will never be known by anyone. Then Jesus won't be able to reproach me 'Couldn't you even stay awake for an hour with me?'

The scourging of Our Lord at the pillar. If you saw the Mel Gibson film the impression will remain with you. The sheer long physicality of the whole proceeding, and how it was normal stuff for a Roman soldier. There is an unconscious irony in the Greek text of St Luke. Pilate says 'I find no cause worthy of death in this man—I will scourge him and let him go.' The word he uses for scourge is *paideusas* which suggests what you do to a *pais*, a boy, when he needs correcting. These days you don't do anything; but within living memory, and way back through history, boys could expect to be whipped or beaten from time to time. They certainly did not expect to be beaten three-quarters to death. But, of course, the boy had all his life still to lead, and Jesus didn't. The scourging was a preliminary to execution, and it would in fact make it easier to kill him. The Passion of the Lord took a perfectly healthy man in the prime of life, and killed him, in stages, over a period of fifteen hours. The scourging was a major component. And he submitted to this. I ponder this as I say this decade of the Rosary. The soldiers who did it must have been deeply cynical and brutalized. They were required to do things which were sickening and destructive to the soul. Himmler, head of the SS, used from time to time to visit the barracks of his men, and congratulate them on what they were doing for the Reich. 'I know it's hard, supervising and killing Jews,' he would say, 'but you really are on the sharp end of a heroic effort, and the time will come when history sees you for the great men you are.' I wonder if the Roman soldiers on execution duty (who, like many of the SS, may well have been from some occupied territory) needed comforting and encouraging? Like the SS, they were trained to see the kind of people they scourged and crucified as racially inferior, so that it didn't really count. You find the same phenomenon in the criminally inhumane treatment of Irish convicts in the Australian penal settlements, back in the nineteenth century. Considerations of class and race slosh around in the human mix in every century, and they are always poisonous. The British are not immune from this. I am not immune to this.

To share the memory of this with Mary seems, on a certain level, indelicate. First, because it's her Son we're talking about; she wasn't present, presumably, but she knew it was happening. Should we expose her to the detail of it? And anyway, it was a grossly male proceeding, the bestial sort of thing men do to one another. We wonder, subconsciously, whether it is not over-strong meat for feminine sensitivity. Yet Our Lady is enormously strong and infinitely generous, and her heart beats so much in time with that of Jesus that if he subjected himself to this for our sake, she does not wish to be left outside.

We need her to intercede for us. *We* cannot afford to leave her outside. It is this disgusting affair of the scourging which brings home to us our own woeful weakness on the physical level. Our sexual weakness, which isn't overtly cruel, but which can be so exploitative. Think of child pornography, which means that at one remove the viewer is putting kids through unimaginable hell; and promiscuous behaviour, which uses and discards people as of no value. Just two examples—obviously there are more. Then there is our violence ... mostly mastered, by social conditioning over generations, but surfacing sometimes in prejudice and contempt for those different from ourselves. The Serbs at Srebrenica: that wasn't ordinary warfare. When American and British troops abuse Iraqi prisoners, does that behaviour come out of nowhere? The bullying inflicted on kids at school, and on new army recruits, is commonplace. Somewhere in our collective subconscious there is a jeering, mocking, implacable thing which delights in inflicting pain and fear. It surfaces in the gang wars of big cities. Watch that Brazilian film about the slums, 'City of God'. You and I may say that we have never had the slightest desire to act violently. Is this simply because our privileged social cushioning has protected us from the triggers which start it off? Human sadism is a horrible thing and it crops up in every century and every country, and Jesus descended right into the pit of this horror. And then there is our greed, and a whole host of physical addictions, and the habit some people have of beating themselves up, despising themselves. That's violence too. We take violence and cruelty for granted, and make jokes about it. Macaulay once wrote, 'Cambridge had the honour of educating those celebrated Protestant bishops whom Oxford had the honour of burning.' When I pray the second mystery I am asking Our Lady to attract Christ's merciful attention to the dark underside of our physical existence, the sexual and the violent, and to heal it. Only he can do it. Holy Mary, Mother of God, pray for us sinners.

When Jesus was crowned with thorns he was humiliated. He was also misunderstood. The whole kingship thing got Our Lord into a lot of trouble, because no-one, least of all the Romans, could conceive of any king who was not a political leader and a threat to the State. Incidentally, the king theme was not a major plank in the proclamation of Jesus. He talks in the Gospel about the Kingdom of God and the Kingdom of Heaven, and some of his parables have a king in them, like the one about the Last Judgment. Not much more than that. But the 'k word', even once, was enough for the paranoid Roman authorities, and the High Priests knew this. It was a sure way to get Jesus eliminated. Neither Jews nor Romans had the slightest notion of kingship which does not coerce, but only appeals. So, on goes the crown of thorns, and with it the purple robe, the laughing, the punching and the slapping. The floor of the room in which all this happened is still marked out with the lines of some sort of game, some sort of hopscotch, which permitted the winner to attack the prisoner. When Pilate washed his hands he in effect transformed Our Lord into a thing rather than a person, a legitimate plaything. Cock-fighting, bear-baiting, dog-fighting, gladiators in the sand of the Colosseum ... it's on a level with all that: depraved amusement, at the expense of someone who no longer matters.

The Church in the secular west is humiliated and misunderstood. And it will certainly happen that in the course of our ministry we personally shall be humiliated and misunderstood. It will probably be about medical-moral and bioethical concerns. I can remember back in 1962 being sent by my parish priest to a public hall in Northampton to defend the Catholic belief about birth control against a very able lady apostle of contraception. There, in front of a large audience, I was made a fool of. Talk about a lamb to the slaughter. There was simply no contest. I trotted out the traditional arguments from the natural law. She told sob-stories about rescuing poor women who were regularly raped by drunken husbands. Forty-four years later the memory still hurts. If the parish priest had been more intelligent he would have got me some help in preparation, but in those days we didn't have communications officers at diocesan level. It was only afterwards that I realized that wild horses on their bended knees would not have got my parish priest himself into that hall. He must have known what he was subjecting me to. These days it's more likely to be the press and the media which put us in a bad light. These days there is help and advice available in advance, if we are wise enough to take it. These days there are models of how to cope in public, like Peter Smith and Vincent Nichols. But the tide of public opinion is running against us, and we are never going to be the flavour of the month. If this happens to you in one way or another, think of the crown of thorns. There is nothing that you and I want more than the well-being and the deep happiness of the human race. We shall, however, be pilloried for inflicting needless suffering on the human race. Well, the disciple is not greater than his master. Mother of God, align me with your Son.

The carrying of the cross. There is a particular cruelty about loading a man with the instrument of his own destruction. It is like making a condemned prisoner dig his own grave, or sending the bill for the bullet to a victim's parents, which is what the Chinese do. The Romans certainly extracted every ounce of deterrence and shame from their public executions.

The message of this mystery, surely, is endurance, perseverance. Keeping on keeping on. Jesus was valiant and brave beyond imagination, because he could so easily have lain down on the road to Calvary and refused to get up. Being killed on the road would, after all, have been no worse than being killed on arrival at Calvary. The fourteen Stations of the Cross spell out for us the prolonged demand of the Via Crucis, and the courage with which Jesus embraced it, so that the Cross could be for us the great symbol of hope. If you have made the pilgrimage to Jerusalem you know that the distance between the Lithostratos, where Jesus was crowned with thorns and mocked, and the site of Calvary, is considerable. The part played by Simon of Cyrene reminds us that we can help, that our support, even if it comes twenty-one centuries later, still counts. We offer that support by being men of endurance ourselves, putting up with adverse conditions when they come and still being there when the dust settles.

I am reminded of the Dutch Jesuit missionaries in Indonesia. They went out there in the late 1930s, when Indonesia was still the Dutch East Indies. At the Japanese invasion they were interned and ill-treated. On their release they had to survive in the middle of a war of independence. When the Republic of Indonesia took shape they were told they could stay only if they took Indonesian nationality. They did this, so that going home to the Netherlands on holiday they had to stand in the 'alien' queue. They became the acknowledged experts in local language, knowing the roots and the history better than the Indonesian themselves. They became gaunt, fragile, very old, often wearing native dress, burned by the sun to a rich walnut; the ones I met in 1989 have probably all died. The word that comes to mind when I think of them is 'constant'. They lived through so much, saw so much, suffered so much, but never for a moment in those sixty years did they waver in their faithfulness to the priesthood and the Gospel.

We cannot see ahead, however much we peer. What sort of world are we destined to live in, what will the values of society be, what shape will the Church have? Will we be reasonably well-off, or will we be poor? Will the ethical rows make the Church deeply unpopular? Will new movements arise in the Church, like the Jesuits at the Reformation, able to put the claims of the Gospel in a new way? Are we destined to be static pastors, or will we be always on the move around our dioceses? von Balthasar, in his book *The Heart of the World* puts these words into the mouth of Jesus:

> Just as a strawberry plant sends out long shoots which soon form roots and finally produce a new plant, so too I have multiplied my inner centre and established new centres in hearts sprung from mine. My children become fathers and new communities blossom from the blood of my Apostles' hearts.*

* H. U. von Balthasar, *Heart of the World*, ch. 4.

Is that how it's going to be? We pray that it is, but we cannot see, and we must live by faith. There will be good times, that's for sure. There may also be some uphill trudge, with some burdens to carry. R. S. Thomas, in 'The Minister', one of his poems about Welsh village life, has this:

> They chose their pastors as they chose their horses
> For hard work. But the last one died
> Sooner than they expected; nothing sinister,
> You understand, but just the natural
> Breaking of the heart beneath a load
> Unfit for horses.

Is that how it's going to be? We pray that it is not, but we cannot see, and we must live by faith. Either way, the keynote of our lives must be faithfulness. In the next few years, you will be celebrating weddings and baptizing babies. My prayer is that you will live long enough, be stable enough and be faithful enough to be baptizing the grand-children of those babies in fifty years' time. One of the translations of the Apocalypse talks of Christ 'pitching his tent' among men. A definitive arrival, hammering in the tent pegs. He's come to stay. We pitch our tent in our diocese. Please God, the tent will still be there in 2050 or even 2060, weatherbeaten and patched in places, but still recognizably itself. And Mary will still be our loving mother, for she will have travelled with us.

And last, the Crucifixion. I approach this subject with sure knowledge of my utter inadequacy. How can I make wise and insightful remarks about the act which saved the world? Pure altruism like the self-gift of Jesus is so foreign to me that I simply cannot enter into the mindset of Our Lord. All I know is that I spend my whole life skirting round what is unendurable, in terms of pain, despair, horror of whatever sort. I dodge and I weave, I take painkillers, I write cheques to pacify my conscience, I use television and DVDs to assuage my loneliness, I construct a lifestyle which, I hope, pleases God while sparing me personally as much suffering as possible. Jesus on the other hand goes right into the pit of pain, dereliction, loneliness: he drinks the cup dry.

He does it so that one day I may see the face of God. He does it so that I may graduate from slavery to sonship, and share in the life of the

Trinity, however unworthy I may be. He does it so that the willful, the wayward, the lazy, the childish may make it home, perhaps without ever realizing the magnitude of the gift, or how near they came to losing it. I am within a hair's breadth of having a life which will trickle out into the sand, meaningless and pointless. Yet because of this man, voluntarily put to death in this slow and squalid way, manipulated by his own religious leaders and pinned up by these gross mercenary soldiers, my life will not be meaningless after all, it will be crowned with fulfillment and bliss, and my thirst for the truth will be satisfied, and my soul will be filled with light.

This I can share with Mary. She has every moment of the Crucifixion indelibly inscribed on her memory, carved on her memory. Yet she recalls it without bitterness and without blame. She is aware of the repulsiveness of sin, the stench and putridity of it, and she knows what it did to her Son; but she has nothing but love and maternal care for the sinner. She knows my motives and reads my heart: she is, after all, a mother. 'Hail our life, our sweetness and our hope.' She is my hope because she is under no illusion about my weakness and selfishness, yet she does not write me off. Because of her prayers, some of the power and life of the Crucifixion can be diverted on to me and those I love, and I can sing

> Heaven's morning breaks, and earth vain shadows flee;
> In life, in death, O Lord, abide with me.

✢

JOHN FISHER

John Fisher was a Yorkshire lad come south. Sent to study at Cambridge, he did so well that he moved from undergraduate to fellow, it seems, effortlessly and seamlessly, and early in his life. His seventeenth-century biographer, Hall, describes him: 'Tall and comely, exceeding the common and middle sort of men, for he was to the quantity of six feet in height, and being therewith very slender and lean, was nevertheless upright and well-formed, straight-backed, big-jointed and strongly sinewed.' Cambridge was his great love. He was twice Vice-Chancellor of the University. By the favour and support of Lady Margaret, Henry VII's mother, he founded Christ's College and St John's. Much her junior, he was appointed her chaplain and confessor. And thus he caught the eye of the King.

His life as bishop at Rochester was austere, especially if you compare it with that of other bishops. He ate and drank with simplicity, he often fasted, and his household was soberly dressed. He was a hard worker, visiting the parishes of his diocese and demanding certain standards of his clergy. He wished above all to be a good shepherd. His biographer depicts him visiting the sick, sitting for hours on end in smoky cottages and climbing precarious ladders to find people living in the loft. He could do this because, unlike his contemporaries, he was relentlessly resident, on the spot all the time, except when the King commanded his presence at Court for state occasions. It was a poor diocese, but Fisher was heard to say 'I would not desert my poor old wife for the richest widow in England.' Erasmus describes his damp house and draughty library. Rochester was on the main road between London and the coast, so he had to do his share of entertaining foreign dignitaries. You get the feeling that he was always glad to see them go, and that they, too, were quite pleased to go; John Fisher must have been a disconcerting host. 'If any strangers came,' says Hall, 'he would entertain them at his own table according to their vocations, with such mirth as stood with the gravity of his person.'

Compared with the balaclava boys hurling bricks at the windows of banks, John Fisher seems an unlikely protestor. But protestor he is. He takes on the prevailing power, and with quiet dignity he challenges it, he shames it. History has given what he did a patina of nobility. Even those who today do not share his ecclesiology would grant him the accolade of great and unflinching courage. At the time, however, government propaganda painted him in quite other colours.

There were not many natural protestors among the bishops at his time. By and large they were appointed by the King, with a nod from the Pope, and Kings tended to select supporters and courtiers. Here, however, is the text of Henry VII's letter to his mother, in 1504:

> 'Madam, An' I thought I should not offend you, which I will never do wilfully, I am well minded to promote Master Fisher, your confessor, to a bishopric; and I assure you, Madam, for none other cause, but for the great and singular virtue, that I know and see in him, as well in cunning and natural wisdom, and specially for his good and virtuous living and conversation. ... I have in my days promoted many a man unadvisedly, and I would now make some recompense, to promote some good and virtuous men, which I doubt not should best please God, who ever preserve you in good health and long life.'

There was a risk in naming bishops of great and singular virtue. John Fisher was just thirty-six when appointed to Rochester, and knew that this might seem a precocious promotion. He wrote a letter of thanks to the King *Quippe qui paucos annos habuerim*, 'Although I am still a young man', but he was already a clear-sighted, courageous and very obstinate character. He would remain the same for thirty years.

A sermon is not the place for a history lecture; and if it were, there are many more qualified than I to deliver it. In broad outline, it is sufficient to say that when Henry VIII asked the bishops to advise him whether his marriage to Catharine of Aragon could be annulled, Fisher gave a decided 'No'; and he never moved from that conviction. When Henry legislated in Parliament to make himself Supreme Head of the Church, Fisher resisted him; and when Henry required all his notables to swear agreement to his supremacy, Fisher said that his conscience would not allow him to do it. He wrote to Cromwell, the Kings's Secretary, 'Not that I condemn any other men's conscience. Their conscience may save them, and mine must save me.' He was grilled by Privy Councillors and pleaded with by his fellow bishops, but to no avail. It was one thing for the King to alter the succession to the throne; it was quite another for him to discard his lawful wife in favour of another, and moreover to break his country's link with Rome. This issue dominated his life. In other circumstances one can imagine him as a saintly and peaceful pastor of his flock. Also as a speculative scholar of note, both in Latin and in Greek. But he was pitched into one of the most painful controversies this country, or Europe, has ever known.

I said that Fisher was a protestor, and he was. He had shown this well before what came to be known as 'The King's Great Matter.' In 1520 he had been swept up into the royal entourage at the Field of the Cloth of Gold, when at unimaginable expense Henry VIII led a cortège across the Channel to swear undying friendship to the King of France. It was Fisher's only trip abroad; his continental experience didn't go much past Calais. He observed the proceedings there with a jaundiced eye, being personally vowed to a life of great austerity. All the more jaundiced three years later, when Henry, now at odds with France, looked for a war chest from the Church. It was Fisher who drily opposed this in the House of Lords. He was overruled, but the memory stuck in the King's mind. Already in 1523 Henry realized that his grandmother's chaplain was an inconvenient old man: just how inconvenient he was yet to discover.

That instinct to protest was extended to abuses in the Church, of which there were many. In his sermons on the Penitential Psalms Fisher said 'All fear of God, also the contempt of God, cometh and is grounded of the clergy.' He looked balefully at dereliction of duty on the part of his fellow priests and bishops. 'Bishops be absent from their dioceses and parsons from their churches ... we use bye-paths and circumlocutions in rebuking. We go nothing nigh to the matter, and so in the mean season the people perish with their sins.' His biographer says that at a synod called by Cardinal Wolsey, 'he reproved very discreetly the ambition and incontinency of the clergy, utterly condemning their vanity in wearing costly apparel, whereby he declared the goods of the Church to be sinfully wasted, and scandal to be raised among the people, seeing the tithes and other oblations, given by the devotion of them and their ancestors to a good purpose, so inordinately spent in indecent and superfluous raiment, delicate fare, and other worldly vanity, which matter he debated so largely, and framed his words after such sort, that the Cardinal perceived himself to be touched to the very quick.' If that was a discreet reproof, an indiscreet one would have been worth hearing. This was in 1518. Well before the King's divorce, he was seen by his colleagues as a difficult man.

The King, even when young, saw himself a theologian, and published a defence of Catholic doctrine of the Seven Sacraments. Fisher wrote a book in support of the King, and against Luther. It was an honest book. He defended the authority of the popes, but said at the same time, 'If the Roman Pontiffs, laying aside pomp and haughtiness, would but practise humility, you would not have a word left to utter against them. Yes, would that they would reform the manners of their court, and drive from it ambition, avarice and luxury.' And again, 'Would then that, if there is anything amiss, they would reform themselves, and remove the scandal from the souls of the weak. For it is greatly to be feared, unless they do so quickly, that divine vengeance will not long be delayed.' That was a bleak and biting Yorkshire wind directed at the Vatican of his day.

We are brought up to see protestors as suspect, eccentric, extremist, and almost certainly wrong. The presumption is in favour of the people currently in power. Both Catholics and the English tend to be anti-disturbance. We know what happened to Savonarola. I remember, as a young curate, listening to a blistering attack from the pulpit by my parish priest, on the anti-nuclear demonstrators who had recently passed the door. Galileo, believers in evolution, imaginative scripture scholars, advocates of vernacular liturgy, opponents of slavery and capital punishment, all have had to endure opprobrium and wait their time. And when history eventually caught up with them, it seldom had the grace to say 'Sorry'. Politicians who, in the 1930s, campaigned against the appeasement of Hitler were viewed as unreliable warmongers. They, at least, were vindicated in their lifetime. The older among us were educated for conformity in every respect: in handwriting, for instance. How many children were told that it was forbidden to be left handed? And in some circles, there was a 'received pronunciation' of English, to breach which was seen as protest.

I do not suggest that all protest, and all manners of protest, are justified. For Catholics, those who set the tone for society are not just a nameless 'them'. Within the Church the Magisterium is clear and focused, and says, in effect, that there is a bottom line of belief and behaviour to which you must subscribe if you want to belong. For all the challenges he threw out to both Church and State, John Fisher believed this. There is a limit to protest, he would have said, and Luther has crossed it, and Henry VIII has crossed it, and what they say and do is not tolerable. Yet, in the context of the England of his time, he had the courage to be a minority of one. Simply by his lifestyle, let alone by his preaching, he was a powerful protestor.

In prison he knew all the trials St Paul describes to us today in the Letter to the Romans: tribulation, distress, persecution, hunger, nakedness. The account of his execution is moving. On his way out of the Tower to the scaffold, he had to wait. He leaned against the wall, opened the bible they allowed him to carry, and found in it the passage from John 17:3: 'This is eternal life, that they may know you, the one true God, and Jesus Christ whom you have sent.' He closed the book and said wryly 'Here is even learning enough for me to my life's end.' They took away his gown and tippet, he was left in his doublet and hose, and his biographer says 'There was to be seen a long, lean and slender body. Having on it little other substance besides skin and bones, in so much as most part of the beholders marvelled much to see a living man so consumed.' He prayed for the King and his realm, and was beheaded.

Retrospect clears the mind. We now see how the King cowed the powerful of the land, and reduced them to ciphers. We can sympathize with them. How well would we have performed in the circumstances? But we have to acknowledge that compared with Fisher they were spiritually impoverished, surrendering to the prevailing wind. Fisher, with his clarity of vision, and his bleak, craggy, gaunt, inconvenient, uncompromising adherence to principle, towers above them all, a giant among men.

On Thursday I visited the church of San Vitale in Rome. It is the church allotted by Pope Paul III to Fisher when he made him a cardinal. It has been extensively made-over since then, with baroque decoration and eighteenth-century frescoes. Fisher would not recognize it. But of course he would not have recognized it anyway, since he never saw it. Indeed, his nomination as cardinal accelerated his execution. While I was there I prayed for Fisher House, and for the chaplaincy. And I pray for the whole University of Cambridge, because it was, and surely is, the apple of his eye. And I reflected that San Vitale is a faithful echo of the spiritual life of John Fisher. It is very old, a fourth-century basilica; and it is half-submerged, well below the level of the street. In both its hiddenness and its antiquity it echoes the spiritual life of a remarkable man.

'He who sits upon the throne will shelter them with his presence. They shall hunger no more, neither thirst any more; the sun shall not strike them, nor any scorching heat. For the Lamb in the midst of the throne will be their shepherd, and he will guide them to springs of living water; and God will wipe away every tear from their eyes.'

CPSIA information can be obtained
at www.ICGtesting.com
Printed in the USA
BVHW070735140620
581357BV00001B/16